THE MINI-ATLAS OF
DOG BREEDS

H-1106

THE MINI-ATLAS
OF
DOG BREEDS

Irish Wolfhounds.

ANDREW DE PRISCO

AND

JAMES B. JOHNSON

Introductory Chapters by Kerry V. Donnelly

Acknowledgments

We thank Dr. Herbert R. Axelrod, whose generosity and vision made this project an immediate reality.

To Isabelle Francais, photographer and friend, whose focused professionalism and four-color skills alarmingly capture the canine prism exposing this book.

To Kerry V. Donnelly, fellow author, whose opening chapters provide sensible recommendations and concise groundwork, appropriately introducing the body of our text.

To typographer Mary Alice Griffin, Merlin at the Miles®, whose wrapping is a gift and whose unselfish magic enables her to translate our hieroglyphic editing.

To artist John R. Quinn, who, at our ever-bellowing "Quiiinnn!!," proves an icon of patience and know-how. Mr. Quinn's body portraits bring to life breeds inaccessible to our photographers; his symbol designs successfully access information to all readers.

To Neal Pronek, for his "pincushion" eloquence, scope and insight.

To Deirdre Connolly, for editing to all hours; to Marcy Myerovich, for editing our editing.

To Dr. Bonnie Wilcox and Chris Walkowicz, pen pals and pedigree pedagogues, whose magnificent mastiff-sized volume inspired the completion of this lap book. *The Atlas of Dog Breeds of the World* uncompromisingly endures as required reading for all dog lovers and scholars.

To all tolerant souls who have supported our endeavors.

Dedicated to Kellie and Michael, "Tip" and "Sam," and the restless partnership awakened by this project.

Contents

How to Use this Mini-Atlas

Just as a map is intended to direct one through an unknown area, so too is this volume designed to guide the reader through the fascinating, though oftimes complicated, world of domesticated canines. To facilitate selection, the authors have arranged the breeds alphabetically within groups according to their origin, purpose and/or geographical development. Most often the breeds treated in each group have distinctive characteristics in common, similar body types, and comparable pet attributes. Although some writers, kennel clubs, or fanciers may categorize a particular breed differently, the authors have judiciously placed each breed in its *most* fitting group. For example, while the Pug is of incontestable mastiff beginnings, it finds its more comfortable home in the toy group; likewise, the Rat Terrier, a toy by size, jockeys among the other terriers for its rightful ground. The ten groups employed are presented in the following order: Sighthounds, Mastiffs, Nordic Dogs, Gundogs, Scenthounds, Toys, Flock Guardians, Herding Dogs, Terriers, and Pariahs. The first chapter of this book describes each group and outlines its history and characteristics.

The main text of the book deals with each of 400+ breeds providing concise physical traits (**Portrait**); history, ancestry and traditional functions (**Development**); major kennel clubs that register the dog (**Recognition**); and psychological characteristics, pet attributes and needs (**Character**). The determination "NR" (Not Recognized) under Recognition indicates that no major registry recognizes the breed. Major registries, for our purposes, include the Fédération Cynologique Internationale (FCI); the American Kennel Club (AKC); the United Kennel Club (UKC); the Kennel Club of Great Britain (KCGB); the Canadian Kennel Club (CKC); and the Australian National Kennel Club (ANKC).

The explanation for symbols can be found on pages 78–79 (Symbol Exposition). Four or more symbols caption the illustration representing each breed. These symbols have been specially conceived and assigned by the authors to assist the reader in breed selection and provide an effective system of quick referencing. The symbols indicate the breed's group of origin and/or current-day functions, general care, and proper accommodations.

The index is the most efficient way of finding a particular breed. Since breeds have different names in different countries, all the common names of each breed are assembled in the index for easy cross-referencing.

The introductory chapters preceding the breed entries were written by Kerry V. Donnelly. These concise, easy-to-read chapters give potential dog owners an idea of the responsibilities and general know-how involved in ownership.

Foreword

Sidati. S'asseoir. Sittan. Sizzen. Sætte sig.
Sitten. Sedere. Seddu. Far sedere.
Hizein. Sentar. Zitten.
Seedet. Sitja.
Sit.*

And through the babble, unrunged tongues ring indiscernibly through tower-ing rubble: Dog squats unknowingly, unaffected, sincere. The blasphe-mous tribe of Man falls.

Man continues to build his towers and walls—sometimes Dog helps and sometimes Dog just sits—still, more knowingly than before, irreverently simple.

Our world is a world of dogs. Revolving, evolving, involving, like man him-self. Red dogs and blue dogs and a lot of black dogs. Bicolored, tricol-ored, or solid white. Mongrels, dingoes, purebreds.

More variations than any other animal on the earth, the dog chooses man—to serve, to befriend, to coexist—without expectation, without apology. Man learns to communicate with this unconditional companion; teaches him, disciplines him, and mythologizes his genesis.

As weapons of war or tokens of peace, chessmen or talismen; tractors; shovels; scarecrows; engines; snowmobiles; and handmuffs—dogs have provided for humankind. It is the dog's many and diversified chores, the tasks which man has set before him, that have lead the authors toward unkennelling the dogs of the world. Ten chores yield the authors' ten groups. Each breed in this book, while admittedly unique, has been placed with other dogs of similar functions or backgrounds. The authors hope that the placement of each is both practical and appropriate.

Herds of sheepless bleary-eyed shepherds, frantic and bankrupt butchers, frost-bitten Eskimos, fat-rat-owning farmers, scalped or starving pio-neers—the likely result had Dog not joined man's forces. Man and dog continue to enjoy a reciprocally pleasing and dependent relationship. To-day, when our eyes fail, when our body sleeps, when our bed is cold, when our child is lost, when our critics curdle, when our therapist vac-ations, our dogs are there—as miraculous a gift to mankind as laughter itself. Dogs in their many moods make us laugh, cry, think.

And with Dog, our dog, we laugh; decidely unaffected by our human follies. Like mutts muddling through puddles of primordial poop, we survive. Our dogs, gratefully indiscriminate and unbiased, free us—uncomplicating the puzzles of our twentieth-century world and reteaching us the simplicity and unqualified love that only children know.

Find a dog.

A.D./J.J.

*Sanskrit. French. Old English. Old High German. Danish.
Middle English. Latin. Welsh. Italian.
Greek. Spanish. German.
Russian. Old Norse.
English.

If the head was smaller . . .
If the tail were longer . . .
If he faced the water . . .
If the paws were hidden . . . ·
If the neck was darker . . .
If the back was curved . . .
More like the parasol . . .

Stephen Sondheim
Sunday in the Park with George

Choosing a Best Friend

Just as phases and crazes in fashion explode, so also do the undulating trends in "in" pedigree puppies. When selecting a companion for your home, do not be seduced by the first litterful of basking eyes and squirming tails. Chinese Shar-Pei puppies may hold the record for most owners wheedled at first glance.

As the oldest domesticated animal, the dog has shared a long-standing relationship with man. In early times man befriended the dog because he realized that this would be a beneficial association, and the dog took naturally to man, becoming a protector and hunting ally. Through the ages, domesticated canines evolved into various forms, adapting to the climate and geography of each particular region and conforming to the task to be served.

Today the dog enjoys universal appeal as "man's best friend" and can be found in all types of homes, from mansion to shack. Like man, there is no easy description of the typical dog. There are more than four hundred distinct dog breeds throughout the world, and each member has its own idiosyncrasies, requirements, and background. Therefore, when deciding which dog is the right one for you, there are many aspects that should be considered.

WILL I BE A GOOD OWNER?

The first question you must ask yourself is whether you are really ready to commit yourself to caring for a pet dog—now and for many years to come. Buying or adopting a dog should be viewed as a long-term commitment, not a trial run. Owning a dog is a responsibility that should be taken seriously, as too many unwanted pets end up in pounds and are destroyed each year. It is also wise to be sure that *all* members of the household look favorably on this new acquisition. This will help to avoid future conflicts and feelings of resentment toward you and the pet.

The basic ingredient for being a good owner is *caring*—caring enough to see that your pet is properly fed, housed, and trained. Not everyone fulfills this basic requirement. Careless owners are those who think feeding their puppy is all that is needed. Such puppies inevitably turn out to be improperly trained, unmanageable adult dogs. Careless owners are those who are away from the home for extended periods of time with little thought given to making arrangements for a substitute caretaker. Leaving a puppy in "solitary confinement" will produce loneliness, and loneliness will manifest itself in messing and any number of destructive habits.

Another point to consider is that a puppy sometimes creates a nuisance. Even the best trained dog will occasionally track in dirt or knock something over —often with an exuberant wag of the tail! Most dogs shed, sometimes heavily. Very neat people should bear these things in mind when considering bringing a puppy into their home.

A happy, obedient dog often resides in a home with a caring owner. American Eskimo.

Through bright blues and some shag do these two toddlers make promising acquaintance. The Old English Sheepdog—or Bobtail to his friends.

WHICH DOG SHOULD I SELECT?

Before you begin the search for that one special puppy, you must take stock of your preferences, lifestyle, and environment. The dog you choose must fit in as a member of your household. Neither owner nor pet should have to make major adjustments to conform with each other's requirements.

Selecting a puppy is selecting a dog: remember that whichever pup you choose will grow into a specific kind of dog with a personality and sense of utility all its own. American Staffordshire Terrier puppies.

Size

If you live in a city or in an apartment in the suburbs, size is an important consideration. Remember that the little puppy will grow into a full-sized dog, and most big dogs require an extensive amount of exercise. Unless you are willing and able to help your dog fulfill his exercise requirements, choose a dog that can thrive in close quarters. Even in the suburbs you should bear in mind that a large dog will have to be carefully confined to keep him from bothering the neighbors. While size is generally a good indicator of how much exercise the dog will require, there are some large dogs that do not have excessive requirements, while there are some smaller breeds that do. Therefore, it is vital that you familiarize yourself with the future space and exercise needs of your prospective puppy.

Many considerations should affect your decision; the size of the dog you choose should "fit" into both your lifestyle and home. The Pomeranian atop this St. Bernard would be the more appropriate choice for an apartment dweller than his mountain-sized buddy.

CHOOSING A BEST FRIEND

Toddlers especially must be taken into account when choosing the right breed. The owner desiring a pint-sized companion and playmate might opt for the toy French Bulldog (above) while the owner looking for a watchdog and "baby sitter" might decide upon the Doberman Pinscher (below).

The Great Pyrenees, though traditionally a flock guardian of undeniable excellence, has become quite a gentle giant, a truly dependable companion of children.

The true giants of the dog world occur mostly within the mastiff group. The Dogue de Bordeaux, or French Mastiff (right), is as giant a mastiff as any dog can aspire to be; his acromegalic features are as wondrous as they are eccentric. The Giant Schnauzer (below) has worked traditionally as a herder and guard dog, and yet he is terrier enough to make the most daring vermin's day. For the right home, both these big doggy dogs can make great pets for great kids.

Purebred or Mongrel?

Both mongrels and purebreds make fine pets, and both offer advantages and disadvantages that you should consider before selecting your puppy or dog. If you are interested in a particular look or a certain trait, you would do best to choose a purebred dog. If your primary interest is in companionship and the ancestry of the dog is of little concern, a mongrel may be a logical choice. The offspring from the mating of non-purebred dogs are generally referred to as mongrels, mixed breeds, or mutts. The offspring of the mating of two different breeds of purebreds are referred to as crossbreeds.

These types of dogs have long been revered as loyal, loving companions. Mongrels are often very attractive, and they are on the whole as intelligent and as healthy as the purebred dogs.

The primary problem with selecting a mongrel puppy is that you can only guess what he will look like when he matures. For example, the mating of a collie-type dog and a terrier-type could produce puppies that are big or small, longhaired or wiry. Also, should you want to replace an old or deceased pet with a new look-alike, you could risk disappointment as your new puppy grows up to look quite different than you hoped. As many mongrels are the result of matings where the sire is unknown, you are then in the dark concerning the personality traits or hereditary factors that your dog will carry. With no pedigree to consult, a new owner has no insurance against the possibility of a sick, unhappy adult dog. Since it is likely that a neighbor may be giving away mixed-breed puppies, a mutt is surely the

Mongrels, mutts, hybrids, or curs—dogs are dogs are dogs, and the right one can make a loving companion. Collie-Lurcher pups.

more affordable option. It should *not* be asserted that you get what you pay for, since mongrels have been known to make equally reliable and loving companions, all things considered.

A good purebred dog, however, represents generations of carefully selected breedings. The

Dalmatian bitch and her whelps. Breeding true, or producing consistent progeny, is one advantage of purebred dogs.

ancestry of the puppy is known and should be traceable. He can be expected to exhibit the bodily structure and carry the traits particular to his breed. However, each puppy must be evaluated on his own. In one litter you may find an assortment of temperaments and variations in size, color, and quality (according to the breed standard). Unlike most mongrels, a purebred puppy will probably have to be purchased from either a breeder or a pet shop. The purchase price can be quite high, depending on the quality of the puppy.

Each breed is judged by a standard that lists as guidelines what the ideal specimen of that breed should look like. The more the dog conforms point by point to the breed standard, the better a specimen he is. While these circumscribed descriptions of breed characteristics refer to the breed as a whole,

Purebred Cocker Spaniel pups take on their parents' characteristics and temperament at an early age.

very few dogs fulfill these exacting specifications, and usually only a trained judge or breeder could tell the difference between several healthy specimens. It is very helpful to read the breed standard when considering the purchase of a purebred dog to acquaint yourself with the major physical characteristics of the breed. A copy of the standard can be obtained from your national kennel club, breeders, or texts avail-

able at your local pet shop.

To provide a general description of each breed, key physical traits of the dogs are presented in the **Portrait** entry of each breed account in this book. These discussions will give the reader an overall sense of a breed's appearance, of course reinforced by the accompanying illustration.

Soft and delicate, the Alaskan Malamute puppy will grow into a sturdy, lively outdoorsman.

The Petit Basset, the jaunty "new" wirehaired basset hound, has opened eyes and arms the world wide.

What Kind of Dog?

Since the world is full of so many wonderful and intriguing dogs, it is difficult to know where to start in choosing the right one for you. The over 400 breeds that this book discusses give the reader a broad perspective of the dogs that man has developed for his purposes. It is important to understand that not all of these breeds are readily available to American or British fanciers, although many of them are. No pet shop in the world could possibly

18

Sporting an appearance similar to his larger cousin the Akita, the Shiba Inu has "sleighed" many a new owner's heart.

stock every breed, but as "rare" breeds become more and more in vogue, the number of possibilities grows. Pet shop dealers, becoming increasingly informed, are often able to direct prospective buyers to a helpful source. Such a buyer must decide which attributes and characteristics are important

This petite Pole has been more than shepherding in recent days. The Polish Lowland Sheepdog is known at home as the Polski Ocwzarek Nizinny.

and then review potential breeds. If you are not familiar with many of the breeds, spend an afternoon visiting an all-breed or rare dog show where you can view quality specimens. A number of dogs are merely international equivalents of beloved American or British breeds, performing similar functions over their given terrain. In order to facilitate the reader's choice, the breeds have been divided into categories. These categories, based on functional and/or historical derivation, are devised to steer the reader toward the type of dog he might like. These groups include: Sighthounds, Mastiffs, Nordic Dogs, Gundogs, Scenthounds, Toys, Flock Guardians, Herding Dogs, Terriers and Pariahs. Each group has individual character traits and abilities that set it apart from another. A closer look at each group reveals the breeds' attributes and personalities.

The Greyhound (left) is the classic prototype of the sighthound group. Among the tallest and sleekest of canines, the Greyhound enjoys moderate popularity in the United States and Great Britain and is most celebrated as the "racehorse of dogdom."

The Toy Fox Terrier (facing), or AmerToy as he is called in the U.S., was America's attempt to produce a toy terrier of her own. The breed's fancy at home is continually growing and Toy Fox owners are ever so enthusiastic about the breed's unmitigated energy and enjoyment of life.

SIGHTHOUNDS

The dogs that we call sighthounds, that is dogs that hunt by sight, are among the oldest known to man. These breeds originated in the Middle East and parts of the southern Soviet Union and Africa. In general, these dogs are lightly boned and sleek in appearance.

As pets, the sighthounds are beautiful and elegant companions. The Borzoi, an example from the group, is becoming increasingly popular with well-to-do persons in the United States and Britain. Sighthounds have never been overly popular—in the U.S., the Afghan Hound boasts the greatest number of fanciers. Because of their relatively large sizes, the sighthounds require a significant amount of space. Most of the breeds are

The sleek, subtly contoured body and the mystic verticality of the sighthound character underlie the Saluki's sudden and pronounced rise in popularity.

smooth-coated, which makes for easy grooming. Exercise is a must. It must be ket in mind that many of the sighthounds or gazehounds were used to course wolves or other large, formidable foes. Their need to stretch their long limbs and run off their frustrations is key to unkinking physical and mental hangups. The sighthounds tend to be dignified and aloof. Never prone to unnecessary cuddling or cooing, they are trustworthy and beguiling companions that always project an unparalleled dignified and regal bearing. A home that is able to house one of these fine canines is well protected and duly ornamented.

The Afghan Hound (right) epitomizes the sighthound's refinement and grace. Owners worthy of such a gracious and regardful canine in their midst find the Afghan an entirely satisfying companion. The Borzoi (below) as a pup captures the more relaxed side of the sighthound personality. Adult Borzois, like a great many of the desert gazers, are aloof and more than a little independent, though rarely condescending toward their human fellows.

MASTIFFS

The mastiffs are generally derived from the molossus-type dogs of ancient times. Many mastiffs are very big and tend to be rather on the aggressive side. The years, however, have substantially mellowed many of them, and they make reliable companions and enviable guard dogs. Historically, the members of the mastiff category were used for fighting or defending purposes. This explains their natural defensive inclinations. Not everyone who is allured by the appeal of these "giants" is a qualified mastiff owner. These dogs require owners that are not afraid to be stern with them. Discipline is a vital component of ownership. One must

The Bernese Mountain Dog pup, in tow with no small amount of appeal or character.

also be fair and consistent with his dogs so that they understand the nature of the correction. In addition to disciplinary measures, the larger of these dogs requires a tremendous amount of food and space in order to thrive. Many mastiff breeds are popular today. Among them are the Bulldog, Doberman Pinscher, and Saint Bernard. These dogs each have personalities of their own. Some are truly gentle giants while others are surly and incorrigible.

The heartwarming St. Bernard has rescued and revived many an astrayed or snowbound human.

CHOOSING A BEST FRIEND

The mastiff group contains the largest and heaviest breeds of dog, although a number of these breeds can be more moderately sized. The Rottweiler's size has not affected its popularity: the personality gleaming from this Rottie youth (right) is singular to the breed and confirms its tremendous popularity. This happy clan of Boxers (below) also moderately sized mastiffs with a growing fancy.

NORDIC DOGS

The breeds from the North are perhaps among the most beautiful and striking of all dogs. These dogs have developed from the sledge dog types. They are mostly of amenable dispositions and revel in the company of their human families. These breeds are distinguished by their plush full coats, curled tails and prick ears. Their coats require a good deal of commitment on the owner's part. Of course, there are exceptions to every rule: the smooth Chow Chow, Norwegian Lundehund, and Norbottenspets are just a few breeds that do not

The plushly coated, blue-tongued Chow Chow is one of the world's most widely embraced nordic breeds.

possess lengthy coats. Many of these breeds have also become popular of late. The Chow Chow, Chinese Shar-Pei, American Eskimo, Finnish Spitz and Shiba Inu are some breeds that have new and growing fancies. Of course, the Alaskan Malamute, Siberian Husky, Akita and Samoyed have enjoyed healthy fancies for quite some time now. As companions, the Nordics are trustworthy and loving dogs that express their affection for their owners in obedience and in their need to be close by. These breeds, having largely originated from vigorous sled-pulling dogs, need a good amount of exercise to keep them healthy and trim.

Never solely a working dog, the Samoyed enjoys a long history of close relationships with man. The unconditional affection and adherence of the Samoyed to its master exceeds the wildest expectations of any new owner.

The Siberian Husky is widely acclaimed today as a robust, faithful working dog as well as a winning, devoted consort.

GUNDOGS

Man has been fortunate in having a dog by his side for his every activity. The breeds that we classify as gundogs are canines that are used to work from the hunter's gun. The group can be further divided by the specific function that a particular dog executes: water

working, pointing, setting, flushing, and retrieving. Many dogs cross these lines and can do any number of tasks. As companion dogs go, these dogs are paramount and have mounted kennel club stats forever. The ever-popular Poodle, Cocker Spaniel, Labrador Retriever and Golden Retriever, to name a few, claim countless canines on both sides of the Atlantic. The gundogs are perhaps the most intelligent of all dogs and resultingly are the most trainable. Their dispositions are even and becoming. In the world of dogs today, most of these breeds are more common as companions only rather than as working gundogs. Not too many Poodle fanciers spend their weekends hunting ducks in the swamp (although some do!). The distinction of "gundog" as a classification reflects the original purpose for which the dogs were bred. Of course, many retriever fans use their

The gundogs comprise the brain trust of the canine world. Handsome as a fox and more cunning, the Nova Scotia Duck Tolling Retriever typifies the swift-minded, swift-moving hunter.

retrievers avidly, and many of these dogs work as well as any of their forefathers. These are active and energetic dogs that need plenty of attention and time spent outdoors. A solely indoor existence is not recommended and can be torturous for these dogs.

CHOOSING A BEST FRIEND

Though elegance is no ordinary barometer of field prowess, the English Springer Spaniel is a happy exception.

Gundogs' devotion to their masters is exemplified in their obedience and stamina on the field. In the home, at their owners' feet, their love and sincerity are unconcealed. Weimaraner.

SCENTHOUNDS

The scenthound group comprises the largest number of dogs. The glory days of hunting in England and France yielded quite a bounty of canines bred to perform that task. America, too, contributed to the pool with its coonhound varieties, which were developed to tree raccoon. Many of these dogs, especially in their native lands, still excel at hunting various and difficult game. Other hounds are cherished as family companions and never experience the high of the hunt. The Beagle,

Dachshund, and Basset Hound are just a few examples of ideal companion dogs—that's not to say that these dogs aren't also quality hunting companions. Hounds are basically easycare animals; their short coats and mild dispositions make them sheer pleasure to

own. Despite many hounds' preference for lying about the house, these dogs need substantial exercise and regular outdoor hours. They can be the most affectionate of all canines.

Hound breeds are the most plenteous. Switzerland offers a lauf-a-thon of hounds: neither of these Berner Laufhund pups will allow a canine fan to walk away without smiling.

The passion for hunting in France traces its roots back for centuries. The foxhounds running with the masters on horseback present a dazzling illustration of the European love for the sport and the scenthound's vigor for the hunt.

Beagles are perhaps the most popular of the scenthounds kept as pets: Beagles and their enamored bugle-blowing beaglers are an important component of the dog fancy in most every country. Ideally sized, obedient and clean, Beagles fit into any lifestyle with beguiling and benevolent ease.

TOYS

The breeds categorized as "toy" are mainly companion animals. Many of the dogs were bred specifically to serve in that capacity while others somehow slipped into the group because of their diminutive size. Most toys have exuberantly friendly personalities and love attention. "Lap" dogs (or dogs that are small enough to fit on one's lap) are conducive to

Overplaying its role, the Chihuahua is a plush delight in any toybox.

fondling and have been popular in Europe and Asia for many centuries. The pampered pets of royalty thrived indoors and were accustomed to the finest treatment. The toy breeds come from a wide divergence of backgrounds, since every functional or historical group has been bantamized to one extent or another. For example, the Pug is a miniature mastiff and the Papillon is a miniature gundog. The toy breeds' need for exercise is easily satisfied, and they are most content indoors. For the longhaired dogs, a quantity of grooming is required. Many toy breeds prosper in the show ring: the Yorkshire Terrier, Lhasa Apso, Maltese and Chihuahua for starters. These are intelligent and hearty companions, but owners must be discretionary with their praise and overflowing affection. Spoiled toy dogs can be real monsters and never allow anyone to touch them (except their "mommies"). Ideally, these dogs are friendly and extroverted companions and not untouchable home ornaments.

Sweatered and cooing, the Italian Greyhound is the original toy dog, feigning no other more strenuous function.

CHOOSING A BEST FRIEND

The Cavalier King Charles Spaniel (right) is a most respected British citizen who has earned the royal seal of approval. A companion that emulates an unfoiled English demeanor, deplete of baseness or the slightest indication of the uncouth. This mini agglomeration of pint-size mastiffs—a litter of Pugs (below)—is as like as like can be, gleaming in faces both pugnacious and proverbial.

FLOCK GUARDIANS

Protective and powerful, the flock guardians are breeds that are employed as sentinels and defenders of sheep or goats. It seems that most every European country has developed a flock guard, since agricultural well-beings are hampered by a number of natural predators. To blend in with the white woolly masses they tend, these dogs are almost invariably white and often tend towards massive. Flock guards have to be sizable and fearless to protect the flock from attacking wolves or other large predators. Guardian angels of sorts, these breeds bond well with their sheep and have no other priority in life. Shepherds relied heavily on these heavy-footed canines. Strength as well as speed are vital to the flock guardian's duty. As companion dogs, many contend that there is no better choice. For the most part, these are gentle and beguiling creatures that can make sublime pets and guard dogs. Some, however, tend to be aloof and perhaps don't quite understand why they're needed around the house with no sheep to protect. Others can be aggressive towards unfamiliar dogs whom they perceive as threats to their homes. The Great Pyrenees, Kuvasz, and Komondor have all excelled as home companions. The general large size of these dogs makes an outdoor pen and/or sufficient exercise area an absolute must.

The Spanish Mastiff is a native flock guardian of Spain. While basically unknown in the U.S. and Britain today, the breed has done well in setting a giant paw forward into the pet world.

CHOOSING A BEST FRIEND

In the Soviet Union, the South Russian Ovtcharka performs wondrous feats of strength in defending its flock and much of its fervor and protective instincts are readily adapted to its human charges, making it a dutiful home guardian and watchdog.

HERDING DOGS

Not to be confused with flock guardians, the herding dogs are used to steer the flock and keep them together. It is not usually the herder's task to protect the flock since its larger workmate handles this with no problem. Herding dogs are perhaps the most industrious and agile of the world's canines. Controlling an unruly gang of wild or semi-wild sheep or cattle requires a dog of both industry and fearlessness.

Herding dogs are easily taught to perform their given chores, and most breeds pick up on their jobs instinctively from the time they are puppies. Although many of the herders today work in their traditional capacities (the Border Collie, Australian Kelpie, and Australian Shepherd are especially noteworthy), many of the dogs have been adapted to other employment. The German Shepherd Dog, Bouvier des Flandres, and Belgian Sheepdog are used variously as police

The Shetland Sheepdog is a warm and sincere home companion that still retains its round-up abilities.

dogs, guide dogs, and search and rescue workers. The Collie, Shetland Sheepdog and Old English Sheepdog are prized companion dogs that are not usually seen maneuvering the ovine masses about the pasture. These dogs require a good amount of exercise but are essentially easy-to-live-with pets.

The Cão da Serra de Aires, as tousled and tantalizing a tot he is, is not seen outside his native Portugal, where he is relied upon as a herder of sheep and goats.

36

The Bouvier des Flandres (above) is a noteworthy cowherder and watchdog that has gained popularity outside Belgium as a pet and companion. The Australian Shepherd, rarely seen in Australia (because he's American), is as competent a sheep herder and faithful a dog as one could wish.

TERRIERS

This energetic group of dogs was developed expressly to go to ground. This task required feisty and fearless dogs with heart and spunk. Size in the group varies extensively: the Airedale Terrier, being the tallest, and the Patterdale Terrier, perhaps the smallest. Yet both dogs have uncompromising vim and controlled aggression. A number of the smaller terriers, rather small to be considered workers, are placed in the toy group.

Terriers have long held the attention of dog fanciers: whether entertaining the masses by speed-killing rats in a pit or elating the terrier-man by holding a badger three times its weight at bay, these energized dogs have always received abundant praise. Terriers are noble in character and highly loyal as companions. Many dogs are worked extensively today and approach their jobs with verve and enthusiasm. The smaller terriers are ideally sized as companion dogs and delight in the company of children.

Going to ground, the Smooth Fox Terrier is a rowdy and industrious companion.

The Cairn Terrier uproots the heart of many a dog fancier; in Great Britain, the breed is especially adored.

CHOOSING A BEST FRIEND

The Welsh Terrier (above) tends to be mindful and decisive as a pet; the Jack Russell Terrier (right) offers the hunting enthusiast astounding ability and the homebody abounding energy.

The Czesky Terrier, a less popular breed of terrier, is as feisty and hell-raising a puppy as one could handle and yet grows into one of the most elegant of canine comrades.

PARIAHS

Granted, pariah in its literal sense is no word anyone would rightly appreciate attached to his dog. Pariah means scavenger or outcast. Such a description is hardly intended, although in the general sense, the word aptly fits the dogs grouped here,

a handful though they may be. Many pariahs derived from the areas of northern Africa and southern Asia. In conformation these dogs vary greatly, and in temperament they are sometimes uneven. The Dingo of Australia is a good example of such a canine. This particular dog is sometimes not even considered a dog and is almost never deemed pet material. The Basenji, however, is a wonderful pet and is believed to be descended from general pariah stock. Also included in this loose grouping are a couple of hairless breeds that can also be ideal housemates for the right owner. The smaller sized hairless breeds are more appropriately grouped with the toy breeds. The pariahs in a domesticated form are fine inside dogs and generally have adapted well to this lifestyle. The Canaan Dog and Basenji are the best known examples.

The Dingoes of Australia (facing) ideally represent the pariah group. These are essentially feral dogs that may or may not have been domesticated at one time. They are very loyal to members of their canine families but have no potential as family pets. Likewise, the New Guinea Singing Dog (right) is of like heritage; these specimens are zoo-kept.

The Basenji, commonly believed to be of pariah origin (although some still purport it is a nordic dog gone off hitch), is the most popular pet in the pariah group. The Basenji is one of the cleanest and most intelligent canines that an owner could hope to adopt.

Show Quality or Pet Quality?

When purchasing your purebred puppy, you must decide whether you want him to be a companion or if you will show him in competition. This is of great importance because only the finest breed specimens should be entered into active competition. Show-quality puppies are the hardest to find and are the most expensive to buy.

With dog shows becoming increasingly popular, more and more owners are becoming stung by the exhibition bug. Any purebred dog, with the necessary registration and pedigree papers, is eligible to compete in the show ring. The dog sport is as professional a sport as any national pastime, and participants, judges and sponsors take the show ring quite seriously. Any owner planning to exhibit his dog should be well aware of the variables involved.

If showing is your intent, you should buy a puppy from a knowledgeable and reputable breeder. The puppies available in pet shops or from most neighborhood owners are generally termed "pet quality," that is, more ideal

Native dogs sometimes become less popular in their homelands as it becomes chic to own an imported equivalent or a foreign rarity. Here at a Japanese Kennel Club exhibition, a British Bulldog takes Best in Show while a Shiba Inu, a native Nipponese, stands off to the side.

CHOOSING A BEST FRIEND

for a household pet than a show ring contender. If you go to a breeder, be sure to make clear your desire to show the dog so that he or she will sell you the best specimen possible. Dedicated breeders strive to produce the best possible dogs, ones that will perpetuate the quality of the breed. Not all dogs owned by even the best breeders are of top quality when compared against the standard. Therefore, a breeder may stipulate that you are not to breed the pet-quality animal and thereby pass on his faulty traits, so bear this in mind and be sure to clarify your intentions at the time of sale. Also be aware that you will pay top prices for show dogs and for those females with brood bitch potential. If you are not interested in dog show exhibiting, any healthy, well-bred specimen should do.

When purchasing a purebred puppy, the new owner should be given the puppy's registration certificate. Breeders generally register their entire litter with the national kennel club, so you may be given a form that you must complete to transfer the ownership of the puppy to your name. If the puppy has not already been registered, you will need to obtain the necessary information from

A small handful of the world's breeds defy both description and equivalents. The Basset Hound, with puddle-warm eyes and its internationally loved personality, celebrates this distinction.

the breeder, fill in the appropriate registration form, and mail this and the fee to your national kennel club. It generally takes three to four weeks to receive the certificate. Your breeder may also be able to supply you with a three-generation pedigree (or an even more detailed one) should you want to trace your dog's ancestry.

If you are purchasing your "pedigreed" dog from a pet shop, you should receive the appropriate papers from the proprietor. Those breeders that sell puppies to pet shops should also provide pedigrees. Most owners like to know where their puppy came from and who its parents were, even if they are not planning to show the dog.

Occasionally a breeder will purposely withhold the registration certificate because the puppy has a fault that would disqualify it according to the breed or dog show standards. In these cases the breeder may sell these pet-quality dogs only after the new owner has agreed not to breed the animal. In this way the breeder hopes to eliminate the disqualifying traits. It does not mean the puppy is not a purebred or that it will make a poor pet.

The necessary forms for registering or transferring ownership of a purebred dog can be obtained by writing to:

AMERICAN KENNEL CLUB
51 Madison Avenue
New York, NY 10010
U.S.A.

THE KENNEL CLUB OF GREAT BRITAIN
1 Clarges Street
Piccadilly, London W1Y 8AB
England

CANADIAN KENNEL CLUB
2150 Bloor Street West
Toronto 12, Ontario, M6S 4V7
Canada

AUSTRALIAN NATIONAL KENNEL CLUB
Royal Show Grounds
Ascot Vale, 3032, Victoria
Australia

FÉDÉRATION CYNOLOGIQUE INTERNATIONALE
Rue Léopold-II
14B-6530 Thuin
Belgium

UNITED KENNEL CLUB
100 East Kilgore Road
Kalamazoo, MI
49001-5598
U.S.A.

A quality purebred and a show-quality purebred are most distinct. While the latter might cost one a good deal, a quality purebred, ideal for life as a pet dog, need not cost much. Pedigreed dogs should be registered with their national kennel club. Miniature Schnauzer.

CHOOSING A BEST FRIEND

No matter how pendant and deep the flews of the English Bulldog are, nothing interferes with this posh gentleman's "stiff upper lip."

Male or Female?

Once you have settled on the breed you want, a choice of sex must be made. While both sexes make good pets, there are a few differences. If you are interested in breeding and raising a litter of puppies, you should, of course, select a female (commonly referred to as a bitch). Those who do not plan on breeding should bear in mind that a non-spayed female will attract males when in season. With most breeds this occurs every six months, lasts two to three weeks, and can be very annoying. Spaying will eliminate this problem. Females are generally regarded as a little more gentle than males and therefore have been acclaimed as better housepets. Males are often larger and more active than their female counterparts and have a stronger tendency to roam. While both sexes are equally loving and loyal, females have been touted as superior watchdogs because they are less likely to be distracted by outside forces. Males, however, are noted for being more aggressive against intruders.

It is a fortunate owner who falls in love with the Dachshund breed. Of all the breeds known to man, the Dachshund has the most varieties: Standards and Miniatures in smooth, wire, and long coats.

CHOOSING A BEST FRIEND

Crinkly seams with unopened fortunes, these two Chinese babies trust their new master to unfold to them the mysteries of the world. The Shar-Pei pup, in all its wrinkly wonder, will soon grow into its oversized skin, leaving only a few folds loose under its neck.

The Clumber Spaniel is renowned for its affectionate and easygoing demeanor, if not for its hunting drive and alacrity. Two Clumbers, therefore, tend to be twice as loving and winning, ever so clumsily demonstrative, although not much faster on the field.

One Dog or More?

Dogs generally prefer the attention of humans to the companionship of another dog, so there is no real need to buy your puppy a companion unless he is to be left alone a great deal of the time. If this is the case, the second dog may help minimize loneliness.

If you are introducing a puppy into a home with an older dog, remember that there will be a period of adjustment for both dogs. The older dog may manifest signs of jealousy and resent the intrusion of the puppy. To

Inherent in the herder's abilities are protectiveness, intelligence and confidence: the Belgian Sheepdog, Tervuren is one of the most industrious and amenable herders anyone could want.

counter this, be sure to give the older dog lots of attention. At feeding time, be sure to watch both dogs, especially the puppy, who—not knowing the rules—may try to steal from the other dog's bowl. Most adult dogs will accept a new dog in the home after some time, but if either dog shows any aggressiveness, you may want to keep them separated. Introduce them to each other for short periods of time until they get accustomed to each other.

Many breeds of dogs, especially the gundogs and hounds, can be raised as kennel dogs, often in large groups. These dogs are trained to function as hunting allies, not primarily as housepets. Dogs that become accustomed to spending all their time with their littermates and companions do not suffer from lack of human attention. They thrive on the time they and their master spend at the hunt or in training for the hunt. These dogs should not, however, be neglected or kept in cramped quarters. They must be given ample opportunity for exercise, be well fed to supply enough energy to sustain this vigorous life, be properly trained, and receive ample love and attention.

Certain breeds or kinds of dogs, however, never take well to other dogs. Whether a protective pit bull sort or a jealous toy dog sort, these sorts do not appreciate the company of other canines and will continually reject a "playmate," no matter how delicately they are acclimated to each other.

What Age is Best?

While puppies are certainly their most adorable at six to eight weeks of age, this may not be the most advantageous age for the owners. At this age, the puppy is like a baby that requires 24-hour-a-day care. He is too

The German Wirehaired Pointer sports one of the most benevolent expressions in dogdom; even at a young age, the Wirehair's appearance is considered gruff and grandfatherly.

CHOOSING A BEST FRIEND

young to house-break, requires four feedings a day, and is undisciplined. In fact, a much higher percentage of four-to six-week-old puppies die shortly after being placed with new owners than eight-week-olds. At three to six months, a puppy can be more easily house-trained and he should have already been wormed and given his primary shots. As a buyer, you should consider how much time you have to devote to the puppy's early care when you set out to purchase that new family member.

For the right owner, the hairless breeds offer a home more than just an exotic conversation piece. These hypoaller-genic, flea-free canines, however, require special care and attention throughout their lives.

Purchase your puppy when you find the one you feel will be best for you—whether he is six weeks old or six months old. One possible solution for dealing with primary puppy care is to leave the six-week-old puppy with the breeder for a month or two after you purchase him and pay board to the breeder. Experienced breeders are generally more adept at dealing with the needs of puppies and may be amenable to this arrangement. If you are considering purchasing an adult dog that has never been kept as a house-pet, be sure to check his disposition carefully, as he may have trouble ad-justing to family life.

WHERE CAN I FIND MY PUPPY?

There are numerous sources to check when looking for a dog. When pur-chasing a purebred dog, you have several options. Pet shops and breeders are the best choices. If your pet shop doesn't have the breed you desire, the proprietor may be able to recommend a reputable breeder. If you choose to select your puppy from a local breeder, you should be able to see both or at least one of the puppy's parents. Visit more than one breeder, even if you think you've found the right dog. You should be able to locate several breed-ers in your area by consulting the ads in your newspaper or in the various publications issued by dog clubs. If you write to your national kennel club, they will also be able to supply you with a list of breeders, but this may take a few weeks. If you are interested in a top-quality specimen, you could attend a dog show and talk to a few of the exhibitors. Some may have puppies or dogs for sale, or may know of some. In some cases exhibitors with a stock of show dogs will sell dogs that have attained their championship title and have been retired from the ring. At the very least, these breed enthusiasts can acquaint you with what to look for and give you helpful suggestions.

Many dog owners acquire their pets when a neighbor's dog has puppies. In the case of mongrels, most are generally given free to good homes. Another major outlet of dogs is the local dog pound or humane society. In some cases animals are kept until suitable homes are found for them, but in many instances the animals are held only for a set number of days before they are destroyed. Because of this, if you are looking for a dog as a companion, the local pound is a good place to start. If you select a dog from this stock, you may be asked for a donation to help defray the costs of maintaining the pound. You may also be asked to sign a form stating that you will have the dog spayed or neutered to avoid future unwanted litters. If this is the case, the organization may be able to arrange for low-cost sterilization.

Poodles are popular. Poodles are friendly. Poodles like people. Poodles are big. Poodles are small. Poodles for hunting. Poodles for tea. Poodles are unique.

WHAT ARE THE SIGNS OF A HEALTHY PUPPY?

When choosing from a group of puppies, what criteria should you use to set one dog apart from the rest? In the case of a litter of well-bred, well-cared-for puppies, it will generally be the pup's temperament. One may stand out as the most jovial or loving—or may do something to get your attention. It should be outgoing and vigorous. Once it has caught your eye, evaluate its physical condition. A puppy should be plump and look well-fed. The ribs and hipbones should not be obviously protruding. A thin or potbellied puppy generally indicates the presence of worms. If it is a smooth-coated dog, the coat should be shiny; if long coated, the coat should be thick.

Don't let bad health sneak up on you: your puppy's vital signs are clear reflections of his healthful condition. This Old English Sheepdog, perky and alert, is the picture of health.

Be aware that many breeds are exceptions to this easy rule. Check the skin for sores, rashes, and the presence of parasites (fleas, ticks). There should be no dry or scaling patches. The eyes should be clear and there should be no discharge from eyes or nose. The typical healthy puppy is full of energy, not listless or shy. If you can, try to see the puppy at mealtime. It should have a good appetite. Have the owner take the puppy's temperature if it shows any sign of illness or fatigue. A normal reading will be from 101° to 102°F (39°C).

Observing the physical state of the dam and sire, if possible, will give you some indication of the quality of animals that they have produced. Keep in mind that the bitch has recently undergone birthing and likely is not looking her best. Nonetheless, her temperament should be steady and her general health sound.

WHEN SHOULD I BUY MY PUPPY?

The best time for buying a puppy is in the late spring or summer, or whenever the weather is pleasant. During temperate seasons you can housebreak the puppy without exposing it to cold and wet weather. At this time, the puppy can get lots of fresh air, exercise, and sunshine—which will be good for its owner too! While puppies make wonderful Christmas presents, this is often a time of great excitement for the whole family and the commotion may intimidate a young puppy. In many geographical areas the weather is at its worst at this

The terriers often get on flawlessly with kids. Their spunk and energy solidify a permanent bond with their starry-eyed toddler companions. In the arms of a friend, this Norfolk Terrier is content and secure.

time of year, making both owner and puppy less than eager to go out for those necessary housebreaking trips. Pets that are given for surprise holiday presents often do not work out, as the family is not prepared for the new addition. Dogs should not be given on a whim or to a small child who may soon tire of him or the care involved.

Regardless of the time of year, it is almost always best to bring the new puppy home over the weekend. In this way the puppy can become acquainted with all members of the household and they will have some time to spend with it.

Getting the puppy adjusted to the family and household is essential. Slowly involve the pup in the house routine, but never rush the acquaintance procedure. Generally, pups are shy when overwhelmed by too much attention—be moderate and let the pup's personality develop naturally.

FINALIZING THE DEAL

Once you've found that perfect puppy, take your time and think over your decision one last time. Before you pay, arrange with the owner to allow you to take the dog to the veterinarian for a health examination. Most breeders or pet shops will let you return the dog within a limited amount of time if the dog should fail the health exam for any reason. Get this in writing, and be sure of the terms. Some owners will return all money and others will replace the ailing puppy with another dog. This agreement does not generally apply for a change of heart about owning a dog but only if the dog is certified as being physically unfit.

Before you take the puppy home, get all shot records and, in the case of purebreds, the dog's registration certificate or application form. Question the owner for any information he or she may have concerning the puppy's habits or personality traits. Is there a favorite toy or blanket that you could take along with you to ease the transition? Ask what and how often the puppy has been fed, and try not to vary the diet very drastically at first. Some owners will send a supply of food home with the new owners. The pet shop owner or breeder should be more than happy to answer any questions you may have on how best to raise the puppy.

A blue-eyed quartet of ghostly delight, these Weimaraner pups promise never a "gray" morning or a restless evening.

General Care

Before the puppy arrives, you should set aside an area of the house for it and buy all the supplies you will need for the early weeks. The basic necessities include: puppy food, food and water bowls, brush and comb, bed or sleeping box, a collar and leash.

Keeshond puppies are popular around the world. Britain favored the Dutch Barge Dog of Holland, the Keeshond, a spin-off of Germany's Wolfspitz.

THE PUPPY'S FIRST DAY

Regardless of the age of your puppy, its first day in a new home is traumatic. Very young puppies can be particularly unnerved. Try to make the transition easy for the puppy by not overtiring it with continuous play or attention. Keep play periods short and allow the pup to take plenty of naps. Be sure all family members, especially children, know the proper way to handle and pick up a puppy. You should place one hand under the hindquarters and the other across the chest—never pick it up by the paws or legs or by the back of the neck.

Start housebreaking the first day, but don't be too stern or expect the puppy to really understand. Mistakes are bound to happen, so confine the puppy to a small area. Use a sleeping box for its naps and try to comfort and reassure it should it start to cry. If the puppy has not been immunized, keep it indoors until this is done.

PUPPY BED OR SLEEPING BOX

The young puppy's bed is an important tool in easing the transition from the security of the mother to the new home. It will also aid in the housebreaking process, as there is a natural instinct for a dog to want to keep his bed clean. A box is best for the four- to eight-week-old puppy. You should hold off buying a bed until your pup is a little older and closer to its adult size. Always place the bed in a warm, dry spot that is free from all drafts.

The puppy's box should be only slightly larger than the pup itself. The bed should allow the pup to stand, turn around, and lie down at full length. The puppy should not be able to make a mess in one end and lie comfortably in another. Be sure there are plenty of ventilation holes and line the bottom of the box with several flat layers of newspaper, which are easily disposable. You should withhold putting a blanket in the box for a week or two, as a blanket may bunch up and just be in the way.

The puppy wants to keep its bed clean, but will be forced to relieve itself if not taken out at regular intervals. Expect a few accidents the first few days. The newspaper should be changed immediately following any such accident. As the puppy grows, you may have to get a larger box, or the pup may do well with early housebreaking and you can move the pup to a more permanent bed.

While it is essential for a new puppy to play with and be loved by the new family, such a creature tires easily and needs many naps each day. Try to place the pup in its box for as many of these naps as possible, as this will help it feel secure in the box and help to keep it from crying at night.

Once the puppy settles into a housebreaking routine, it is a good time to consider buying a permanent bed. Be sure to place the bed in an area that the dog likes, or it may not use it. Some beds come with mattresses that contain scented materials, such as cedar. Many dogs do

An American Cocker Spaniel pup nestled in its bed.

not like the smell and will not use the bed. Other dogs just don't enjoy a bed and often prefer the rugs or furniture. Hopefully the pup's preference and yours will be mutually agreeable! If not, correct the dog each time it breaks the rules of where it can and cannot sleep. For the old dog, a foam rubber mattress may be soothing and help it to sleep easier. Pet shops stock a wide variety of ideal accommodations.

DOGHOUSES

If your dog spends much time outdoors, it should be supplied with the protection of a doghouse. This house should not be so heavy as to be immovable, as it should be placed in the shade in the summer and in the sun in the winter. If possible, it should be well insulated to keep warm in cold weather and stay cool in the heat of the summer.

The doghouse should be placed in an area that drains well. The

Nordic dogs, more than any other group of dogs, enjoy a snow-covered outdoors, but even such hardy breeds as the Siberian Husky appreciate the convenience of an outside doghouse.

bottom of the house should never be placed directly on the ground but should be slightly elevated, perhaps by placing two or three bricks under each corner or by building legs that extend six to eight inches from the bottom.

Pet shops are often well stocked with a number of commercial dog houses. These typically hard plastic or fiberglass structures come in a variety of colors, shapes and sizes and may even give your backyard a new zing. Designed to be parasite-free and withstand the elements, these "home-away-from-homes" can save you time and money in the long run.

Whether you are building your own doghouse or purchasing a ready-made one, there are several important features to consider. There are various methods to draftproof the doghouse. Nail carpeting across the door to act as a curtain against the wind. A more effective method is to partition the house into two separate compartments. The inner wall will keep the inside compartment shielded from the elements. A section of roof or one side should be hinged for ease in changing the bedding.

Bedding is an important part of the doghouse. It provides warmth and comfort and helps protect the dog from getting sores and callouses on his elbows, hocks, and tail. The bedding should be changed frequently, as soiled bedding will attract fleas, ticks, and lice.

FEEDING

Although one generous meal a day will suffice, the most common feeding pattern among today's dog owners is to give a small meal in the morning and a big meal in the late afternoon or early evening. This system originated with the use of herding dogs. Since food tended to make the dog sluggish, he was fed after he finished his day's work. Owners of guard dogs which work primarily at night reverse the usual pattern and feed the dog his big meal in the morning—which is after work for the dog. This pattern should not be followed for growing puppies that may need up to four meals a day. Most dogs grow, in the first two years, the equivalent of a human's first twenty-four years, so maintain an adequate diet during this high growth period.

Types of Food

Dogs have tolerant digestive systems that are well adapted to handling concentrated foods, such as meat. Their diet must be high in protein and have a sufficient amount of carbohydrates, fats, vitamins, and minerals. Today's commercially prepared name-brand foods are the result of years of research in nutrition. They are also convenient and economical. These products are generally fortified with vitamins and minerals to supplement the basic ingredients, which can suffer a substantial vitamin loss during processing.

Some meats—canned or fresh—can be irritants to the dog's system. A small number of dogs have been found to be allergic to beef products that contain chemical additives to prevent spoilage. Pork is hard to digest, and some dogs experience diarrhea after eating liver. Be alert for signs of distress if you feed these meats to your dog. Older dogs can suffer from kidney problems, and heavy meat often overloads their systems with wastes and excess protein. Your veterinarian will generally prescribe modifications to the diet of older dogs to avoid health complications.

A balanced diet is essential for any dog. This Shih Tzu's chow mein treat, however, sets no model.

How Much Is Enough?

A growing puppy should be plump, but as it grows it should lose its "baby fat" and grow into a lean, firm adult. To determine if your adult dog is properly fed, run your hands over its ribs and hipbones (do this after a bath in the case of heavy-coated dogs). If these bones are easily seen or felt, the dog is probably underweight. If the bones are padded and hard to find, it may be overweight.

An overweight dog is the product of too much food and too little activity. To help a dog regain proper weight, cut back slightly on the amount of food you give. Increase the dog's physical activity slowly at first, and maintain the desired level to keep off all lost weight.

All dogs will benefit from receiving healthy table scraps, such as vegetables and cereal. Do not give any sweets or products with sugar, seasoned meats, or vegetables that can be gas producing (brussels sprouts, cabbage, or broccoli).

Fresh water should regularly be made available to your puppy. However, like this Rottweiler, puppies have notions of their own as to its proper use.

While most dogs will eat the same food every day without complaint, it is advisable to offer a slight variation every now and again. By serving a variety of foods, you can avoid stomach or bowel trouble when the dog's diet is forced to change due to travel plans or shortages of its usual food.

Puppies require daily multiple feedings for energy and development. Samoyed pups.

GENERAL CARE

Vitamin and Mineral Supplements

Nutritionists claim that vitamin and mineral supplements can help pets live longer and healthier lives. If you are decreasing the amount of food you are giving your overweight dog, you are also decreasing the amount of vitamins and minerals in his diet. Therefore, you should consider giving a vitamin supplement if the dog is to remain on this low-calorie diet for an extended period of time.

Various claims have been made concerning the benefits of supplementing a dog's diet. Vitamin E has been shown to help improve a poor coat, and vitamin supplementation is generally used to help bitches whelp easier and faster by replacing the elements that are diverted from the mother to the puppies during pregnancy.

EXERCISE

A proper diet and adequate exercise are necessary requirements for keeping a dog fit. The most obvious sign that your dog is not getting enough exercise is excess weight, but there are other indications. If your dog is overactive or restless in the house, he may need more time outside for vigorous activity. Pets with excess energy may show signs of anxiety or exhibit destructive tendencies.

To test your dog's physical trim, feel his muscles in the shoulder and thighs. They should be firm and not soft and flabby. A droopy undercarriage is also evidence that more exercise is needed.

On summer, sunny days, water must be provided. Active, outside breeds in particular, such as the Standard Schnauzer, will need fresh water constantly.

Probably if given the choice, most dogs, especially the working and sporting dogs, would prefer to live in the country. The open space, clean air and water contribute to a dog's well-being (and the owner's too). The larger breeds have greater exercise requirements and country life agrees with them winningly. Terriers, scenthounds, and all other dogs that enjoy the smells of the good earth riot and rejoice when given the opportunity to indulge their sniffers. Additionally, even the smaller breeds—Westies, Shih Tzus, Lhasas and Cavs, for instance—have deceptive exercise needs. The Pug concept of *multum in parvo*, a lot in a small package, exemplifies the small dogs' concentrated energy supplies. While such breeds commonly do well as urban citizens, these dogs also thrive in the great outdoors.

If you live in the city, daily workouts may necessarily be limited to walks and an occasional run in a park. Several walks each day may be necessary to satisfy your dog's needs if he is a dog with high exercise requirements. Country dogs have greater opportunities. Swimming is an excellent activity

Some breeds require more exercise than others. Generally, the large breeds (such as the Doberman Pinscher) will need substantially more exercise than the small ones.

that works all the muscles, and many dogs love it. Another favorite exercise that is easy on the owner is to have your dog chase and retrieve a ball or disc.

If your dog has a sedentary life and you wish to help him get back in shape, begin a regularly scheduled, gradually increasing exercise program. Consider your dog's age, weight, and degree of fitness when determining the starting level and rate of increase for the activity. A gradual progression is especially important for older dogs and for all dogs working out in hot weather. Walking is an often recommended activity for most dogs. An extra walk each day can quickly condition the dog, tone his muscles, and build his stamina. Keep in mind that as the dog's daily activity increases so too does his water requirement. Exercise is an enjoyable way to spend quality time with your pet and is recommended to all owners.

The great sedentary sentinel of Central America, the Fila Brasileiro is said to sit (or stand) anywhere he likes, for who's to question the comfort requirement of a 200-pound Fila (no less propose a rigorous exercise regimen).

A rugged gundog, the Wirehaired Pointing Griffon is a gentleman with the children.

Chesapeake Bay Retriever, a la carte, is a choice companion for any adult or child.

A yellow Labrador Retriever
receiving a healthful workout
with a quality Nyladisc® from
an industrious toddler.

Pointer patiently awaiting his master to
reconsider his hold.

GROOMING

To keep your dog looking his best, you will need to perform such routine care as brushing and combing; trimming nails; bathing; checking and cleaning teeth, eyes, and ears; and removing burrs or clumps of hair that form in the coat. If you do these things regularly, they won't become a difficult chore, as you can catch all problems in the beginning stages. A burr that remains undiscovered in your pet's coat can get more deeply embedded and, if left unattended, will need to be cut out of the coat. Such drastic action often mars the coat's appearance.

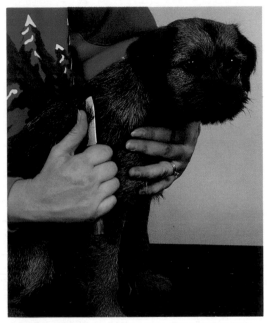

Wirehaired breeds require stripping, The stripping knife grips the hair without cutting it. The terrier look depends on the properly groomed coat. Border Terrier.

Frequent grooming is not only good for the coat—your dog may enjoy it and appreciate the personal massage! Such handling will benefit your dog by putting him at ease when being held, touched, or examined. Examination is especially important in such areas as the paws, ears, mouth, and around the eyes, as these are places where health problems occasionally occur that may need attention by owner or veterinarian.

Besides keeping your pet neat and attractive, regular grooming sessions give you the chance to look for other medical problems. Be on the alert for sores, rashes, bald spots, excessive shedding, or lumps on or under the skin. If you should spot any of these conditions, a visit to the veterinarian may be in order.

Grooming Tools

The following items should aid in keeping your dog's coat in top condition. Some tools are used on particular types and lengths of coats that require special attention. Grooming equipment is available at your local pet shop.

- wide-tooth comb
- protein coat conditioner
- ear cleaner
- scissors
- natural bristle brush
- nail trimmer
- nail file or emery board
- dog shampoo

- wire pin brush
- grooming glove
- stripping knife
- mat splitter
- grooming table
- undercoat rake
- utility comb
- chamois cloth
- rubber curry brush
- ear forceps
- electric clipper

Brushing

Regular brushing will keep your dog's coat clean and free of that "doggy" odor. The amount of brushing your dog requires will depend on the type of coat and how much exposure it has to the environment. The main objective of brushing is to keep the coat free of knots and in a healthy condition. For ease and efficiency, it is recommended to have your dog stand for the brushing. If possible,

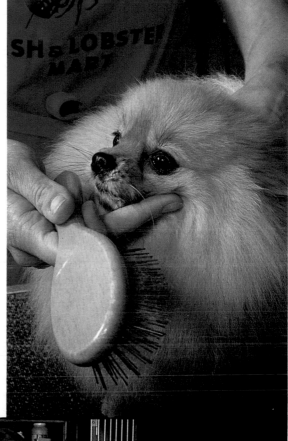

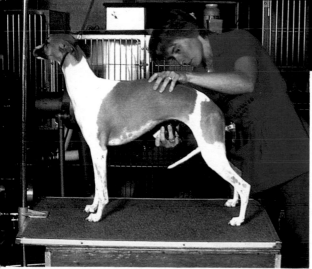

The Pomeranian (above), like other longhaired dogs, requires brushing on a daily basis. The Whippet (left), as a smooth-haired, sleek-coated dog, needs far less grooming attention.

have the dog stand on a table, as this will help you to avoid back strain.

If you find a mat or tangle, gently try to pull the hairs apart with your fingers. If this fails, apply a grooming preparation and try to work the knot out using the end of a comb. Work toward the skin. If this is unsuccessful, use a mat splitter or cut the mat out, being very careful not to cut the skin—but this is best handled by a professional groomer.

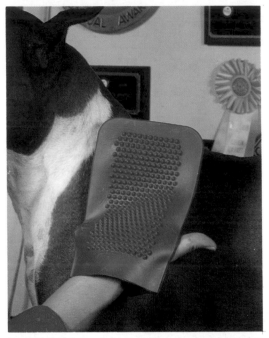

Smoothhaired dogs require very little in the way of grooming. A quick once-over with a hound glove does this Boxer's coat well.

Nail Trimming

If your dog does not get sufficient exercise on hard ground to keep his nails worn down, you may have to clip them regularly. Long nails can cause sore feet and lameness, so they cannot be ignored. Dogs' nails are very tough and require specially designed clippers, which are available from your veterinarian or pet shop. Do not use ordinary clippers or scissors. Cut off all excess nail and file it smooth, but do not go as far as the quick (the vein in the nail), as this will cause bleeding. Should you cut the quick, apply pressure to the area with a cotton ball dipped in powdered alum or dab a moistened styptic pencil on the end of the nail. If

In tow with his Rolls, the elegant and czarlike Borzoi—groomed for success.

bleeding persists, consult your veterinarian.

Bathing

It is generally unnecessary to maintain a monthly or routine schedule of bathing. Combing or brushing the coat several times a week should keep it in good condition, so bathe your dog only when the coat becomes dirty or infected with parasites.

While puppies or very small dogs can be washed in the sink, most dogs will need to be bathed in a tub or outdoors (weather permitting). Have your shampoo, comb, and towels close at hand and always avoid letting your dog get chilled. Begin by thoroughly soaking the coat with lukewarm water. Apply a dog shampoo and work it into a

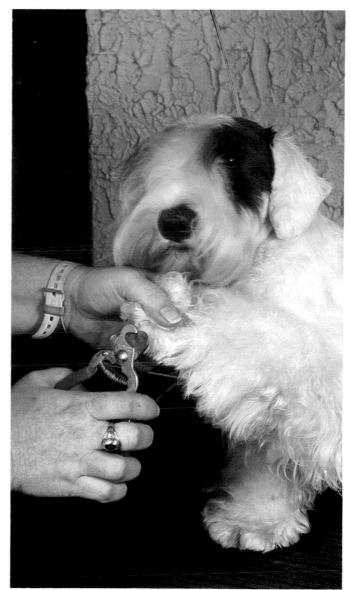

Your dog's nails need regular attention. When properly trained, as is this Sealyham Terrier, a dog sits patiently and quietly through this routine.

lather. Nylon leashes are recommended to hold the dog steady. It is important that the dog be well trained; often the dog's natural inclination is to shake its coat clear of the soap, much before drying time. A premature, impatient shake from the dog can result in the owner also sharing his dog's lather. Here again, be sure to use a product designed for dogs, as other shampoos are too harsh and may cause dandruff or damage to the coat. You may want to shampoo the coat twice if it is highly soiled or if you need to apply a lotion to rid the coat of fleas or other parasites. Rinse the coat very thoroughly to remove all traces of shampoo. Squeeze all excess water from the coat—and look out for the inevitable shake that your dog will give himself! Cover the dog with towels and gently rub until as much water as possible has been absorbed. Run a comb through the coat to be sure that knots have not formed. With long-coated dogs,

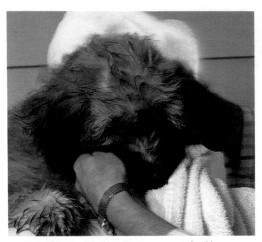

To keep his soon-to-be-wheaten coat soft, this Soft Coated Wheaten Terrier pup enjoys a bath.

you may use a hair dryer—on a low-heat setting—held at least twelve inches from the skin to help speed drying. In cold weather, be sure the dog is adequately dry before allowing him out into possible drafts.

TOOTH CARE

If tartar or plaque is allowed to build up on your dog's teeth, this scaly deposit will push the gums back and eventually cause the teeth to loosen and fall out. Check the dog's teeth monthly for signs of tartar at the gum line. If you should notice a build-up, have it removed by a professional. If your dog is prone to a tartar problem, scraping the teeth will be necessary. This is best handled by your veterinarian.

If your dog develops offensive breath, this may be a sign of dirty or decayed teeth or diseased tonsils. If it persists for more than a few days, consult your veterinarian. Remember that a dog needs his teeth throughout his life, so take special care not to injure them or let them deteriorate. An easy way to remove tartar from your dog's teeth is to provide

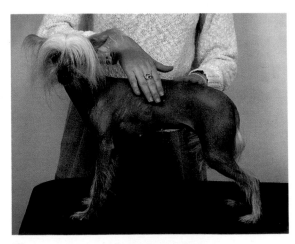

While owners of hairless dogs save time brushing their dogs, they invest a similar effort on skin care. Applying lotion to the Chinese Crested's skin softens it and protects it from chapping.

GENERAL CARE

him with a safe, effective canine chew product. Specially designed products are the only items you should use for this.

The good health of your pet's teeth can be maintained by his regular use of a chew product such as Nylabone® or Gumabone®, which serves to clean the teeth of tartar accumulation and massage and stimulate the gums. With puppies, a chew product helps to relieve the discomfort of the teething stage and prevents the pup's chewing of your furniture and slippers!

Tooth care, however, cannot be taken too lightly by owners. Dogs take care of their teeth differently than humans ... and most dogs seem to derive more pleasure from a chew bone than the average human gets from his toothbrush or dental floss. Just as in humans, poor dental health can lead to a bounty of other physical problems, including heart and kidney disorders. Owners

The Shiba Inu, upon entering the Western World, finds many new wonders and learns the value of proper tooth hygiene. A savory and salutary discovery—the Gumaknot®.

must take the necessary precautions to prevent these avoidable difficulties. One new product worth mentioning is the Nylafloss®, a fun nylon ropelike device designed to remove plaque accumulation between the teeth. Pet shops carry this and other Nylabone® products.

It is amazing how many long-time dog owners are not aware that rawhide and biscuits do not provide a dog with the necessary chewing stimulation. This is not to say that these products have no use—undoubtedly dogs like them. However, it is the owner's responsibility to provide the proper chew devices to facilitate the good healthkeeping of his pet's teeth.

Health Care

SIGNS OF ILLNESS

Should you notice that your dog is not acting normally, perhaps appearing overly tired and sluggish, take his temperature by using a rectal thermometer. Listlessness is often a sign of fever. Most major ailments cause a rise in temperature above the normal 101° to 102° Fahrenheit range. A reading of more than one degree above or below the normal is cause for concern and you should consult your veterinarian.

Sometimes an itch is but an itch and other times it's worth looking into. Be in tune with your puppy's everyday physical habits.

A sudden loss of appetite can be a sign of various ailments: fever, a sore mouth, diseased teeth, or an upset stomach. If it should continue for more than twenty-four hours, a trip to the vet is in order; likewise with persistent vomiting or diarrhea. While most upsets pass quickly, do not delay in seeking help.

Good healthkeeping entails regular exercise and time outdoors with your dog. This Komondor, in dangling tangles, gets a good morning workout.

DISEASES

Most communicable diseases to which dogs are susceptible can be prevented by obtaining the necessary series of vaccinations during your puppy's initial visits to the veterinarian.

These vaccinations will immunize the puppy against rabies, distemper, hepatitis, leptospirosis, infectious canine tracheobronchitis, and parvovirus.

It is very common for dogs to become infected with internal parasites (worms). The most common types are roundworms, hookworms, whipworms, tapeworms, and heartworms.

Much of your dog's health depends upon your responsible consideration and fulfillment of his needs. A well-cared-for and healthy Rhodesian Ridgeback.

Heartworm infestation can be a very serious problem. Most infestations are not severe and are easily cured by medication. If left unchecked, worms can cause permanent damage and death. During your puppy's first check-up, your veterinarian will look for the presence of worms by examining a stool sample under the microscope. Testing for heartworms requires a blood test. As the number of heartworm cases has been increasing in recent years, even if the test shows no present infestation it is advisable to give your dog daily heartworm medication during the mosquito season to help prevent this deadly disease. It is spread by bites from mosquitoes that carry the microscopic heartworm larvae.

As the dog ages, you should have routine tests for worms performed when your dog receives his yearly shots. Be on the lookout for signs of worms, such as small worms clinging to the dog's bedding, stools, or hair around the rectum. The dog may also "scoot" across the floor. Scooting can also be a sign of overfilled or infected anal glands.

EMERGENCIES

Accidents, such as being hit by a car, require immediate action. Until you can get the dog to the veterinarian, you must try to stop all bleeding by applying pressure to the wound. Tightly wrap the cut in a clean bandage, if possible, and try not to move the animal any more than absolutely necessary. Talk to the dog in a reassuring tone and try to keep him calm and still.

If you suspect that your dog has swallowed a poisonous substance, first try to locate the source. If you find the container, read the label for instructions on how to deal with accidental poisoning. The procedures can vary. Making the dog vomit may be the proper treatment for some types of poisonings, but this can be very damaging for other types that call for you to feed the dog milk or other substances to help neutralize the poison's effects. Time is of the essence, so get the dog to the veterinarian as quickly as possible.

Smart owners should have a well-furnished first-aid kit on hand at all times. Since it is impossible to predict all emergencies, a variety of ointments, bandages, and medications should be included. Talking to a veterinarian or a similarly experienced dog person will give you helpful insight. Further, it is necessary to keep on top of expiration dates and the conditions under which substances must be kept (some may require refrigeration, others, room temperature or darkness).

Some breeds, such as the Finnish Spitz, abound with high energy and thrive on vigorous outdoor activity.

CARE OF THE OLDER DOG

To help your dog live a long, healthy life, watch his diet from puppyhood on. Don't let your pet get overweight, as this taxes the heart. Exercise is necessary throughout the dog's life, but, as he ages, his activities should be slightly decreased to keep from overexertion. This is especially important in hot weather. Painful, arthritic joints are common in the older dog, and you can offer some relief by supplying a comfortable bed to rest on. Vitamin supplements have also been acclaimed as helpful in alleviating joint discomfort.

Enjoying a quiet and relaxing afternoon around the pool, this Bearded Collie glistens with contentment.

Your veterinarian can discuss which vitamins and minerals might be useful, or may prescribe medicines that restrict swelling in the joints.

Remember that your aging canine friend becomes ever more dependent upon your watchful care. Senior citizen dogs appreciate their masters' attention now more than ever. Older dogs are not aware that their bodies are slowing down, but rather that the world revolves at a slower daily rate. In return for the many years of dedicated companionship, proper care and daily affection are but a small price for an owner to pay.

The teeth can be a major problem in older dogs. You should regularly check for tartar and remove all build-up. An abscessed tooth is a common malady that often goes undetected until visible signs, such as a pussy wound on the cheek or a loss of appetite, appear. Inspect your dog's mouth and have all diseased teeth removed as soon as detected, as infection can result from neglected dental problems.

The older dog needs special care when exposed to the extremes of weather. The animal should be covered with a coat or sweater in cold weather and kept dry to avoid sudden chills. Keep your pet indoors as much as possible in very hot weather to avoid heat stroke and dehydration. The dog's naps may become more frequent and longer, and changes in his diet may have to be made to keep from overtaxing the digestive system. Take your dog to the vet for regular checkups, including examinations of eyes and ears for signs of vision and hearing problems.

A cropped-ear Great Dane, subtly equine. Many of the larger breeds do not live as long as the smaller breeds. Owners are reminded to capitalize on quality time with their animal, no matter what kind of dog or how old he is.

HEALTH CARE

LIFE EXPECTANCY

Small dog breeds generally live longer than large breeds. This is a reversal of the pattern common to many animals, such as elephants and mice. In most cases, animals that take a long time to mature (elephants, humans) live longer than the quickly maturing animals (mice). Small dogs, such as the Pekingese, commonly live fifteen or more years, while the large breeds, such as the St. Bernard, average only ten years.

The long-standing adage that one year of a dog's life is equal to seven human years is not quite accurate. Recent studies have shown that the first year of a dog's life is a highly formative one, comparable to the growth experienced in sixteen years of human life. At age two, a dog compares with a twenty-four-year-old; at age three, he equals thirty hu-

The West Highland White Terrier, one of the smaller dogs, is a happy, long-lived terrier and companion.

man years. From this point on, each year in a dog's life is comparable to five human years. Nonetheless, make your dog's every year a memorable, happy one.

Symbol Exposition

Sighthound

Ratter/Terrier

Of **Bullbaiter** ancestry

Nordic **Draft** dog

Scenthound

Of **Pariah** origin

Sheep Herder

Ideally suited as **Companion** dog

Cow Herder

Well suited as **Watchdog**

Flock Guardian

Needs regular **Exercise**

Gundog

Ideally suited for **Indoor** life

Toy dog

Potential **Man-stopper**

Aggressive dog

Pointer

Flusher

Setter

Water Dog

Retriever

Raccoon Hunter

Special Coat Care
required

All-Weather Coat

Easycare Coat

Trainable as
Seeing Eye
or assistance dog

Trainable for
Search & Rescue
or service work

Rare dog breed

Small game hunter

Large game hunter

Feral or uneven in
nature

Race dog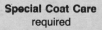

Azawakh.

SIGHTHOUNDS

AFGHAN HOUND
Tazi, Baluchi Hound

PORTRAIT: The proudly held head, eyes gazing into the distance, and an unmistakably aristocratic carriage comprise the Afghan's exotic and dignified air. Thick silky hair, fine in texture, and abundant all-encompassing feathering adorn the Afghan's graceful and well in-lined body. The head is of good length and absolute refinement. The feet are sizable and furnished to appear as pom poms. The tail, moderately fringed, has a ring or curve at the tip. Height: 24–28 inches (61–71 cm). Weight: 50–60 pounds (23–28 kg). The breed is variously colored in solids, bicolors, and tricolors.

DEVELOPMENT: "Yet no man knoweth whence they came, but there they are and there they stay." Afghan Shikaris claim that the Afghan Hound was the breed favored by Noah and taken on the Ark with him. Although the whole truth may never be told, the Afghan's pedigree is without a doubt pre-Christian in age. Portraits of the Afghan's ancestors appear engraved upon cuneiform pillars and tablets. So priceless are the dogs in their native lands that some hounds provoke theft after their sale to another fancier. The breed is used to guard sheep and cattle, to hunt deer and other animals, and to serve as a companion and show dog. To speak of its courage and ability, dogs have been known to attack and kill both leopards and panthers.

RECOGNITION: FCI, AKC, UKC, KCGB, CKC, ANKC

CHARACTER: The Afghan Hound is a kind and considerate soul, seemingly possessing wisdom acquired from his desert-faring ancestors. He may tend to be aloof and reserved but is gay and cheerful with his kind. Exercise is requisite, as is appropriate space.

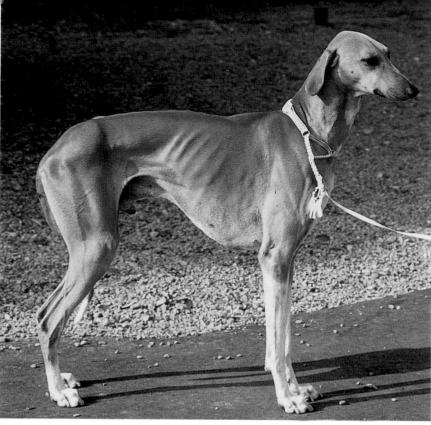

AZAWAKH
Tuareg Sloughi, Azawakh Hound

PORTRAIT: An elegance, a uniqueness wedded to unfaltering exquisiteness, bestills the Azawakh, a breed that defies description. The body is slim with unconventional and stern delicacy. On long and muscular legs, the Azawakh stands high with small feet, much like the conformation of a fine Arabian horse; the tail, thin and curling. Height: 23–29 inches (58–74 cm). Weight: 37–55 pounds (17–25 kg). The coat is soft and short in various shades of sable with white markings. The head is slender and pear-shaped and embellished by no fewer than five warts.

DEVELOPMENT: The Tuareg tribes of the southern Sahara cultivated their Sloughi to work as a hunter and guardsman. The dogs are "fleet footed enough to catch gazelles, hares and the European mouflon, courageous enough to ward off big predators, untiring like a camel and beautiful like an Arab horse." The Azawakh's hunting method is pure sighthound: he does not kill the prey, but rather hamstrings the quarry until the master arrives. Seated in the master's saddle at the onset of the hunt, the Azawakh is released when the gazelle is sighted. Reaching speeds of over 40 mph, the Azawakh can course for over five hours.

RECOGNITION: FCI

CHARACTER: The Azawakh is a commanding and somewhat pretentious dog who is accustomed to receiving respect and admiration from his human contacts. The breed has strong footholds in a number of European countries, with fanciers working to further the breed.

BANJARA GREYHOUND

PORTRAIT: This sighthound is a fine upstanding hound with a sturdy, defined conformation. The head, long and narrow, is high-held and houndy; the neck is lengthy and supple. The back is medium broad and muscular. He is described as being stouter than the Saluki with a squarer muzzle. The coat is rough but silky and generally black, mottled with grey or blue. The ears, legs, and tail are feathered generously. Height: 27–29 inches (68–74 cm). Weight: 50–65 pounds (23–30 kg).

DEVELOPMENT: The Banjara is one of the greyhounds indigenous to India. It finds its origin in either the Sloughi or the Afghan Hound. The general body type does not differentiate this sighthound from others of the group. As dog exhibition and the fancy in general have not evolved in India as they have in the West, and as a dog's function affords its following (instead of its following's defining its function), the working coursing hounds of India may not breed true for the sake of breeding true. A traveler to India conveys that pure Banjaras are difficult to locate since most dogs indiscreetly breed with the common pariah dogs.

RECOGNITION: NR

CHARACTER: The Banjara's relationship to his master is proverbial: a mutual respect and admiration breeds pure. The dogs are used for various hunting and general work jobs. No Banjaras are known outside of India.

BORZOI
Russian Wolfhound, Psowaya Barsaya

PORTRAIT: He is gracefulness and beauty with every suggestion of speed: symmetry and perfect proportion, every part flawlessly placed and distanced from the other to preserve the beauty which is the Borzoi's own. The body is marked by flowing lines and developed musculature. The head is slightly domed, long and narrow. The coat is long and silky (never woolly), flat and wavy. Height: 28–31 inches (71–79 cm). Weight: 75–105 pounds (34–48 kg). Although white usually predominates in the coat pattern, any color is acceptable.

DEVELOPMENT: The importance of aesthetics and symmetry in the Borzoi has not always been a quintessential concern. Speed, strength, fearlessness and coursing intelligence were the most valued Borzoi traits, as coursing wolves was a dangerous and difficult sport. The Russian royal family favored the Borzoi, much the way the British royal family embraced the Greyhound. Wolf-coursing became the national sport of Russia and the Borzoi was bred for prowess in the sport. Two Borzois, of compatible speed and stamina, were needed to course one wolf, both simultaneously gripping the wolf behind its ears, throwing it over, and pinning it to the ground. The hunter then takes over the gagging and tying. The Borzoi, upon arrival to England, found no wolves to course and, because of its natural beauty, became an ornament in elegant homes and a favorite in the show ring.

RECOGNITION: FCI, AKC, UKC, KCGB, CKC, ANKC

CHARACTER: The Borzoi is a beautiful and exquisite dog but not ideal for every lifestyle. For owners with adequate space, here is a dog of unparalleled style and grace. He is even-tempered and always a perfect gentleman.

CHORTAJ
Eastern Greyhound

PORTRAIT: A large hard-coated dog with a long neck and an arched body. The build is stouter and coarser than the Greyhound with which the Western World is acquainted. The coat is super-efficient, thick and smooth to the touch. In color the Chortaj is usually solid, but this is of no importance. The conformation is well-balanced and sinewy. The head is long, without stop, and narrow. The chest is broad and deep; the tuck-up is severe. The ears are rose. Height: 25–26 inches (63–66 cm).

DEVELOPMENT: The sighthounds of Russia have withstood the sands of time and still can be found hunting on the wide open steppes. The tradition of hunting on horseback, accompanied by a pair of gazehounds and a falcon, comes from the Cossacks and Tartars and is upheld by Soviet huntsmen today. The Chortaj, along with the South Russian Steppe Hound, is still used to hunt the abundant game found in these open plains.

RECOGNITION: NR

CHARACTER: The 1952 Cynological Congress chose the Chortaj as one of the indigenous Russian breeds worthy of preservation. His keen hunting abilities and hardiness make him a choice for the avid hunter; his sleek, easycare coat and moderate appetite make him an ideal companion.

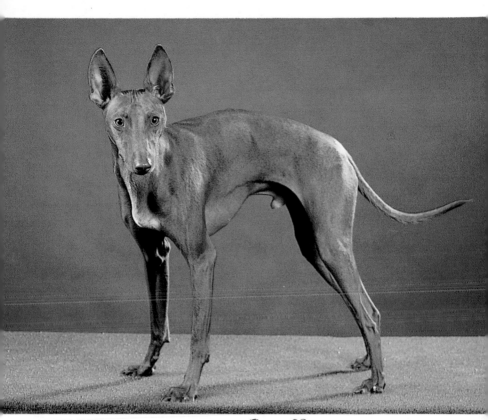

CIRNECO DELL'ETNA
Sicilian Hound

PORTRAIT: A finely built sighthound with upright ears placed prominently on his head, the Cirneco dell'Etna is miraculously sleek and clean-cut. The head is well chiseled; the nose self-colored. The coat is short and smooth. In color the Cirneco is fawn-red, with white markings permissible. Height: 17–19 inches (43–48 cm). Weight: 18–26 pounds (8–12 kg). The chest is fairly broad and the tuck-up is more moderate than many of his fellow sighthounds.

DEVELOPMENT: Like the Ibizan Hound and Pharaoh Hound, the Cirneco dell'Etna likely had an older ancestor of the coursing type that originated in the Mediterranean region. In Sicily the Cirneco has bred true to type for many years, free from the persuasion of outside dogs; he is the only dog that hunts on the hills of Mount Etna. Compared to the Pharaoh and Ibizan, the Cirneco is smaller. Its hunting acumen rests in coursing hare and rabbit. Its light-footed and delicate approach also makes it effective on ground birds.

RECOGNITION: FCI

CHARACTER: A playful and lighthearted sighthound, this native Sicilian is hardy and undaunted by cold and rain. The interest in the Cirneco dell'Etna has been steadily waning in its native Italy. It is hoped that new dog enthusiasts will actively pursue this ideally sized easycare dog and not let the breed enter into oblivion.

GALGO ESPAÑOL
Spanish Greyhound

PORTRAIT: Symmetrical formation: the body is lithe and balanced; the head is long and narrow. The ears are small and rose shaped; they hang straight down. The legs are long, and the tuck-up is defined. Height: 26–28 inches (66–71 cm). Weight: 60–66 pounds (27–30 kg). Color variations include: cinnamon, chestnut, red, black, and brindle; solid or in combination with white. The conformation is practically identical to the English Greyhound but on a proportionately smaller scale.

DEVELOPMENT: Named for the Gallic peoples that once inhabited the Iberian peninsula, the Galgo is an ancient breed of running hound. It is plausible that the Galgo shares like roots with the Ibizan Hound. For many centuries, the Galgo bred true and was employed on farms in Castile and Andalusia as a guard and hunter of small game. On the race track, the Galgo is a professional and *el favorito* of Spanish dog-race enthusiasts.

RECOGNITION: FCI

CHARACTER: This is a sturdy and adaptable hound that is most apropos for the sport of racing. Additionally, he is a fine home companion, gentle and fraternal. Older dogs tend to be more aloof and nonchalant than do youngsters—insouciance, the wisdom of days.

GRANDE PODENGO PORTUGUESO
Large Portuguese Hound, Portuguese Rabbit Dog

PORTRAIT: The Grande Podengo Portugueso is a large sighthound type with a well-proportioned head, flat skull and pronounced stop. The muzzle is straight; the eyes small and oblique, ranging in color from light honey to dark chestnut. The ears are pricked, triangular, and sizable. The back is level; the legs are straight, with cat feet. Height: 22–28 inches (56–71 cm). Weight: 66 pounds (30 kg). The breed occurs in two coat types: short coat, which is hard and longer than most sighthounds; wire coat, which is medium long, shaggy and coarse. Yellow, fawn, and black with white markings are the color options.

DEVELOPMENT: Employed by the Portuguese as rabbit hunters—setting and tracking—the Portuguese Hounds or Rabbit Dogs find their running hound ancestors in northern Africa. Hunting in packs or singly, the Portuguese Hounds became specialists on rabbits. The Portuguese Podengos come in three size varieties: the Grande is the largest and therefore is able to cover more ground, possesses greater strength and can hunt large game.

RECOGNITION: FCI

CHARACTER: A dog of great character and ability, the Grande is a delightful companion and a hunter of superior skill. In either coat, the breed is hardy and adaptable and loves to be outdoors. Exercise is essential as is time with the owner.

GREYHOUND
English Greyhound

PORTRAIT: Generously proportioned and upstanding, the Greyhound is symmetrical and powerful. The body is capacious, with an arched loin and powerful quarters. The lengthy legs and feet are sound and supple, ever important to the dog's traditional function. The coat is short and smooth and can be colored in any shade, solid or brindle. Height: 27–30 inches (68–76 cm). Weight: 60–70 pounds (27–31½ kg).

DEVELOPMENT: The "speed merchant" of the canine world, the Greyhound needed not to dig, fight, or scent—only to run, and of course to see where it was running. The breed has the keenest eyesight of any dog, just as the Bloodhound has the keenest nose. The breed, isolated by the treeless expanse of open desert, was able to ingrain exactitude of type with no interference from other dogs. The Arabs, thus, are the originators of the dogs we know as Greyhounds. The "sport" of coursing hares developed and was certainly a dubious one. Its purpose initially was to entertain the dog's owners and his friends, none of whom wanted to dine on the kill. As a matter of fact, it became no more than a matter of killing rabbits, since the owners could never tell which dog reached and killed the rabbit first. Perhaps the answer to the folly of hare coursing comes to us in the sport of dog racing, where the rabbit is a decoy and the winner is the fastest and the first disappointed to discover the course was a fluke, further baffled by his owner's bounteous praise. And yet Greyhounds remain a noble breed, despite their having to engage in the mindless diversion of men.

RECOGNITION: FCI, AKC, UKC, KCGB, CKC, ANKC

CHARACTER: The Greyhound is a gentle and loving companion animal. With his family he is even tempered and affectionate. In order to maintain his health, it is essential that suitable exercise and space be provided.

IBIZAN HOUND
Podenco Ibicenco, Ca Eivissencs

PORTRAIT: The tall and narrow Ibizan Hound is distinguished by his outstanding upstanding ears. The head is fine and long, and the clear amber eyes possess an expression unique to the breed. The coat can be shorthaired or wirehaired; in both varieties the coat is hard, close and dense. The wire coat is 1–3 inches (2½–8 cm) in length, with a mustache and slight feathering on the back, thighs and tail. In color the Ibizan is white, chestnut (lion tawny) or, most commonly, a combination of these colors. Height: 22–29 inches (56–74 cm). Weight: 42–55 pounds (19–25 kg).

DEVELOPMENT: Resembling the large-eared type greyhound that kicked up sand in Egypt circa 2000 BC, the Ibizan Hound gazes at the 20th century with eyes wide and ears cocked. Unlike the Greyhound, the Ibizan, founded on the island of Majorca, can hunt by sight or scent. Nonetheless, the Greyhound and Saluki are his likely ancestors. A touch of Egyptian Mastiff would account for his stouter physique, and the relative isolation of ancient Egypt would facilitate the purity of the Ibizan type. History finds the Ibizan s wearing prominent collars, suggestive of their somewhat deceptive strength, and riding side-saddle on Hannibal's elephant in his Italian invasion.

RECOGNITION: FCI, AKC, UKC, KCGB, CKC

CHARACTER: The Ibizan is a clean and companionable animal. The small-game hunter who chooses the Ibizan as his partner wisely leaves his gun home, along with any other unnecessary implements.

IRISH WOLFHOUND

PORTRAIT: The tallest breed of dog, the Irish Wolfhound, ideally stands up to 34 inches (86 cm) tall. The commanding and tousled appearance is nothing short of impressive. The head is long and carried high; the chest is not too broad. The muzzle is long and somewhat pointed. The coat is rough and harsh, especially wiry on the head. The body is muscular and massive. The chest is very deep, the breast wide, and the back longish. Gray, brindle, red, black, pure white, fawn and other dark self-colors. Weight: at minimum, 90–120 pounds (40½–55 kg).

DEVELOPMENT: Standards through the ages have compared the Irish Wolfhound to the lighter Deerhound and the heavier Great Dane. These two comparable breeds apparently have contributed to the Irish Wolfhound; the Wolfhound's history parallels that of the Deerhounds, say many well-respected cynologists. Having fascinated 4th-century Rome with its size and very presence, the breed has always been venerated for its massiveness. In the 15th and 16th century, its hunting of wolves was foremost. Wild boar, stag and elk are also among its ill-fated quarry.

RECOGNITION: FCI, AKC, UKC, KCGB, CKC, ANKC

CHARACTER: "Gentle when stroked, fierce when provoked"—the ring and pleasant rhyme is true through the present time. The Irish Wolfhound is friendly and kindly. The tallest dog in the world needs plenty of room to stretch his record-making limbs and is therefore not the choice for apartment dwellers or condo inhabitants.

KANGAROO HOUND
Australian Greyhound, Kangaroo Dog

PORTRAIT: The robust and powerful Kangaroo Hound is well ribbed with a deep chest. The dog is comparable to an oversized English Greyhound and can weigh as much as 80 pounds (36 kg). The head is narrow and lengthy; the ears tiny and rose shaped. The legs are long and powerful. Height: 27–30 inches (68–76 cm). These hounds can be any color, often with white predominating, although solid black dogs are known. The coat appears smooth but is actually coarse.

DEVELOPMENT: The Kangaroo Hound was derived from selective crosses of Greyhounds and Deerhounds to hunt kangaroo. Although this springy marsupial is protected by Australian conservation laws today, at one time it was a verifiable pest and destroyer of crops. Dogs were needed to course and diminish the high kangaroo population. The kangaroo can travel at unbelievable velocities; and, when it is overtaken by one of these powerful running hounds, it has the good sense to hop into the water and thus force its assailant to attack swimming. Backed against a tree, the kangaroo is formidable, equipped with invincible legs and a sweeping Godzilla-like tail. A kangaroo willingly fights to the death. The dog bred to hunt the kangaroo had to be equally quick-footed and quick-witted—and plenty strong.

RECOGNITION: NR

CHARACTER: If any Kangaroo Hounds exist today, they are found on remote stations in Australia, where employed to catch small game for the ranchers. Even so, the Kangaroo Hound would make a basically nasty companion dog because of his ruthless, single-minded approach to life.

LURCHER

PORTRAIT: The tall and firm Lurcher is a rough-coated dog. Not much else can be definitely asserted about the size, since it is dependent on the variables plugged in. Ideally, the Lurcher should have the nose of a foxhound, the feet of a greyhound, and the eye of a hawk. His hard coat is necessary for performance over harsh thick-thicketed terrain. Important features of the Lurcher include a long strong back, good spring of rib, and a lengthy neck. Color is of no importance.

DEVELOPMENT: The name *Lurcher* derives from the Romany word meaning to rob or plunder; the nomenclature was determined by the Romanies although the tinkers of Ireland also favored the dog. Often not considered a breed as such, the Lurcher is more of a crossbreed, usually three-quarters sighthound. The most common combinations are Greyhound/Terrier and Greyhound/Collie. The Collie crosses often are not sizable enough for the Lurcher's intended work. Gypsies traditionally scoff at any Lurcher that is not predominantly Greyhound, since the lesser Lurchers are ineffective for a day-long hare hunt. The stringent training method of the gypsies is frowned upon in some Lurcher circles, since the pups begin working at six months. Only the top-producing pups are kept; the rest are sold at traditional bargain rates.

RECOGNITION: NR

CHARACTER: Lurchers were an important part of gypsy lifestyle and inherited many of these wanderers' traits: they are shrewd, good-humored, coarse, and run best when the heat is on.

MAGYAR AGĂR
Hungarian Greyhound

PORTRAIT: The Magyar is a lean and elegant dog that closely resembles the Greyhound proper. He stands between 25–27½ inches (63–70 cm), slightly smaller than the Greyhound. He weighs 49–68 pounds (22–31 kg). The head and muzzle are wide for a sighthound, but they contribute to his prey-gripping ability on the hunt. Coat: short and coarse, providing good protection. Color possibilities encompass solid and brindles.

DEVELOPMENT: The present-day Hungarians are largely descended from the Magyar people who invaded and settled, in the 9th century, the area of Europe known today as Hungary. The Magyar people brought, along with their traditions and customs, their dogs. These dogs likely resembled the Sloughi and other Eastern greyhound types. In later centuries, however, the Agărs were crossbred with the Greyhound proper and hence closely resemble that breed today. The Agăr's primary job was (and still is) coursing hare and fox, although with the ecological changes of the modern world, hare is more commonly coursed today. The quickness of the Magyar's feet is only rivaled by the quickness of his mind; his sight is far superior to his scenting ability.

RECOGNITION: FCI

CHARACTER: The Agăr is a fun-loving dog, always enjoying the company of man. He takes his job seriously, though, and needs regular runs, preferably of the coursing kind. With proper care, he is a calm, affectionate canine.

MAHRATTA GREYHOUND

PORTRAIT: This rare breed, unknown outside his native province of Mahratta, is best described as resembling the smooth-coated Saluki, for he gives the impression of enduring speed coupled with active strength. Standing only 21 inches (53 cm) at the shoulder, the Mahratta is, however, slightly smaller than the Saluki. The Mahratta is a compact sighthound, well muscled, deep chested, and strong backed. The common color pattern consists of dark blue and tan. The coat is short and provides good protection against the various Indian elements. **DEVELOP-MENT:** Uncertainty prevails over the Mahratta's lineage. Whether the Mahratta is a descendant of the Saluki or a localization of other indigenous Indian sighthounds remains the essential question. The Mahratta's small size, in relation to the Rampur and other Indian dogs, makes either Saluki descendancy or a pure, ancient origin the most likely hypothesis concerning development. With exceptional speed and concentrated strength, the Mahratta is used successfully for coursing small and medium-sized game in his indigenous province after which he was named. **RECOGNITION:** NR **CHARACTER:** The Mahratta possesses instinctive courage and ability for the hunt. He uses these to full advantage in conjunction with his excellent eyesight, fleet feet, and able muscle. The Mahratta is used almost exclusively for the hunt; life in India makes owning a dog solely as a pet a frivolous venture, though, if given the chance, these high-strung working canines could make faithful companions.

MEDIO PODENGO PORTUGUESO
Medium Portuguese Hound, Portuguese Rabbit Dog

PORTRAIT: The Medio Podengo Portugueso is a moderately sized sight-hound type with a well proportioned head, flat skull and pronounced stop. The muzzle is straight, the eyes small and oblique; eye color varies from light honey to dark chestnut. The ears are pricked, triangular, and sizable. The back is level; the legs are straight, with cat feet. Height: 15–22 inches (38–56 cm). Weight: 35–44 pounds (16–20 kg). The breed occurs in two coat types: short coat, which is hard and longer than that of most sight-hounds; wire coat, which is medium long, shaggy and coarse. Color may be: yellow, fawn, or black with white markings.

DEVELOPMENT: Employed by the Portuguese as rabbit hunters—setting and tracking—the Portuguese Hounds, or Warren Dogs, find their running hound ancestors in northern Africa. Hunting in packs or singly, the Portu-guese Hounds became specialists on rabbits. The Portuguese Podengos come in three size varieties: the Grande is the largest and therefore able to cover more ground, possesses greater strength, and hunts large game. The Medio is probably the fastest of the three *hermanos* and has exquisite ma-neuverability on rough ground. The Pequeño, for all its petiteness, is still an eager hunter.

RECOGNITION: FCI

CHARACTER: Many Portuguese owners favor the Medio over both of its brothers because they feel its size is ideal, not too big and not too small. Regardless of its size, the Medio is a wonderful companion dog and a super-efficient hunter.

PHARAOH HOUND
Kelb-tal Fenek

PORTRAIT: As does a lover's glow, the Pharaoh Hound's blush of happiness evokes amorous unity between himself and his admirer. When excited or happy, the Pharaoh Hound's nose and ears become flushed with a deep rose color, and his amber eyes grow in intensity. Always he suggests grace, power, freedom, and dignity. His skull is long, lean, and chiseled; his body is lithe and elegant. Height: 21–25 inches (53–64 cm). The coat is short and glossy, ranging in texture from fine to slightly harsh. Color possibilities pass from tan through rich tan to chestnut, with some white markings.

DEVELOPMENT: Perhaps the oldest, but certainly the most honorably recorded dog in history, the Pharaoh Hound graces the tombs of ancient Egyptian pharaohs with his much retained beauty and elegance. His lineage can be traced to circa 3000 BC. Much about the type and abilities of these ancient dogs is revealed through observing early paintings and working out the kinks in surviving hieroglyphics. The Pharaoh Hound retains both this enthusiasm for the hunt and the distinctive blushing trait. Merchant traders brought the dog to the island of Malta sometime before Christ, where his type was retained through the multitude of centuries, for he closely resembles his ancient forepharaohs.

RECOGNITION: FCI, AKC, UKC, KCGB, CKC, ANKC

CHARACTER: Having both speed and power, scent and sight, the Pharaoh Hound is a versatile hunter. Having lived for centuries with civilized man, he is a natural companion.

RAMPUR DOG
Rampur Greyhound

PORTRAIT: Immediately striking is the Rampur's head, with its very pronounced stop and light-colored eyes, which contrast with the mouse-gray coat to wield a disarming impression. He is deep chested and strong backed. His limbs are muscular, allowing for speed over otherwise exhausting distances. He is strong boned, built for the punishment served in the hunt. Height: 25½–28½ inches (65–71 cm). Weight: 50–66 pounds (22½–30 kg).

DEVELOPMENT: The question remains: Is the Rampur Dog a descendant of the Afghan Hound or the Sloughi? Based on the Rampur's entirely smooth coat, the evidence seems to point to the latter breed, yet the Rampur is both bigger and more powerful than the Sloughi. Crosses with the English Greyhounds could easily account for the added bulk, but the evidence is too unsubstantial to state with certainty anything pertaining to component stock. The Rampur Dog, believably enough, originated in the Indian province of Rampur. He is rarely seen outside of his native land; he is, however, an able hunter worthy of consideration by coursing fanciers.

RECOGNITION: NR

CHARACTER: The Rampur has the coursing instinct ingrained within him. He uses it to full advantage with his excellent eyesight, good speed, and powerful body. The Rampur is bred for the hunt; it is a rare owner who owns one solely as a pet, though they can make fine companions.

RHODESIAN RIDGEBACK
African Lion Hound

PORTRAIT: The dagger-forming and name-giving ridge of this Zimbabwe native is singularly distinctive to the breed. The smooth tight muscles of the Ridgeback's body and the strong-boned symmetrical carriage combine to give him free and efficient movement over great distances at good speeds. With a flat skull, the head should be fairly long and rather broad. The brow is typically wrinkled. The ears are of medium size. Height: 24–27 inches (61–69 cm). Weight: 65–75 pounds (29–34 kg). Coat: short, dense, sleek and glossy. Color: wheaten, from light through red.

DEVELOPMENT: The name "Lion Dog" comes from the Rhodesian's ability to harass a lion through constant strategic attacks which lure the preoccupied "king" towards the hunter's cocked rifle. Standing patiently at an unmissable distance, men revel in their enviable rifleman skills. The requisite skills for this line of canine work include: courage, agility, stamina, and strong instincts. It was not until the 1920s that type began to standardize; for centuries prior there existed many varieties of the Ridgeback dogs. The curious ridge is now unique to this dog alone and suggests the possible link to the now extinct Hottentots dog.

RECOGNITION: FCI, AKC, KCGB, CKC, ANKC

CHARACTER: The Ridgeback is intensely loyal and affectionate. Though he is receptive to strangers, he remains suspicious and ready to defend. A natural performer, he will delight his owner by conquering all tasks set before him.

SALUKI
Persian Greyhound

PORTRAIT: "The fine-trained lop-eared hounds, with slender sides, who lightly outrun the sharp-horned white antelope." The whole appearance of the Saluki suggests grace, speed, endurance, and symmetry. The head is long and narrow; the nose is black or liver in color. Height: 23–28 inches (58–71 cm). Coat: smooth and silky, with light feathering on the legs, back of thighs, and sometimes shoulders; the ears are covered with long silky hair; the smooth variety has no feathering. Color: cream, white, golden, fawn, red, black/tan, grizzle/tan, and tricolor.

DEVELOPMENT: From the pre-dynastic periods, about 6000–5000 BC, before the pharaohs, there exists a carved ivory head of a Saluki, with the long neck graced by the traditional collar. There also exists an engraving on slate of three Salukis attacking a gazelle. Indeed, Salukis are historically renowned for their hunting ability. In writings of the Greek expeditions of Xenophon in Arabia: "These swift hounds were known to the Greeks, and their methods of a 'straight forward chase' without employing 'net or wily inventions' are extolled." Salukis are also seen in ancient Egyptian records dating between 2000 and 3000 BC.

RECOGNITION: FCI, AKC, UKC, KCGB, CKC, ANKC

CHARACTER: The Saluki is a prized companion. The hunting skills and canine instincts so deeply imbedded within this beautifully elegant dog impress even the mildest of canine fanciers. They are clean, naturally affectionate, and always willing to earn their master's attention.

SCOTTISH DEERHOUND
Deerhound

PORTRAIT: The Scottish Deerhound appears as a rough-coated Greyhound; he is, however, larger in size and bigger in bone. Height 28–32 inches (71–81 cm). Weight: 75–110 pounds (34–50 kg). The head, which is carried high, is long, level, and in balance with the whole dog. The body, too, is long; there is great depth to the chest which provides maximum endurance. The coat is rough and hard, with a beard and brow of softer hair. The ears are small and carried as a Greyhound's. Colors include a variety of dark self-colors, with dark blue-gray being preferred.

DEVELOPMENT: The Greyhound is a centuries-old inhabitant of the British Isles. The Scottish breed's development closely jockeys its English counterpart's: in Scotland, the Greyhound developed into quite a distinctive dog and became known as the Scottish Deerhound. Bred to hunt the native and indigenous deer of Scotland, the dog gained size and strength. To flourish in the harsh climate, it also sprouted a rough protective coat. Long maintained only by Scottish nobility, the Deerhound of today remains in limited hands.

RECOGNITION: FCI, AKC, UKC, KCGB, CKC, ANKC

CHARACTER: A gentle and gentlemanly dog is he, with elegant ways and polite affection. All Deerhounds are said to be born under Gemini, the twins, for they possess the dual personality that allows them success on the rowdy hunt and love in the quiet home. His large size and need for roomy "roaming" grounds deter many captivated witnesses from acquiring the breed.

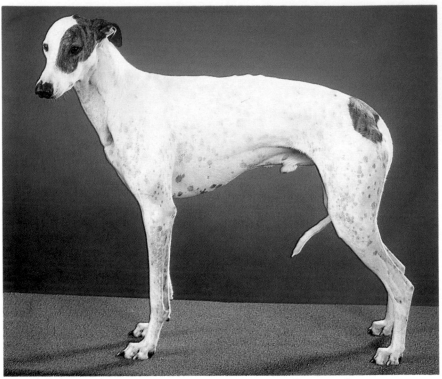

SLOUGHI
Slougui, Arabian Greyhound

PORTRAIT: Entering the world labeled as unsightly would be enough to make any sighthound puppy slip its chin under its collar and cower to the corner, never to emerge again—not so for the Sloughi. Such judgment proves premature as the Sloughi grows into quite an eye-stopping animal: racy and elegant, well contoured in musculation, and slender. The Sloughi is entirely smooth coated; the coat hair is tough and fine. The mountain type is heavier boned than the desert type. Height: 24–28½ inches (61–72 cm). Weight: 45–60 pounds (20–27 kg). Color: all shades of sable or fawn; also possible are various brindles, white, and black with tan points.

DEVELOPMENT: This Arabian star made its European debut in 1898, when the breed entered the Netherlands only three strong under the discerning eye of artist August Legras. Their impact was so great, however, that the breed has never left the minds nor the homes of European fanciers and has orbited its grace and beauty around the globe. The Sloughi, an ancient Arabian, proved courageously capable at coursing hare. Arabs believe that by two years of age a Sloughi should be able to kill a wild gazelle and at three years a wild boar.

RECOGNITION: FCI, KCGB

CHARACTER: The aristocrat of the canine world appreciates the best in life. Zealous care and fine mutton are among the breed's absolute requisites. This deserving dog makes a fine companion, despite its rather intellectually aloof air.

TAIGAN
Kirghiz Borzoi, Tajgan

PORTRAIT: The sleekness, the grace, the elegance, the beautiful coat, the courage, strength, endurance, and long history of dedicated service are all qualities of the Taigan which make it undeserving of the near extinction it now faces. The Taigan is bred for work at high altitudes; his chest is deep, allowing for excellent lung capacity; his build is lithe, with fine bone, tight muscle, lean neck, and good tuck-up. The head is lean and tapered; the eyes, commonly hazel in color, express determination. The warm coat is thick and double, with heavy feathering on the tail, ears, thighs, shoulders, and front legs. Height: 22–28 inches (56–71 cm).

DEVELOPMENT: Along the Russo-Chinese border extends a land rugged and steep. Elevations can exceed 7000 feet (2100 m). For coursing the fox, marmot, badger, hare, wildcat, wolf, and various hooved game of the area, a strong enduring dog was required. Inhabitants of the area selectively bred a classic sighthound type to yield a hunter effective in this terrain. The Taigan was for many years a commonly sighted sighthound in his native land. However, as the game and necessity of procuring food by the hunt waned, the ancient Taigan ironically found himself becoming a thing of the past.

RECOGNITION: NR

CHARACTER: The Taigan blends outward beauty with inner strength: the unebbing love to lead the chase and undying affection for his master are truly worthy of preservation.

TASY
Mid-Asiatic Borzoi

PORTRAIT: The tapered head, the lissome body, the deep chest, good tuck, and runner's legs all suggest coursing hound. Though a tough, enduring fleet hound, the Tasy lacks the refinement desired in most westernized Greyhounds. Some notable features are his ringed tail and silky yet protective coat, with heavy fringe on the ears, legs and tail. Height: 22–28 inches (56–71 cm). Color: Tan, black and tan, or gray.

DEVELOPMENT: Like a strong breeze off the Caspian Sea, the Tasy courses the vast deserts of this windswept area, where he is used to great effect on hare, marmot, fox, various hooved game, and even an occasional wolf. Unlike many coursing hounds, who rely purely on their acute eyesight for effectiveness, the Tasy has a nose sensitive enough to track game and begin the chase before the victim is in sight. So necessary were these dogs to the survival of men in years past that they were prized above any other animal as a possession. A report states that a purebred Tasy could once command a price of 47 horses in his native land. The incessant march of modernization, however, has trampled the breed to near extinction. Presently a few individuals are working hard to preserve this deserving breed.

RECOGNITION: NR

CHARACTER: Independent and untiring, the Tasy requires a human companion who can appreciate his abilities, will, life-sacrificing courage. He is a rewarding dog to own and has much to teach mankind about our long-time relationship with canines.

WHIPPET

PORTRAIT: The Whippet is built for the race. His moderate size, balance, and force allow maximum ground coverage with a minimum of superfluous motion. He is a lean yet muscular dog, with excellent cardiovascular capacity, enabled by his deep chest and aerodynamic body design. Height: 18–22 inches (46–56 kg). Weight: 28 pounds (13 kg). The coat is short, fine, and close; the color is unimportant, and any color is accepted.

DEVELOPMENT: For his weight, the Whippet is the fastest domesticated animal, attaining speeds up to 35 miles (56 km) per hour. This ability is primarily directed to the dog tracks, where the Whippet is renowned for its competitive nature and awesome ability to excite those inclined to dog racing. He is also a fine coursing hound, especially capable on rabbits; his ratting ability puts many proud terriers to shame. The Whippet is a rather recent creation, originating in the 1800s, during the lull of bull- and bear-baiting, for the gentry's dog racing desires. They were created by crosses of small English Greyhounds and various terriers. At a later date, Italian Greyhound blood was infused and helped to perfect type. Recently, a long-haired version has stirred great controversy among fanciers.

RECOGNITION: FCI, AKC, UKC, KCGB, CKC, ANKC

CHARACTER: Though graceful, affectionate, and willing to please, the Whippet may be high-strung. His racing heritage necessitates substantial exercise. His coat requires little care, and he is essentially a hardy dog.

American Bulldog.

MASTIFFS

ALAPAHA BLUE BLOOD BULLDOG
Otto

PORTRAIT: A well-developed, unexaggerated bulldog with a broad head, natural drop ears, and a prominent muzzle. The Alapaha weighs approximately 100 pounds (47 kg) and is 24 inches (61 cm) at the shoulders. Females are usually substantially smaller and weigh an average of 78 pounds (34 kg). In color the Alapaha can be black, white, blu marbling (*sic*), buff, brown and spotted. The ears and tail are never trimmed or docked. The body is sturdy and unquestionably muscled.

DEVELOPMENT: The Alapaha Blue Blood Bulldog results from the generations-old breeding program of PaPa Buck Lane of Rebecca, Georgia. The program intended to rescue the "plantation dog" of Southern Georgia that was nearly extinct. Lana Lou speaks of her granddaddy as always having had an "Otto" about the estate. One Otto was all one needed since these bulldogs were capable of guard work and woods work. When PaPa Buck was killed by a train in 1943, his Otto proved his undying devotion by constant visitation and guard duty over the grave.

RECOGNITION: NR

CHARACTER: Dutiful and quickly trainable, the Alapaha Blue Blood Bulldogs are named as such for their streak of "royalty." Owners claim that they are aggressive for defense only and needn't be restrained with a chain (provided the property is fenced). These are active, athletic and mindful dogs with a lot of heart.

AMERICAN BULLDOG
Old Country Bulldog, Old English White

PORTRAIT: The head is large, with a broad skull and a tenacious set of jaws; the small high-set ears, when uncropped, are flap or rolled; the muzzle is short, and the lips are loose. Complementing the broad skull are intensely well-muscled wide shoulders. The tail is usually docked, but, if not, is low lying and long. Height: 19–25 inches (45–64 cm). Weight: 65–105 pounds (30–48 kg). The short, smooth coat is colored (in order of preference): red brindle, all other brindles, solid white, red, fawn, and piebald.

DEVELOPMENT: First brought to America in the early 18th century, he, unlike his English counterpart, is continuously bred for utility and action, whether it be guard work, farm work, pit fighting, or other; he has never been accepted into the show circles. Despite his versatility and proven worth in a vast number of areas and his ability to pass type with reliability, he remains unrecognized by the major registries of the world. The American Bulldog is registered by the Game American Bulldog Club. He is the chosen mascot of the U.S. Marine Corps. A number of working "American Bulldog" varieties have evolved in the 20th century; they too remain unrecognized.

RECOGNITION: NR

CHARACTER: The American Bulldog is one of the few, the proud, and the mighty working dogs good enough for the show scene but lucky enough to be excluded and therefore not have his type or ability altered or reduced. From the halls of Montezuma to the shores of Tripoli, one can find no better all-around ready, willing, and able-to-please canine.

AMERICAN PIT BULL TERRIER
American Pit Bull, Pit Bull Terrier

PORTRAIT: The Pit Bull immediately strikes one as being a dog of power, passion, and undying willingness. The brick-like head, which is especially broad between the cheeks (to house the powerful jaws), is carried upon a thickly muscled, well-defined neck. The neck runs into a deep, thick, well-sprung chest that bursts with raw dynamism, sure affection, and pure game. The length of the dog exceeds slightly the height of between 18–22 inches (46–56 cm). Weight is varied, even among dogs of the same height; weight can be between 30–80 pounds (14–36 kg), with 35–55 (16–25 kg) being common. The coat is short, glossy, and stiff to the touch. All colors are acceptable, with or without markings. The ears set high on the skull can be cropped or uncropped; docked tails, though they occur, are not accepted by the UKC.

DEVELOPMENT: Developed from the bull and terrier types of yesterday, the American Pit Bull Terrier comes from an undeniable history of pitfighting. The breed's tenacity and accompanying strength are unparalleled in the canine world. As rich and captivating as the breed's history is, the Pit Bull's future is more worthy of commentary. The APBT, as registered by the UKC, is an individual breed of dog and does not refer to just any ill-bred, mindless warrior-type mongrel. In the America of times unfortunately gone by, the Pit Bull was a much loved, much trusted worthy companion. The loveless unworthies who have capitalized on the breed's abilities for illegal dogfighting activities or other comparable lowlife goings-on are chiefly responsible for the banning and witchhunting that have begun sweeping the U.S. The media, however, should not go unscathed, for it is also responsible for escalating isolated incidences in an unrelenting and attention-getting way. The Pit Bull's future has been perhaps irreparably undone and everyone is to blame except the dog itself. The "little rascal" is too set on pleasing his owner, and ironically this is the root of his own undoing. Accompanying this need to please are remarkable abilities of all kinds. Pit Bulls excel in practically every canine task: herding, guarding, hunting, policing, and ratting.

RECOGNITION: UKC

CHARACTER: That sly smile, those determined eyes, that unwaning pleasure to please, the mere quality and characteristics of the APBT have evoked more human emotional, rational, and irrational response than any breed that exists today. By no means are these dogs people-haters or people-eaters: their natural aggressive tendencies are towards other dogs and animals, not people. These are truly quality companions for quality owners—*only!*

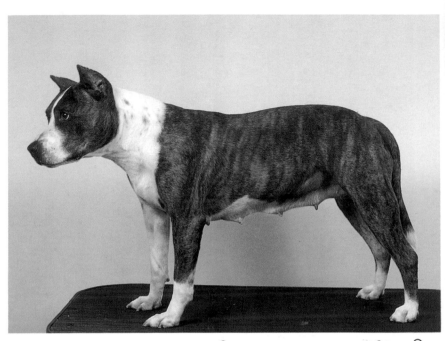

AMERICAN STAFFORDSHIRE TERRIER

PORTRAIT: Well-put together, muscular and stocky, the American Staffordshire Terrier should project the impression of tremendous power for his size. Height: 17–19 inches (43–48 cm). Weight: 40–50 pounds (18–23 kg). The skull is broad, and the cheek (or jaw) muscles are clearly noticeable. Uncropped ears are preferred. The tail is short in proportion to body size; it is not docked or curled. Coat: short and glossy; close lying and harsh to the touch. The Staff is seen in all colors, including solid, parti, and patched.

DEVELOPMENT: The American Staff is first cousin to the Staffordshire Bull Terrier of England, which is a cross between the Old Bulldogge of England (who was for many years the premier bullbaiter) and, most likely, the Fox Terrier. The Old Bulldogge is not to be confused with the Old English Bulldog; if there is a resemblance, it is more between the Staffordshire Terriers, especially the larger American Staff, and the Old Bulldogge. American fanciers desired traits that differed from those of the English fanciers, i.e., greater height and weight and more substantial body features, especially the head. Thus, the two Staffs grew apart in type. In 1936, the American Staff was recognized as a separate breed by the AKC.

RECOGNITION: FCI, AKC, CKC

CHARACTER: Despite their pit fighting history and the harsh criticism that they are vicious, these dogs are loyal, trustworthy, and above all affectionate. Even in the heyday of pit fighting, these dogs were known by those who knew them well as gentle with humans. AmStaffs are known as "pleasers" and not as maulers. Their willingness and ability to achieve the desired goals of their master are renowned.

APPENZELLER
Appenzell Mountain Dog, Appenzeller Sennenhund

PORTRAIT: Necessarily a strong, well-built, and hardy animal, the Appenzeller is a versatile working dog. The dog's length slightly exceeds his height of 19–23 inches (48–59 cm). His weight is between 50 and 55 pounds (23–25 kg). He is a good-looking dog, a doggy dog as some say, with a short, smooth, and considerably tight coat, well-muscled limbs, strong jaw, and powerful neck. Color is "tricolored," black and tan with white on the chest, blaze, tail, and toes. The tan is always between the black and the white.

DEVELOPMENT: According to a most respected thesis, the ancient molossus, introduced to the Swiss Alpine region by the Roman legions sometime in the 1st century BC, yielded today's Appenzeller. The Appenzeller contributes to the belief in the Roman's capability to breed dogs of outstanding ability. The Appenzeller's type was perfected centuries ago, probably through crossings with various herders and, likely, the Puli. The Appenzeller has performed well as a guard dog, a cart puller, and as both a cattle drover and a livestock guard. The coupling of herd droving and guarding excellence is not to be taken lightly. In most other cases, two breeds are necessary for successful herding—one to drive and one to protect. The Appenzeller remains a dog of outstanding ability and versatility.

RECOGNITION: FCI

CHARACTER: This guy is athletic and always aroused; therefore, he needs his space and his exercise. Intensely loyal and very territorial, the Appenzeller needs a caring family to love and protect.

BELGIAN MASTIFF
Mâtin Belge, Chien de Trait

PORTRAIT: The Belgian Mastiff is a bobtailed mastiff: this quality is one of his distinguishing characteristics. The coat is brindle or fawn, and there may be a dark mask and/or infrequent white markings. The dog's strength is superb and can be witnessed in his brawny musculature, thick neck, big bones, and impressive skull. Height: 27–32 inches (69–78 cm). Weight: 100–110 pounds (45–50 kg). The coat is short, smooth, and rather loose fitting.

DEVELOPMENT: The Belgian Mastiff was a leash dog, used for comparable work to the Saint Hubert type hounds, i.e., tracking and search work. Undoubtedly, he was also used as a guard. Because of his remarkable resemblance to the large French hounds, he likely originated in France, and changed type specifics during his residence in Belgium. The FCI places him on the suspended list; the Belgian Kennel Club states that he may be extinct; the Société Royal Saint Hubert claims the Chien de Trait to be extinct. In short, none of these dogs is known to exist today.

RECOGNITION: FCI (suspended)

CHARACTER: The Belgian Mastiff is (or was) an untiring worker. His locomotion is free and powerful, steady and sure. Not known as a friendly dog, he is still loving towards his immediate human family and loyal towards his master. With strong drives of protectiveness, he must be allowed to vent his energy and anxiety.

BERNESE MOUNTAIN DOG
Berner Sennenhund, Bouvier Bernois

PORTRAIT: The mountainous regions of Switzerland demand that a dog be hardy. The Bernese Mountain Dog has the unpampered look of the rugged mountaineer. His coloring is pure Swiss: black and tan with white markings. His coat is of medium length, with slightly wavy hair that protects against harsh breezes and falling snows. The skull is flat. The muzzle is strong and straight. The eyes are dark brown and almond shaped, expressing loyalty. The body is compact. The chest is large. Height: 23–27½ inches (59–70 cm). Weight: 87–90 pounds (40–44 kg).

DEVELOPMENT: The Berner Sennenhund, like all other sennenhunden, is descended from the ancient molossus dogs introduced to Switzerland by the Roman legions sometime during the first century before Christ. From these ancient guard dogs, with the crossbreeding of native or available working stock, the Berner Sennenhund was created. He is the Swiss dog that has achieved the greatest popularity outside of his native land.

RECOGNITION: FCI, AKC, UKC, KCGB, CKC

CHARACTER: The temperament of the Bernese Mountain Dog is that of a truly hard-working, completely domesticated dog. He has come a long way from his ancient molossus forefathers, yet he still retains much of their courage, strength, and hardiness.

BOXER

PORTRAIT: The Boxer is of very refined mastiff type; great attention is paid to the quality of the unique head and the fine points of the body. Though he has retained much ability, strength and gameness, he is a much different dog from his ancestors: more lithe, stylish, and chiseled. The skull is lean, without exaggeration, and shows no wrinkle. The muzzle is broad, deep and powerful. The upper jaw has a slight taper. The body is square; the chest is deep; and the ribs are well arched but not barrel shaped. The tail is set on high and usually docked. The limbs are strong and well-boned. Height: 22½–25 inches (57–64 cm). Weight: 53–71 pounds (24–28 kg). The coat is tight to the body, short, smooth, and glossy. Colors are fawn or brindle and can be with or without white markings.

DEVELOPMENT: He invariably begins the fight with his front paws, like a real pugilist. The Boxer is a polished adaptation of the old *bullenbeiser* that frequented the animal-baiting rings of 17th-, 18th-, and 19th-century Europe. Among his possible ancestors are the Great Dane and the Old English Bulldog, and he certainly has some terrier in him. Knowledgeable fanciers believe that the Boxer is related to most breeds of the bulldog type, whether by close or distant relation. The Boxer has transformed from a rough, feisty scrapper to a refined member of the civilized world.

RECOGNITION: FCI, AKC, UKC, KCGB, CKC, ANKC

CHARACTER: Self-confident and proud, the Boxer has a cocky way about him. Many love him; many fear him. The Boxer is able to guard well and conquer many obedience tasks. He is a fine companion to be trusted always.

BULLDOG
English Bulldog, British Bulldog

PORTRAIT: The image is of a tug boat, powerful and compact; the determination of a steam locomotive, well-fueled and strong. Height: 12–14 inches (31–36 cm). Weight: 40–55 pounds (19–25 kg). The head's circumference is equal to the dog's height. The eyes are very dark and set low down on the skull; the ears are rose and set high. The close, short, smooth coat comes in various brindles (commonly red), white and pied (white with any of the various brindles). Dudley (black and black with tan) is most undesireable.

DEVELOPMENT: Of all the dogs sharing the ancient molossus type, the Bulldog is probably the one who has taken the blood the farthest. Bulldog, as the name may imply, refers to a dog who is (or was) especially apt at baiting a bull. The sport of pitting one animal against another was quite in vogue through the 18th and 19th centuries and was practiced at least since the Roman era. In 1835, bullbaiting was made illegal in England, and the bulldogs in general suffered decline in numbers. 1860 is the year that this bulldog entered the show ring and began his new era.

RECOGNITION: FCI, AKC, UKC, KCGB, CKC, ANKC

CHARACTER: Despite extremes in physical bearing, the Bulldog maintains a surprising degree of subtlety and subdued fierceness. Endowed with both charm and modesty, Britain's national pride is an icon of determination, boldness, and loyalty. He is affectionate, loving people young and old; and he is intelligent and trainable. Volumes could be written about the charming Bulldog of old and new.

BULLMASTIFF

PORTRAIT: This silent, fearless watchman in the night would combat un-aidedly his often armed opponents. He is, necessarily, a quick and agile, strong and determined dog. Height: 24–27 inches (61–69 cm). Weight: 110–130 pounds (50–59 kg). A short hard coat covers the richly muscled body. The head is large and square; the muzzle is short, broad, and nearly without taper. His appearance alone is a deterrent to intrusion. Color possibilities include: fawn, brindle, or red, with a black mask common.

DEVELOPMENT: In the 1860s, the Bullmastiff was bred to be the superlative protector of game from poachers. The original crosses produced a 60-percent Mastiff to 40-percent Bulldog breed type. The Bullmastiff was to track, run down, and secure a poacher until the proper authorities arrived. Poaching was punishable by death, and one can imagine the desperate struggles that must have resulted from the fear of being caught in the act. The Bullmastiff, with his strength, speed, and determination, was awesome at estate policing. He was originally known as the "Gamekeeper's Night Dog." These original dogs were more brawny than today's more refined dogs. The great majority were dark brindle colored, to conceal them in the night, as opposed to the popular fawn color of today.

RECOGNITION: FCI, AKC, KCGB, CKC, ANKC

CHARACTER: The Bullmastiff, though a big dog with a dark history, is a loving dog that you can trust with your person and your property. Ever watchful and always enduring, his spirited ways delight the owner. Fanciers are strongly advised to seek a dedicated breeder with proven stock.

BULL TERRIER

PORTRAIT: Aesthetically speaking, it is hard to find another breed of dog that satiates the eye more than the perfectly balanced Bull Terrier. Poised on his toes, with his steely muscles firm beneath the tightly fitting coat and his small triangular eyes glistening, he is truly the white cavalier. Height: 21–22 inches (53–56 cm). Weight: 52–62 pounds (24–28 kg). Color: white or any color other than white, with or without white markings. The head is long, strong, and deep, from the back of the skull to the tip of the muzzle. The ears, standing alert, are small, thin, and placed close together. The body is well rounded, with a noticeable spring to the rib. The legs should be big boned but in balance with the body. The forelegs should be straight.

DEVELOPMENT: In the 1850s, after years of experimentation, James Hinks of Birmingham, England, thrust upon the world a new bull-and-terrier dog, one who further removed some of the undesirable traits of the then existing Bulldog (the roach back, the overly angulated legs, and the undershot jaw). The Bull Terrier was bred in a large part from crosses of the bullbaiting bulldogs and the now extinct English White Terrier.

RECOGNITION: FCI, AKC, UKC, KCGB, CKC, ANKC

CHARACTER: The Bull Terrier has class, and he has style. Long favored by the gentlemen of England, the Bull Terrier is a refined dog with good manners, a quick wit, and a jaunty demeanor. Easily trained, fearless, and clean, he makes a fine companion and guard for the home or apartment.

CANARY DOG
Perro de Presa Canario

PORTRAIT: Immediately catching the eye is the powerful square head that is nearly as wide as it is long. This dog has a broad muzzle, a strong jaw, and ears that are usually cropped. The rump is slightly raised (set higher than the withers), giving a curved impression to the indestructible back. Great power emanates from the broad, deep chest and the thick-boned, well-muscled legs. Height: 21½–25½ inches (54–65 cm). Weight: 84–106 pounds (38–48 kg). The coat is short and rough. Color: fawn or various brindles, with white markings sometimes seen.

DEVELOPMENT: Developed on the Canary Islands, the modern Canary Dog is a cross between the native and indigenous Bardino Majero (now extinct) and the Mastiff of England, brought over in the 1800s. These cross-bred dogs were selectively bred for fighting ability. With the outlawing of dogfighting on the island and the introduction of foreign dogs such as the German Shepherd Dog, the Canary Dog faced extinction by the 1960s. Thanks to dedicated breeders, the Canary Dog was saved and enjoys today renewed popularity. Dr. Carl Semencic is responsible for the breed's growing American fancy and the name "Canary Dog," employed in this book.

RECOGNITION: NR

CHARACTER: The Canary Dog requires a dominant master and an attentive human family; no member can be uncomfortable around dogs. Canaries make outstanding guards; their appearance is a deterrent and their ability a detriment to any intruder.

DANISH BROHOLMER

PORTRAIT: The Broholmer is a compact mastiff, standing 27½–29½ inches (70–75 cm) tall and weighing 115–140 pounds (52–63 kg). The head, though broad in both skull and muzzle, is neither of German nor English Mastiff resemblance; it is distinctively refined yet functionally useful. The chest is large, broad, and deep. The back is straight and powerful. The coat is short and coarse. Color: a fawnish brown, or brownish yellow, or black, with white markings on feet, tail, and chest allowed.

DEVELOPMENT: The Danes accepted the gifts of English Mastiffs from the English royalty, just as they had accepted gifts of German Mastiffs from the German royalty. The Danish Broholmer is the result of the crossing of English Mastiffs with "local dogs," which were received from Germany years earlier. The breed was likely established sometime in the 19th century. These robust dogs were popular throughout Denmark for many years. The World Wars changed the face of Europe, and they changed the practicality of a Dane's keeping such a large dog with such a big appetite. It was not until the 1970s that activity was focused on preserving the breed. The current breed base is small, yet type is well established.

RECOGNITION: FCI

CHARACTER: The Danish Broholmer is a watchful, faithful, and fearless dog who remains affectionate and easily trained. His size and power, however, require that an owner be sure of himself as a master, willing to give the dog the necessary training, discipline, and exercise.

DOBERMAN PINSCHER
Dobermann

PORTRAIT: He is a dog of sculpted elegance, resembling fine marble crafted to denote power, courage, stamina, and nobility. Standing 23–28 inches (59–71 cm) tall and weighing 66–88 pounds (30–40 kg), the Dobie is a mid-sized dog and a mid-sized mastiff. The build is compact and powerful, showing no exaggeration of muscle or bone. The head is long and dry, with a gradual taper from between the ears to the point of the muzzle. The jaws must be solid and powerful, never hinting at snipiness. Coat: smooth, short, hard, thick, and close lying. Color: solid ground color of either black, red, fawn, or blue, all with tan markings. The ears are usually cropped and held erect in the U.S.A. and uncropped and held naturally in Great Britain.

DEVELOPMENT: Originated in Apolda, in Thueringen, in Germany, through the definitive breeding efforts of Herr Louis Dobermann, a tax collector and dog catcher, the Wagner of the canine universe. Dobermann had the need for a dog that would protect himself from both the irate, negligent tax payers and their snarling guard dogs. Remember that Germany is famous for its ready, willing, and able heart-stopping canines. His access to all dogs that he brought in through his employment plus his own fine kennel stock afforded Dobermann the opportunity to develop the canine par excellence. At this task Herr Dobermann admirably succeeded. In a remarkably short period of time, the Doberman's type was perfected. He remains today a dog of outstanding quality and ability, used for guard, police, military, and obedience work—despite the wanton breeding practices of some money-minded individuals.

RECOGNITION: FCI, AKC, UKC, KCGB, CKC, ANKC

CHARACTER: Though the breed has come under fire in recent years as an overbred and failing type, today many flawless, well-bred specimens grace the dog world. In the hands of a conscientious owner, the Doberman Pinscher is an unbeatable companion, worker, and showman.

DOGO ARGENTINO
Argentinian Mastiff

PORTRAIT: The Dogo is a concentrated conglomerate of attributes from ten able breeds. His smooth-muscled, symmetrical appearance appeals to the esthetic minded, while his massive skull, unrelenting jaws and unbreakable neck make him an indomitable hunter. Height: 23½–25½ inches (60–65 cm). Weight: 82–95 pounds (37–43 kg). The coat is very short, smooth, thick, and glossy.

DEVELOPMENT: Dr. Antonio Nores Martinez, in the 1920s, distinguished himself and Argentina by producing Argentina's first native purebred dog, the Dogo Argentino. The Dogo was bred to hunt in packs the vicious big game of wild boar, mountain lion, and jaguar. The terrain of his native land is demanding on the most fit of animals, yet the Dogo can traverse great distances at considerable speeds and retain enough strength to conquer his quarry. Though we recommend that you don't concoct this potentially volatile mixture at home, the recipe reads like this: base stock, Old Fighting Dog of Cordoba (a rich brew of Spanish Mastiff, Bull Terrier, old Bulldogge, and early Boxer); for height, add harlequin Great Dane; for bulk, weather resistance, and white color, pour in the Great Pyrenees; for scenting, add a dash of the English Pointer; and for speed, a pinch of Irish Wolfhound; nearly completed, crosses with the Bordeaux fortify strength and courage.

RECOGNITION: FCI

CHARACTER: The Dogo is intrepid and untiring. The essential requirements are exercise and obedience training. An impassable guard, the Dogo is gaining international respect and popularity.

MASTIFFS

DOGUE DE BORDEAUX
French Mastiff, Bordeaux Bulldog

PORTRAIT: As far as giants go, the Dogue de Bordeaux is a lesser giant; nonetheless, his massive head, superabundant wrinkles, exaggerated paws and general, though congenial, passivity qualify him to loiter with the most molasses-like of molossus types. The breed's acromegalic features are not subtle and give it strong, if perverse, appeal to the general public. The body is well balanced and muscular. Furrowed with wrinkles, the broad round head is tremendous and the largest in the canine world. Height: 23–27 inches (59–69 cm). Weight: 84–100 pounds (38–46 kg). The coat is fine, short and soft to the touch, if one were to pet it (which is not regularly advised). In color the Dogue is fawn, mahogany, golden, or black speckled—warm tones desirable. Black or red mask a must.

DEVELOPMENT: A frequent sight on French estates for centuries, the Bordeaux Dog is a fearless guardian. Employed as a hunter of pigs, bears, boars and wolves, these formidable titans were never overly esteemed by their 12th-century French masters. During the Middle Ages, the dogs were used for cattle droving.

RECOGNITION: FCI

CHARACTER: Fairly lazy, the Dogue adheres to a *laissez faire* attitude towards life. Thick-skinned and strong-willed, the Dogue is aggressive with other dogs but, if handled properly, makes a fine companion dog. Not nearly as bad-tempered as its ancestors, the breed gets on well with children.

ENTELBUCHER
Entelbuch Mountain Dog, Entelbucher Sennenhund

PORTRAIT: The classic Swiss coloration adorns the smooth coat of the Entelbucher. He is a square, sturdy dog with typical working dog features. The head is well proportioned to the body, strong with a flat skull. The body is robust and compact and most efficiently conceived. Height: under 20 inches (51 cm). Weight: 55–66 pounds (25–30 kg). The tricolor coat is black and tan with white on toes, tail tip, chest and blaze; the tan always lies between the black and white. Tails are sometimes docked.

DEVELOPMENT: Brought to Helvetia circa 2000 years ago by the Romans, the Swiss mountain dogs are among the oldest of Switzerland's dogs. The Entelbucher finds its original home in Entelbuch in the Canton of Lucerne. He is the smallest of the four Swiss mountain dogs. The Greater Swiss Mountain Dog and the Bernese Mountain Dog each have larger international followings; the Appenzeller and the Entelbucher remain popular primarily in Switzerland. The Entelbucher was embraced by Lucernese shepherds as guard dogs and was used as a farm dog and cattle drover. The Entelbucher's size makes him a superior all-purpose dog.

RECOGNITION: FCI

CHARACTER: A people-person dog, the Entelbucher is entirely comfortable surrounded by his family and friends. He delights in pleasing his human acquaintances and is a sincere easykeeper, able to remain clean on his own.

FILA BRASILEIRO
Brazilian Mastiff, Brasilian Molosser, Cão de Fila

PORTRAIT: Well boned and rectangularly structured, the Fila is compact yet harmonic and symmetrical in outline. The head is big, heavy and massive. The muzzle is strong, broad and deep; the lips are thick and pendulous. The neck is tremendously powerful. The Fila can be any color, solid or brindle, except white or mouse gray. The skin is thick and loose all over the body. At the neck it forms a generous and prominent dewlap, which might be more aptly described as a lap! Height: 24–30 inches (61–76 cm). Weight: 95 pounds (43 kg) and over.

DEVELOPMENT: The mastiff-types indigenous to the Iberian peninsula were transported with the Portuguese and the Spaniard conquerors into Central America. These new-in-town flewy mastiffs crossed with indigenous dogs to create the Fila Brasileiro. Somewhere along the line, the Bloodhound may have joined in this Latino orgy of crossbreeding as the abundant facial skin would seem to indicate. Their size doesn't hinder their agility. Originally the hunters of the jaguar and runaway slaves, they are used to drove untamed cattle and are commonly employed on ranches.

RECOGNITION: FCI

CHARACTER: A valuable guard dog, the Fila is suspicious of strangers and dedicated to his owner. Brazilian breeders are promoting the Fila's acceptance abroad. Proper socialization is the key to ownership with the Filas.

GREAT DANE
Deutsche Dogge, German Boarhound, Alano, Dogo Aleman

PORTRAIT: Smoothly muscled and well formed, the Great Dane accomplishes a distinguished appearance with elegance and ease. The head is long and narrow, refined as if chiseled by a fine sculptor. The ears should be high and of medium size. Sufficiency of bone and tremendous substance are paramount with this breed. Height: 28–32 inches (71–80 cm). Weight: 100 pounds (45 kg) and over. The Great Dane comes in five coat colors: black, blue, brindle, fawn and harlequin. The coat should be short and thick, smooth and glossy.

DEVELOPMENT: No Dane at all (though surely Great), the Great Dane is pure *Deutsche*, the Germans having astutely laid claim to the development of the ancient molossus/alaunt type. The Alans brought their mastiffs with them upon invading Gaul, Italy and Spain in the 5th century. His old British name, German Boarhound, reminds us of his once passionate pursuit of wild boars. It is believed that a cross to the Greyhound may be responsible for the breed's agility and slenderish body type.

RECOGNITION: FCI, AKC, UKC, KCGB, CKC, ANKC

CHARACTER: To be or not to be a Great Dane owner is contingent upon the size of one's home, yard, and pocketbook. They need to feel involved with the home life activities—dinnertime is a unanimous favorite! Many believe that the Great Dane is too gentle to be a man-stopper, although his size and strength would qualify him for this work were he properly raised.

GREATER SWISS MOUNTAIN DOG
Grosser Schweizer Sennenhund, Large Swiss Mountain Dog

PORTRAIT: A very short, shiny coat waves the traditional Swiss Mountain Dog flag—black and tan with white. Weighing as much as 130 pounds (59 kg), the Swissy is the largest of the four Swiss mountain dogs. The coat is practically water- and weatherproof. Height: 23–29 inches (59–74 cm). Rectangular and well put-together, the body is well ribbed with strong loins. The back is flat and not too long. The chest is broad.

DEVELOPMENT: The relation of the Greater Swiss Mountain Dog and the Smooth-coated St. Bernard became intertwined as the latter became more popular and the former fazed out of favor. Crossbreeding to Saints explains the large size in the Mountain Dog today. The dogs were used as pullers of small carts and as general purpose farm dogs. Second only to the Bernese Mountain Dog in popularity, the Greater Swiss Mountain Dog has found friends in the United States, where it is recognized, as well as Great Britain and Canada.

RECOGNITION: FCI, AKC

CHARACTER: Good natured and friendly, the Greater Swiss makes a marvelous house pet and loves to be outdoors. He is self-assured and fearless; he responds best to a confident though equable approach. Grooming is a cinch and never a chore.

MASTIFFS

LANDSEER
Landseer Newfoundland

PORTRAIT: Clear nobility and power in black and white—the Landseer is mountainous and mountainously majestic. The coat is black and white particolor, dense, flat and double; it is also waterproof. The head is broad and grand in size. The body is muscular and well ribbed; the chest is fairly broad. The feet are webbed and well shaped. The coat pattern preferably consists of a black head with a narrow white blaze and an evenly marked saddle; the black rump extends to the tail. The Landseer is slightly taller than the Newfoundland and lighter in frame. Height: 26–31½ (66–80 cm). Weight: 110–150 pounds (50–68 kg). The gait is free and rolling.

DEVELOPMENT: Named for the artist whose renderings brought fame to the black and white particolor Newfoundland, this breed owes much to the romantic realism of Sir Edwin Landseer's canvasses. Like the Newfoundlands (that they are), the Landseer was developed to give assistance to fishermen on the shores of the island of Newfoundland. The dog's ancestor is clearly the Greater St. John's Dog, the larger of the two types of St. John's Dogs that were the first stage of evolution of these fish-fishing swimmers. The dogs are natural rescue dogs and are greatly inclined to the water.

RECOGNITION: FCI

CHARACTER: For the owner seeking a dog of singular beauty, strength and unequaled faithfulness, the Landseer is indeed an ideal choice. Owners are advised to give their Landseer as much time in the water as possible. This is unparalleled exercise for the dog, which he appreciates swimmingly.

LEONBERGER

PORTRAIT: The Leonberger is strong and muscular. The skull is tolerably wide and moderately deep. The stop is slight; no wrinkles should be noticeable on the head. The ears are set on high and lay close to the head. The body is slightly longer than high. The coat is medium soft to hard, fairly long, lying close to the body despite a rather well-endowed undercoat. Height: 29–32 inches (72–80 cm). Weight: 80–150 pounds (37–67 kg). Color: light yellow, golden to red-brown preferably with black mask. The tail is well furnished and flown at half mast.

DEVELOPMENT: For purely aesthetic reasons, the lion-loving Mayor of Leonberg, Herr Heinrich Essig, decided to emulate the "King of the Jungle" (a cat!) in the canine species. The cross between a Landseer Newfoundland and a Saint Bernard, then crossed to a Great Pyrenees, in 1907, produced a strong, furry leonine emblem to be unfurled with lion-hearted pride over the city of Leonberg. At one time the dogs were said to have worked as herders, but this theory is basically unqualified and undeveloped.

RECOGNITION: FCI, KCGB

CHARACTER: A force to be reckoned with, this canine resembles the mighty lion in appearance and attitude. He is laid-back and content, though livelier than his Saint Bernard ancestors. Gentle and genial, he enjoys the company of children and makes a wary and able watchdog.

MASTIFF
English Mastiff, Old English Mastiff

PORTRAIT: Massive and symmetrical in appearance, the Mastiff possesses an imposing and well-knit frame. The head is broad with noticeable wrinkles—breadth is desired greatly. The mask is black and ever-present. The muzzle is short and squared off. The outer coat is moderately coarse; the undercoat is close lying and dense. In color the Mastiff is apricot, silver fawn, or dark fawn-brindle. Height: at least 27½–30 inches (70–76 cm). Weight: 175–190 pounds (80–86 kg).

DEVELOPMENT: There is no doubt that the Mastiff is an ancient type; the dogs roamed around Europe and Asia a few millennia before Christ. These massive canines were employed in the hunting of wild horses and lions, as well as in protecting the homes of Babylonians. The burying of terra-cotta Mastiff figures under the thresholds of houses was a custom the Assyrian peoples practiced to invoke the canine spirits to ward off evil. Mastiff prototypes, such as the Molossus of Epirus and Babylonian Mastiff, were used as flock guards against wolves and other predators. Romans found the Mastiff in England when they first arrived—how the dogs got to England escapes our knowledge—and took them to Rome to participate in arenas.

RECOGNITION: FCI, AKC, UKC, KCGB, CKC, ANKC

CHARACTER: The Mastiff needs a good deal of exercise and lots of room to move—and a lot of food too. Mastiffs aren't too fond of the show ring; although many participate, they would rather meander around an estate, looking noble and being omnipotent.

MINIATURE BULL TERRIER

PORTRAIT: Well balanced and powerfully built, the Miniature Bull Terrier stands from 10–14 inches (26–36 cm) tall and is the spitting image of his big brother, the Bull Terrier, as perceived from the flip side of the telescope. The down-faced, egg-shaped head, distinctive among the Bull Terriers, is rippingly endowed with strong sound teeth. The body is well rounded, with great depth from withers to brisket. The back is short and strong, as is the tail. Weight must be in proportion to the height.

DEVELOPMENT: Bred down from the smaller standard-sized Bull Terrier, the Miniature Bull Terrier was developed to assist his big brother in ratting. The present Mini Bull remains free of the problems that often haunt the miniaturized breeds. At one time, the breed was considered but a variety of the standard-sized Bull Terrier, but more recently the kennel clubs register them separately. At the end of the 19th century in Britain, eight-pound Mini Bulls were all the rage, but this waned in time. A movement to rebuild the variety took place in the 1930s; the emergent specimens weighed about 18 pounds but lacked good quality heads and the gladiator fire so denoting of the Bull Terrier breed.

RECOGNITION: FCI, AKC, KCGB, CKC, ANKC

CHARACTER: The Mini Bull today, not bantamized to toy extremes, preserves the Bull Terrier's spirit and even disposition. These are ideal apartment dwellers due to their convenient size and alert demeanor. When reared properly in a household with children, the breed demonstrates great consideration and protectiveness over its allotted charges.

MOSCOW WATCHDOG
Moskovskaya Storodzevay Sobaka

PORTRAIT: A big-boned but not clumsy dog with a marvelously massive head and powerful legs. The Moscow Watchdog is well developed, muscularly and mentally. The coat is thick with fringing and of moderate length. The color is always red and white. Height: 25–27 inches (64–69 cm). Weight: 100–150 pounds (45–68 kg). The tail is generously plumed and practically floor length. The expression is confident and knowing.

DEVELOPMENT: A product of Soviet dog breeders of the 1950s, the Moscow Watchdog is much of a crossbreed. Beginning with the Caucasian Ovtcharka for its obvious watchful and assertive traits, these determined canine concocters crossed in a Saint Bernard to increase size. That Alpine Mastiff was too supine and slow in manner to meet the needs of these fanciers. The result, the Moscow Watchdog, possesses the mental and physical attributes desired.

RECOGNITION: NR

CHARACTER: This strong and able-bodied mastiff is both a companionable comrade and a watchdog—the latter feature evident in the translation of the dog's name. He is fine in temperament, if properly reared, and a suitable choice for Russian owners who have the space to keep him. The need for exercise and room to stretch the limbs precludes his use by Russian apartment dwellers. No dogs are known outside the U.S.S.R.

NEAPOLITAN MASTIFF
Mastino Napoletano

PORTRAIT: Quadrupled chinned, with the lilt of a hippopotamus, the Neapolitan Mastiff is as beguiling and commanding as a 150-pound brachymorph can be. His appearance is massive, strong, and coarse and yet synchronously majestic. The broad flat skull is abundant in wrinkles and folds. The nose is large with well-opened nostrils. The muzzle and lips are copious and heavy. The chest is broad and well developed. The coat is dense, the texture coarse. Permissible colors are black, blue, gray, mahogany, and brindle. Height: 23–30 inches (59–76 cm). Weight: 110–154 pounds (50–70 kg).

DEVELOPMENT: The rustic Neo has been protecting and performing in southern Italy since Roman times. The breed is a descendant of the ancient molossus that were transported to Rome to fight in the arenas. In their pit days, stoicism was key although the type of pugnacity with which the Pit Bull Terrier approaches the match was never achieved. Piero Scanziani, after witnessing the first Neos to enter the show ring in 1946 (Naples), became an avid breeder and is honored for his efforts that brought the dogs to the public's eye.

RECOGNITION: FCI, KCGB

CHARACTER: This is an unsurpassed defender of home and property. However, he is never aggressive or tenacious with people. His docility and even temperament make him a lovable and lovingly bumbling companion. He is not clumsy by foot or by heart. Not the ideal dog for a condo or mini apartment complex, he needs room and air to live, and he is quite the messy eater.

NEWFOUNDLAND

PORTRAIT: August and stately, the Newfoundland is the incarnation of imposing beauty. He is a large dog with big bone but never appears heavily inactive. The head is broad and massive; the body is muscular and well ribbed, with a fairly broad chest. The bear-sized feet are webbed and well shaped. The Newfy's coat is medium in length and very dense. Some feathering occurs on the forelegs and hind legs. The undercoat is substantial and the outer coat is water resistant. Height: 26–30 inches (66–76 cm). Weight: 110–150 (50–68 kg). In color the Newfoundland is painted in solid black, bronze, and black and white particolor. The latter coloration is called Landseer and is recognized by the FCI as an individual breed.

DEVELOPMENT: Developed from the fishermen's dogs, the Greater St. John's Dogs, the Newfoundland was prized by shore and sea dwellers on the island of Newfoundland. Possibly the companions of ancient Beothuk Indians on the island, the Newfoundland's big black water-wallowing ancestors dwelt with humans before the settling of Newfoundland by white men. The large mastiff-like Newfoundland today possesses an unquenchable affinity for the water and is a natural rescue dog.

RECOGNITION: FCI, AKC, UKC, KCGB, CKC, ANKC

CHARACTER: This happy-camper canine is a unanimously loved member of the dog world, with a character that is second to none. A dog of discriminating style and majesty, he is able to protect himself against would-be enemies yet is actually indiscriminative about his candidates for rescue—unfalteringly volunteering to save a drowning fellow canine with whom he is not friendly.

OLDE ENGLISH BULLDOGGE

PORTRAIT: This medium-sized dog looks like his creator's personal conception of the "original Bulldogge." Great strength and athletic refinery are evident in his conformation. The moderately wrinkled head is large in proportion to the body. The skull is deeply sunken between the eyes, extending up the forehead. Two-fold dewlap and semi-pendulous flews are desired. The ears are rose or button. The muzzle is short and broad. The body is cobby and muscular. The back is slightly roached and strong. The short, close coat is colored with brindles of red; gray or black on white; solid white; or fawn, red or black, with or without white.

DEVELOPMENT: Disenchanted by the English Bulldog and its breeding and breathing hang-ups, David Leavitt of Pennsylvania began a project to recreate the 18th-century Bulldog. Not so impressed by that ancient breed's fighting career as he was enamored with its tenacity and fierce appearance, Leavitt set out to reconstruct the dog which the present-day Bulldog no longer resembles. A linebreeding scheme involving Bullmastiffs, Pit Bull Terriers, American Bulldogs and the Bulldog have reaped a modern protection dog that looks and is man-stopping, able to impede an assailant without having to bite.

RECOGNITION: NR

CHARACTER: A Bulldog that is functional and traditional at the same time, the Olde English Bulldogge is courageous and determined without being overly aggressive. He is a genuinely friendly soul and a natural watchdog. His strength makes him ideal only for those who can control and curb such a powerpack.

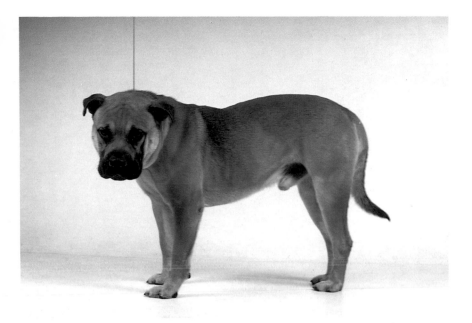

PERRO DE PRESA MALLORQUIN
Ca de Bou, Mallorquin Bulldog

PORTRAIT: An impressive, broad-chested bulldog with an imposing mastiff presence. The dog's musculation is formidable; the jaws are punishing. The size of the Perro de Presa Mallorquin does not exceed 150 pounds (68 kg) and the height is no less than 23 inches (59 cm). Coloration varies and is not of tremendous importance; conformation and balance are more vital to the Ca de Bou. Colors are usually shades of yellow, tan and fawn; brindles occur. The head is massive but not excessively wrinkled, appearing more like a Canary Dog. The coat is short and smooth.

DEVELOPMENT: *España* regaled in dog fights—the Spaniards, who have never been renowned for their love of the bull, were engrossed in bullbaiting as a spectator sport. Even today, while bullbaiting has been outlawed, dogfights are still supported by certain, thankfully small, circles. Mallorca, one of the Balearic islands off of the coast of Spain, developed this "gripping" canine to participate in its dogfighting ring. Organized dogfights on Mallorca have waned and with it, the population of Mallorquin Bulldogs. A number of dogs still exists, but residents believe that most of them are mainly crosses of the original dog.

RECOGNITION: FCI

CHARACTER: Were one to find a purebred Mallorquin Bulldog, one would possess a guard dog of unsurpassable ability—a dog that would require discipline and attention. *Grande y fuerte*, this *perro* is strong-minded but obedient if properly reared from puppyhood.

ROTTWEILER

PORTRAIT: Fine proportion, good size, attractive coat, and inherent confidence illustrate the Rottweiler. His form is compact and powerful, and his chest is roomy and deep. The back is straight and not too long, complementing the compact build. The head is medium in length, with the skull broad between the ears. The top coat is of moderate length; the undercoat is not visible. Color is quintessential: a glistening black with markedly defined rich tan markings. Height: 22–27 inches (56–69 cm). Weight: 90–110 pounds (41–50 kg).

DEVELOPMENT: The extinct Hatzrüden, a powerfully built mastiff used to hunt boar in Germany, bore a close resemblance to the present-day Rottweiler. The Rottweiler is named for the southern German town in which he originated. In Rottweil, the dogs were used as butcher's dogs—droving, herding and protecting cattle. He was called at that time the Rottweiler Metzgerhund. In the early 1900s, the breed was scarcely known, and even in the 1930s, when the breed had established a following in America, Austria and Switzerland, the Rottweiler was "totally unknown" in Great Britain. Today the breed enjoys great acclaim and popularity. Breeders strive for evenness in temperament as well as sound conformation.

RECOGNITION: FCI, AKC, UKC, KCGB, CKC, ANKC

CHARACTER: The Rottie is not excitable or quarrelsome; he is faithful, friendly and able: his calm expression suggests his good nature and soft humor. As a guard dog and family companion, the breed excels. Natural obedience, dependability and genuine intelligence disclose the breed's ever-increasing popularity.

144

SAINT BERNARD
St. Bernhardshund

PORTRAIT: A mighty and proportionately tall dog, the Saint's musculation is impressive on his every part. The head is imposing and massive and the expression is unmistakably dignified. The coat is very dense: smooth coats lie close; long coats are medium in length and slightly wavy. In color the St. Bernard is white with red or red with white is the St. Bernard in color. Red and brown-yellow are equally desired. Height: 25½–27½ inches (65–70 cm). Weight: 110–over 200 pounds (50–90 kg).

DEVELOPMENT: Buried under a few miles of snow, the origin of his kind is surely the only escapee that "Old Barry" has been unable to dig up and rescue. Many colorful and pardonably romantic themes persist on the origin of the St. Bernard. Great Dane and Newfoundland blood at one time or another entered the veins of the breed. He claims fame as a rescue dog, plowing through the deepest snow, at the Hospice of St. Bernard. Although it is not likely that the St. Bernard ever met St. Bernard (the monk who lived during the 12th century), these Barry Hounds began assisting the brothers at the Hospice in the third quarter of the 18th century. Today the Hospice preserves tradition and the dogs are busy charming the enchanted visitors who, much to the dogs' relief, rarely need rescuing.

RECOGNITION: FCI, AKC, UKC, KCGB, CKC, ANKC

CHARACTER: The somber and never ill-natured expression of the St. Bernard modifies one of the most benevolent of canines. His disposition is steady and kindly, making a fine companion for children and adults alike.

STAFFORDSHIRE BULL TERRIER

PORTRAIT: A neat and refined smooth-coated dog of tremendous musculature and accompanying strength and confidence. The head is short with pronounced cheek muscles and distinct stop. The medium-sized ears are rose or half-prick—they are never cropped. The body is close coupled, with a level topline and a wide front. The coat is smooth, short and close lying. Red, fawn, white, black or blue or any combination of these colors with white comprise the color variations. Height: 14–16 inches (36–41 cm). Weight: 24–38 pounds (11–17½ kg).

DEVELOPMENT: Squirming and squirting, the rhythmic disfiguring and dismembering of rats, rats, rats in the choppers of champion terrier-bred chompers was a popular pastime of British working classes in the 19th century, who cringed in the putrid excitement of the over-piling vermin carnage. The Staffordshire was bred to participate in this "sport" as well as in dog fights. The outlawing of both these dubious diversions ushered the Staff out of the pits and into the more respectable arena of the show ring. This dog is smaller than the American Staffordshire Terrier, his close relative.

RECOGNITION: FCI, AKC, UKC, KCGB, CKC, ANKC

CHARACTER: Although there is a tendency to joust with fellow canines, this is one of the friendliest of man's best friends. His devotion and faithfulness are proverbial. If properly reared, he is an affectionate, outgoing, even witty pet that promises years of delight.

TIBETAN MASTIFF

PORTRAIT: From Tibet comes this well-built and heavy dog with undeniably good looks and a kindly expression. A straight back, well-developed musculature, deep chest, well-laid shoulders, fairly broad head: the Tibetan Mastiff's body is a phenomenon of the dog world. European owners have led fanciers to think that the dog can grow to weigh over 220 pounds (99 kg), although a maximum of 140 pounds (60 kg) is more reasonable. The coat is thick and double and fairly long. The hair is fine but hard, stand-offish and straight. In color the dog is rich black, black and tan, brown, various shades of gold or gray. Height: 22–28 inches (56–71 cm).

DEVELOPMENT: Originating in the central tableland of Asia and occurring in Syria and Arabia, the Tibetan Mastiff is a real mountain dog and a true mastiff. Prized for their bravery and tremendous size (Marco Polo reported dogs as big as donkeys), Tibetan Mastiffs were presented to Alexander by an Asiatic king to combat lion and elephants and were warmly smiled upon by the Romans in the height of their hallowed decadence. They were employed in the Himalayas and around Central Asia as guard dogs and herders of flocks.

RECOGNITION: FCI, KCGB

CHARACTER: Possessing little of the innate ferocity of the mastiff group, the Tibetan Mastiff is docile and very attached to his owner. As a family guard dog he is brave, and his size alone deters both determined and ill-prepared intruders alike.

TOSA INU

*Tosa Ken, Tosa Token, Tosa Fighting Dog,
Japanese Tosa*

PORTRAIT: A stately manner and robust build impose the Tosa's presence. The body is solid muscle with little excess—moderate wrinkles on the head give the dog an inquiring and intelligent expression. The chest is broad and deep. The skull too is broad—the jaws are punishing and powerful. The coat is short, hard and dense. The ideal color is solid red on which white markings are tolerated; brindles, fawns and dull blacks also occur. Height: 24½–25½ inches (62–65 cm). Weight: up to 200 pounds (90 kg).

DEVELOPMENT: Dog-fighting enthusiasts in the Kochi prefecture in Japan set out to produce an unconquerable pit fighter, since the Japanese mastiffs were not fending well against occidental imports. Their efforts in the middle of the 19th century resulted in the Tosa Inu. Bull Terriers, Bulldogs, and Mastiffs were crossbred with the indigenous dogs, which were probably descendants of the ancient Molossus. The dogs were bred to fight to the death in the silent, stoic, obedient way that is aphoristically Japanese. The Tosa never disappointed the congregated spectators and attacked its opponent head-on, relentlessly, unceasingly.

RECOGNITION: FCI

CHARACTER: As a defender of one's home, the Tosa is extremely committed and effective. With proper handling, the breed is an excellent choice as a guard dog. It is people-oriented and more demonstrative than one might expect of a such stoic scrapper.

Siberian Huskies.

NORDIC DOGS

AINU DOG
Hokkaido Dog, Ainu-Ken

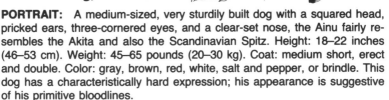

PORTRAIT: A medium-sized, very sturdily built dog with a squared head, pricked ears, three-cornered eyes, and a clear-set nose, the Ainu fairly resembles the Akita and also the Scandinavian Spitz. Height: 18–22 inches (46–53 cm). Weight: 45–65 pounds (20–30 kg). Coat: medium short, erect and double. Color: gray, brown, red, white, salt and pepper, or brindle. This dog has a characteristically hard expression; his appearance is suggestive of his primitive bloodlines.

DEVELOPMENT: The history of this dog is very closely tied with the history of the Ainu tribe. This old tribe first settled in Japan some three thousand years ago—apparently with their dogs. The dog has played an important role in the history of dog breeds in Japan. The Ainu's ferocity, courage, and loyalty are very appealing characteristics and were probably bred to through the years.

RECOGNITION: FCI

CHARACTER: The dog's character is packed full of desirable qualities. He has proven a fearless and determined hunter, guard, and defender, and at the same time a loyal and well-behaved dog. The dog's ever alert and suspicious nature lent itself to the required role of village guardian.

AKITA
Japanese Akita, Akita Inu

PORTRAIT: A large dog with a bear-like expression created by the massive skull, broad muzzle and black nose, stand-offish coat, and small, triangular, slightly rounded ears. Height: 24–28 inches (61–71 cm). Weight: 75–110 pounds (34–50 kg). Coat: medium short, harsh and double, with no feathering. Any color is acceptable, including pied and brindle. The Akita has a solid build that could be likened to a well-muscled gymnast; the dog's keen expression and proud way give him a noble appearance.

DEVELOPMENT: The Akita represents an ancient Japanese breed type. The common belief is that these dogs were originally bred for the hunt. In fact, Akitas have been commonly and successfully used for hunting such prey as bear. Others, however, feel that Akitas were developed for fighting. Supporting their claim, they refer to the Japanese zest for the dog pits and cite examples of same-sex hunting pairs being too hostile and aggressive to work together effectively. The Akita was so rare in the 1930s that only the very wealthy could afford or the very lucky could acquire a specimen.

RECOGNITION: FCI, AKC, UKC, KCGB, CKC

CHARACTER: These dogs are very proud in their way and somewhat independent. While they prove even-tempered companions for many and effective guardians for others, Akitas can be sometimes somewhat detached in nature; this quiet aloofness is often misinterpreted as a lack of loyalty or affection.

ALASKAN MALAMUTE

PORTRAIT: The Alaskan Malamute gives a strong, dense, power-packed impression. His coat appears ready for the coldest of weather; his tail plumage, carried over his back when relaxed, gives him an unmistakably northern-type appearance. Height: 23–25 inches (59–64 cm). Weight: 75–85 pounds (34–39 kg). Coat varies in length; medium short most common. Color: gray through black, with white markings. At first glance, the breed may have a rather wolf-like appearance; however, on closer inspection, the breed's expression is at once affectionate and trustworthy.

DEVELOPMENT: A native of Alaska and the arctic region, the Malamute as a breed can be traced back to the Mahlemut tribe that inhabited Alaska as far back as can be determined—they are never mentioned without their dogs. These early Malamutes were highly prized as workers and beloved companions. It is no wonder that today's breed is such an affectionate companion that has retained a good share of its working abilities.

RECOGNITION: FCI, AKC, UKC, KCGB, CKC

CHARACTER: The Alaskan Malamute must combine the grueling endurance and untiring dedication to work (especially as a sled dog) and the docile nature required of a companion/family/team dog. It is a dual-natured dog possessing two highly esteemed characteristics: love of work and love of man.

AMERICAN ESKIMO
"Spitz"

PORTRAIT: Proportionate and balanced, the American Eskimo, in any size, is the typical model of the northern working-type dog. Triangular ears, slightly rounded at the tips, ring with the celebrated nordic character. A thick coat and a richly plumed tail carried over the back complete this picture of elegance, alertness and beauty. The head should denote power in its wedge shape and perfect proportion to the body. The body is strong and compactly built. The coat is preferably pure white; cream or biscuit is permissible. The coat covers the body with soft straight hair, with a noticeably thicker mane forming a ruff on the neck. The Standard American Eskimo is 18–35 pounds (9–16 kg) and stands 15–19 inches (38–48 cm). The Miniature is 10–20 pounds (4½–9 kg) and stands 11–14 inches (28–36 cm).

DEVELOPMENT: The spitz family can trace its lineage back six millennia to the Peat Dog of the New Stone Age lake dwellers. Remains of these prototypes have been uncovered in various European countries. The American Eskimo resulted from Americans' breeding of white German Spitz and promoting the variety. This fostering began about 100 years ago. Although the American Eskimo, once referred to simply as "Spitz," is a keen part of America's native-dog heritage, to this day, it is only registered by the United Kennel Club. Its popularity in its homeland is continually growing. A Toy variety has also been developed but is not registered by the UKC. It is unfortunate that more show rings aren't graced by these snow beauties' presence. Europeans may favor the tiny pure white Pomeranians or Toy German Spitzes, but these really do not compare to the American version of the spitz type.

RECOGNITION: UKC

CHARACTER: The Eskie's agreeable temperament makes him ideal for most any living situation. These are principally companion dogs and are rarely used for any work purpose. They are intelligent and hardy dogs that are trainable and obedient. In the snow, they are most content.

Left: *Standard American Eskimo.*
Above right: *Miniature American Eskimo.*
Below right: *Standard American Eskimo.*

CHINESE SHAR-PEI
Shar-Pei, Chinese Fighting Dog

PORTRAIT: Imparting a unique and intriguingly uncanine appearance, the Shar-Pei puppy's superabundant skin, which it seems to wiggle in and out of, gives the breed an appeal all its own. The general impression of the Shar-Pei toddler may be that of a diminutive hippopotamus or a wondrously wrinkled porcine miniature. The extremely oversized coat, prickly and stand-offish, is but one of the breed's peculiarities: a bluish (preferably black) tongue and mouth; a wide, blunt muzzle, well padded to cause a bulge at the base of the nose; petite, rounded equilateral triangular ears that drop close to the head; canine teeth, curved like scimitars. The head is large for the size of the body, which is medium sized and powerful. Height: 18–20 inches (46–51 cm). Weight: 35–45 pounds (16–21 kg). The color is solid in fawn, chocolate, cream, red or black.

DEVELOPMENT: The Chinese Fighting Dog, as it was called, by its very nature is a cross of mastiffs and nordic breeds. The blue tongue is a feature that it shares with the Chow Chow, an obvious contributor to the Shar-Pei's make-up. For the residents of the Chinese southern provinces (Dah Let and Kwantung), the dogs were not just gladiators vaudevilling in the pits for entertainment purposes. That was their night job—during the day they hunted, herded and protected the Chinese, who were their captivated audience later that night. The dog's pig-like pliable skin gave it an advantage over its opponents, who found it most distasteful and uncomfortable when grabbed. Contrary to previous cynologists' beliefs that the Shar-Pei's interest is in violence, needing no provocation to attack, the breed was less successful in the pits due to its discerning and basically disinterested demeanor. Being intelligent canines, lordly and sober, the Shar-Pei left the pits to the more suitable bull-like mentalities. The outlawing of pets on mainland China forced the breed into near extinction. Matgo Law, a concerned breeder, was able to stir up Western interest in the breed and effectively rescue it from mortality.

RECOGNITION: FCI, AKC, UKC, KCGB, ANKC

CHARACTER: Alert and dignified, the Shar-Pei is affectionate with his own but is usually aloof and independent. His frowning expression is no fair indicator of his disposition: he is mostly delighted to be in the presence of the people to whom he is extremely devoted. However, this living Pound Puppy® isn't for everyone, no matter how irresistible he appears. Shar-Peis tend to be one-person dogs and can sometimes be less than hospitable.

Above right: *Shar-Pei, puppy.*
Below right: *Shar-Pei, adult.*

CHINOOK

PORTRAIT: A compact muscular frame well suits this amazing performer of a sled dog. The body is well balanced; the chest is deep; moderate bone and flexible musculature are prominent. The coat is medium and close lying. The muzzle is powerful, and the teeth are enduring. In color the Chinook is tawny (a golden fawn). The breed's ear carriage, rather wind-blown and bending, gives the dogs a curious and entreating glint. Weight: 65–90 pounds (29–40 kg). Height: 21–26 inches (53–66).

DEVELOPMENT: An early 20th-century American creation, the Chinook was the brainchild of Arthur Walden. Walden desired a dog that was as fast as the arctic husky dogs and as strong as the larger sledge pullers. Walden considered the dog a "half-bred Eskimo," part mongrel and part St. Bernard. The Chinook possesses a pulling power comparable to any snow-shoed arctic horse. The name was given to the breed to commemorate "Chinook," the founder's favorite and most untiring sled dog. Admiral Byrd's Antarctic expedition was powered by Chinook dogs, each of which towed an average load of over 150 pounds.

RECOGNITION: NR

CHARACTER: These are dedicated and hard-working sled dogs. Performing their given task is their primary concern in life. In addition to sledge pulling, the breed also excels at protection work. A tad strong willed, these dogs need to be taught early who is head dog. Chinook fanciers presently work hard to increase the breed's numbers and popularity.

CHOW CHOW

PORTRAIT: The Chow is a perfectly balanced dog. His massive muscular body is squarely built (body squares at the shoulder). The head is large and proportionate. The characteristic expression is essentially of independence. A distinguishing characteristic, shared with the Shar-Pei and the polar bear, is the blue-black tongue. The ears are small and carried stiffly. Two coat types exist: a long coat which is dense, abundant, stand-offish, and, of course, long; and a smooth coat which is shorter and more plush. The color may be any clear color, including black, tan, cream, blue, and red. Height: 19–20 inches (48–51 cm). Weight: 45–70 pounds (21–32 kg).

DEVELOPMENT: The Chow is the principal indigenous dog of China and its menu of chores is impressive: hunters, caravan guards, nightwatchmen for the sampans and junks, sled pullers. An unpalatable truth must be added to the above carte—the omnivorous Chinese also used the Chow for sustenance (i.e., chow). On a high feast day or most any day, the Chow could be found offered at the butchers' or grocery store. A union of northern breeds of the arctic and heavy Eastern mastiffs probably produced the Chow. The less popular smooth coat variety followed the long coat's 1870 entry into England and was promoted as a curiosity, labeled "the Edible Dog." Today the smooth is gaining much ground.

RECOGNITION: FCI, AKC, UKC, KCGB, CKC, ANKC

CHARACTER: The teddy-bear-like Chow has seemingly unlimited appeal in the U.S. and Great Britain. In physical abilities and intelligence, he is sure-footed and powerful. The long coat requires substantial grooming. In the summer months, he must not be left without shade. He is both independent and quiet and makes a reliable guard.

EAST SIBERIAN LAIKA

PORTRAIT: Upon this large, tough dog lies a short-medium stand-offish coat of either solid or piebald white, gray, tan, red, or black. This coat is plush; the tail is thickly furred and curls over the dog's back. The neck is thickly muscled and incredibly strong, capable of breaking the back or snapping the neck of prey held within the dog's unrelenting jaws. The head is covered with shorter fur; the ears are carried erect. Height: 22–25 inches (56–64 cm). Weight: 40–50 pounds (18–23 kg).

DEVELOPMENT: The working laikas of the Soviet Union may indeed represent the link between the wolf-like spitzen and the world's dog-like dogs. The East Siberian Laika today is more of a conglomeration of these working "barkers" than an individual breed. Soviet breeders are working sedulously to establish type. Historically the laikas were used for pulling and hunting. Among their quarry are the bear, elk, reindeer and marten. Only the strongest of the pack is used on the larger game. It is the assurance of Prince Shiriminsky that Orientals also had a fancy for the Laika, and that many tons of tender Laika flesh were fondled by the Orient's indiscriminative eating sticks.

RECOGNITION: NR

CHARACTER: Despite the more or less wolf-like resemblance, the Siberian Laikas possess calm and even temperaments. Many of the dogs are seen as city companions. They are highly trainable and, with appropriate discipline, very obedient.

ESKIMO DOG
Husky, Esquimaux, Canadian Eskimo Dog

PORTRAIT: Heavy coated and powerful, the Eskimo Dog is a hardy working and sledge dog. Its tremendous freight capacity is evident in its broad big-boned shoulders, heavily muscled legs, deep chest and overall balance. The head is broad and wedge shaped. This is a compact and efficiently built canine. Height: 20–27 inches (51–69 cm). Weight: 60–105 pounds (27–48 kg). The outer coat is long, 3–6 inches (7–15 cm) in length, and coarse; the undercoat is impenetrable and abundant. Dogs come in any color or combination.

DEVELOPMENT: Considered by many to be the most genuinely useful sledge dog of all the arctic breeds, the Eskimo Dog finds its fountainhead in Greenland. To the northern Canadians and the Inuit people, the breed is known as Kingmik. When first discovered, the Eskimo Dog provided the long-searched-for answer to the transport problem that Eskimos faced. The Eskimo Dog is the legitimate Husky, the name loosely used to refer to the Siberian Husky who has effectively usurped much of the fame that the Eskimo rightly deserves. The Siberian dog is a shrimp in comparison to the mighty Husky of Canada. Among the breed's game, the polar bear is its most impressive object of pursuit.

RECOGNITION: FCI, KCGB, CKC

CHARACTER: The breed's power and tremendous size avail it to a great number of people. As a working sledge dog, he is peerless; as a companion, he is a loyal friend and a favorite among the children.

EURASIER
Eurasian

PORTRAIT: This handsome, well-coated spitz is a beautifully balanced dog, in both physical conformation and temperament. Graceful and medium sized, the Eurasier possesses an abundant stand-off coat that is long enough to withstand the cold yet short enough to reveal the muscular contours of the body. Height: 19–24 inches (48–61 cm). Weight: 40–70 pounds (19–32 kg). Dogs can be red, fawn, mahogany, wolf-gray, or black in color; white and pintos also occur. Only solids are registerable by the FCI.

DEVELOPMENT: The recreation of the ancient German Wolfspitz was the chosen whim of one Julius Wipfel of Bergstrass in Weinheim, Germany. Crossing the Chow Chow and the present-day German Wolfspitz, Wipfel whipped up his first batch of "Wolf-Chows," as he called them. The selected pups were crossed with a Samoyed-type sledge dog, and this cross begot the Eurasier. By the 1960s the breed was established and popular in its native country.

RECOGNITION: FCI

CHARACTER: Very people- and affection-oriented, the Eurasier is a flawless companion. He is an easily trained animal that is docile and peace-loving. Owners know not to approach discipline boldly—the Eurasier responds best to a soft reprimand. A heart so meek can be broken by a brazen hand.

FINNISH LAPPHUND
Lapinkoira

PORTRAIT: A strikingly beautiful canine with a gloriously plush coat, the Finnish Lapphund is medium sized and very active. The head is square and the muzzle is slightly elongated. The neck is long, without dewlap. The chest is deep, and the shoulders are well angulated and long. In color the Finnish dog is most any color, provided that it dominates over any white symmetrical markings present. Height: 18–21 inches (46–53 cm). Weight: 44–47 pounds (20–21 kg). The coat is long and thick, with heavy underwool. Fringing is generous on the legs and tail; a mane adorns the neck and head.

DEVELOPMENT: The development of the breed known today as the Finnish Lapphund traces back to the dogs kept by the Lapp people. These European natives lived in the area known as Lapland, which includes Sweden, Finland and parts of northern Russia and Norway. The Lapland Dog, as it was once known, was brought to England by the Normans. The dogs that were adopted by Finnish dog lovers became known as the Finnish Lapphund, while the dogs that endeared themselves to the Swedes became known as the Swedish Lapphund. To avoid creating unnecessary animosity, the FCI recognizes each as a separate breed, whether or not they are actually different dogs.

RECOGNITION: FCI

CHARACTER: Because of their hearty constitutions and good-natured dispositions, Finnish Lapphunds are a welcome part of many European households and fine draught dogs.

FINNISH SPITZ
Suomenpystykorva, Finsk Spets, Loulou Finnoi

PORTRAIT: A lively dog of medium size and striking, brilliant red coloration. The Finnish Spitz has small, cocked, sharply pointed ears, medium-sized eyes, set slightly askew, and a generously plumed tail, curving vigorously from the root into an arch. All of these features add to its alert bearing. The body is almost square in outline; the back is straight and strong; the chest deep. The coat varies in thickness; overall, it is dense, moderately short and stand-offish. The undercoat is soft, short and dense. Height: 15–20 inches (38–53 cm). Weight: 25–35 pounds (12–16 kg).

DEVELOPMENT: The Finsk Spets is a descendant of the dog which, centuries ago, accompanied the ancestors of the Finns, who lived in small clans in their primeval forests and subsisted by hunting and fishing. Following the arrival of newcomers to the area (and their hot-to-trot canines), the Finsk Spets followed their owners north, and hence the only purebred specimens were to be found in northern Finland, Lapland, and Russian Karelia. The individual efforts of two foresters, both sharing the name Hugo, are hailed as the breed's modern-day fathers: Hugo R. Sandberg and Hugo Roos. This Norseman, sometimes called the Finnish Cock-eared Hunting Dog and the Barking Bird Dog, is used for hunting bird as well as squirrel and hare. In Finland he is highly loved for his wonderful voice, capable of yodeling with the best of them.

RECOGNITION: FCI, AKC, KCGB, ANKC

CHARACTER: Courageous though cautious, the Finnish Spitz is a mindful, independent soul. As a pup, he is not as prone to fondling. Rather cat-like in his distribution of affection, the breed is strong-minded and sensitive.

GERMAN SPITZ
Deutscher Spitz

PORTRAIT: A well-knit, nearly square outline befits the active and alert German Spitz. Its profuse fur coat does not cover the dog's substance; the body is compact, well ribbed up and rounded. Overall body proportion is of utmost importance. The coat is double, consisting of a soft dense undercoat and a long, rough-to-the-touch outer coat. In color the German Spitz is most typically solid—black, orange, brown, wolf gray or white. Particolors exist. Size: Klein—9–11 inches (23–28 cm); Mittel—11½–14 inches (29–35½ cm). The Klein is regally *y-clept* by British fanciers as the Victorian Pom.

DEVELOPMENT: Developed in Germanic countries as companion and utility dogs, the spitz breeds were popular in Germany, Austria, Holland and Great Britain. The spitz-type dogs are considered to be among the most ancient of canines known to man. Fossils of prehistoric dogs found in Scandinavia, Russia and Switzerland bear likeness to these spitz types. The family of German spitz is large and divided not so much by differences in conformation as by those in color and size.

RECOGNITION: FCI, KCGB

CHARACTER: The German Spitz's popularity in America (and for the most part, Great Britain) is limited by the favoritism shown to the Pomeranian, Keeshond, and American Eskimo—all of whom stem from German Spitz stock. The German Spitzen are of equable disposition, exhibiting a healthy amount of confidence; they are happy and up-beat companions.

GERMAN WOLFSPITZ
German Spitz

PORTRAIT: A richly composed dog, with a stand-off coat in a wolf-gray color that supplies its name. The appearance is fox-like, with pointed ears and a well-plumed tail. The body is compact and exhibits an assured carriage. As a distinguishing feature from the other Spitz breeds of Germany, this dog must be at least 18 inches (46 cm) at the shoulder. The coat is long and hard, most profuse on forelegs and trousers.

DEVELOPMENT: Ancestors of the German Wolfspitz, the nordic herding dogs with profuse harsh coats, were probably transported to the Germanic countries during the Middle Ages. These dogs spread throughout the European continent and progenerated the shepherd breeds as well as the spitz varieties, of which this breed is the oldest. The Wolfspitz once frequented a number of German and French neighborhoods, particularly Elberfeld, Düsseldorf, Aix-la-Chapelle, and Credfeld. The French referred to him as Chien Loup, which translates roughly to the current-day name. These dogs were agile workers and proficient herders. Their given tasks acquired them names of "dogs of the vine grower" and "dogs of the carrier."

RECOGNITION: FCI

CHARACTER: Adaptable and energetic, the Wolfspitz is a real outdoors dog who enjoys a hardy hiking expedition or trot through an open field. Less reserved than some of the other nordic dogs, he is a fanciful companion who genuinely enjoys the company of his owners and friends.

GIANT GERMAN SPITZ
Deutscher Grossspitz, Great Spitz

PORTRAIT: Although standing no less than 16 inches (41 cm) high, the Great Spitz is hardly the "giant" that his name indicates. Compared to the mastiffs and larger flock guards, the breed's lot of 40 pounds (18 kg) is not an impressive one. Among the German Spitz family, if we exclude the Wolf-spitz, the Giant is quite big. The color of the breed can vary but is always in solid colors. Black, white and brown are most common. The head shape is fox-like, the tail is graciously plumed. The coat is double, long, dense and harsh; the undercoat is substantial and soft.

DEVELOPMENT: With the exception of size, members of the German Spitz family share most every trait, as well as breed development. Viking travelers' bringing dogs into Germany and Holland briefly explains these dogs' root taking. Around Germany, the different colored spitzen were each associated with specific areas: the grays were found along the Rhine in the districts of Mannheim and Stuttgart; the blacks in Wurtenberg; and the whites in Elberfeld. English exports of the larger sized spitzen are now known as the Keeshonds.

RECOGNITION: FCI

CHARACTER: Hardy and eager, the Giant German Spitz is a dog of a gentle disposition, ready to please and always ready to walk. The German Spitzen, especially the larger ones, love the outdoors life and thrive on plenty of exercise and fresh air.

NORDIC DOGS

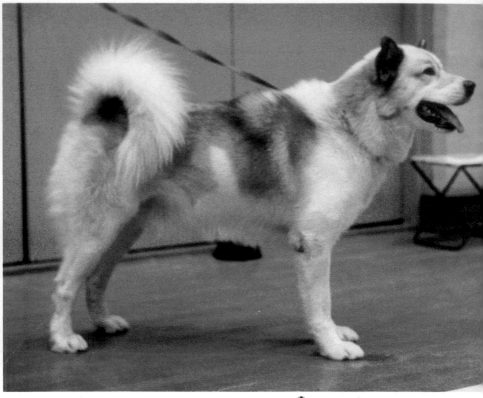

GREENLAND DOG
Grølandshund

PORTRAIT: The Greenland Dog possesses the typical robust nordic dog conformation and appearance: a muscular body, well defined and rigorous; a profuse hard coat; a rather sizable head topped by pointed triangular ears; and a fully plumed tail, curled over its back. Height: up to 25 inches (64 cm). Weight: at least 66 pounds (60 kg). Members of the breed can be any color: white, gray, or black, and a little tan in any proportion. The coat is dense and stand-offish; the undercoat is thick and woolly.

DEVELOPMENT: Although recognized today as an individual breed, the Greenland Dog represents the standard working "husky-type" dog. It is one of the nordic hauling breeds that has survived until the current day. Modern innovations on the ice-laden landscape (snowmobiles and other mechanically propelled vehicles) have broached the disappearance of dozens of husky breeds and varieties. Even today, with the dedicated efforts of concerned individuals, the Greenland Dog is not populous in native Greenland.

RECOGNITION: FCI

CHARACTER: A sled dog's loyalty is traditionally measured by his stamina and indefatigable desire to work. For pet owners who do not work their dogs, this is a foreign concept. Pack dogs especially, never given the opportunity to establish a personal relation with the lead human, must show their loyalty and even affection in their unstinting work ethic. This breed is a rigorous and faithful canine of unending drive that is still used principally as a working dog.

ICELAND DOG
Icelandic Sheepdog, Iceland Spitz

PORTRAIT: The compact Iceland Dog is dramatic in his appearance, with an arched head, short snipy muzzle, ears with their tips hanging down, and an efficient coat. This coat is thick and not as long as those of many of the other northern breeds; the hair is of medium length and tight to the body; the undercoat is dense. The legs are of medium size, high and slender. Wheaten, black, wolf-sable, off-white, and black are the color possibilities. White markings and black mask often accompany. Height: 12–16 inches (31–41 cm). Weight: 20–30 pounds (9–14 kg).

DEVELOPMENT: More of a herder than a hunter, the Iceland Dog was conceivably introduced to Iceland by Norwegians, who referred to the ancient breed as the "Friaar-Dog." Studies of the breed done in 1877 by Dr. Fitzinger divided it into two categories, a division which no longer persists in Iceland. The coat and undercoat are its principal divergences from the Greenland Dog. The Icelandic breed's coat is not quite as long as its polar cousin's jacket. The Sirjanskaja Laika is believed to resemble the breed in many respects as well. Thanks to native and British breeders, the Iceland Dog still survives; these dedicated fanciers were faced with reconstructing the breed after a severe outburst of distemper in the early 1900s.

RECOGNITION: FCI

CHARACTER: Vivacious and good-humored, the Iceland Dog is a prime pet. His need for working is less intense than many of the other nordic herders. In his heyday, he was a confirmed enemy of the snow fox and crow; today, however, his hunting instincts are quite dormant, making him a fine companion.

JÄMTHUND
Swedish Elkhound, Norwegian Bearhound

PORTRAIT: The Jämthund is the taller and heavier brother of his close-resembling and more popular relative, the Norwegian Elkhound. The Jämthund weighs around 66 pounds (30 kg) and stands between 23 and 25 inches (59–64 cm) tall. His long legs are thick boned; his hind legs are especially well muscled with slight angulation. The deep chest, moderate tuck, and brawny shoulders give an athletic look, which is substantiated by his vigorousness on the hunt. He has, as do the other elkhounds, a narrowing taper to the skull, beginning at the erectly carried ears, and a curling tail carried over the body. The coat color may be any shade of gray, with white or lighter markings common.

DEVELOPMENT: The ever so difficult task of categorizing local breeds that have been existent for centuries becomes folly ridden when discussing the nordic big game hunters of the Scandinavian area. The Jämthund may find its origin as a hunter of bear in Norway, but history finds him more commonly hunting moose in Sweden. Since the sport of bear hunting is no longer common practice, the elkhounds stake their fame on such quarry as lynx, wolf, and moose. The Elkhound breeds are as ancient as any breed of dog known to man.

RECOGNITION: FCI

CHARACTER: Popular in its homeland of Sweden as a hunter and companion, these are lively hardy dogs that thrive on the hunt, love the great outdoors and adore their masters above all else.

KAI DOG
Tora (Tiger) Dog

PORTRAIT: The Kai is a medium-sized dog, standing 18–23 inches (46–59 cm) tall, and is of the classic Japanese canine type. He is distinguishable from his other mid-sized Japanese relatives by his narrower skull, sightly more tapered head, and less than domesticated nature. Dogs found in the mountainous regions are extensively worked and may weigh between 35–45 pounds (16–21 kg); some dogs may weigh up to 60 pounds (27 kg). Coat is short, straight, and coarse. The most common colors are: black brindle, red brindle and tan brindle.

DEVELOPMENT: A discussion about dogs in 20th-century Japan must begin with the large importation of Western breeds into Japan after WWI. The Japanese were so greatly impressed by the abilities of the Pointer and Alsatian that native breeders took to these newcomer canines and abandoned their Japanese dogs. A study done by Mr. Haruo Isogai in the 1930s divided the nation's dogs by size and attempted to regroup and revive the native breeds of the land. The Kai Dog was often referred to as a "deerhound" and is a fine hunter, though rarely seen outside his native country.

RECOGNITION: FCI

CHARACTER: The Kai of today is more docile and mild than his forefathers. The name Tiger Dog was derived likely from the brindle coat, although some believe the dog's untamable disposition influenced the choice.

KARELIAN BEAR DOG
Karelsk Bjornhund. Karjalankarhukoira, Karelischer Barenhund

PORTRAIT: Robustly built, well boned and of moderate size, the Karelian Bear Dog is slightly longer than he is high. The outer coat is straight and stiff; the undercoat is soft and dense. In color he is black with a slight brownish or dull cast preferred. White markings are distinct and occur on the head, neck, chest, abdomen and legs. The head is shaped as a blunt wedge. The ears are cocked and point outward slightly. The body is sturdy and the back is well developed. Height: 19–23 inches (48–59 cm). Weight: 44–50 pounds (20–23 kg).

DEVELOPMENT: The area once known as Karelia in northern Europe (now the Karelio-Finnish republic of the U.S.S.R.) has always been populated by tough big game hunting canines. Among this avid hunter's game are the buck, hare, and moose. He is also fearless enough to fight the wolf and therefore functioned as a protector by hunting these large wild canids. In Finland, his homeland, the dog is used mostly on elk and is the favored dog of native big-game hunters.

RECOGNITION: FCI, CKC

CHARACTER: Not the choice for the casual pet owner, the Karelian Bear Dog is a hunter of unyielding bravery and determination. The true outdoors enthusiast and dedicated hunter can look to this hard-working breed with delight and unmitigated satisfaction. Owners must be willing to handle this very forceful canine. Proper training and socialization are absolute musts.

KARELO-FINNISH LAIKA
Finlandskaja, Karelskaja

PORTRAIT: Unlike many other nordic breeds, the Karelo-Finnish Laika has a skull that is not broad between the ears; this feature coupled with the circular eyes, appearing mistrustful rather than sly, gives the breed a more jackal-like, rather than fox-like, expression. The neck appears disproportionately thick, due to the long profuse ruff which extends to the cheeks. The back is moderately long, slightly exceeding the dog's height of 15–19 inches (38–48 cm). He is a lightly built dog, with a bushy tail. Weight: 25–30 pounds (11½–14 kg). The coat is dense and stand-offish. Common colors are red with a white chest, intermingled with gray or black hair, and fawn of various shades.

DEVELOPMENT: Finnish doglore refers to the Finlandskaja as a cross between a fox and a nordic-type dog; indeed, the muzzle has a very fox-like suggestion. The breed originated long before the national boundaries of the present-day Scandinavian countries or Soviet Union. The Karelo-Finnish Laika and the Finnish Spitz once were probably the same breed. Later, however, with the drawing of hard-line national parameters, and the claiming of all existing within them as the given country's, two distinguishable breeds emerged. The Karelo-Finnish Laika hunts small game, including various birds and hare, at which it proves exceptional.

RECOGNITION: NR

CHARACTER: Although he is quick to mature, he never loses his adolescent excitability. He is zealous to please and makes a fine hunter. Firm but fair discipline is necessary to keep this powerful dog in tow.

KEESHOND
Wolfspitz, Chien Loup

PORTRAIT: The distinguishing characteristic of the breed is the "bespectacled" face. These "spectacles" are actually a delicately drawn line that angles slightly upward from the outer corner of each eye to the lower corner of the ear; completing the spectacled effect are distinct markings and shadings that form short but expressive eyebrows. This highly expressive, distinctly marked head is set upon a well-balanced, medium-sized short-coupled body. The coat is harsh, straight, and stand-offish. A dense ruff on the neck and profuse trousers on the hind quarters are formed by the coat. Color is a mixture of gray and black, with no black below the wrist or hocks. Dutch specimens at one time could be seen in solid black and solid white, the latter color being more common. Height: 17–19 inches (43–48 cm). Weight: 55–66 pounds (25–30 kg).

DEVELOPMENT: A descendant of the German Wolfspitz, the Keeshond entered the British dog scene as the Dutch Barge Dog, named for its producing Netherlands. In that country, the dog was used as a good-luck companion on sea-faring vessels and as a handy guard and vermin controller. The spitz dog in wolf gray was most favored in the Netherlands (particularly in the southern provinces of Brabant and Limburg) and became the mascot of the common Dutch Patriot Party. The British Keeshond (now popular the world over) is the progeny of the Wolfspitz of Germany crossed with a negligible percentage of Dutch imports. In Holland, the dog is smaller and darker in coat color. In the 1930s, Holland could not boast a great number of Keeshonden and most of their dogs were discovered on farms "running in circles round and round their wooden kennels, tied to these by heavy, cumbersome chains," or an occasional specimen would be a vendible of gypsies and tinkers.

RECOGNITION: AKC, UKC, KCGB, CKC, ANKC

CHARACTER: The breed makes a fine pet, being one of two popular German Spitz varieties to grace the British and American dog fancy (meaning the toy-sized Pomeranian). The Keeshond's sporting instincts may be developed or restrained at will. With training, this incisive rabbitter and ratter will either ignore or pursue the given quarry. Content with small doses of exercise, he is an adaptable city dweller or country bumpkin. This dog's attachment to his master is keen.

KISHU
Kyushu

PORTRAIT: The Kishu is a mid-sized dog of classic Japanese type. His closest relatives are the Kai Dog and the Shikoku; he is also related to the Ainu Dog. There are only subtle differences between these dogs. The Kishu is distinguished from the Kai by his broader skull, although it is narrower than the Shikoku; and from the Ainu by his more lengthy body. Each breed possesses the short, straight, coarse coat, the curled over the back tail, the erect ears, and tapered skull. In height the Kishu is 17–22 inches (43–46 cm) tall. He is fringed on the cheeks and tail. His most common color is white but he can be red, sesame or brindle.

DEVELOPMENT: The Kishu, one among the Shika-Inu classification of Japanese dogs, has its beginnings in the mountainous areas of the Mie and Wakayama prefectures, where it is the *matagi's* dog. Neglected like the Kai after WWI, these ancient dogs depended upon Mr. Isogai's efforts to resuscitate the national Japanese dogs for its survival. The mid-sized dogs couldn't compete with the larger, jauntier German Shepherd Dog that had recently captured the public's squint. Although once used primarily on deer, the Kishu is marvelously skilled at hunting the boar.

RECOGNITION: FCI

CHARACTER: Like the Japanese philosophers of old, the Kishu is pensive and silent. As a home companion, he is docile and content. These dogs primarily are hunters but have adjusted to life as a companion dog considerably well.

NENETS HERDING LAIKA
Russian Samoyed Laika, Reindeer Herding Laika

PORTRAIT: Medium in size and symmetrical in balance, the Nenets Laika is very close in type and appearance to the Samoyed. Never bred for color; the Nenets can be gray, black, white or tan as a solid or in piebald pattern with white. The head is powerful and wedge shaped. The ears are triangular and erect. The coat is inordinately profuse, often obscuring the muscular conformation and stunning outline of the dog. The coat forms a ruff and thick breeches. Height: over 16–18 inches (41–46 cm). Weight: 40–50 pounds (19–23 kg).

DEVELOPMENT: Just as the Samoyede nomads were developing and employing the Samoyed, the Nentsy tribe, an equally ancient group, fostered the Nenets Herding Laika. Granted, this is an over-simplification, since these nomads didn't give the concept of "breed" a moment's thought. A working and yet warm dog, the Nenets fulfilled the tribe's guard and herding necessities. It is also suggested that the Nenets dog actually represents the Samoyed of today in its native land, where color variation exists. The Soviet Cynological Council established the national interest in this laika as their only chosen herding breed. It has since entered reindeer herding programs and continued use is encouraged.

RECOGNITION: NR

CHARACTER: A dog that loves to work, he is intelligent and free thinking, needing little guidance to execute the task at hand. Like the Samoyed, continual exposure to humans has made this ancient laika extremely devoted and people-oriented.

NORBOTTENSPETS
Nordic Spitz, Pohjanpystykorva

PORTRAIT: The Norbottenspets is a small spitz with an uncharacteristically short coat for a northern breed. His other point of dissension from the nordic type is his loose curled tail that hangs more toward the thigh than tightly across the back. He is short, squarely built, and of strong body. His stand-offish double coat, although short, provides good all-weather protection. Color is white with limited spots of cream or brown (black and red are also seen). Height: 16–17 inches (41–43 cm). Weight: 26–33 pounds (12–15 kg).

DEVELOPMENT: The Norbottenspets's close resemblance to the Norwegian Lundehund suggests his being a descendant of similar arctic spitz types. Conjecture has it that there may be a touch of the German Spitz in the Nordic Spitz's lineage. More contemporary studies, however, relate a more direct bloodline connection to the ancient spitz-type dogs of the Vikings. For many years, he was commonly employed as a hunter of small game and as an all-around farm helper. Then, with the waning of the hunt and the farm and the introduction of foreign dogs to Sweden, the Norbottenspets became nearly extinct in the middle of the 20th century. He is again a breed popular with native Swedes, more common as a companion than a hunter.

RECOGNITION: FCI

CHARACTER: To the glee and good behavior of this dog is added an uncharacteristic quietness. These qualities, plus his affection and sedulity, make him an outstanding pet.

NORWEGIAN BUHUND
Norsk Buhund, Norwegian Sheepdog, Nordiske Sitz-hunde

PORTRAIT: The short body, although compact, is lightly built. The head, too, is lean, light and wedge shaped. The ears are placed high and carried erect. Overall, the breed is free from exaggeration and built for arduous work. The legs, though lean, are strong; the hind legs are only slightly angulated. The double coat is made of a harsh, close but smooth outer coat and a soft and woolly undercoat. Height: 17–18 inches (43–46 cm). Weight: 53–58 pounds (24–26 kg). Color can be wheaten, black, red, or wolf; small symmetrical markings and black masks allowed.

DEVELOPMENT: Belonging to same variety as the sheepdogs of Greenland, Siberia and Kamchatka, the Norwegian Sheepdog was once employed as a *kometik*-puller (a type of sleigh) and hunter's companion, who possessed a subtle nose. As time and necessity should dictate, these dogs were adapted for work on farms as general hands and herders. Since the Middle Ages, the breed has been known to fulfill this capacity and was designated the *Buhund* (translating variously as farm dog). Slightly smaller than the Norse herder of old, today's Buhund is employed mostly as a guard dog.

RECOGNITION: FCI, KCGB, ANKC

CHARACTER: The Norwegian Buhund is an ideally sized and tempered pet. As a watchdog, he is completely reliable, always on duty and always prepared to protect his own. They are legion in their courage and dedication to their owners, and they are especially easykeepers.

NORWEGIAN ELKHOUND
Elkhound

PORTRAIT: A proportionately short body with a thick and rich but not bristling gray coat. Powerful and compact, the body is broad chested, with a straight back and well-developed loins. The ears are prick and the tail is curled over the back. The head is considered "dry," that is without loose skin. The Elkhound's color is gray with black tips—a solid coat should be a medium-gray tone. Height: 18–20 inches (46–51 cm). Weight: 44 pounds (40 kg).

DEVELOPMENT: The Elkhound of Norway, as known in the U.S. and Great Britain, is a gray, thickly coated dog. The Scandinavian elkhound breeds, three in number, are among the world's most historic breeds and have changed the least from the pristine dog type through ages of development. The Norwegian Elkhound actually can be gray or black. The black breed is a little smaller and much rarer. In Norwegian *elghund,* the dog's name, really translates to moosedog, which more accurately describes the group since there is no hound in their blood. "Moose" is as appropriate a word choice as elk, since the dogs were used on both animals, plus lynx, bear, wolf and a host of small game. Granted, in translation, "Elkhound" has a more mellifluous ring than "Moosedog."

RECOGNITION: FCI, AKC, UKC, KCGB, CKC, ANKC

CHARACTER: Many current-day owners are unaware of his hunting prowess and the unique fashion in which he executes it. Barking at bay, dodging attack, and soundless creeping encompass his versatile approach to the hunt. Normally friendly, they are natural protectors with great dignity and independence.

NORWEGIAN LUNDEHUND
Lundehund, Norwegian Puffin Dog

PORTRAIT: At first glance, the Norwegian Lundehund may appear just another nordic dog—nothing could be farther from the truth! Its short, rough coat, curled tail, pointed ears and wedge-shaped skull are the extent of the similarities. This dog has a double-jointed neck, allowing the head to bend backwards to nearly lay on its back; feet which have at least six multiple-jointed toes on each, two large functional dewclaws, and eight plantar cushions on each foot; and ears that are closeable. Height: 12–15½ (31–40 cm). Weight: 13 pounds (6 kg). In color it is reddish brown to fallow, with black-tipped hairs preferred, black or gray. Whites with black tips also occur.

DEVELOPMENT: Originating in Vaerog, an island off the coast of Norway, the Lundehund was developed for the specific task of hunting the puffin bird. The puffin bird could only be caught by reaching into tight crevices in the rocks and the Lundehund is specially equipped for this difficult task. The described characteristics each equip the Lundehund with a particular ability that is vital in its very specialized task. He was also trained to search and retrieve the puffin bird's abandoned nest. An ancient theory that this dog survived the Ice Age by feeding on sea birds is unlikely, even though the dog's purity and antiquity cannot be challenged.

RECOGNITION: FCI, KCGB

CHARACTER: For his size, the Lundehund is wonderfully robust and lively, often bordering on boisterous, but never nervous or aggressive. As can be surmised from his greatly detailed hunting methods, he is highly intelligent and equally industrious. He has been well-acclimated to life as a pet, since the call for puffin extractors is quite limited in 20th-century society.

RUSSO-EUROPEAN LAIKA
Lajka Ruissisch Europaisch, Karelian Bear Laika

PORTRAIT: A good-sized, strong working dog, the Russo-European Laika is short-coated and usually black and white in color. Height: 21–24 inches (53–61 cm). Weight: 45–50 pounds (20–23 kg). The muzzle is rather elongated and the jaws are punishing and strong. The tail tends to curl up although many are born tailless, a condition breeders do not favor but to which they concede. The ears are prominently placed on the top of the head and are large.

DEVELOPMENT: The awesome Russo-European Laika is closely related to the Finnish dog, the Karelian Bear Laika. The Soviets, upon claiming the Karelia area, embraced the indigenous big-game hunter as their own. In an attempt to increase the Karelian Bear Laika's power and aggressive nature, Russian breeders crossed the breed with the Utchak Sheepdog, an absolutely fearless and intrepid animal that needn't think twice when encountering Cerberus or a similarly formidable beast. The result, the Russo-European Laika, is an intrepid bear hunter, also used on boar, moose, and wolf.

RECOGNITION: FCI

CHARACTER: By no means is he a family pet; the Russo-European Laika acquired much of the Utchak's fearless nature and is qualmless to attack a full-grown animal. If this audacity could be focused, the breed would be a true man-stopping guard dog. Hunters must regularly exercise these dogs for continual fitness.

SAMOYED
Samoyedskaja

PORTRAIT: Substantiating the strikingly luxuriant appearance is a strong, active, graceful dog capable of awesome endurance. The well-balanced, medium-sized body is blanketed by a thick, soft undercoat which is penetrated only by the harsh, stand-offish hairs composing the weather resistant outer coat. This 18–22 inch (46–56 cm) dog is exceptionally strong and well muscled. At a weight of 50–65 pounds (23–30 kg), he is able to pull by sled many times his weight. The Sammy's coat is unparalleled in the dog world, being as white as the snow that blankets the tundra of his native land.

DEVELOPMENT: The pure and ancient lineage which the Samoyed enjoys, untampered by man's experiments for improvement or stability, is a rare case in the dog world. The Samoyed, named after the great nomadic tribe with whom it dwelled, celebrates a heritage of close intercourse with Nature and remains today "unimproved by man." The breed's pure coloration was greatly loved by the Samoyede people: "a coat of dazzling white with silver-tipped ends which gleam like glacier points, or with a pure white coat delicately tinted with biscuit, as though reflecting the rays of the sun." Historically, however, the breed could also be found in black and white and rich sable. Early British fanciers (around 1900) favored the white and biscuit dogs. These dogs did not hunt but instead were used as reindeer herders, guards, and intimate pets—occasionally they were sledge dogs.

RECOGNITION: FCI, AKC, UKC, KCGB, CKC, ANKC

CHARACTER: The Samoyed's long history of human association has emphatically shaped its fine character. This is a noble, kind and friendly dog that is exceptionally people-loving. Owners must dedicate time daily to care for his luxuriant coat, but the dog's indelible character makes this chore a pleasure.

SANSHU DOG
Japanese Middle Size Dog

PORTRAIT: A beautifully constructed dog with a sturdy squarish body and straight stout limbs. A rather large head for his proportionately smaller body—full with the robust expression of the Akita (which is considerably larger). In color the Sanshu varies in shades of red, tan, white, gray, fawn, and pied, as well as black/tan and salt/pepper. Height: 16–18 inches (41–46 cm). Weight: 44–55 pounds (20–25 kg). The tail, rather feathered, curls loosely over the back. A smaller version of the Sanshu exists, which maintains these same physical traits but is about 4 inches (10 cm) smaller.

DEVELOPMENT: Picture it—Honshu, 1912, breeders on the Japanese mainland decide a medium-sized guard dog is of the essence and cross various Shika-Inus with smooth-coated Chows to yield the Sanshu Dog. Much to their surprise, their creation bears an enviable resemblance to the extinct Indo-Chinese Phu Quoc Dog, which too was a guard dog of great ability. Today the breed functions as both a guard and companion.

RECOGNITION: NR

CHARACTER: Dedicated to his family and an able guard dog, the Sanshu is a greatly esteemed member of the Shika-Inu group. He is a sought after companion dog around the world, and the popularity the Shiba seems to be instrumental in the West's interest in other Japanese breeds.

SCHIPPERKE

PORTRAIT: The medium-sized Schipperke possesses a short, thick-set body that is broad behind the shoulders. The head is fox-like and fairly wide; the muzzle is tapering, not too elongated or blunt. The outer coat is abundant and somewhat harsh to the touch—the longer hair around the neck forms a ruff while the longer hair on the rear forms a culotte and jabot. The British standard does not emphasize these touches as much as the American does. In England, "peg top trousers are taboo." In color the Skipperke is solid black, which is the only color accepted by the AKC; however, the breed also comes in a handsome range of tans and fawns, which are acceptable abroad. He is typically tailless. Weight: up to 18 pounds (10 kg).

DEVELOPMENT: The "Little Skipper," with his prick ears and nordic body shape, is most probably a descendant of spitz types and not a miniaturization of the black Belgian Leauvenaar, a province herder, as was once asserted. Used on barge ships in Belgium, the Schipperke likely has always been little. As a breed, it   has been around for centuries and continues to breed pure. He is believed to have participated in the world's first specialty show which took place in Brussels in 1690. Though traditionally a shipmate, the Schip has been popular with landlubbers and shows an impressive propensity as a ratter, if trained. He can also hunt effectively on rabbit and mole.

RECOGNITION: FCI, AKC, UKC, KCGB, CKC, ANKC

CHARACTER: Hardly a "non-sportsman," the Schip is an active, lively dog that thrives on outdoor adventures. The breed's hardy nature and convenient size (between a terrier and a toy) make him an ideal choice for a home companion.

SHIBA INU
Japanese Shiba Inu, Japanese Small Size Dog

PORTRAIT: The small Shiba Inu, appearing much like a dwarf-size Akita, is well balanced and sturdy. The head, appearing like a blunt triangle, is broad with well-developed cheeks. The muzzle is straight and of good depth. The coat is plush, hard and straight, with a warm soft undercoat; coat is slightly longer on the sickle-curved, curled tail. Completing the spitz portrait, the Shiba has erect triangular ears, inclining slightly forward. The most preferred of the Japanese colors are deep red and red sesame; black, black and tan, brindle, white with red or gray tinge, and lighter red also occur. Height: 14–15½ inches (36–40 cm). Weight: 20–30 pounds (9–14 kg).

DEVELOPMENT: Surely able to trace its roots to primitive times, the Shiba developed in the landlocked areas of Japan some 3000 years ago, possibly from dogs that originated in the South Seas. Hunters, who used the little dogs on a variety of game (usually ground birds and small game but sometimes an assistant on the bear or deer hunt), crossbred and inbred the small-sized native dogs to concentrate on the desired traits. Such ancient types as the Shinshu, Mino and Sanin were used.

RECOGNITION: FCI, KCGB

CHARACTER: The Shiba Inu is perfectly cat-like in many respects: he is clean, independent, and industrious enough to amuse himself for hours on end. His striking appearance and ideal size make him one of the jauntiest and brightest Nipponese to arrive on the Western scene in many years. Fanciers, who favor the Akita for its unique qualities, have found the Shiba to offer those same traits in a more conveniently sized package.

SHIKOKU

PORTRAIT: The Shikoku is distinguishable from its fellow Shika-Inu by its smaller size and coat color. The Shikoku stands 17–21 inches (43–53 cm) high and comes in only brindle or red coloration. Like the other middle-sized Japanese breeds, the coat is short, harsh and straight with a soft dense undercoat. The body conformation is typically nordic: the feathered, curled tail; the prick triangular ears; the fairly good-sized head and medium-length muzzle.

DEVELOPMENT: The Shikoku originates on the Shikoku Islands, across the inland near Osaka. The Japanese, so taken by the abilities of the Pointer and German Shepherd Dog, promoted these newly discovered dogs and all but ignored the native breeds. A study done by Mr. Haruo Isogai in the 1930s divided the nation's dogs by size and attempted to revive the indigenous Japanese breeds. The Shikoku was one of the most ignored dogs, being larger than the less neglected Chins and Shibas and less substantial than the large Akita, which remained favored and sacred. The Shikoku is a specialist on deer and has been referred to as a "deerhound," although it bears no resemblance whatsoever to the Western conception of the Deerhound (i.e., of Scotland).

RECOGNITION: FCI

CHARACTER: The Shikoku is a loyal hunter and an all-weather companion. He is rather on the independent side and may be quite aloof and reserved. If properly trained, he is quite obedient and, with appropriate acclimatization, can get along with most any house pet.

SIBERIAN HUSKY
Arctic Husky

PORTRAIT: Quick and light on his feet, the Siberian Husky is a medium-sized working dog with a moderately compact and fur-covered body. His beautifully balanced and perfectly proportionate structure is a tribute to his power, speed and endurance. Height: 21–23½ (53–60 cm). Weight: 35–60 pounds (16–27 kg). The gait is effortless and smooth. A well-muscled, well-made dog with good bone: the head is of medium size, as is the muzzle in length; the coat is well furred and pelt-like, but not so thick as to obscure the dog's clean cut outline. The dense soft undercoat is long enough to support the straight smooth-lying guard hairs. Any color is acceptable—black, grays, red and pied are usual. The correct tail is well furred and fox-brush in shape.

DEVELOPMENT: The Siberian Husky, the Alaskan Malamute, and the Eskimo Dog are but a few of the world's Arctic husky-type dogs. There is considerable reason to believe that these "huskies," a coined degenerate term, all stem from the same dogs but were each fostered by a different region and group of hunters. The Chukchis of far north-eastern Asia employed what is today the Siberian Husky and fostered it as a pure "breed" throughout the 19th century. As dog sledges were the principal means of transport in Alaska, the huskies were most vital. The Siberian, being 30 pounds (14 kg) smaller than the dominant Alaskan Malamute, became favored by Russian explorers as sled dogs of speed, agility and endurance, the same qualities valued by the Chukchis.

RECOGNITION: FCI, AKC, UKC, KCGB, CKC, ANKC

CHARACTER: A ready and able worker, the Siberian is adept at his age-old sled dog role as well as an eager and friendly companion. Adult dogs may tend to be reserved, with an unmistakably dignified air. Gentle and alert, these are heartily agreeable, tractable companions.

SWEDISH LAPPHUND
Lapplandska Spetz, Swedish Lapp Spitz

PORTRAIT: A medium-sized, well-coated nordic-type dog with a sturdy square body and squarish head, high set triangular ears and a prominent muzzle. The coat is abundant and harsh, feathers persist throughout, even onto the legs. The tail is fully plumed and rests on the back. Height: 17½–19½ inches (44–49 cm). Weight: 44 pounds (20 kg). The undercoat is thick and woolly. In color the breed is usually solid black or liver, although white marks are neither uncommon nor objectionable.

DEVELOPMENT: The development of the breed today known as the Swedish Lapphund traces back to the dogs that were kept by the Lapp people. These European natives lived in the area known as Lapland, which includes Sweden, Finland and parts of northern Russia and Norway. The Lapland Dogs, as they were once known, were brought to England by the Normans. The dogs that were adopted by Swedish dog lovers became known as the Swedish Lapphund, while the dogs that endeared themselves to the Finns became known as the Finnish Lapphund. The FCI recognizes each as a separate breed. They are especially useful as draught dogs and adept at reindeer herding.

RECOGNITION: FCI

CHARACTER: The dog's moderate size and alert disposition make him a natural alarm dog. Although not a man-stopper, this dog can be courageous and assertive. In the home, he is affectionate and personable.

WEST SIBERIAN LAIKA

PORTRAIT: The brawny and robust West Siberian Laika is a picture of immense power and stamina. The Siberian hunting/sledding laikas are rather long-legged and light, giving them agility and endurance in the deep snow. Height: 21–24 inches (53–61 cm). Weight: 40–50 pounds (18–23 kg). The coat, short and stand-off, is solid or piebald in white, tan, red, white, or black in color.

DEVELOPMENT: Of the two Siberian Laikas, the West dog is more numerous and more firmly established in type. The Russian laikas are used over ice-ridden terrain as sledge dogs and hunters of large game (including bear, elk and reindeer). The prized sable or ermine, however, is this sturdy hunter's specialty. The hunters from Khantu and Mansi breed the dogs for their working purposes. In origin, the West Siberian Laika comes from the indigenous stock from which the other laikas also descend. The individual dog works less than the span of a decade because the work is so demanding. Without the laikas, the hunters surely would not survive.

RECOGNITION: FCI

CHARACTER: These are devoted hunters from the hardiest of stock. Their mind-boggling speed and ceaseless endurance make them highly praised by the hunters, whose reliance on them is proverbial. Although companions to their keepers, they are not kept for their pleasing dispositions as much as for their stupendous acumen in the hunt.

Labrador Retriever.

GUNDOGS

AMERICAN COCKER SPANIEL
Cocker Spaniel

PORTRAIT: The Cocker Spaniel is a small gundog of sturdy and compact build. His cleanly chiseled and refined head is a most appealing physical feature. Although he is small, his muscular quarters allow for considerable speed and endurance. The skull is rounded and there is no protuberance to the cheeks. The eyes are round, although their rims give them a slightly almond-shaped appearance. The ears are lobular, long, and well feathered. The coat is long, silky, and abundant. Color may be solid black, including black with tan points; any solid color other than black, all with tan points allowed; or particolors (roans are classified as partis). Height: 14–15 inches (35–38 cm). Weight: 24–28 pounds (11–12½ kg).

DEVELOPMENT: The American Cocker Spaniel is of direct relation to the English Cocker Spaniel. Spaniels in America probably go back farther than the United States; and spaniels in England go back at least 400 years more. Cockers in America were bred for desired traits (size, head, body, build, etc.), and through the years they changed from both the original cockers and the modern English Cockers. It was in the 1940s that the two breeds were recognized as separate. The American Cocker is today the smallest member of the sporting family.

RECOGNITION: FCI, AKC, UKC, KCGB, CKC, ANKC

CHARACTER: Although still called an effective hunter's helper, the Cocker certainly makes more vocation of companionship and showmanship than field work. His outstanding attributes are intelligence and affection.

AMERICAN WATER SPANIEL

PORTRAIT: The physical characteristics of emphasis are size, head properties, and coat texture and color. Height: 15–18 inches (36–46 cm). Weight: 25–45 pounds (11–20 kg). The body, although sturdy and muscular, is not too compact. The head is of moderate length; the skull is rather broad and full. The forehead is covered with short smooth hair. The muzzle is square; the jaws are strong and of good length. The remarkable coat is closely curled and of sufficient density to resist the intrusion of weather and water; it is not coarse, however. The powerful legs have a medium-short curly feather. Color: solid liver or dark chocolate, small amount of white on the toes or chest permissible. The general appearance is of a medium-sized, sturdy dog of typical spaniel character.

DEVELOPMENT: Although unrecorded, judging from his physical type, the American Water Spaniel's lineage is composed of various water spaniels, including the Irish and the old English water spaniels and the Curly-Coated Retriever. It is very likely that other breeds played various roles in his development; as should be the case with other dogs bred for utility, most any dog can be justifiably bred into a line if it will better the functional ability of the breed or breed line.

RECOGNITION: FCI, AKC, UKC, CKC

CHARACTER: Of amicable disposition and typical spaniel character, the American Water Spaniel must be quick, intelligent, obliging, and enduring.

BARBET
Griffon d'arret a poil laineux

PORTRAIT: The Barbet is essentially a generic water dog. His long, woolly coat is given to waviness or curling; some specimens may even possess a slightly corded coat. The coat is impenetrable by harsh weather and cold water. His size is medium, standing about 22 inches (56 cm). His weight is also medium, 35–55 pounds (16–25 kg). Made for the water, his feet are large and round. Color possibilities include black, chestnut, fawn, gray, and white with or without markings; mixed colors are common.

DEVELOPMENT: At one time the Barbet was probably *the* water dog of Europe, for the frequency of references and illustrations suggests great popularity. He is one of the most ancient of all French breeds, but his exact origin is irretrievably submerged; he is said to remarkably resemble the old English Water Dog. From the high-flying French ornithologist M. Buffon, we learn that the Barbet of the 18th century had a tight, curly coat. The Barbet is most likely the forerunner of the modern Poodle but has remained unclipped for nearly 200 years! (Some show specimens are clipped today in the manner of the Poodle.) The Barbet is said to be the ancestor of the Bichon and some of the sheepdogs.

RECOGNITION: FCI

CHARACTER: He is excellent at waterfowl work; and icy conditions never slow him down. His determination turns his retrieving abilities and hunting instincts into pliable tools for land hunting as well. The Barbet is a companionable dog, though if kept in the home he will require considerable care to keep him clean and odor free.

BELGIAN SHORTHAIRED POINTER
Braque Belge

PORTRAIT: This good-sized and strong pointer is closely related to and closely resembles the French braques. He is distinguished from them mostly by his color: a heavily ticked white (appearing slate gray) with varied brown patches. He is also a more thickly built dog than the typically lighter French pointers. Height: 24–26 inches (61–66 cm). Weight: 55 pounds (25 kg). The head is rather broad and has a less defined stop. The ears are small and the tail is usually docked. The legs are rather long and built more for power than speed. He has an overall appearance of well-directed power in a discerning dog of good hunting ability.

DEVELOPMENT: His distinctive color is likely the result of crossing the Grand Bleu de Gascogne with the Old Danish Pointer. The Belgian Pointer was selectively bred to hunt over Belgian terrain, a task which requires power rather than quickness. With the diminution of quarry and the influx of German and French pointers to this hunter's world, the Braque Belge fell from favor in his native land. He is probably extinct today, and has been placed on the FCI suspended list.

RECOGNITION: FCI (suspended)

CHARACTER: Thoughtful, easily trained and a natural hunter, what the Belgian Shorthaired Pointer lacked in speed he made up for in both strength and intelligence.

BOURBONNAIS POINTER
Braque du Bourbonnais

PORTRAIT: Handsomely dressed in lilac-white with claret markings, the Bourbonnais's debonair vestments were almost his undoing. The Braque is a fairly large, muscular dog who combines hardiness and elegance. The head is rather pear-shaped and smooth in outline. The ears are medium length and triangular. The muzzle is strong, and the jaw overshot. Sometimes referred to as the tailless pointer, the Braque is born with either a rudimentary or an absent tail. Height: 22 inches (56 cm). Weight: 40–57 pounds (18–26 kg).

DEVELOPMENT: A sporting dog that evolved from the old French braques, the Bourbonnais Pointer originated in the province of Bourbon. An old breed, it is believed to be represented in a 16th-century artwork. This depiction closely resembles the Bourbonnais in its present form. The breed's history was disrupted by the French Revolution. However, throughout the 1800s, breed purity was carefully preserved. Unfortunately, commercialized breedings were conducted at the turn of the 19th century to meet the demands of a suddenly ravenous Bourbonnais public. These once outstanding hunters had their instincts ousted in the name of the show. WWI and WWII took a toll on the breed as well. To make a happy ending, dedicated fanciers pooled their efforts and the breed today is one of the finer Continental pointers.

RECOGNITION: Useful, intelligent, affectionate, though slightly capricious, the Bourbonnais makes an excellent companion. Not needing to be confined to the marshlands and woods, this all-around hunter can be used on all types of game.

BOYKIN SPANIEL

PORTRAIT: Larger than a Cocker, he is, without coincidence, similar in size to both the American Water Spaniel and the Springer Spaniel (two important contributing breeds). Height: 15–18 inches (36–46 cm). Weight: 30–38 pounds (14–17 kg). His coat, however, is less dense and straighter than the Water Spaniel's. The large ears are set high and covered with long wavy hair. The muzzle is broad and elongated. The wavy or curly coat varies in its degree of tightness; it is waterproof. The tail is curled and feathered. Color is solid liver.

DEVELOPMENT: During the early 20th century, dog fanciers from South Carolina witnessed the creation of a new breed of dog. Two ambitious hunters of the Boykin community in search of the premier turkey dog began with a stray; this dog proved so responsive to the experienced training of these men that it was bred to spaniel bitches of various breeds (of special importance were the obliging Springers and American Water Spaniels). Other contributors were Pointers and Chesapeake Bay Retrievers. Turkey dogs needed patience to remain quiet and alert until the fowl was called and shot; not until then could the dog move or make noise. Being no butterball, the Boykin fits wonderfully into the small crafts used by southern hunters of water fowl. So successful is he that South Carolina made the Boykin its official state dog.

RECOGNITION: UKC

CHARACTER: The Boykin is a fantastic swimmer. His fine nose and enthusiasm in the field make him a versatile hunter. He is docile, pleasant, and obedient but requires considerable exercise.

BRAQUE D'AUVERGNE
Bleu d'Auvergne, Auvergne Pointer

PORTRAIT: Although a large medium-sized dog and very powerful, the Blue has a lean appearance. He is a tough dog with good length of leg; he is built for enduring the challenging hunt over rugged terrain. The chest is deep and large, the loins are short. He is hare-footed. The coat is spotted black on white, forming a blue shading with large black patches; he is without any tan markings. Although the black markings are not prescribed, they must appear on the head, covering the ears and eyes. A body color of speckled black on white is also seen. Height: 22–24 inches (56–61 cm). Weight: 50–62 pounds (23–28 kg).

DEVELOPMENT: An idea that goes back many years is that this braque is actually the Braque Francais transformed under the influence of the surroundings or by skillful selection. Another equally interesting suggestion is that he came from Malta—a hypothesis based on the simple idea that members of the Maltese Order, which once contained French knights, brought these dogs back to France with them when that Order was dissolved in 1798. Unfortunately, both of these suggestions lack convincing evidence. The fact remains, however, that the Auvergne is a fine breed of excellent ability.

RECOGNITION: FCI

CHARACTER: This dog trains with a breeze. He has a hard mouth but remains a good retriever. His high intelligence, fearless display of affection, and unending enthusiasm on the field make him a treasure among gundogs.

BRAQUE DUPUY
Dupuy Pointer

PORTRAIT: Large and somewhat high on the leg, the Braque Dupuy possesses a chestnut and white coat that cannot be aptly described as brilliant. The head is long, fine and dry. The ears are high set. The muzzle is ram-like, and little stop is present. The chest is large, and there is a noticeable tuck to the belly. The tail is set low. The general appearance is light and graceful. Height: 25–27 inches (63–68 cm). Weight: 49–62 pounds (22–28 kg).

DEVELOPMENT: The older of the French braques gave way to a more houndy appearance, and the Braque Dupuy, one of the oldest of the braque types, is surely more houndy than his *frères*. He is tall, uncommonly fast, and elegant, as braques go, which leads some to believe that a Greyhound (or Sloughi) cross occurred. The French Revolution nearly decimated the Dupuy population, and only a few specimens were preserved in the Abbey of Argensols. Although this braque is willing to work in water, owners relay that he would really prefer not.

RECOGNITION: FCI

CHARACTER: Though workman-like and no-nonsense, this braque is somewhat hasty in his character. He owns a good nose, and is always active on the hunt. The Dupuy can blaze enviable speed over open ground.

BRAQUE FRANCAIS DE GRANDE TAILLE
Large French Pointer, French Pointer–Pyrenees type

PORTRAIT: His head is as imposing as his nose is tender. The Large French Pointer maintains a tall appearance and is in fact taller than the English Pointer, the breed that has become the "yardstick" for all European gundogs. The Braque Francais is duly deep chested; his head is broad and his skull is slightly convex. The body is muscular and athletic in appearance. The coat is short, thick and dense. In color the Large Braque is white with chestnut patches, with or without ticking. Height: 22–27 inches (56–68 cm). Weight: 45–71 pounds (20–32 kg).

DEVELOPMENT: The Pyrenees area is graced by this sizable gundog that has been a popular hunting dog there for many years. He is closely related to the Spanish Pointer and is described as looking like the extinct and much talked about Southern Hound. His appearance certainly verifies any supposition of hound in his blood. With his nose lifted high into the air, this dog is keen on a scent while expressing a wonderfully French *noblesse oblige* attitude to the sport, which he takes seriously and professionally.

RECOGNITION: FCI

CHARACTER: The dog's temperament, like his conformation, is well balanced and durable. He is a much admired gundog in France and an equally loved home companion.

BRAQUE FRANCAIS DE PETITE TAILLE
Small French Pointer, French Pointer–Gascony type

PORTRAIT: The smaller version French Pointer, although more *petite* than his other half, is no less handsome or striking. This Braque Francais's muzzle is shorter than the larger French Pointer and his ears, set higher and shorter, hang flatter to the head. Both breeds share the same white and chestnut coloration, although the Petite's chestnut markings are often more extensive. The head is slightly more tapered and refined. Height: 19–23 inches (48–58 cm). Weight: 37–55 pounds (17–25 kg).

DEVELOPMENT: The Braque Francais de Petite Taille, like the Grande Taille, developed from the Spanish Pointer (and likely the Italian Pointer as well). This dog is a more refined version of the Pyrenees-type Braque Francais and was fostered in the Gascony region. His hunting style is also high-nosed; he is particularly good in harsh marsh and and thick cover. This dog's small size makes him an agile and easily maneuvering hunter.

RECOGNITION: FCI

CHARACTER: This is an obedient, respectful hunting companion of worthy abilities and sound disposition. He is clean cut and easy to keep. Owners relay what a joy he is to have indoors, although he loves to be outside too.

BRACCO ITALIANO
Italian Pointer

PORTRAIT: Squarely built and very agile, the preferred specimens are "dry" limbed and packed with muscle. The Bracco has long folded ears, a round skull, and a nearly convex muzzle. His truly distinguishing feature, however, is his unchanging nervous expression. The coat is short, dense, and fine; it is finer on the head, the neck, and the lower parts of the body. Tail is docked short. Color possibilities are: white, orange and white, chestnut and white, orange roan, and chestnut roan. Color faults are: all black or chestnut, black and white, tricolor, and black and tan. Height: 22–26 inches (56–66 cm). Weight: 55–88 pounds (25–40 kg).

DEVELOPMENT: The Bracco Italiano is possibly the oldest of the Italian gundog types, and he is certainly the oldest surviving and the most successful of those who have come to the fore. Many assert that the Bracco descended from the same stock as the Segugio. The likely scenario is that native Italian hounds were bred to old gundogs, and dogs were selected for retrieving, scenting, swimming and other abilities. The breed originated some time in the early 1700s. He has changed little over the years and, with the Segugio, remains one of the characteristic hunting dogs of Italy.

RECOGNITION: FCI

CHARACTER: Having changed little in his long history, the Bracco holds on to some of that characteristic stubbornness. Like a true gundog though, he is "coolly elated" in the field, excited but always keeping his head. Besides his outstanding field abilities, his attributes of docility and level-headedness make him an enjoyable and worthy companion.

JRQuinn

BRAQUE D'ARIÉGE
Ariége Pointer, Braque de Toulouse

PORTRAIT: Big and virile, the Ariége was once a slow steady hunter but is now more fleet footed and graceful. He remains, however, one of the largest and most powerful of the French pointers. The low set tail is docked—as is common with most continental pointers. His rather houndy features include: the possible dewlap, the scroll ears, the hare feet, and the convex muzzle. Powerful, elegant, and graceful, he is a tireless worker of slow pace designed for work in rough terrain. Height: 23–27 inches (58–68 cm). Weight: 55–65 pounds (25–30 kg). The short coat is fine and rather tight fitting. Color is white with orange or chestnut spots; ticking is a very likely possibility.

DEVELOPMENT: Unlike most of the other French pointers that were named for the locale in which they originated, the Braque D'Ariége is not descended from native hounds of his origin. This is certain because the local hound of Ariége is strictly a 20th-century development. The most acceptable theory regarding their creation is that they represent an old cross between the Spanish Pointer and the Bracco Italiano. The Ariége received new blood during the 20th century, mostly from the Braque Saint-Germain but also from the Braque Francais. These crossings resulted in a sleeker and quicker dog.

RECOGNITION: FCI

CHARACTER: This big dog can sometimes be a bit of a bull. He requires a dominant personality as his master. He is quite intelligent and responds well to proper training. If set straight from the beginning, his elegance, even temper, and clean coat make him a fine dog to have in the home.

BRAQUE SAINT-GERMAIN
Saint Germain Pointer, Compiègne Pointer

PORTRAIT: Arguably the most beautiful of the more useful French pointers, the Braque Saint-Germain is elegant and well proportioned. This is a dog of supple build and no fewer heavy bones than his fellow pointers. The chest is broad and deep. The stop is less pronounced than the English Pointer's; the Saint-Germain's snout is less elevated, and his muzzle is less square. The nose is wide-nostriled, broad and dark pink. The ears are medium sized and attached on a level with the eyes, standing well out from the head. The neck is strong and fairly long. The coat is short, not too fine, and never hard. In color the Saint-Germain invariably is a dull base with bright orange splashes. Height: 20–24 inches (51–61 cm). Weight: 40–57 pounds (18–26 kg). The tail is long and tapering.

DEVELOPMENT: Like the English Pointer, the French pointers owe their heritage to the Spanish Pointer. The Braque Saint-Germain can be traced to the dim time of Louis XV or before. Paintings hanging in the Louvre today indicate the breed's sure antiquity and type consistency through the ages. In the 18th century, these early braques were all basically considered a single "breed." The Saint-Germain as a breed first appeared during the reign of Charles X.

RECOGNITION: FCI

CHARACTER: The Braque Saint-Germain fulfills completely the desires of the sportsman who wishes to have an effective hunter and an unbeatable companion. Rather reserved and quiet, this dog is a willing performer and an obedient pet.

BRITTANY
Epagneul Breton, Brittany Spaniel

PORTRAIT: The deep chest, short but strong loin, broad hind quarters, and sloping forequarters are all essential qualities for this active and energetic canine. The tail, which is customarily docked to 4 inches (10 cm), is carried level and has a small twist of hair on the end. The coat, which is fairly fine but dense, lies rather flat and is slightly wavy. Color: orange and white, liver and white, black and white, roan, or any of these colors in a tricolor pattern. The nose is dark and its pigmentation corresponds to the coat color (is in harmony with it). Height: 18–20 inches (47–50 cm). Weight: 28–33 pounds (13–15 kg).

DEVELOPMENT: Hunting accounts and illustrations dating back to the 1700s depict the Breton (or Brittany) Spaniel. This Brittany, however, is not the Brittany of today. The modern Brittany begins his history at the start of the 1900s, when one Arthur Enaud devised a breeding program to rejuvenate the old Breton, which at that time was waning into obscurity. The old dog was physically and temperamentally suited to his native habitat—rough and thicketed country. Today's Brittany may be more suited for the show ring but is still a versatile hunter of good ability.

RECOGNITION: FCI, AKC, UKC, KCGB, CKC, ANKC

CHARACTER: An all-around hunter, pointer, and retriever, the Brittany is also affectionate and eager to please. He makes an excellent companion, being gentle and trustworthy. He is a dog for all seasons; owners cite multitudes of reasons why no other dog can compare to the Brittany.

CHESAPEAKE BAY RETRIEVER

PORTRAIT: The Chessie was bred with a specific purpose in mind—duck hunting. It is for this purpose that his features are ideally billed. His broad skull, wedged forehead, and powerful jaw make him ideal for retrieving fallen water fowl; he is perhaps more effective than any other dog at this in icy water conditions. His high set ears and less refined, rather thick appearance have been the targets of many mark-missing condescending remarks in "hoi polloi" show circles. The ears, however, while not exaggerated in any esthetically inane way, are ideally set for a dog to work unpredictable waters. His short neck, though disproportionate to some other features, is powerful and well suited for towing heavy fowl. The coat is short, thick, and very coarse; it may give the appearance of a shag rug. A deadgrass color is most desirable, though liver and hay colors are acceptable. Height: 23–26 inches (58–66 cm). Weight: 64–75 pounds (29–34 kg). Eyes are yellow.

DEVELOPMENT: It was on the famous ducking shores of the Chesapeake Bay of Virginia and Maryland that these dogs were conceived and bred, and on those shores the first Chessies prospered. It all began sometime in the late 19th century, and the perfection continued into the 20th century. The true origin of the Chessie wanes yarnfully yawnful in comparison to the well-knit, well-loved tale of the stranded Newfoundland vessel. The captain of this tossed ship gave two Newfoundland-type dogs to a Mr. George Law, who had aided the sailors of the vessel in their time of need. The tale continues with these Newfie-type dogs' being bred to the then-common yellow and tan coonhounds, thus happily yielding the Chesapeake. Feasibly, the yellow and tan hounds have contributed to the spinning of the Chessie, since both the coat and eye color of the breed suggest such a bloodline. This breed is revered as the unsurpassed water retriever. First-hand data speaks of individuals of the breed retrieving 1000-plus fowl in a given season.

RECOGNITION: FCI, AKC, UKC, KCGB, CKC

CHARACTER: The Chessie is a relentless worker, with great courage and power and a will of tempered steel. He is a loyal and enjoyable companion, but he needs a commanding master to really get his all extracted.

CLUMBER SPANIEL

PORTRAIT: The low-to-the-ground Clumber is a unique spaniel, rather long and heavy. These dogs weigh between 55 and 85 pounds (25–38 kg). Height is 19 to 20 inches (48–51 cm). One can easily spot a Clumber by his massive head and heavy-boned body. The head has a marked stop, a flat top skull, and a large protuberance at the occiput. The muzzle is medium in length. The nose is large and square. The ears are broad and set low at about eye level; they are triangular in shape and slightly feathered. The dense, weather-resistant coat is straight and flat but not harsh. There is noticeable feathering of the underbelly and legs; a neck frill is also present. The coat color is predominantly white, with either lemon or orange markings. The muzzle and ears are often freckled with such markings.

DEVELOPMENT: Based on physical qualities, assumptions have been made concerning the Clumber's origin: the long and low body might indicate the use of the Basset Hound; the heavy head and visible haw suggest the infusion of the early Alpine Spaniels (thus a relation to the St. Bernard). Some surmise just by the Clumber's quaintness and charm that he is of French origin (or should be). Not much can be ascertained as fact, but the need for heavier spaniels to work denser terrain is one acceptable impetus for the Clumber's inception. A second, more entertaining if not more reliable, reclines on the notion that supine hunters desired a more sluggish gundog in order for them to keep up with him, flattering their snail's pace style and thereby avoiding any overexertion during their weekend exhibitions.

RECOGNITION: FCI, AKC, UKC, KCGB, CKC, ANKC

CHARACTER: The Clumber Spaniel responds well to training and, although slow, makes a fine tracker and retriever. As a companion, the Clumber is excellent; his qualities are loyalty, affection, and discrimination.

CURLY-COATED RETRIEVER

PORTRAIT: This breed deserves its name, for its mass of crisp, small curls is its most distinctive and important feature; even the tail, which is left at its natural length, is covered with curls, though the muzzle and foreface have shorter, smoother hair. Coat color is either black or liver. Beneath the coat is a strong and active dog with a deep chest, muscular hindquarters, and a back that is never long. The skull is long and well proportioned. Eyes are large but not prominent and either of black or dark brown color. Height: 25–27 inches (63–69 cm). Weight: 70–80 pounds (32–36 kg). The build is square.

DEVELOPMENT: It is suggested that smaller Newfoundlands played a part in the early development of the breed. The other oft-stated component breed is the Irish Water Spaniel, though the old English Water Spaniel is possibly the water spaniel contributor. This breed is an old one, with written descriptions dating to 1803. The Curly-Coated Retriever is likely the first dog used for serious and extensive retrieving work in England. The breed's success has made it known around the world.

RECOGNITION: FCI, AKC, UKC, KCGB, CKC, ANKC

CHARACTER: This is a dog who is easy to get along with; he is kind and friendly, intelligent and loyal. Even his coat is easy to care for, as it requires little grooming. He is also an enthusiastic and athletic working dog.

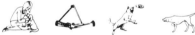

CZESKY FOUSEK
Rough-coated Bohemian Pointer, Czech Coarsehaired Pointer, Slovakian Wirehaired Pointer

PORTRAIT: This is a large and rather tall dog, with good length of leg, deep chest, thick neck, well-muscled hind quarters, and angulated hind legs. The tail is docked. The ears are medium-high set; the dark eyes are alert in expression; the muzzle on the sides and undersides is bearded. Height: 24–26 inches (61–66 cm). Weight: 60–75 pounds (27–34 kg). Coat: rough outer, soft and thick inner; bristly in feel and appearance. Color: brown or brown and white; ticking or markings may be present.

DEVELOPMENT: In all likelihood, the breed originated in the Slovak region today called Czechoslovakia. It enjoyed grand popularity in Bohemia from the mid-19th century until the First World War. The breed does contain both German Wirehaired and German Shorthaired Pointer blood. We know that Shorthair blood was infused in the 1930s. All German breed crossings with the Czesky probably were done after the breed was established.

RECOGNITION: FCI

CHARACTER: Only after a hardy day on the field does the Czesky have time to rest at the hearth of his master's fireplace. Dogs of this breed like to feel that they have earned their daily bread. They need plenty of exercise and a master willing to share rewarding times with them.

DALMATIAN

PORTRAIT: Grace and stature aflame, a breed of truly unique beauty and character. All Dalmatians have a coat coloration of a virgin white base with defined round black or liver spots. The coat hairs are short, hard, and close set. The overall picture of the dog is one of balance and symmetry. He is a strong and muscular dog, weighing 50–55 pounds (23–25 kg) at a height of 19–23 inches (48–58 cm). His chest is not too wide but is deep. The ears are set high, of medium size, and round.

DEVELOPMENT: The Dalmatian has been known in England since the 1700s, and models of a spotted dog have been found in ancient Greek friezes. E.C. Ash, the notable author of *Dogs and Their History*, refers to spotted dogs that appear on a tablet dated circa 2000 BC. No doubt Dalmations are an ancient breed, and no doubt they have passed through many changes over the centuries. These dogs were adopted by the fire departments of the 1800s because of their outstanding way with horses. Dalmatians have been used with great success since the Middle Ages. In the age of horse-drawn carriages, they would stride alongside them to protect the travelers within and would clear the road ahead should the carriage come upon a populated area. Later they became more of a status symbol, skipping gaily under carriage axles.

RECOGNITION: FCI, AKC, UKC, KCGB, CKC, ANKC

CHARACTER: There are at least 101 good reasons to own a Dalmatian. He is a congenial and pliable pet, although his strength and stamina can be too much of a challenge for some owners. He is dedicated and loyal, and he is always eager to please. The absolute incarnation of man's best friend!

DEUTSCHER WACHTELHUND
German Spaniel

PORTRAIT: The German Spaniel is solid dog that stands on medium-short legs; he is about 16–20 inches (40–51 cm) tall. His brawn is compacted, giving him a robust look at a weight of 44–66 pounds (20–30 kg). He is slightly longer than he is high. The wavy coat grows thick and medium long. The coat on the muzzle and foreface is shorter and smooth. The muzzle and the skull are equal in length, and there is a slight arch to the upper head; however, there is no stop. The muzzle is not pointed but is elongated. Ears set high and wide hang flat behind the eyes, touching the eyes when pulled to them. The tail is docked. Color is dark brown, often with white markings on the chest and toes; other colors are white with brown patches and white mottled with brown. Brown roans and brown harlequins are preferred to the caille-colored dogs.

DEVELOPMENT: *Watchel* in German means "quail," and these dogs are certainly schooled in hunting fowl, with a masterful ability in quail. Little else is definite. Based on use and ability, it seems only logical that Continental water dogs were employed, although the breed resembles old English water dogs. It is likely that various sporting spaniels, including the Cocker, are also in his blood.

RECOGNITION: FCI

CHARACTER: The breed is one of the choice bird-hunting dogs. Performing well at retrieving, flushing, and bloodtrailing he is, however, an all-around hunting dog. He is durable and and responsive—always heeding a command and forever following a call.

DRENTSE PATRIJSHOND
Dutch Partridge Dog

PORTRAIT: This breed of medium build is strong enough to retrieve even large felled game. The refined head, not large, is set thick and placed on an incredibly strong neck. The tail is left long, resembling a setter. His height is between 23–26 inches (58–66 cm). He weighs between 45–50 pounds (21–23 kg). The coat is coarse and straight. The extensive feathering on the legs, feet, tail, and ears gives the coat a longer overall appearance.

DEVELOPMENT: This is an all-purpose gundog, although his name may suggest a certain specialization. Known at least since the mid-1500s, few dogs survive today that are true to type. The breed is facing a serious challenge as interest in its survival wanes. A head study by Henrick Goltzius (1558–1617) shows a Dutch Partridge Dog that appears much like today's breed. Originated in the Dutch province of Drente, from which he takes his name, the Drentse Patrijshond represents the half-spaniel and half-setter dogs that are the believed ancestors of most gundogs—justifying somewhat the claim of his descent from these dogs.

RECOGNITION: FCI

CHARACTER: Both a pointer and good retriever, he takes well to water and quite naturally to the gun. Gentle, meek and obedient, he does not respond well to aggressive training. He makes a fine companion and is ideal for the sporting but sensitive hunter.

ENGLISH COCKER SPANIEL
Cocker Spaniel

PORTRAIT: The English Cocker is distinguished from the American Cocker by size and head type, among other things. The English Cocker weighs between 26–34 pounds (12–16 kg). He is sturdy, well balanced, compact, and square. The Cocker has a square muzzle, a cleanly chiseled head and a nose sufficiently wide for scenting. The bright and merry eyes are dark colored and express intelligence and gentleness. Overall, the dog is well built, concentrated, and able. Height: 15–16 inches (38–41 cm). The coat is flat and has a silky texture; it is not profuse or ever curly. The legs and body are well feathered above the hocks; the ears are also covered with a fine feathering. Colors are various, including self, parti, and roan.

DEVELOPMENT: From Chaucer's *The Canterbury Tales*: "...for as a Spaynel she would on him lepe." Prior to the late 1800s, all spaniels were held as one group. These dogs began more specialized work—the larger, flushing game and the smaller, hunting woodcock. In time, separate breeds began to emerge: large were bred to large and small to small until type became uniform. The KCGB recognized these separate breeds (cockers and flushers) in 1892. The modern English Cocker remains a fine hunter, lively and intense on the field with good hunting instinct and sense.

RECOGNITION: FCI, AKC, UKC, KCGB, CKC, ANKC

CHARACTER: He is, of course, a merry dog, always on the move, willing to please and loving to learn. The English Cocker is a functional worker and an unbeatable companion.

ENGLISH SETTER

PORTRAIT: Here is a dog of exquisite style and graceful movement: quick, easy, and true. The English Setter is a mid-sized, active dog. He denotes balance and symmetry and has no exaggerated points. Height: 24–25 inches (61–64 cm). Weight: 40–70 pounds (18–32 kg). The coat is flat and of good length; feathering is seen on the body, legs, and tail. Color possibilities: blue, liver, orange belton, lemon belton, black, lemon, liver, and orange and white; also all white. Heavy dark patches and solid coloring are avoided by most fanciers. The long lean head, with its well-defined stop, gives the characteristic expression of the breed; the skull is oval from ear to ear; the muzzle should be long and square, of width in harmony with the skull.

DEVELOPMENT: Evidence suggests that the old English Setter was created by crosses between the Water Spaniel, the Spanish Pointer, and the Springer Spaniel. Selective breedings over the years for desired type produced the modern-day English Setter. Though we can only guess, these crossings likely took place some time in the 16th century in England. Edward Laverack is the one most credited for the development of the modern setter's breed type. His breeding program began around 1825 and continued for some 35 years. The turning point for today's Setter is set at January 28, 1859, when the first show for English Setters took place, at Newcastle-on-Tyne, England. From that day on, the English Setter has maintained a steady following of loyal enthusiasts who are captured by the dog's coupling of usefulness and beauty.

RECOGNITION: FCI, AKC, UKC, KCGB, CKC, ANKC

CHARACTER: An ideal companion of distinguished elegance, he is less excitable than the Irish Setter. Devoid of vice and never vicious, he is also intelligent and easily trainable.

ENGLISH SPRINGER SPANIEL

PORTRAIT: This canine is symmetrical, compact, strong, and, like his cocker cousin, quite merry. Of all the British land spaniels, the English Springer is highest on the leg and raciest in build. This translates to a strong body, neither too long nor short, a deep chest, well-muscled loins, and a skull of medium length and fair broadness. Height: 19–20 inches (48–51 cm). Weight: 50–55 pounds (23–25 kg). The coat is straight, close lying, and never coarse; extensive feathering can be seen under the body and on the legs and ears. Colors are liver and white, black and white, and either color with tan or liver markings (tricolor).

DEVELOPMENT: Until the late 19th century, all spaniels of England and the United States were considered a single breed (or group). They did, however, come in a variety of sizes, often within the same litter. The largest of these spaniels were used for flushing game. They were called springers because they would spring the game from its hideout. In 1902, the English Springer Spaniel was given breed status by the KCGB. It is certain that the breed is quite old. A description of the springing Spaniel is found in the 1576 publication *Treatise of Englishe Dogges* by Dr. Johannes Caius.

RECOGNITION: FCI, AKC, UKC, KCGB, CKC, ANKC

CHARACTER: The proper English Springer must be a dog of ability. He is a fine hunter, excelling at springing game. He is hardy yet well behaved and quick to learn and respond. He is a fine showman and an unbeatable companion. In short, he is an all-around dog—even making his way to the White House under President George Bush.

ÉPAGNEUL BLEU DE PICARDIE
Blue Picardy Spaniel

PORTRAIT: Fairly tall, up to 25 inches (64 cm), and built for stength. The coat is fairly long, dense, and hard; on the ears and tall it is finer and longer. Color: black (often called blue) and white, with heavy ticking but without red markings; red on head and feet is more acceptable. Weight: 44 pounds (20 kg). He has a gentle nature which is expressed in his deep brown eyes and candid facial movements.

DEVELOPMENT: The Bleu was created by crossing the blue belton English Setter with the Picard. In considering the English Setter a descendant of the Picard, the Bleu is but a Picard spin-off. The Picard probably stretches his origin to Spain, although, like the Épagneul Francais, he may be of northern descent. He most likely traces back to the Chien d'Oyssel and came into being somctime in the 14th century. Really not a spaniel, the Bleu is closer to a setter in physical characteristics. The Épagneul Bleu de Picardie, like his close relative the Épagneul Picard, is lighter in bone, better in nose, and more prolonged in stamina than thc old French Spaniel type.

RECOGNITION: FCI

CHARACTER: Specially suited for hunting in the wood and marsh, he is responsive, obedient, and bonding with his master. His work ethics are astounding. His specialty is snipe in the marsh.

ÉPAGNEUL FRANCAIS
French Spaniel

PORTRAIT: In general appearance, the French Spaniel is a sturdy dog of calm disposition; his expression is unusually sensitive and seemingly empathetic for a canine. The head is squared; the skull is slightly domed; it is joined to a short though strong neck, which runs into the deep, rather broad chest and the broad, straight back. Height: 21–24 inches (53–61 cm). Weight: 44–55 pounds (20–25 kg). Coat: short, tight, flat, and straight, with feathering on the legs, ears, underbelly and tail. Color: white with liver markings.

DEVELOPMENT: Two rather interesting theories exist concerning the origin of this breed. One purports that the breed was formed on the Barbary Coast, whence it spread to Spain and then to France, where it was bred with type in mind. A second asserts that the breed is of Scandinavian descent, probably Danish; this is supported by the institution of the Order of the Elephant, by King Christian I in 1478, in memory of the spaniel named "Wildbrat." It is assumed that Wildbrat is the forefather of the Épagneul type. Although nothing is certain, the fact remains that these dogs are popular in France today and are fine hunters and companions.

RECOGNITION: FCI

CHARACTER: With hunting becoming more and more of a sport and less of a necessity in France—as it is most of the world over—these dogs are more popular companions than ever before. They are docile and friendly, though they may be wary of strangers. They are quiet, only barking for reason.

GUNDOGS

ÉPAGNEUL PICARD
Picardy Spaniel

PORTRAIT: Standing up to 25 inches (64 cm) tall and weighing around 44 pounds (20 kg), the Picardy is an enduring dog built for strength and stamina. The long coat is fairly dense and hard; the ears and tail are covered with finer and longer hair. Coloration is a liver, tan, and white tricolor with heavy ticking. The eyes are a rich brown; they are set fair on a moderately rounded head. The nose is well designed for sufficient scenting ability.

DEVELOPMENT: The Épagneul Picard probably stretches its origin to Spain, although, like the Épagneul Francais, it may be of northern descent. The likely lineage trails back to the Chien d'Oyssel. The Épagneul came into being in the 14th century. Really not a spaniel, the Épagneul is closer to a setter in physical characteristics. The Épagneul Picard is lighter in bone, better in nose, and more prolonged in stamina than standard French spaniel types.

RECOGNITION: FCI

CHARACTER: Specializing in hunting snipe in the marsh, the Picardy also does very well when hunting other water fowl and even some land game. He is an especially affectionate mate, bonding closely to his master and family. The Picard requires moderate exercise for an active dog and is gentle and undemanding.

ÉPAGNEUL PONT-AUDEMER
Pont-Audemer Spaniel

PORTRAIT: The Pont-Audemer is a marvelously handsome spaniel. The coat is long with slightly "snappy" curls. A rather long head is draped by wavy light curls, and the face is smooth with a topknot on his head. Despite this clownish tuft, the dog still appears tough and vigorous. In color the Pont-Audemer is solid liver or liver and white (with or without ticking). The body is thick set and moderately sized. Height: 20–23 inches (51–59 cm). Weight: 40–53 pounds (18–24 kg).

DEVELOPMENT: The Pont-Audemer's aptitude for water work suggests that the old English Water Spaniel or the Irish Water Spaniel played an important part in the development of this French spaniel breed. It is also reasonably asserted that perhaps the Poodle or Barbet had a paw in the Pont-Audemer. We do know that because the numbers have always been limited, inbreeding has sometimes been a problem. The Irish Water Spaniel was once used to help regenerate the breed; hence, that dog, at least in later times, has contributed blood. The breed is a water dog par excellence and is beautifully suited to handle the marshes. His land abilities are also notable.

RECOGNITION: FCI

CHARACTER: The Pont-Audemer, scarce as he may be, is a sublime hunting companion. He enjoys the hunt as a sport and approaches a weekend with his master with an eager and light heart. He loves the water and captivates many a land hunter with his natural ability to point.

FIELD SPANIEL

PORTRAIT: Without exaggeration or coarseness, the Field Spaniel should be the picture of sound breeding and refinement. The body is of moderate length; the back is strong and brawny, and the legs are of fairly good length with flat straight bone. The coat is flat or slightly waved—not too short. Feathering is abundant but not hyperbolic. In color the Field Spaniel is black, liver, golden liver or mahogany red, or roan; or any of these with tan. The breed also comes in bicolors (with white). Height: 18 inches (46 cm). Weight: 35–50 pounds (16–22 kg).

DEVELOPMENT: Although modern-day dog show buffs would wince winningly at the suggestion, historically the Field Spaniel is nothing more than a Cocker Spaniel. Admittedly, "nothing more than a Cocker Spaniel" here can be interpreted as a high compliment to any breed of canine. Essentially a diversion in Cocker Spaniel type brought about today's Field Spaniel. The Field was once a ludicrously proportioned, functionally inept dog with an exaggerated long body, sagging tummy, cumbrous head, and crooked legs. Sensible breeders returned the dog to working condition. The breed has always enjoyed but a fraction of the Cocker's unshakable popularity.

RECOGNITION: FCI, AKC, UKC, KCGB, CKC, ANKC

CHARACTER: This sporting dog is the epitome of utility and nobility. He is a handsome home companion, graced with a saint's docility and patience.

FLAT-COATED RETRIEVER

PORTRAIT: The ideal appearance of the Flat-Coated is "power without lumber and raciness without weediness." This is a gundog of strength and substance with unmistakable refinement and elegance. The head is long and clean; the body symmetrical, with wiry muscling and a deep chest; proud carriage; and a waving tail to project its undaunted style—all of these in silhouette comprise the breed's uniqueness. Height: 22–23 inches (56–59 cm). Weight: 60–70 pounds (27–32 kg). The Flat-Coated can be solid black or liver. The proper coat is of moderate length, dense and full, with a high luster—as inferred, the ideal is flat-lying and straight.

DEVELOPMENT: The breed-in-progress was first called the "Wavy-Coated Retriever" but as the type became set and the variety progressed, the coat *flattened* out and the initial denomination was duly deleted and replaced by the present name. And yet the Flat's origin can be traced to the waves in British ports on which arrived lumber ships carrying Lesser Newfoundland dogs. These dogs were sold to British gamekeepers, who were hopeful that they would make ideal house or "flat" companions. The imported dogs were crossed to setters in order to improve matters and preserve the black coats. The combination (needless to say) proved successful.

RECOGNITION: FCI, AKC, UKC, KCGB, CKC, ANKC

CHARACTER: Outgoing and devoted, the Flat-Coated makes a wonderful family dog. His versatility and adaptability are key to his character. Friendly, watchful and cheerful, the breed attaches itself strongly to its owner.

GERMAN BROKEN-COATED POINTER
Stichelhaar, Deutscher Stichelhaariger Vorstehhund,
German Roughhaired Pointer

PORTRAIT: A wire coat appearing most moderate in length is accentuated by this Deutscher's bearded chin and brow. The Stichelhaar is relatively indistinguishable from the German Wirehaired Pointer. He is medium sized, standing 22–26 inches (56–66 cm) and the picture of good proportion and balance. The coat deceptively measures 1½ inches (4 cm), although it appears much shorter since it lays flat against the body. Coat quality is paramount with the Broken-Coat as is the appropriate feathering on the muzzle, eyebrows, hind legs and tail. In color the Stichelhaar is white and brown in a roan pattern. Weight: 44 pounds (20 kg).

DEVELOPMENT: The present-day Stichelhaar is much different than it was in the Germany of old. The breed's close resemblance with the Griffon is no coincidence: crosses between the two were unavoidable and frequent; even today, they share very similar heads. Additionally, the infusion of German Shepherd blood has made for the Stichelhaar's less narrow and long muzzle. Ironically, with all the emphasis on coat type, the breed has undergone a few name changes, each of which attempted to describe the coat more accurately. Straufhaarig (hard-haired) and Stichelhaarig (prick-haired) are among the names that still stick out from yesterday. Many Stichelhaars today are registered as Drahthaars (wire-haired) and the differences between the two are continually dissolving.

RECOGNITION: FCI

CHARACTER: Active and able, the German Broken-Coated Pointer is an effective gundog and a faithful companion. He is a tad removed from the home environment but can never be called unfriendly.

GERMAN LONGHAIRED POINTER
Deutscher Langhaariger Vorstehhund, Langhaar

PORTRAIT: The Langhaar is a sturdy, never coarse-appearing pointer with a solid liver coat that is shiny and wavy. In size he is comparable to the other German pointers, but his long coat sets him apart. Height: 24–27 inches (61–69 cm). Weight: 55–77 pounds (25–35 kg). Never silky, the coat is of moderate length and rather harsh in texture. White spots or a white chest often occur, although a solid-colored dog is the desired norm.

DEVELOPMENT: Not simply a German Shorthaired Pointer with long hair, the Langhaar descends from similar ancestors as the Shorthair and the Wirehair: most probably the Water Spaniel of old. Westphalia, if no other city in Germany, once had a tremendous number of these dogs as hunters and companions. The Longhair, in order to be true, should avoid both red and black coloration—such colors would indicate the bloodline's being violated by the Irish Setter, Newfoundland, or Gordon Setter. Each of these three admittedly handsome dogs were often carelessly crossed with the Longhair, with the result being coarser, improperly colored dogs. His hunting affinity centers on feathered game and he is a pro in the water. At one time, he was a notorious falconer and hawker.

RECOGNITION: FCI, CKC

CHARACTER: This enthusiastic hunter must be provided an outlet for his energy. He is a fun-loving, easygoing dog that enjoys being with his master. Although hunting is a passion for him, other outdoor diversions can be undertaken and enjoyed. The coat is not so long as to require extended grooming sessions.

GERMAN SHORTHAIRED POINTER
Deutscher Kurzhaariger Vorstehhund, Kurzhaar

PORTRAIT: A symmetrical and power-suggesting conformation well suits this agile and animated hunter. The Shorthair's nobility is produced by the sum of its parts, all in absolute proportion to one another: deep chest, powerful back, good quarters, cleanly cut head, adequate muscle, good bone, well-carried tail, and hard coat. The dog's outline is graceful and well balanced. The size of the Shorthair is of prime importance: he must be neither too large nor too small. Height: 23–25 inches (58–64 cm). Weight: 55–70 pounds (25–32 kg). Solid liver or liver and white (with or without ticking) are the desired colors. A true water dog, this breed has webbed feet.

DEVELOPMENT: Prior to the 1870 Kurzhaar Stud Book, no actual records were kept of the breed. *Schweisshunds*, that is slow working scent hunters, were popular in Germany for countless generations, as were bird dogs (*huehnerhunden*). The early Shorthair likely resulted from crosses between the Spanish Pointer, English foxhounds and a variety of German scenthounds. The dog that resulted from these careful crosses was much heavier, longer eared and slower than today's breed. Crossing the English Pointer to this dog effectively made it lighter and faster. No one can deny this gundog's abilities or intelligence.

RECOGNITION: FCI, AKC, UKC, KCGB, CKC, ANKC

CHARACTER: Efficient and no-nonsense, like his taut coat, the Shorthair is an unbeatable field dog, with a subtle nose and the ability to work on water or land. As a companion, he is keen and easily trained in addition to being affectionate and approachable.

GERMAN WIREHAIRED POINTER
Deutscher Drahthaariger Vorstehhund, Drahthaar

PORTRAIT: The sturdy German Drahthaar is exceptional for his rough coat—harsh and wiry, rather flat lying—and grandfather-like facial furnishings (beard and brow). The outline of the dog is muscular and defined and is never obscured by the coat's bushiness. The head is moderately long; the body is a little longer than high; the back is straight; the chest deep and capacious. Height: 24–26 inches (61–66 cm). Weight: 60–70 pounds (27–32 kg). In color the Wirehair is solid liver or any combination of liver and white. Although not accepted in the AKC registry, the breed can also be black and white. Other color possibilities which are frowned on by all registries include solid black and tricolor.

DEVELOPMENT: Recognized in his native Germany in 1870, the Wirehair is a fairly new breed of dog. The demands of European sportsmen ceaselessly implored more diversified gundogs, namely retrieving pointers. The development of the German pointers was an essentially simultaneous concurrence, each developing from the same stock but becoming individualized with the efforts of regional breeders. Compiling the Pointer, Poodle and Foxhound abilities and traits yields this multi-talented Wirehair.

RECOGNITION: FCI, AKC, UKC, KCGB, CKC

CHARACTER: Whether boorish or boar-like, the Wirehair has a personality that is all his own and all to his owner's delight. This is an active breed that needs plenty of exercise. His hunting abilities are keen and he will relish impressing you with his prowess and obedience.

GOLDEN RETRIEVER

PORTRAIT: The best of all possible worlds: symmetry, power, beauty and grace. The Golden Retriever is a beautifully balanced, sound canine of imposing elegance and kindly expression. The body is short coupled and the chest deep. The coat is dense and water repellent with good undercoat. The quality of the coat and the wealth of free-flowing feathering are essential for the Golden. In color the breed is rich, lustrous golden in various shades. Height: 21–24 inches (53–61 cm). Weight: 60–75 pounds (27–34 kg).

DEVELOPMENT: The Golden's ancestors, ancient Caucasus sheepdogs, were the much trusted flock guards for Russian shepherds who entrusted their charges to these slow working enduring dogs. So impressed by a troupe of these dogs in a circus, the persuasive Lord Tweedmouth dryly talked his way into ownership of the performing canines. Transported to Scotland, they became known as Guisachan Retrievers. More recent discoveries, however, take a little sparkle out of the Golden's delicious beginnings. The presently accepted origin doesn't rely on Tweedmouth's fleeting circus fancy nor does it get caught up in the question of what six heavy set, slow working flock guards could possibly muster to regale the likes of a circus tent audience. The Golden was developed through crosses of the Tweed Water Spaniel, a light-weight Newfoundland and other setter crosses.

RECOGNITION: FCI, AKC, UKC, KCGB, CKC, ANKC

CHARACTER: Affectionate and uncommonly good-natured. His retrieving and upland game abilities combined with his flawless disposition and inspiring beauty are indicative of his unparalleled popularity. Despite the breed's enviable obedience trial records, many pet Goldens tend to be fuzzy-minded and should be kept active and free of a monotonous routine.

GORDON SETTER

PORTRAIT: Marked by good size and developed musculature, the Gordon is perhaps the most "meaty" of the setters—his head, rather broad, large and nicely rounded, is the heaviest in the setter group. Sturdy with solid bone, the Gordon is a well-built black and tan bird dog. Height: 23–27 inches (58–69 cm). Weight: 45–80 pounds (20–36 kg). The coat, with its clearly defined mahogany on sleek black, is moderately long and flat. The feathering is long and fine.

DEVELOPMENT: The Gordon Castle in 18th-century Scotland, famed for its fine setting dogs of various colors, became enraptured by stories of a black and tan shepherd bitch with an unusual proclivity to uncover grouse. The fourth Duke of the Castle ascertained these facts and originated the black and tan breed from this Scotch Collie bitch. "Black and fallow" setters were commonplace in Scotland and were esteemed "the hardest to endure labour." In black, white and tan combinations, these Setters occurred. Ticking, as deemed by his grace, was a Gordon *faux pas*. This Scotsman is an excellent bird dog with a fine nose.

RECOGNITION: FCI, AKC, UKC, KCGB, CKC, ANKC

CHARACTER: "A most pettable dog," the Gordon Setter is celebrated both for his loyalty and obedience. A quiet and serene dignity graces this handsome setter, who is a biddable and kind companion.

HERTHA POINTER

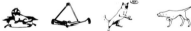

PORTRAIT: The moderately sized Hertha is a solid orange-red dog of typical pointer type. A minimum of white markings may occur on feet, tail, chest and muzzle. This dog is comparable to the Pointer of Great Britain in size, although the Hertha tends to look slightly sleeker. Height: 23–26 inches (58–66 cm). Weight: 45–60 pounds (21–27 kg).

DEVELOPMENT: This is essentially the harmonious result of crossing a stray bitch named "Hertha," who was found by Danish soldiers, and "Sport," a Pointer owned by the Duke Frederik Christian. Hertha was of a standard gundog type, obviously not a Pointer of British breeding. These dogs have bred true ever since 1864 and are continually increasing in numbers in Denmark. The breed's parent association has had no success in achieving official recognition but is not discouraged. Time will tell if Lady Hertha's line will soon achieve the status it deserves.

RECOGNITION: NR

CHARACTER: These are athletic and robust hunters who are praised by their Danish owners for their keen desire to work and undaunted ability to learn. Their hunting instincts are sharp, and they use them to full advantage on the hunt. They are readily adaptable to the home environment, and prefer to sleep indoors.

IRISH RED AND WHITE SETTER

PORTRAIT: The athletic and powerful Red and White is a well-proportioned dog, without lumber. The head is broad with a noticeable stop. As the name indicates, the coat color is a clear particolor—a pure white base with solid patches in red; roaning is not permitted but mottling and flecking are common and pardonable. The coat, slightly coarse, is finely textured with thin feathering. Height: 23–27 inches (58–69 cm). Height: 40–70 pounds (18–32 kg).

DEVELOPMENT: Preferred for years over the solid red Irish Setter, the Red and White is more easily discerned on the field. Naturally the advocates of both breeds claim that their breed is the "proper setter color." Nevertheless, the once-called "Parti-Coloured Setter" actually predates the Irish Red Setter but has never established as firm a fancy. The last original R&W was reported at the Strabane show in 1908, in Ireland. In the 1920s, the breed could be seen with one Rev. Noble Huston of County Down as working field dogs, not exhibition dogs. A different Catholic priest, Rev. Doherty, represented a group that wanted to revive the breed some decades later. Their determination and success brought forth today's breed, which was created from white whelps from the solid Red's breeding, begrudgingly contributed.

RECOGNITION: KCGB

CHARACTER: If not as graceful as the Irish Setter, the Red and White is equally as proficient in field work and as untiring and jubilant in enthusiasm. As a companion, he is friendly and devoted.

IRISH SETTER
Irish Red Setter

PORTRAIT: Unlike his Red and White cousin, the Irish Setter is a racy dog—full of balance and quality—standing well up in front. The striking appearance of the Irish Setter is refined and handsome. The head is long and lean; the muzzle is moderately deep. The body is efficient: the chest deep, the ribs well sprung, the legs muscular. The coat, short and fine on top with long, silky feathering on ears, legs and chest, is rich chestnut or mahogany, with no sign of black. White on chest, forehead, etc., shall not disqualify. Height: 25–27 inches (63–69 cm). Weight: 60–70 pounds (27–32 kg). Feathering as straight and flat as possible.

DEVELOPMENT: The "Modder Rhu," as he was called in Gaelic, or "Red Dog" traces his history back to the 15th century. In Ireland, the Red Setters (or Red Spaniels of the early 19th century) were always integral to the pursuits of Irish sportsmen. Although not the oldest canine known to man, many contend he is the oldest pure breed and the most elegant and athletic of sporting dogs. Still today, the Setter's pace is of utmost importance to field performance. This Red sportsman is built on galloping lines.

RECOGNITION: FCI, AKC, UKC, KCGB, CKC, ANKC

CHARACTER: A trainable hard worker, the Irish Setter is a thorough gentleman and a beguiling canine friend. Tractable and handsome, this is the ideal dog for the weekend hunter or owner seeking a loving, faithful companion with elegant good looks.

IRISH WATER SPANIEL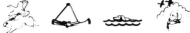

PORTRAIT: A strongly built, upstanding dog that should not appear leggy or tucked. The body is of medium length, pear-shaped at the brisket, and muscular. The head, rather sizable and high in dome with a prominent occiput, peaks in a top knot that consists of long, loose curls that do not bewig it. Height: 21–24 inches (53–61 cm). Weight: 45–65 pounds (21–30 kg). The proper coat is vital: it should be tight with crisp ringlets on the body, neck and slightly down rat-tail; it is longer with loose curls on the legs, and smooth on face and elsewhere. In color he is rich dark liver with a plumish tint peculiar to the breed (sometimes called puce-liver).

DEVELOPMENT: Persian manuscripts dating 4000 BC indicate the presence of "Water Dogs" in Ireland. Legal documents from the Christian era specifically mention "Irish Spaniels"—many believe that these writings (circa 17 AD) are the first references to spaniels in black and white history. Pinpointing the ancestry of the Irish Water Spaniel is quite problematic. The Poodle was probably a Water Spaniel and therefore isn't the progenitor as once believed. The most reliable theory purports that the breed is the result of dogs brought into Ireland through Spain from beyond the Caucasus by the earliest inhabitants of Ireland.

RECOGNITION: FCI, AKC, UKC, KCGB, CKC, ANKC

CHARACTER: Never shy, the Water Spaniel is bold and eager. He is courageous and effective in the field, especially when retrieving waterfowl. Grooming is a necessity but never a tortuous chore.

KOOIKERHONDJE
Kooiker Dog

PORTRAIT: A light and graceful Dutchman, the Kooikerhondje flies a beautiful spaniel-like coat in red and white. The head is proportionate to the body; the stop is defined; the ears are set high. With a slight wave, the Kooiker's coat is moderately long with fringe adorning the legs, ears, chest, and tail. The ears, well feathered, are jeweled by black tips that are referred to as earrings. In size the breed is medium sized and resembles a small setter. Height: 14–16 inches (35–41 cm). Weight: 20–24 pounds (9–11 kg).

DEVELOPMENT: Although believed to have been a common companion of Dutch duck hunters for many years, the Kooiker, as we know him today, is a rather new addition to the gundog group. In 1942, the Baroness v. Hardenbroek van Ammerstool sought specimens to reestablish the Kooiker Dog that had saved Prince William of Orange and that was illustrated by 17th-century Dutch painters. The Baroness was successful in creating the modern-day Kooiker within a few years. In hunting style, the Kooikerhondje is unique. He functions as a decoy, attracting wild ducks into traps with his fringed white tail. The hunters, admirably concerned in natural reserves, net the birds and ring young or endangered specimens.

RECOGNITION: NR

CHARACTER: The Kooiker is an industrious and imaginative sportsman. In intelligence he can be compared to the quickest witted of the gundogs. A companion dog, he can execute any number of household chores.

LABRADOR RETRIEVER

PORTRAIT: A strongly built, very active dog with a broad skull and deep chest. The body is short coupled and muscular. The hind quarters are well developed. One of the breed's distinctive features is its otter tail: very thick towards the base and gradually tapering to the tip, with no feathering. The coat is also distinctive in its weather resistant quality; it is comprised of short dense hair, without wave or feathering. Height: 21½–24½ (54–62 cm). Weight: 55–75 pounds (25–34 kg). Labradors come in three solid colors: black, chocolate/liver, and yellow (from light cream to red fox).

DEVELOPMENT: Carrying salt cod from Newfoundland to Poole Harbour, boats in 1800 transported the Labrador's ancestors to Great Britain. These dogs were sturdy swimmers and probably employed by the fishermen to paddle ropes ashore. One of these small, splashing, otter-tailed canines was spotted by the Earl of Malmesbury who muttered on the spot (to himself) "Labradors." The name was written in a letter and later adopted to refer to the breed. In Greenland, its country of origin (which, to the Earl's dismay, was once called Labrador), these fishermen's dogs were basically taxed out of existence, since their nautical, seafaring owners would not pay a high dog tax. Meanwhile in Britain, the dogs flourished where they were used for field work and water retrieving.

RECOGNITION: FCI, AKC, UKC, KCGB, CKC, ANKC

CHARACTER: A most devoted and intelligent companion, the Labrador is among the most biddable and dependable dogs in the canine world. A very keen working dog that is both sensible and sensitive. Long walks with this eager-to-please samaritan prove rewarding and healthful.

LARGE MÜNSTERLÄNDER
Grosser Münsterländer Vorstehhund

PORTRAIT: The Large Münsterländer possesses a well-balanced conformation suggestive of easy, steady movement and drive. The breed's head is sufficiently broad and slightly rounded; it is solid black with a white snip or star allowed. The coat is long and dense, not curly or coarse. Feathers on ears, front and hind legs and tail. The body is white with black patches, flecked and/or ticked. Height 23–25½ inches (58–65 cm). Weight: 50–70 pounds (23–32 kg).

DEVELOPMENT: In the late 18th-century, Germany's interest in bird dogs brought countless *huenerhunden* into the hands of hunters. The Large Münsterländer, although a German bird dog, has not been around quite that long. Its excellent nose properly indicates the correlation to the Lower Saxon area; its similar conformation to the German Longhaired Pointer and Continental setters suggests that connection as well. The German Pointer fanciers traditionally seem to ignore black-colored progeny—this controversy occurs in the Longhaired and the Wirehaired Pointers. Many insist that the Grosser Münster was once simply the black and white Longhaired Pointer. The breed club was formed in 1919 and hails its dog as an all-purpose hunter, capable of pointing/retrieving and general utility work.

RECOGNITION: FCI, KCGB

CHARACTER: Reliable on both land and water, the breed is equally reckoned as a companion and home guardian. Although not plenteous, this breed is a recognizable and valued hunter in England, Germany and Canada.

MARKIESJE
Hollandse Tulphond

PORTRAIT: This smallish spaniel-type Dutchie is an intelligent and well-balanced multi-purpose dog. The head is medium sized, with a flat skull and a pointed muzzle. The coat is long and silky; feathering is generous on the ears, legs and tail. In color the Markiesje is solid black, with or without white markings. Height: 14 inches (35 cm). Weight: 20–22 pounds (9–10 kg). The expression is undeniably clear and intelligent. The body is finely built with a well-developed chest.

DEVELOPMENT: A new creation of Dutch dog fanciers, the Markiesje has yet to receive FCI recognition. True to its spaniel heritage, the Markiesje works as a gundog and retriever. The dog is also used by various Holland native plant breeders as a guard for the highly prized tulip fields. The dog is delicately footed and most industrious to perform this function with the requisite professionalism and tip-toed elegance. This new Dutch blossom is a hybrid: Miniature Poodle, Continental Toy Spaniel, and possibly a diminutive Brittany were cultivated to bloom the Markiesje.

RECOGNITION: NR

CHARACTER: The breed's charm and intelligence are unmistakable. It is easily trainable and, once taught, never forgets. The breed tends to be independent and can be aloof with strangers, often quiet and reserved.

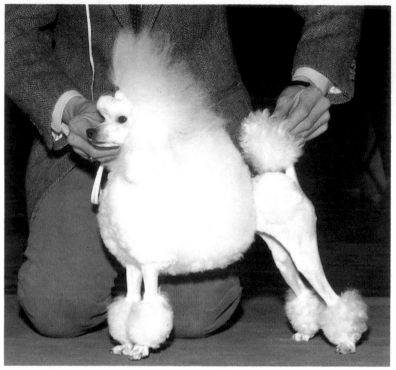

MINIATURE POODLE
Caniche, Barbone

PORTRAIT: The squarely built, well-proportioned Miniature Poodle possesses all the elegance, grace and intelligence of its larger sibling, although in a considerably smaller package. The Poodle coat is profuse, harsh, dense and closely curling. Traditional clipping gives the breed an appearance that is distinctive and prototypical. Standards for the breed describe in detail the four clips that are acceptable. If the curly coat is not clipped properly, it will cord. Poodles must be solid in color: white, black, red, blue. Particolor dogs occur in breeding programs but cannot be registered. Height: 10–15 inches (11–15 cm).

DEVELOPMENT: The development of the Miniature Poodle seems quite obvious. The breed was scaled down from the larger Standard variety for fanciers desiring the same intelligence and abilities in a smaller, more affordable package. They became quite well loved in circuses as trick and stunt dogs and popular in homes. Many years ago, a blending of Maltese blood with the Poodle was used to re-perfect the Mini whites—but this cross was unsatisfactory and has been thoroughly bred out. The Miniature is not to be confused with the even smaller Toy Poodle, which is exclusively a companion dog, too totlike to tote a duck, take to the tides, or till truffle.

RECOGNITION: FCI, AKC, UKC, KCGB, CKC, ANKC

CHARACTER: The Miniature Poodle makes the ideal home companion; his small size and lively disposition make him both easy to keep and easy to enjoy. Grooming and coat care are required but not to the extent that many overboard enthusiasts venture.

NOVA SCOTIA DUCK TOLLING RETRIEVER

PORTRAIT: A well-muscled, medium-sized dog; medium to heavy bone. The coat is water-repellent, double, of medium length. It may have a slight wave on the back but is otherwise straight. In color the Toller is various shades of red and orange, with lighter feathering. The body is deep chested with good spring of rib; the head is clean cut and slightly wedge shaped. Height: 17–21 inches (43–53 cm). Weight 37–51 pounds (17–23 kg).

DEVELOPMENT: Developed to toll (or lure) ducks in the manner of the fox, the Nova Scotia Duck Tolling Retriever is the creation of cunning Canadian hunters. The dog prances and plays on the shore for the deceptive entertainment and subsequent attraction of off-shore ducks. The overly inquisitive ducks bagged by concealed hunters are then retrieved by their canine charmers.

RECOGNITION: FCI, UKC, CKC

CHARACTER: The same charming way this dog has with his game, he demonstrates with his owner. He is industrious and clever and enjoys being with his master. His expression can be perceived as slightly doleful, but once on the hunt he is the happy hunter.

OLD DANISH BIRD DOG
Old Danish Pointer, Gammel Dansk Honsehund

PORTRAIT: For a pointer, the Old Danish is quite small, standing only 22 inches (56 cm) in height. Weight: 40–53 pounds (18–24 kg). The head is rather heavy and broad; the neck is thick-skinned. The coat is short and dense and colored in brown and white, with a small amount of ticking permitted. The dog's appearance is sleek and symmetrically put together. Its height and weight make maneuvering in tall grass entirely do-able.

DEVELOPMENT: The probable contribution of the Spanish Pointer, brought with gypsy travelers into Denmark, to bloodhound types created today's Old Danish Bird Dog. Evidence of bloodhound blood include the breed's heavy neck and superior nose. The Old Danish is often used in *schweisshund* work, that is the locating of wounded deer. Morten Bak is hailed for his contribution to the dog's development.

RECOGNITION: FCI

CHARACTER: Rarely seen outside of Denmark, the Old Danish Pointer is an intelligent and trainable companion and hunter. His coat requires minimal care and he makes a fine watchdog. He is serious in his work and serious in his devotion to his master and household.

PERDIGUERO DE BURGOS
Spanish Pointer, Perdiguero Burgales

PORTRAIT: A giant head atop a brawny, slender body, the Spanish Pointer is an able-bodied hunter that is tough and paradoxically docile. The coat is liver and white, usually with heavy ticking. In length and texture, it is short and fine. Flew and dewlap are evident. Height: 20–24 inches (51–61 cm). Weight: 55–66 pounds (25–30 kg). The muzzle is square, the ears are sizable and the expression is of decisive melancholy.

DEVELOPMENT: Just as gundogs, and particularly pointers, have long existed in other European countries, Spain has profited by these efficient hunters' companions as well. The Perdiguero de Burgos, commonly called the Spanish Pointer, does not feign possession of a pure, ancient lineage and is a fairly new creation in his present form. His ancestors were more heavily built and less elegant. Most likely, the infusion of Pointer blood into the stream helped lighten the strain. Once used on larger game, such as deer, today   used mostly on hare, partridge and smaller game.

RECOGNITION: FCI

CHARACTER: This is an adaptable, likable dog that is obedient and consistent. As a hunter, the Perdiguero is sublime, able to retrieve from water and rough it over mountainous terrain. Hardy yet elegant, he is a fine companion.

PERDIGUERO NAVARRO
Old Spanish Pointer, Navarro Pointer, Pachon de Vitoria

PORTRAIT: With a bony yet sinewy conformation, the Perdiguero Navarro exonerates the ancient pointer body type. In appearance the Navarro lacks refinement: the muzzle is block-like, the stop is abrupt, dewlap and heavy skin hang from the neck while the body's skin remains taut. Like no other breed of extant canine, the Navarro possesses the split or double nose, giving the dog a most unique expression. Height: 20–24 inches (51–61 cm). Weight: 55–66 pounds (25–30 kg). The coat can be short or long. In color the base is white with orange markings or liver/white with ticking.

DEVELOPMENT: More important than uncovering the Navarro's ancestry is realizing how extensively the Old Spanish Pointer contributed to the gene pool of Continental gundogs. Once thought to be lost, this very old breed of dog is fortunate to have an active group of fanciers to revitalize it. The present type is virtually identical to the dog that helped produce the European setters, vorstehhunds and braques of Germany and France.

RECOGNITION: NR

CHARACTER: Not known outside of Spain, this double-nostriled, no-nonsense breed is perceived by non-Spaniards as quite a novelty. Its oddly formed nose was referred to in the histories of other gundogs, but only the Navarro brings this feature to modern-day hunters, whom he delights with his energy and natural abilities.

POINTER
English Pointer

PORTRAIT: The symmetrical and efficient appearance of the Pointer are indicative of the dog's keen abilities on the field. The body is muscular, accentuated by graceful curves and a sleek, economical coat. The head is proportionate, the skull of medium breadth, the stop well defined, the muzzle concave, ending with the nostrils to produce a slightly "dish-faced" appearance. Height: 22–27 inches (56–69 cm). Weight: 42–67 pounds (19–30 kg). The colors are usually lemon and white, orange and white, liver and white, and black and white. Self and tricolors also occur and are accepted.

DEVELOPMENT: Believed to be of Spanish extraction, the Pointer arrived to the hunters of Great Britain in the early 1700s—for what that's worth! The breed was known in both France and Italy before its arrival on the British Isles and had already been refined into a lighter and more graceful dog than the Spanish Pointer, from whom he was derived. With the increasing improvement of firearms came the need for a faster dog. The graceful Continental pointing dog was bred to foxhounds to produce a swifter, stouter dog. Eighteenth-century hunters experienced the Pointer in its hunting prime. An irrepressible desire to hunt, exceptional nose, size and speed combine to form a staunch gundog.

RECOGNITION: FCI, AKC, UKC, KCGB, CKC, ANKC

CHARACTER: Pointers are celebrated for their even and kind dispositions. The breed's bearing is decidedly aristocratic. In intelligence and trainability, owners simultaneously stick their noses way out to point his being second to none.

PORTUGUESE POINTER
Perdigueiro Portugueso

PORTRAIT: The body is well balanced and sturdily boned. The head is broad and the chest is moderate. Built for endurance and tiresome work, the breed is muscular and indefatigable. Height: 20–22 inches (51–56 cm). Weight: 35–60 pounds (16–26 kg). This dog is usually seen sporting a short and smooth coat, which lies tightly on its body revealing his slender muscling; an older type coat also occurs, it is longer haired with feathering on ears, underside and tail. In color the breed is yellow or chestnut, varying in intensities—solid colors as well as Irish patterned whites.

DEVELOPMENT: Like most of Portugal's breeds, the Perdigueiro is derived from Spanish dogs. These dogs were used centuries ago as hawking dogs. Some look on the extinct Podengo de Mastra, a pointing hound, as the ancient prototype. The Podengo's versatility on the field extends to pointing and retrieving abilities.

RECOGNITION: FCI

CHARACTER: The Portuguese Pointer is no run-of-the-mill hunter. He is able to withstand the most severe climates and terrains. Naturally hardy and intensely committed to the hunt, the breed is a joy to hunters and is a popular house pet in native Portugal.

PORTUGUESE WATER DOG
Cão de Agua

PORTRAIT: Robust and well endowed with a strong, compact build, the Portuguese Water Dog sports the conformation of a fine Olympic swimmer: his musculature should be indicative of his constant natation. He is moderately sized, standing from 16–22 inches (40–56 cm). In weight he ranges widely from 35–55 pounds (16–25 kg). The coat is profuse, covering the entire body except on the forelegs and thighs. Two types are distinct: long, loosely waved, with sheen; or short, harsh and dense. Two clips are also common: the lion clip and the working-retriever clip. In color the Portie is white or black or brown, with or without white markings.

DEVELOPMENT: In actuality, the Portuguese Water Dog could be accurately categorized as a herder—a herder of fish! For an unknown length of time, the Portie has been used by Portuguese fishermen to herd fish into nets, retrieve overboard tackle (or escaped codfish), and guard nets and board on shore. His appearance and type suggest similar ancestors to the Irish Water Spaniel and other European water dogs. Sources claim that thousands of years ago the dogs were also used as herders of cattle, sheep and camels on the central Asian steppes. Despite his growing number of show-ring fanciers, the Portie remains a hardy and inspiring water dog.

RECOGNITION: FCI, AKC, UKC, KCGB, CKC

CHARACTER: The breed's jaunty expression and captivating looks have brought many newcomers to investigate the Portuguese Water Dogs. These neophytes invariably find a highly intelligent, courageous and untiring companion and sportsman.

Portuguese Water Dog

PUDELPOINTER
Poodle Pointer

PORTRAIT: Standing plenty of ground, powerful and taut, the Pudel-pointer is a sufficiently tall hunter. The dog stands to 26 inches (66 cm). The coat, of medium length, is dense and hard, rather tight to the body with a fine, woolly undercoat. Chestnut to deadleaf, dark liver to autumn leaf, are the desired colors, but black occurs in dogs with concentrated Pointer blood. The chest is deep and wide, and the loins are strong. The shoulders and upper arms sufficiently angulated for good movement. Weight: 55–70 (25–32 kg).

DEVELOPMENT: Although his appearance doesn't let on so, this robust, macho hunter is half-Poodle, yet no French powderpuff or poof ever gets close to this half-Caniche. As the name has given away, his "better half" is, of course, Pointer. This seemingly unlikely cross took place in the late 1800s, conducted by hunters that wanted a fit gundog with water abilities and supreme intelligence. The Poodles of yesteryear were well equipped with these latter qualities. Because of the great divergence in type between these two breeds, it took a few good decades to establish type definitively, but the result was worth the wait.

RECOGNITION: FCI, CKC

CHARACTER: The Pudelpointer today graces the likes of German and Canadian hunters with endurance, adaptability, and physical and mental swiftness. He is able to hunt fox, big cat and deer. His courage and prowess in the hunt are still a pleasant surprise to his outdoors-loving owners.

RUSSIAN SPANIEL
Russkaja Spaniel

PORTRAIT: The moderately small working spaniel of Russia may stand only 15–17 inches (38–43 cm) high but is no less able bodied and balanced than the larger, more brawny gundogs. The desired coat is silky with good feathering on the ears and loose fringe on the belly and legs. In color the Russian Spaniel is usually white with dark marks (black, brown, liver) occurring on the body and most usually on the head and ears.

DEVELOPMENT: Gundogs in Russia have existed for countless generations. Many Russian dogs of old were said to have resembled European breeds: for instance, the Russian Retriever could have nearly passed for the Golden Retrievers of its day; the Russian Setter for the English Setter. The Russian Spaniel is not nearly so old as these but surely results from similar Continental gundog offspring and the ever-popular English Pointer, the usual speed ingredient. He is multi-faceted in his hunting abilities—able to search out, flush, and retrieve. The duck, quail, corncrake, and sandpiper are among his feathered quarry; the wild goat and hare, his land quarry.

RECOGNITION: NR

CHARACTER: To their Russian owners, these Spaniels are unparalleled in devotion and ability. In addition to providing impressive work on the field, these spaniels make good-natured house pets and reliable alarm dogs.

SMALL MÜNSTERLÄNDER
Kleiner Münsterländer Vorstehhund,
Heidewachtel, Spion

PORTRAIT: Essentially setter-like in appearance, the Small Münsterländer is a tightly skinned, sleekly coated gundog. In coloration he is invariably brown (liver) and white, with variable amounts of ticking. The coat is of moderate length with considerable feathering. Height: 19–22 inches (48–59 cm). Weight: 33 pounds (15 kg). The tightly lying skin prohibits the existence of dewlap.

DEVELOPMENT: A 20th-century creation from old-time Spanish types of spaniels, the Kleiner was developed in Westphalia, Germany, from small gundogs related to the Dutch Partridge Dog and French and Spanish gundogs. The breed was "discovered" by Herr Edmund Loens who recognized its above-average abilities and worked toward the establishment of a parent club in 1912. In Germany, he is called the Spion.

RECOGNITION: FCI

CHARACTER: This is a happy, carefree dog who is equally at home hunting in the woods as he is playing in the back yard. He gets on well with children and has an overall, consistently pleasing disposition. His natural retrieving inclinations are strong but can be used effectively in the home as a slipper- or newspaper-fetcher.

SPINONE ITALIANO

Italian Spinone, Italian Coarsehaired Pointer

PORTRAIT: Squarely built and solid, the Spinone Italiano is possessed of strong bone and firm musculature. The coat, one of the breed's chief traits, is tough, thick and slightly wiry, fitting closely to the body. Eyebrows, moustache and beard comprise the facial furnishings. In color the Spinone is all-white, white with orange, white with chestnut, or either coloration with roan. Height: 24–26 inches (61–66 cm). Weight: 71–82 pounds (32–37 kg).

DEVELOPMENT: There are two worthwhile theories about the Spinone's origin. The first makes the breed a descendant of the Segugio Italiano, an ancient hound from the Middle Ages. The second purports that the breed originates in the Alps of Piedmont from the Barbet, Korthals Griffon and other hound types. The dog's physical and mental abilities afford quite a variation of hunting proclivities. He is adaptable to any kind of shooting and is particularly suited for heavy cover. He is noted for his subtle nose and supple mouth.

RECOGNITION: FCI, AKC, KCGB, CKC

CHARACTER: The breed's expression is surely a direct line to its temperament. The distinguished, well-salted, great-grandfather look indicates that this is a noble, wise and protective canine companion. It can be either reserved or rowdy and playful.

STABYHOUN

PORTRAIT: In black, chocolate, or orange—all with white markings—the Stabyhoun is a well-balanced, well-feathered moderately sized dog. He stands 19–21 inches (48–53 cm) and weighs in from 33–44 pounds (15–20 kg). The coat is somewhat on the long side and sleek; it appears bushy on the tail and breeches. The coat may or may not be ticked or roaned. In bone, he is moderate; the skull is broad, and the jaws are powerful.

DEVELOPMENT: Originating in the Friesland province of Holland, the Stabyhoun probably descends from the larger Dutch gundog, the Patrijshond, combined with other French and German spaniels. In his native Holland, the breed is frequently seen larger than the standard indicates—these dogs are used for draft work. The Dutch breeds were often captured by artists and writers, and many renditions of the local *Hollandse* dogs seemingly have bred true for many centuries.

RECOGNITION: FCI

CHARACTER: With retrieving and pointing abilities to boot, the Stabyhoun is a fine guardian and companion dog. He is affectionate in the home and always even-tempered. Additionally, his sensitive nose makes him an excellent locator (and retriever) of wounded game.

STANDARD POODLE
Caniche, Barbone, Chien Canne

PORTRAIT: The squarely built, well-proportioned Standard Poodle possesses elegance, dignity and intelligence. The Poodle coat is profuse, harsh, dense and closely curling. Traditional clipping gives the breed an appearance that is distinctive and prototypical. Standards for the breed describe in detail the four clips that are acceptable. If the curly coat is not clipped properly, it will cord. Poodles must be solid in color: white, black, red, blue. Particolor dogs occur in breeding programs but cannot be registered. Height: over 15 inches (38 cm). Weight: 45–70 pounds (21–34 kg). The body is muscular and sinewy: the show clip should accenuate this well-developed conformation.

DEVELOPMENT: The Poodle comes to us from ancient France, where it was used as a marvelously skilled duck hunter. The breed was worshiped for its superb nose and uncanny intelligence, together enabling it to continue collecting wounded game in the dark. The Poodle's coat, inordinately profuse, is said to have hindered the dog in its water work. The tradition of clipping the coat (originally shaving from ribs to the stern) stems from this facilitation of the Poodle's work abilities. Scientists attest to the breed's supercanine intelligence: a most capacious cerebral cavity and the fully developed frontal sinuses are indications of the dog's extreme mental capacity. This acumen has been utilized variously by man: a circus dog in carousel apparel, a trained "truffle-untuffler," an informed lace smuggler for Belgian owners, an obedience worker, a hunter of difficult game, a noble and confident companion.

RECOGNITION: FCI, AKC, UKC, KCGB, CKC, ANKC

CHARACTER: It is a noble and confident dog that can still maintain all of its positive attributes while donning such a peculiar "do." Non-poodle people do not understand why the breed's lovers persist in grooming their dogs so perversely. The practice is deeply implanted in tradition and cannot be uprooted. Admittedly, the dogs themselves thrive on attention and are able to shine above all their fellow canines as companions and pets.

SUSSEX SPANIEL

PORTRAIT: Light liver tinged with gold, low stationed and long, the Sussex Spaniel is truly a one-of-a-kind kind of dog. The coat is abundant and flat with a slight wave. Feathering is generous. The color is unique to him alone and golden liver is the only acceptable color. Height: 13–15½ inches (33–38 cm). Weight 40–45 pounds (18–20 kg). The body is solid—the back is long and well developed; the chest is round; and the legs are heavily boned and muscular.

DEVELOPMENT: The Sussex can be truthfully described as a hard-working dog, although today and historically he has been perceived as a companion dog first. The truth is that he is an extraordinary flusher in dense undergrowth, equally able to undo feather or fur. In the early days of the "toy spaniels," owners didn't give up on their working abilities: these "carpet" spaniels *could* hunt, just not all day! This race of spaniels has been peculiar to Sussex County, England, for many generations. Its physical characteristics—the heavy skin, long low-set ears, compact massiveness, and prominent flew—would suggest that the low-stationed hounds were important contributing ancestors of the Sussex.

RECOGNITION: FCI, AKC, KCGB, CKC

CHARACTER: Perhaps the breed's similarities to the Cocker Spaniels or its meandering between working and toy dog explain the breed's moderate popularity. It certainly cannot be attributed to its abilities or personality. He is cheerful and easily trained.

VIZSLA
Hungarian Vizsla, Magyar Vizsla, Hungarian Pointer

PORTRAIT: The lean but muscular Vizsla is a medium-sized dog of power and drive in the field. In color the Vizsla is solid golden rust in different shadings. Height: 22–24 inches (56–61 cm). Weight: 49–62 pounds (22–28 kg). The Vizsla's coat is shorthaired, smooth, dense, and close-lying, without woolly undercoat; the wirehaired Vizsla (Drótszörü Magyar Vizsla), although not accepted in the U.S. or Britain (but accepted in Canada), is coarse and bristly but not very long. Hair on the muzzle and skull is short and coarse but smooth lying, except for the beard and the eyebrows, which are prominent and bushy.

DEVELOPMENT: This slim Hungarian hunting dog thrives in the plain area of the country, an area that is highly agricultural and whose hunters necessitated such a hardy gundog. It is believed that the Vizsla is the same ancient dog that accompanied the Magyars in their invasion of Hungary. Other sources point to similar dogs from the Central European area as falconers and huntsmen during the Middle Ages. Type was preserved, with or without intention, by the early barons and warlords who favored the breed. The Vizsla is a multi-functional dog that is particularly useful on upland game and the retrieving of waterfowl.

RECOGNITION: FCI, AKC, UKC, KCGB, CKC, ANKC

CHARACTER: An impressively intelligent and gentle-mannered dog, the Vizsla is a natural hunter that is most easy to train. As a home companion, he is clean, and his protective nature makes him a reliable home guardian.

WEIMARANER
Weimaraner Vorstehhund

PORTRAIT: The light gray coloration of the Weimaraner is surely the "gray ghost's" hallmark. The eyes, in shades of amber, gray or blue-gray, complement the ghost's unique appearance. The coat can be shorthaired or longhaired. The smooth coat is short, fine and hard; the long coat is about 1–2 inches (3–6 cm) in length and fringed like a setter's coat. Height: 23–28 inches (58–66 cm). Weight: 70–85 pounds (32–38 kg). The dog is essentially medium sized. The back is moderate in length; the forelegs straight and strong; the tail is docked.

DEVELOPMENT: The history of the gray ghost is an unsolved mystery. Although he was conjured by 19th-century German hunters, the potion has remained shrouded. The Weimar Pointer, as he was originally christened, probably comes out of European brackes and schweisshunds—the Spanish Pointer often receives a majority vote. A cross to the *huenerhunden* (bird dogs) improved the dog's wing ability. The dog's silver-gray color is unique in the dog world and no explanation really   solves the true mystery of the gray ghost. The longhaired Weimaraner is not accepted in the U.S. but enjoys recognition in Europe.

RECOGNITION: FCI, AKC, UKC, KCGB, CKC, ANKC

CHARACTER: A loving family dog of unstinting devotion to his household members, the Weimaraner is also a competent hunter of small game and a skilled tracker of large game. He is adaptable and highly trainable.

WELSH SPRINGER SPANIEL

PORTRAIT: Built for endurance, the Welsh Springer is symmetrical and compact. The head is slightly domed, with a clearly defined stop. The pear-shaped ears are moderately long and hang close to the cheeks. The body is of proportionate length—strong and muscular. The coat is straight and flat, with a silky texture. It is not wiry or wavy. In color the Welsh dog must be white with rich red markings. Height: 18–19 inches (46–48 cm). Weight: 35–45 pounds (16–20 kg). The tail is well set on low and carried above level of back. It is customarily docked.

DEVELOPMENT: " . . . the Spanniells whose skynnes are white, and if they are marcked with any spottes, they are commonly red. . . " Dr. Caius's volume, *English Dogges*, of 1570 gives us some evidence that the Springer of Wales has been known in a compatible form for many centuries. From what scanty (and admittedly vague) details we can cull from historical references and artistic renderings, we can surmise that these little Springers (sometimes called Starters) sprung up all over the United Kingdom, not just Wales. We cannot be certain that the dogs were always used as gundogs but do know that they were also used for shepherding and cattle droving. It can also be surmised that crosses were conducted between the Springer and the Welsh Sheepdog and Corgi. Before acceptance into The Kennel Club in 1902, they were exhibited as "Welsh Cockers."

RECOGNITION: FCI, AKC, UKC, KCGB, CKC, ANKC

CHARACTER: With kind and careful handling, these dogs can be tireless and efficient hunters. They are high-spirited and good-natured companions that resent inappropriate harsh treatment, expecting their delightful, polite manners to be reciprocated by their human master.

WETTERHOUN
Otterhoun, Dutch Spaniel

PORTRAIT: This rugged and soundly built working water dog is an unsinkably capable canine. Its appearance should suggest endurance and wearability. The coat is thick, with tight curls covering the body (except the head and legs, which are smooth). The head is strong and sizable; the body is broad and deep, standing stoutly and square on four legs. In color the Wetterhoun can be liver or black or a combination of either with white—with or without ticking or roaning. Height: 21–23 inches (53–59 cm). Weight: 33–44 pounds (15–20 kg). It is not all together a super large dog but, judging from its abilities, is unbeatable for its size.

DEVELOPMENT: The developed dog of the Frisian people, the Wetterhoun (literally water dog) was a pursuer of otters—locating and killing them. Today such hunting is less common and its focus has been changed to small land game, which the dog flushes closely. He usually hunts singly and hunters attest that he is fearless enough to go face to face with a polecat. The Frisian dog most likely descended from the Old Water Dog, a breed that contributed to a number of modern-day spaniel types but is now extinct.

RECOGNITION: FCI

CHARACTER: This is an all-purpose, all-weather dog that is a popular canine companion and farmhand in its native Holland. When properly trained, this is a highly biddable guard dog with a strong will and a sometimes coarse temperament.

WIREHAIRED POINTING GRIFFON
Korthals Griffon, Wirehaired Continental Pointer

PORTRAIT: A strongly limbed, medium-sized dog that is rather low on the leg. His coat is coarse and harsh—the standard compares the coat to "the bristles on a wild boar," a helpful analogy if you've ever had the opportunity to pet a wild boar. Height: 22–24 inches (56–61 cm). Weight: 50–60 pounds (23–27 kg). The head is long and covered with harsh hair that forms the beard and moustache. The tail, generally cut to one-third its length, is carried straight. The overall appearance is of an unkempt, rugged workman with a Yale education.

DEVELOPMENT: The Korthals of France had to be a truly diversified hunter—"Pointing" in its English name scarcely grazes the surface. The Griffon d'arret á poil dur had to point and retrieve partridge and small game, beat hedgerow and brush, chase the wily ducks; it pursued roebuck, fox, and cat and functioned as a vermin-ridder. The Griffon breed in 1860s France needed regeneration if it were to survive. One Eduard Karel Korthals of Amsterdam gathered seven specimens and began a zesty breed program that achieved high success and public attention. Korthal advanced selection and training and never crossed in a non-Korthal dog for the sake of improvement. The Korthals were as fast and enduring as the finest bred English Pointer.

RECOGNITION: FCI, AKC, CKC

CHARACTER: The breed's smarts and physical abilities make it a remarkable hunting companion and home guardian. The Korthal's history of working alone makes it an independent and decisive canine with the intelligence and skills to back up its confidence and determination.

Basset Hound.

SCENTHOUNDS

ALPINE DACHSBRACKE
Alpenlandischer Dachsbracke

PORTRAIT: A hardy, solidly built hound with short but not contorted legs. The head is broad and of moderate size. The breed is most commonly seen in stag red, although black/tan and red with black ticking are also typical. The coat is described in the standard as dense and coarse but not wire. White on the body is undesirable; chocolate, black or gray-blue disqualifies. Height: 13–17 inches (33–43 cm). Weight: 33–40 pounds (15–18 kg).

DEVELOPMENT: For the purpose of pursuing deer, rabbit and fox, Austria, like its European neighbors, needed a larger dachsbracke, with the requisite robustness and drive to withstand the high-altitude Alps. The Alpine Dachsbracke's hunting method is coldnosed and its bag of quarry overflows as a rule. This many faceted, multi-utility dog is pure Austrian, developed strictly from indigenous dachsbrackes.

RECOGNITION: FCI

CHARACTER: A working dog personality well befits this versatile little gentleman. Never popular as a pet, the Alpine boasts an impressive following of hunters and gamesmen in the areas that he is popular. Knowing well the task he was bred to do, this hound is an easykeeper for his master. Quick-thinking and industrious describe him aptly.

AMERICAN BLUE GASCON HOUND
Big n' Blue

PORTRAIT: An extremely large, big-voiced, houndy hound, the Big n' Blue stands up to 32 inches (81 cm) in height and weighs up to 110 pounds (50 kg). The breed is heavily ticked; the roaning and ticking over its usually well-speckled white coat give the impression of a grizzled appearance. Color, though important to the appearance, doesn't much affect this hunter's performance.

DEVELOPMENT: The Gascony-type hounds of France—very large, well-voiced, and cold-nosed—acquired countless hunters as fans. These hunters, who favored the blue-ticked hounds of the Old Line strain, broke away to promote the Big n' Blue. "Bluetick Bill" Harshman receives credit for giving the breed its nickname. Its cold-nosed excellence was focused on game from fox to mountain lion and every ill-fated creature in between.

RECOGNITION: NR

CHARACTER: By no means is the American Blue Gascon for everyone, or even for every hunter. He is a very able hound and possesses specialized skill. His hunting desire cannot (and should not) be curbed. With people, he is audacious; with his friends, he is outwardly familiar; with strangers, he remains aloof.

AMERICAN FOXHOUND

PORTRAIT: This long-eared hound is sufficiently tall and lightly boned for a hound. The head is fairly long; the ears are of no moderate length; the eyes large and set well apart. The shoulders are sloping, clean and muscular. The medium-length coat is close and hard and comes in any color. The tricolor combination is believed to be the most popular and is frequently seen in the show ring. Height: 21–25 inches (53–64 cm).

DEVELOPMENT: In 1650, Robert Brooke transported a pack of working hounds to the Crown colony. These hounds remained in the Brooke family for three centuries. English hounds, imported by the Gloucester Foxhunting Club, along with hounds from France and Kerry Beagle-type hounds from Ireland form the basis of the American Foxhound. This hot-nosed American hound has both speed and endurance and, true to its namesake, hunts fox well.

RECOGNITION: FCI, AKC, CKC

CHARACTER: Independent and willful, the American Foxhounds excel in pack hunting and yet maintain their individual personalities. Their cheerful tail-wagging way can also be competition-oriented. As these dogs get older, they oftimes tend to be less attentive to their master's requests (or demands).

ANGLO-FRANCAIS, DE MOYENNE VENERIE
Middle-sized French-English Hound, Anglo-Francais Tricolor

PORTRAIT: A tidy size, not too big and not too small, makes this 20-inch (51-cm) hound efficient and ideal. Weight: 49–55 pounds (22–25 kg). In appearance, the Middle-sized French-English Hound is the spitting image of his larger *confrere*, being only a tad shorter. The head is moderate in comparison to the body; the ears are pendulous and appear to spring from the head. The breed comes in three color varieties: black and white, tricolor, and orange and white. Its coat is typically hound: short and sleek.

DEVELOPMENT: This English-French hound enjoys a clean-cut derivation: crossing the Harrier with the Poitevin and Porcelaine. The result of this cross was a moderately sized hound that thrives on pack work and is potentially unstoppable on a myriad of hopping, crawling, and flying game. As is the case with all three sizes of the Anglos-Francaises, a wirehaired version once existed. These dogs have effectively disappeared as interest waned.

RECOGNITION: FCI

CHARACTER: With dark eyes and melodious voice, this Anglo-Francais is sensible and indefatigable. As a pet, he is a pleasant and easygoing companion.

ANGLO-FRANCAIS, DE PETITE VENERIE
Small French-English Hound, Petit Anglo-Francais

PORTRAIT: The most compact of the Anglo-Francaises, the Petit is conveniently sized between the French and English hounds. The breed has a short, smooth coat; an occasional wire coat may still occur. Height: 16–18 inches (40–46 cm). Weight: 35–44 pounds (16–20 kg). Three color varieties: black and white, orange and white, and tricolor. The Petit is the most graceful in appearance of the Anglos-Francaises. The body is muscular and efficiently constructed; the head is small in comparison to the body and the ears are medium in size.

DEVELOPMENT: Developed for work on smaller game, the Petit Anglo-Francais is a direct cross between the Beagle and a few smaller French hounds. On tracks and in packs, the Petits are superb on rabbit, quail, and pheasant. This dog is considered the "least pure" of the French-English Hounds and is probably the youngest as well as the smallest. Type is essentially set, but many an overly cautious Frenchman still labels him a hound-in-progress.

RECOGNITION: FCI

CHARACTER: Perhaps more reserved than his larger brothers, this hound is a calm and tidy home companion. He loves to work, however, and doubles well as a hunter and a pet. Of the three sizes of Anglos-Francaises, the Petit adapts the most readily to life indoors. He has made this transition to house companion more gracefully than either of his big brothers.

ARIEGEOIS

PORTRAIT: Perhaps the pinnacle of elegance in the French hound family, the Ariégeois is a finely built and mostly slender dog. He is rather small, standing 22–24 inches (56–61 cm) tall and weighing about 66 pounds (30 kg). His short coat is tricolored: black patches with a few scattered tan markings (mostly on the head) mottling a white background. The Ariégeois's head is surely the key to the breed's elegance: it sports a soft, intelligent expression. The ears are long, easily extending past the muzzle when outstretched.

DEVELOPMENT: Not feigning an ancient origin, the Ariégeois emerged in 1912 from three French medium–small-sized hounds. Those used were the Bleu de Gascogne, the Gascon-Saintongeois, and the Chien d'Artois. In southern France, he is sometimes referred to as the Bastard Hound, but he is hardy enough that even sticks and stones don't hurt him. His acumen in pack hunting over most any terrain cannot be denied.

RECOGNITION: FCI

CHARACTER: An affectionate and reticent companion, this hound doesn't abuse or showoff his sonorous voice in the home. Although originally developed for hunting small game, the Ariégeois adapts to family living. His medium size makes him an easy-to-live-with, easy-to-step-over kind of canine.

AUSTRIAN BRANDLBRACKE
Austrian Smoothhaired Hound, Austrian Hound, Carinthian Brandlbracke

PORTRAIT: With flat pendant ears, a deep chest and a thick coat, the Austrian Hound stands from 18–23 inches (46–59 cm) and weighs in at up to 50 pounds (23 kg). This hound possesses surprising strength, despite its loosely limbed body. In color the breed is unexceptionally black and tan with white markings tolerated.

DEVELOPMENT: Probably a spin-off of the black and tan hounds popular throughout Europe and France in times past, the Brandlbracke brings to 20th-century hunters an acute sense of smell and the ability to track a large variety of game. In trailing, the breed is silent and marvelously effective. At home, the breed goes by two rather long, rather "brickety-bracke-like" names: Österreichischer Glatthaariger Bracke and Österreichischer Bracke-Brandlbracke.

RECOGNITION: FCI

CHARACTER: Although not known outside his native Austria, the Brandl-bracke is prized by hunters who desire an efficient and industrious sports-man. Although a hunter full of vim and activity, he possesses a quiet and placid disposition in the home.

J R Quinn

BALKAN HOUND
Balkanski Gonič

PORTRAIT: The flat-headed Balkan Hound is black and tan saddled or red with the same black saddle, with black marks over his eyes. The head is sloping, and the muzzle is pointed. Invariably, the Balkan Hound is muscular, particularly in the shoulders and limbs. Height: 17–21 inches (43–53 cm). Weight: 44 pounds (20 kg). The coat is coarse and pliant.

DEVELOPMENT: Believed by most a descendant of hounds left by the Phoenicians, the Balkan serves Yugoslavian hunters with diligence and accuracy. Selective breeding by these hunters, who hunted equally for sport and necessity, perfected and perpetuated the Balkan type. Today the Balkan is a favorite pack-hound choice of many regional Yugoslavian hunters, who perceive hunting as more than a weekend pastime.

RECOGNITION: FCI

CHARACTER: This Yugoslavian hound is pleasant natured and obedient. In his homeland, he spends much time with the hunter. If not focused, this dog's energy spreads towards tenacity and unruliness. Generally though, he is serene and content.

BASSET ARTESIAN NORMAND
Artesian Norman Basset

PORTRAIT: A short, straight-legged hound. Cone-shaped ears, in generous proportion, give the head a noble and aesthetic appearance. Its short coat is either tricolor or bicolor (orange and white). Height: 10–14 inches (25–36 cm). Weight: 33 pounds (15 kg). The muzzle is long, refined, and arched. Smooth muscles and a moderate amount of wrinkles and dewlap are appropriate.

DEVELOPMENT: In order to work in unruly terrain, brush and briar, the Artésian Basset needed straight legs that would neither hinder his speed nor drain his energy. These strong-bodied dogs, though considered handsome by their owners, were developed strictly for utility. Short-legged hounds always seem to have been there for the French hunter.

RECOGNITION: FCI

CHARACTER: Although brave and determined in the hunt, the Artésian is gentle with children and makes a fine, trustworthy pet. Obliging and obedient, he is valued as a companion. Many French owners embrace this dwarfish hunter and welcome him into their home as a wholly deserving member of their family.

BASSET BLEU DE GASCOGNE
Blue Gascony Basset

PORTRAIT: A big hound in a small package, this melodiously voiced basset boasts a unique coat. Considered a tricolor—mostly white, with tan on parts of head and black spots on head and body—this coat is heavily roaned, creating a blue effect. Height: 12–14 inches (30–36 cm). Weight: 35–40 pounds (16–18 kg). The head is strong, and the topskull and muzzle are well formed. The body is sufficiently muscled and compact. With plenty of ear leather and a good nose, the Basset Bleu is a true basset.

DEVELOPMENT: Like its other small Bleu brothers, this hound was bred down from the Grand Bleu de Gascogne. Pack hunting in France was quite the rave in the early 17th century, and the French couldn't have enough variations on this glorious theme. The Basset Bleu is one such variation that pursues hare and smaller quarry. The Basset Bleu delightfully maintains much of its larger siblings' ability on the hunt; his size is hardly a hindrance but gives him stupendous ability to maneuver in heavy thicket. Set low to the ground, he is the "short-legged version," not the "small version" of the Grand Bleu; his heart, strength and enthusiasm make him a giant among the low-set hunters.

RECOGNITION: FCI

CHARACTER: The breed's diminutive size and delight in the hunt make him the choice of countless rabbit-bagging Frenchmen. His good-natured and charming demeanor make him a welcome housemate.

BASSET FAUVE DE BRETAGNE

PORTRAIT: Sporting a coarse, hard coat of varying shades from fawn to golden wheat, this dwarfed but sturdy hound stands about 14 inches (35–36 cm) high and can weigh from 36–40 pounds (16–18 kg). Its elongated head is outlined by medium-length ears and rests on a short muscular neck. The chest is wide and deep; the sternum prominent; the ribs are slightly barrelled. The tail, set on high, is thick at the base and tapers to a point. Color variations include red-wheaten and fawn. The coat is never long or woolly.

DEVELOPMENT: To achieve the desired shorter legged and coarse-coated hound, enthusiasts crossed the Grand Griffon Fauve de Bretagne and the Basset Griffon Vendeen. The breed's stubby, somewhat crooked legs have warranted extensive usage as a hunter in briars and heaths. In addition to its French homeland, the breed is becoming popular in Great Britain, where it is also recognized by the KCGB.

RECOGNITION: FCI, KCGB

CHARACTER: With vigor and stout-heartedness, the Basset Fauve revels in the hunt; however, his affectionate and personable demeanor has earned him a continually expanding group of fanciers. In Britain, the breed has gained the active, admiring following that it deserves.

BASSET HOUND

PORTRAIT: Distinct wrinkles adorn a large, well-proportioned head; the breed's expression is aristocratic and intelligent. Relative to size, this is the most heavily boned dog in dogdom, standing 14 inches (35–36 cm) or less and weighing 40–60 pounds (18–27 kg). The coat is short and smooth, lying close without being too fine. In color the Basset Hound is typically black, white and tan (tricolor) or lemon and white (bicolor), but any hound color is accepted. Its undocked tail is carried gaily.

DEVELOPMENT: This "crook-kneed" hound boasts a long and celebrated history, tracing back to medieval monks. The breed is directly related to the French bassets. British nobility, like French royalty, favored the short-legged hounds. The British Basset Hound branched off from the original bassets as French importation ceased. If given the choice, the Basset will trail deer, but he can be used on a variety of game, including rabbit, pheasant, and even raccoon. Basset Hounds are hunted in packs; they are slow but irrefutably effective.

RECOGNITION: FCI, AKC, UKC, KCGB, CKC, ANKC

CHARACTER: A popular home companion and hunter in both England and America, the Basset Hound is most often brotherly and warm-hearted. Such attributes are attestable to the pack existence, explaining why these hounds often make great pets. Despite their charm and classic appearance, Bassets can be stubborn and lazy, so proper discipline and regular exercise are imperative.

BAVARIAN MOUNTAIN HOUND
Bayrischer Gebirgsschweisshund, Bavarian Schweisshund

PORTRAIT: This bloodhound is shorter and lighter than others. Although standing only 20 inches (51 cm) high, he has the endurance and persistence of a much larger hunter. And although he is comparatively light for a bloodhound, he is in possession of an impressive musculature. Weight: 55–77 pounds (25–35 kg). Black-masked fawn to red and brindle are two color possibilities for his glossy, short, thick coat.

DEVELOPMENT: Various crosses of Bavarian hounds brought forth the Bavarian Mountain Hound. Popular conjecture contends that the Hanoverian Hound and Tyroler Hound are the most probable forebears. Tracking in the mountainous regions of Bavaria requires the most agile and coldtrailing ability. This schweisshund (or simply bloodhound) fulfills this need with a vengeance. He is dear on deer but can trail other game besides his favorite antlered specialty.

RECOGNITION: FCI

CHARACTER: The Bavarian Mountain Hound bonds closely to master and owner. This trait alone cannot warrant its popularization as a pet: the Bavarian is a specialist who must be worked consistently for maximum utilization of talents. Not for the part-time or weekend sportsman, the Bavarian is chiefly employed by foresters and game wardens.

BEAGLE
English Beagle

PORTRAIT: One of the world's most recognizable hounds and dogs, the Beagle is essentially a small foxhound, solid and "big for his inches." His inches can be under 13 (33 cm) or 13–15 (33–38 cm)—two varieties. Any true hound color is allowed; the coat is close, hard and of medium length. Weight: 18–30 pounds (8–13½ kg). The Beagle is sturdy and compact, conveying high quality with no hint of coarseness.

DEVELOPMENT: The Beagle may have been begotten from Celtic hounds crossed with smaller French and British hounds. For centuries in England, Beagles or Beagle prototypes are reported to have been hunted in packs by royalty. When present-day type was firmly established is pure conjecture. Beagles arrived in the U.S. during colonial times and have excelled in hunting quail, hare, and pheasant in America as they did (and do) in Europe.

RECOGNITION: FCI, AKC, UKC, KCGB, CKC, ANKC

CHARACTER: Beagles are happy dogs: happy to be hunting, happy to be home, happy to be with their people. This disposition explains only a part of the breed's tremendous popularity. Longevity, good looks, and intelligence are also notable pluses. Over-vocalization and a trace of stubbornness are cited by some owners as potential concerns.

BEAGLE HARRIER

PORTRAIT: Heavily boned, sturdy, and stocky is this breed. In size the Beagle Harrier stands between 15–19 inches (38–48 cm), conveniently filling the gap between its two closest foxhound relatives. Weight: 44 pounds (20 kg). The typical hound coat, short, smooth, and thick, can be any color under the hound's sun. Although no importance is placed on color, a tan-dominated tri is common. Its V-shaped ears are set high and goodly sized, though not large.

DEVELOPMENT: No conjecture needs to be conjured in the Beagle Harrier's origin. Baron Gerard crossed a Beagle with a Harrier to acquire a foxhound of the two breeds' average height. Interestingly, the two breeds which comprise the Beagle Harrier's make-up were once considered one and the same breed. In thus crossing them, Gerard unknowingly completed the circle. This mid-sized breed is best on deer and hare.

RECOGNITION: FCI

CHARACTER: A rare but delightful appearance at rare breed dog shows, the Beagle Harrier is more frequently seen in small packs in France. His abilities are surely top-notch; his temperament is lively and pleasant.

BERNER LAUFHUND
Bernese Hound

PORTRAIT: The Berner Laufhund and the Berner Neiderlaufhund comprise the two types of Bernese Hounds; the latter is also called the Small Bernese Hound. Both breeds possess a soft undercoat covered by a dense, hard outer coat in black and white (with prescribed tan markings), often considered a tricolor. Ticking or roaning is minimal. The taller stands from 18–23 inches (46–59 cm) and weighs 34–44 pounds (15½–20 kg); the smaller stands 13–17 inches (33–43 cm) and weighs 30–40 pounds (13½–18 kg). Both breeds possess elongated body trunks, a lean head and a strong muzzle. The Neider is more compact and short-legged compared to the well-boned yet lighter body of the Laufhund. The Neider is the only Swiss hound that can be seen in a wire coat.

DEVELOPMENT: The scenthounds of Switzerland are all very similar, barring colors and sizes. These hounds are believed to have been used by hunters for at least 900 years. Named for the Alps in which they are apt to hunt, the Bernese excels on roe deer, stag and a variety of other game.

RECOGNITION: FCI

CHARACTER: Subdued and calm when not hunting, these hounds are not recommended as just pets or home guardians. To be happy and healthy, these tireless laufhunds must hunt to gratify their constant desire to hunt. When "off-season," plenty of exercise must top the daily agenda. Owners find them diligent and responsive.

BILLY

PORTRAIT: This elegant, handsome Frenchman is distinguished by his lemon/orange spotted white sports jacket; the coat is short and smooth. His expression denotes intelligence and alacrity. Height: 23–26 inches (58–66 cm). Weight: 55–66 pounds (25–30 kg). The Billy has a lean head and slightly curled flat ears. A light, well-placed trumpet quality marks his vocal timbre, which is capable of great variation in volume and intensity.

DEVELOPMENT: This beautifully conceived 19th-century creation combined three now extinct French hunters: the Céris, Montaimboeuf, and Larrye. Respectively, these pack hounds contributed small size and orange spots, fortitude and speed, and a superlative nose. M.G. Hublot du Rivault's described recipe brought forth the Billy. He is a pack hunter, like his forebears, and is superior on deer.

RECOGNITION: FCI

CHARACTER: Industrious and cunning, as his expression reveals, the Billy is a passionate professional in the hunt, but never a hero. As a pet, the Billy is obedient to its master but is reportedly contentious with pack mates. His short coat needs little grooming but is meager protection from cold weather and thorny brush.

SCENTHOUNDS

BLACK AND TAN COONHOUND
American Black and Tan Coonhound

PORTRAIT: Solid carriage: a muscular and well-proportioned body structure. The graceful droop of loosely fitting skin and extensive ear leather give the Black and Tan a distinctive quality. Height: 23–27 inches (58–69 cm). Weight: 55–75 pounds (25–34 kg). As the breed name subtly discloses, this dog is coal black with rich tan markings. The coat is dense and short. Fundamentally a working dog, this hound should not appear racy or thin, as have many show-ring specimens (and winners!); rather, he should be strong, sturdy and powerful.

DEVELOPMENT: The roster of the Black and Tan's forebears is surely impressive: the 11th-century Talbot Hound, the Kerry Beagle of Ireland, the Foxhound, the Bloodhound, and the American Virginia Foxhound. Selectively bred for his famous coat color, the Black and Tan is cold-nosed and methodical in the hunt. He was crafted on American soil for the task of treeing coon and opossum.

RECOGNITION: FCI, AKC, UKC, CKC

CHARACTER: A quick-to-follow, bright, loyal and good-natured hunter and companion, the Black and Tan pleases hunter and owner alike. Although he can be assertive, this is an obedient, watchful dog. Owners must be wary of grooming and exercise requirements. In order to keep the ears clean and infection-free, regular attention is a must.

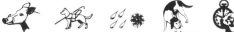

BLACK FOREST HOUND
Slovensky Kopov, Slovakian Hound

PORTRAIT: A sleek-looking though wirehaired hound in a black/tan coat pattern. The coat can be 2 inches (5 cm) in length but remains close to the body. Structurally the body is somewhat elongated and lightly boned but sufficiently strong. Height: 18–20 inches (46–51 cm). Weight: 44–49 pounds (20–22 kg).

DEVELOPMENT: The oldest and only indigenous scenthound of Czechoslovakia, the Black Forest Hound is still used today on wild boar. He is a tracker par excellence. His similarities to the Polish Hound make his close relationship with that breed seem probable. Other sources speculate that the Balkan Hound and the Transylvanian Hound crossed with the Czesky Fousek or similar gundogs yielded this popular hound.

RECOGNITION: FCI

CHARACTER: The Black Forest Hound is an obedient and inspired hunter who doubles well as a pet and guard dog. His genuine intelligence makes him a widely used hunter and popular companion. He is even beginning to make a mark on the show dog world. Owners advise sufficient early training to acclimate the dog to his purpose, be it hunting, guard work, police duty or other.

BLACK MOUTH CUR
Southern Cur, Yellow Black Mouth Cur

PORTRAIT: This brawny and rugged Southern gentleman is capably structured and unquestionably sturdy. Height: 16–25 inches (40–64 cm). Weight: 45–95 pounds (20–43 kg). The short coat comes in a variety of shades of yellows and fawns. The irrefutably powerful muzzle is black, giving this cur his name. The tail is left natural and can be quite lengthy. This dog's chest is deep and solid.

DEVELOPMENT: The southern United States is well populated with cur-type dogs that are used by local hunters and sportsmen. Boar, bear, coon, and deer are among the Black Mouth's quarry. With medium-sized game, the Black Mouth catches and kills it (no questions asked). It is also proficient at treeing and baying.

RECOGNITION: NR

CHARACTER: For the people who hunt, no other dog will do. These are workmen's dogs. Male dogs are particularly manly, preferring the ladies for company and being especially protective of children. Loyalty and fearlessness are the norm. As with other hunting breeds, exercise is essential.

BLOODHOUND
St. Hubert Hound, Chien de St. Hubert

PORTRAIT: The largest and most powerful of the hounds, the Bloodhound can weigh up to 110 pounds (50 kg) and stand as high as 27 inches (69 cm). The head is among the breed's most impressive features, perhaps the most beautiful in all dogdom. Wrinkles, dewlap and excessive skin adorn a noble head that epitomizes character, indelibly. The coat, thick, hard and short, can be black/tan, tawny, or red/tan. The Bloodhound's eyes are neither sunken nor prominent. Big boned sound legs "stand over more ground than usual." The ears hang low and are enormous.

DEVELOPMENT: This distinctive hound descends from the hounds kept by St. Hubert in the 1200s. Hubert's hounds were black/tan or white, and these dogs were fostered by his fellow monks after his death. Used exclusively for hunting, these slow, deliberate hounds form the stock of today's Bloodhound. In the 19th century, the breed was used on deer in addition to its usual game of wolf and big cats. The breed's nose is so exquisite that it has been frequently used for tracking criminals and sheep swipers. Evidence found by a Bloodhound stands up in court.

RECOGNITION: FCI, AKC, UKC, KCGB, CKC, ANKC

CHARACTER: Despite its formidable strength and persistence, this is not a killer. One of the friendliest of dogs is more likely to greet a tracked criminal with a muddy paw and a slobbery kiss. Its even disposition is as solemn as the deep-mouthed notes on a cathedral organ, which incidentally aptly describes its glorious voice. A personality sometimes arrogant but reconcilably courteous, this miraculous canine is not recommended for uncouths.

BLUETICK COONHOUND

PORTRAIT: Speckled in blue, this tricolor coonhound boasts a wonderfully unique, shiny, medium-length coat. Its heavy ticking is actually composed of black-colored hairs on a white background, creating a bluing effect. This is a middle-sized, rather racy hound with longish, lightly boned legs. Height: 20–27 inches (51–69 cm). Weight: 45–80 pounds (20–36 kg).

DEVELOPMENT: Capital scenthounds from the famed cities of France were continually imported into America. These Gascony-type hounds were crossed with working dogs in the Louisiana area (foxhounds and curs alike) and afforded us the Bluetick Coonhound. This versatile hunter can be used to tree raccoon or track fox or even cougar. Now hailed as a native American, the Bluetick displays what appears to be a streak of Indian warpaint between its eyes, a sure indicator of this dog's fearless and warrior-like approach to the hunt.

RECOGNITION: UKC

CHARACTER: A competitive and arduous sportsman, the Bluetick is the choice of many American hunters. It does remarkably well indoors and promises a fine companion and guardian to the family it loves. The breed's devotion to its family is only rivaled by its fervor on the field.

BOSNIAN ROUGHHAIRED HOUND
Bosnian Hound, Bosanski Barak

PORTRAIT: This tousy wirehaired hound sports a long (4 inch/10 cm) coat of a stubbly texture, covering a thick undercoat. This is the classic wire coat, complete with beard and mustache. Height: 18–22 inches (46–56 cm). Weight: 35–53 pounds (16–24 kg). Shades of gray, yellow, tricolors and bicolors are acceptable for colors.

DEVELOPMENT: This dog's ingenuity and adaptability in the hunt can be attributed to his diverse background. Not purely a scenthound, the Bosnian may indeed have a touch of sighthound or pariah in his blood. Hunters of the 19th century strove for a dog with keen hunting abilities and a wire coat to withstand foul weather and difficult terrain. Boar, fox and hare are among his quarry.

RECOGNITION: FCI

CHARACTER: The breed's versatility in the field crosses over to its personality as well. This is a good-natured, insouciant companion who enjoys home life as well as work. Some owners warn against letting the dog go idle too long. His industriousness can manifest itself in his rearranging the garage or flower garden.

BRUNO JURA LAUFHUND
Jura Hound, Bruno de Jura

PORTRAIT: Ambling close to the ground, the Jura Hound is an elongated, robust little mountain dweller. He stands from 17–23 inches (43–59 cm) high and weighs from 33–44 pounds (15–20 kg). His short coat is most commonly seen in a classic black/tan or saddled pattern, but it can also occur in solid bronze, yellow or red. He is not as heavily boned or exaggerated as his relative the St. Hubert variety. The breed's expression is peaceful and seductively good-natured.

DEVELOPMENT: The walking dogs of Switzerland that developed in the Jura area are very similar to the French hounds. Their coats, many occurring originally in smooths and wires, are free of white markings. The Bruno Jura Laufhund's oversized ears and skull size point to the St. Hubert-type hounds common in Belgium. For its reputation as a finder of game and hunter of unstinting energy, the breed's Swiss masters yodel extollingly for hours.

RECOGNITION: FCI

CHARACTER: Although this hound is a persistent and dedicated hunter, his personable, lovable way makes him highly desirable as a home companion. He is a pleasure to have in one's abode and abides by the house rules with minimal instruction.

CHIEN D'ARTOIS
Briquet

PORTRAIT: An efficiently bodied and fine-proportioned little hound with a broad skull, dark eyes, and a merry tail. The Briquet has a smooth dense coat comprised of fine hairs. The tricolor pattern is broken and brilliantly colored in white, dark fawn, and charcoal. Height: 20–23 inches (51–59 cm). Weight: 40–53 pounds (18–24 kg). The flat, large ears and slightly creased facial skin give this hound an unmistakably likeable expression.

DEVELOPMENT: The Chien d'Artois is one of the oldest of the French scenthounds; its history parallels the Normand, Vendeen and Poitou, all of which are scarcely found. 19th-century French hunters boasted *"les chiens de petit équipage"* (packs of small dogs) made up of the sprightly and Anglo-bright Briquets. Its over-chicness and incalculable crosses to British gundogs nearly decimated the purity of the Artois type. Today the descendants of the remaining pure Artois are growing in number. They are used on hare and other small quarry in small packs.

RECOGNITION: FCI

CHARACTER: No ordinary hound: the inevitable crosses to British gundogs equipped the new *équipage* with pointing instincts. Today they spoil French hunters with their versatility: to hunt, to point, to scent. Penetrating impenetrable briars, bristles, and brush, the Briquet knows no bounds.

CHIEN FRANCAIS
French Hound

PORTRAIT: Well balanced and sturdy, these French Hounds are pack hunters: there is little concern for an "ideal" conformation; functional, working concerns are foremost. The Chien Francais comes in three colors: orange and white, black and white, and tricolor. Each color is recognized as an individual breed, named respectively: Le Chien Francais Blanc et Noir, Le Chien Francais Blanc et Orange, et Le Chien Francais Tricolore. The coat is always short and smooth. Bicolor dogs weigh up to 66 pounds (30 kg) and stand 29 inches (74 cm) high; the Tricolor is ten percent smaller.

DEVELOPMENT: The determination of the Chien Francais grouping resulted from the 1957 pack surveys conducted in France. These purely Celtic descendants developed variously from the Gascon-Saintongeois and the Levesque and were once countless. Today they specialize on deer but are efficient on practically everything.

RECOGNITION: FCI

CHARACTER: The Chien Francais has been smiled on graciously by Mother Nature. Coming to modern man exclusively as a hunter, these dogs are both elegant in appearance and affectionate in personality. No hunter can ask for a better behaved, better looking dog.

DEUTSCHE BRACKE
German Hound, Deutsche Sauerlandbracke

PORTRAIT: A tricolor, smoothhaired bracke, the German Hound is low stationed and well boned. For his inches, this hound is a powerful and robust dog of superior ability. Height: 16–21 inches (40–53 cm). Like many of the other German hounds, the Deutsche Bracke possesses stiff ears that lie close to his head and the standard ram's nose profile. In size he is closest to the British Harrier, while in appearance he resembles the Scandinavian Stövare.

DEVELOPMENT: At one time, western Germany was well inhabited by packs of hounds that resembled this basic type. Said to evolve from generic Celtic hot-nosed hounds, this breed worked in the German forests. Only the Deutsche Bracke still exists to remind us of the type of hounds that once flourished. Extinct relations include the Sauerlander Holzbracke and the Westphalian Bracke. The breed is used today on both hot and cold trails, silently and giving tongue.

RECOGNITION: FCI

CHARACTER: This is a huntsman's dog that hasn't received much attention as a show dog or as an exclusive home companion. Hunters reveal that he is a dog without limitations on the field and, with patience, can even be trained to retrieve.

DREVER
Swedish Dachsbracke

PORTRAIT: A solidly built dog close to the ground, the Drever flaunts characteristic white markings on his face, feet, neck, chest and tail tip. He stands from 11½–16 inches (29–41 cm) high and weighs about 33 pounds (15 kg). A well-proportioned head is placed atop a long, strong neck. The legs are straight and not crooked like the Dachshund's. This dog is standardly described as somewhat less than medium size. In appearance he is rectangular, compact and of good stature. The coat is complete with hair straight and close.

DEVELOPMENT: Dachsbrackes begetting dachsbracke: the Westphalian Dachsbracke crossed backed to the Strellufstövare, the Danish Dachsbracke (whence it came) created the Swedish Dachsbracke or Drever. Born to hunt, the Drever is a vociferous and industrious worker with capabilities far beyond one's expectations. He is rarely shown but has turned up at an occasional exhibition.

RECOGNITION: FCI, CKC

CHARACTER: The Drever's swishing tail is said to be a reliable barometer of his continually good disposition. Not subject to outbursts or unpredictable behavior, he is a fine home companion and watchdog. Owners prize him for his alert and self-possessed demeanor.

DUNKER
Norwegian Hound

PORTRAIT: A dog of striking elegance and extraordinary balance, the Dunker illustrates the paragon, cleanly lined, sleek scenthound conformation. Height: 18–22 inches (46–56 cm). Weight 35–49 pounds (16–22 kg). The breed's short coat is uniquely colored: tan with a black (splotchy) or blue-marbled saddle. His ears are soft and thin. Despite his moderate size, he is sufficiently powerful.

DEVELOPMENT: Towards the middle of the 19th century, Herr Wilhelm Dunker crossed his most competent scenthounds with the Anglo-Russian Hound (now referred to as the Russian Harlequin Hound) to create a hound that would be able to hunt rabbit by scent instead of sight. Dunker was pleased with his creation's abilities and distinctive appearance. The merle gene's transferring from the Harlequin Hound explains the unique saddle the breed wears. His deep chest and robust lungs give him endurance in the hunt.

RECOGNITION: FCI

CHARACTER: Although not known outside of his native Norway, the Dunker delights hunters and owners with his trustworthy and reliable conduct. As a watchdog, he is valuable, comfortably served by his confidence and quick wit.

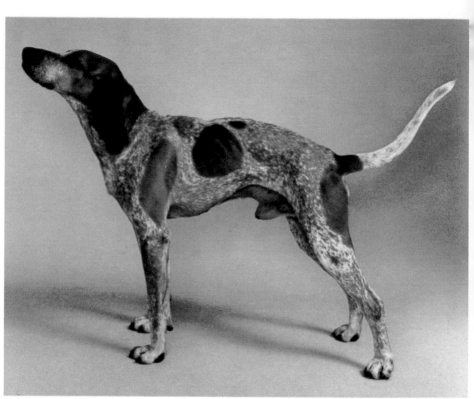

ENGLISH COONHOUND
Redtick Coonhound

PORTRAIT: A thinly boned, slender hound with an elongated head and longish tail. As his alternative name suggests, the breed usually occurs in redtick (a white background marked by copperish red patches and specks); however, it can also be bluetick, tricolor, white-red, white-black, white-lemon or brindle. Height: 20–27 inches (51–69 cm). Weight: 40–65 pounds (18–29 kg). His slender conformation is no measurement of his strength or endurance.

DEVELOPMENT: The English Coonhound is English only in name and the probable ancestors that contributed to the coonhound breeds. This coonhound is related to the Virginia hounds and was originally called the English Fox and Coonhound—in an attempt to describe its capabilities. In reality he should have been called the English Fox and Opossum and Cougar and Bear and Coonhound, since this describes (more accurately) his abilities. Gratefully such an untidy name was not adopted. These dogs are large and hot-nosed.

RECOGNITION: UKC

CHARACTER: The breed has perfectly adapted to the laid-back lifestyle that stills the American South. These dogs are mild-mannered gentlemen with good looks and manly drive. With children they are affectionate and gentle.

ENGLISH FOXHOUND

PORTRAIT: A medium-sized foxhound, the English Foxhound has a level back and rather angulated hind quarters. His short coat is either tricolor or bicolor. The body is well muscled and tight. The limbs are lightly boned. Good depth of rib, most symmetrical in body, and brainy in expression all describe the ideal dog. Height: 23–27 inches (58–69 cm). Weight: 55–75 pounds (25–34 kg). Grace and strength must prevail. The English Foxhound is a few inches larger than its cousin, the American Foxhound.

DEVELOPMENT: The need for foxhounds in Great Britain did not originate from the love and pep-pep of the sportsmen but instead developed out of the need to rid the countryside of a vile varmint (as it was then perceived): the fox. This "varmint" was so wily and evasive that the sporting aspect of fox extermination became paramount. At the sport's golden age, well over 200 packs of foxhound reportedly existed. The English Foxhound descends from these pack dogs and is still able to function in that hot-nosed, solid-voiced capacity.

RECOGNITION: FCI, AKC, CKC

CHARACTER: The breed is affectionate and obedient. The English Foxhound is quiet and mannerly; his even disposition makes him an ideal home companion, while his attentive nature and solid voice make him a guard dog par excellence. Hunters' horns acclaim his endurance and professionalism wherever he goes.

ESTONIAN HOUND
Gontchaja Estonskaja

PORTRAIT: Not excessively tall or heavy, the Estonian is an ideal-sized hound who flashes a brilliant black/tan jacket that is short and dense. The muzzle is somewhat long and the teeth are of maximum strength. His ears are long and tend to fold as they hang. Standing only 18–21 inches (46–53) high, he is longer than he is tall.

DEVELOPMENT: As the need for a low-stationed, smaller scenthound arose in the Estonian Republic (north of Moscow, on the Baltic Sea), Soviet hunters began developing the Estonian Hound. Crossing Beagles to local hounds effectively reduced the dog's size; mixing in the Swiss Neiderlaufhund contributed early maturation and voice; and a splash of the English Foxhound for endurance culminated in the present-day breed.

RECOGNITION: NR

CHARACTER: This hound is good-natured and personable with his own but tends to be wary of strangers. This quality and his convenient size have made him an increasingly popular watchdog in the Soviet Union. Unfortunately, Westerners probably won't have the opportunity to meet or adopt this hound, as no specimens have successfully defected from the Motherland. Perhaps this *gontchaja* will begin to cover new ground as Gorby's *Perestroyka* takes effect.

FINNISH HOUND
Suomenajokoira, Finsk Stövare

PORTRAIT: A large, robust hound with moderately loose skin and generously proportioned ears. In color pattern he is always tricolor, with white markings on the front and under body (including feet and tail tip). Height: 22–25 inches (56–64 cm). Weight: 55 pounds (25 kg). He is taller than his Scandinavian brothers and resembles the American Foxhound in size.

DEVELOPMENT: Originally shown in Finland in 1870, the Finnish Hound may feign an ancient heritage but has only been known to man for a good hundred years. He has a mixed ancestry like most of the scenthounds; crossing of the English Foxhound as well as French, German and Swedish hounds brought forth this handsome, finely finished Finn. He is very much the hunter and approaches the sport with enthusiasm and skill.

RECOGNITION: FCI

CHARACTER: An energized hunter in warm weather, the Finnish Hound loves a master who also enjoys the great outdoors. He does not relish cold weather and will contend (quite effectively) for his favorite couch in the winter. He is a choice family dog but maintains a streak of independence. Additionally, he is generous and good-natured and will usually share his sofa.

GRAND ANGLO-FRANCAIS
Large French-English Hound

PORTRAIT: The largest of the Anglo-Francais breeds of hound, the Grand Anglo-Francais is a big-boned dog with a solid body trunk. His expressive eyes are superscribed by delicate tan shadings. These tan markings complement the black and white coat; tricolor and orange and white are also color options. Height 24–27 inches (61–69 cm). Weight: 66–71 pounds (30–32 kg). Rather generous ear leather adorns an aristocratic head.

DEVELOPMENT: The breed name in translation reveals the origin of these fine dogs. The Anglo-Francais or English-French derived from crosses of French hounds with the English Foxhound. These very elegant hounds hunt in packs and are capable of working most any game, big or small. Most hunters attest that these dogs have an inbred knowledge of the game they hunt and possess spectacular noses.

RECOGNITION: FCI

CHARACTER: This dog is gentle and kind but is primarily utilitarian. The noble and appealing appearance of the dog may attract non-hunters to the breed, but it should be emphasized that this is a pack hunter who must be worked to be happy. An exclusively suburban existence would be hell indescribable. French hunters brand members of their pack with the family initial for identification purposes.

GRAND BLEU DE GASCOGNE
Large Blue Gascony Hound

PORTRAIT: Reaching 28 inches (71 cm) in height, the Grand Bleu is one of the world's tallest scenthounds. He is efficiently built (on the leggy side) with a strong, large head. Weight: 71–78 pounds (32–35 kg). His coat is thick but not too short. The coat color is *bleu*—that is, white ticked with black, complemented by tan markings.

DEVELOPMENT: The Phoenician hound trade is cited as the source of these Gascony Hounds; the Grand was modified and thereby perfected by crossings to the Bloodhound. His silky oversized ears, sunken eyes and melancholy personality are testament to this cross. Incidentally, the breed doesn't possess the Bloodhound's heaviness. The Grand is hunted in packs and has an ice-cube nose—the coldest in the family.

RECOGNITION: FCI, KCGB

CHARACTER: The coldness of his nose does not extend into his temperament. The Grand possesses a typical hound warmth with his owners. He is eager to please and very dignified in his manner. On the hunt, this dog is no pussy cat—his loving temperament is reserved for the family.

GRAND GASCON-SAINTONGEOIS
Virelade

PORTRAIT: A robust, big and leggy hound with long, exaggerated ears and a handsome head, occipital peak of which is very pronounced. Like many of the scenthounds, the tricolor pattern is specifically detailed with tan spots on the head only and black spots on the upper body. Oftimes the white background has black ticking throughout. Height: 25–28 inches (63–71 cm). Weight: 66–71 pounds (30–32 kg).

DEVELOPMENT: Baron de Virelade created the Grand Gascon-Saintongeois by crossing the few remaining specimens of the Grand Gasconies and the Saintongeois. Both of these breeds were large hunting dogs that worked roe deer and other large game. The Grand Gascon-Saintongeois adapted well to its forebears' quarry. A smaller version of the breed called the Petit Gascon-Saintongeois was developed for work on rabbit and smaller game. The Grand is often referred to as the Virelade.

RECOGNITION: FCI

CHARACTER: A kind and gentle nature well befits this easygoing companion. He is not known outside of France, but in his native land he is still a popular pack hunter. To see a pack of these large hounds gallop on the chase is truly a wondrous sight.

GRAND GRIFFON VENDEEN
Large Vendeen Griffon

PORTRAIT: Displaying patches of orange, gray, tawny, or black/tan on a bright white background, the Grand Griffon Vendeen can stand as high as 27 inches (69 cm). His coat is wire—hard and rough—never woolly or soft. Weight: 66–77 pounds (30–35 kg). The Grand Basset Vendeen (Large Vendeen Basset) is shorter, standing about 15 inches (38 cm). A third variation is the Briquet Griffon Vendeen (Medium Vendeen Griffon), which stands only about 22 inches (56 cm) tall and weighs no more than 53 pounds (24 kg).

DEVELOPMENT: As outstretching hunting ground in France diminishes, so too does the call for large swift running hounds. The Grand was bred from the white Southern Hound (now extinct) and the Griffon Nivernais to hunt boar and wolf. For centuries, French kings used the Chien Blanc du Roi, as the Grand was formerly known, in the region of Vendee.

RECOGNITION: FCI

CHARACTER: This hound is irascible and all agog at the incipience of the hunt and may tire out ever so momentarily before the rakish rabbit is reached. This shortcoming makes him an option for the part-time hunter who likes to sleep after lunch. Some Grands reportedly like to sleep through lunch as well.

JR Quinn

GREEK HAREHOUND
Hellinikos Ichnilatis, Hellenic Hound

PORTRAIT: Distinctive for his elongated head and ram-shaped nasal canal, the Greek Harehound stands from 18–22 inches (46–56 cm) high and weighs 38–44 pounds (17–20 kg). The coat is short and coarse and reddish tan in color with black saddle and white markings. The breed has moderate-sized ears and coffee-brown eyes that project an intelligent and alert expression.

DEVELOPMENT: Indigenous to Greece, the Greek Harehound is an ancient breed that shares its root with the Balkan Hound of Yugoslavia. Its extraordinary inclination to hare has lent itself to high specialization. The dog possesses a fine nose and beautifully resonant voice. Once used specifically as a pack hound, the breed is used today in duos or trios.

RECOGNITION: FCI

CHARACTER: The Greek Harehound's alert and perky disposition makes him an enthusiastic and untiring hunter and a devoted companion. His pleasant and good-willed personality continues to satisfy Greek sportsmen, who will do with no other. He is not known outside of his native Greece.

GRIFFON NIVERNAIS
Chien de Pays

PORTRAIT: A woolly, rugged coat bedecks a sturdy well-muscled body. The Griffon Nivernais sports a bushy appearance, led off by a wiry beard and mustache. Whether closer in appearance to the Spinone Italiano or the Otter Hound, this dog is still unique. Height: 21–25 inches (53–64 cm). Weight: 50–55 pounds (22–25 kg). The breed comes in a variety of colors— the preferred color is gray (in varying shades), but black/tan, tawny, fawn, and roan may occur as well.

DEVELOPMENT: The exact origination of the Nivernais's wire coat is unknown but likely connected to the Eastern shepherds. One popular contention purports that the modern breed is a direct descendant of the Chien Gris de St. Louis that roamed France 800 years ago. A smaller variety known as the Griffon Nivernais de Petit Taille existed at one time but is no longer locatable. The breed contributed to the gene pool of the original scenthounds. Specifically bred for hunting boar, they are used in a number of countries today on various quarry, including bear.

RECOGNITION: FCI

CHARACTER: The unshakable hardiness and durable coat make this dog adaptable to any environment. He is a courageous, active and strong hunter, ever so willing to earn his day's pay.

HALDENSTÖVARE
Halden Hound

PORTRAIT: This deeply chested, able-bodied hound possesses a distinctive tricolor coat: a short, shiny jacket of predominating white blotched by black spots and brown shadings. Height: 20–25 inches (51–64 cm). Weight: 45–60 pounds (20–27 kg). The dog's feet receive particular emphasis in breeding programs; breeders strive to attain a specialized foot construction capable of propelling the dog through the treacherous Norwegian terrain.

DEVELOPMENT: The breed's roots are implanted in the scenthounds (especially foxhounds) of various European countries. It still, however, possesses a distinguishing appearance unlike any other recognized hound and has been deemed purely Norwegian. This is a hound of remarkable scenting ability, so proficient it can work by itself on the varying game of Norway.

RECOGNITION: FCI

CHARACTER: A family companion par excellence, this demonstrative, extroverted hound is affectionate in the home. He appears pleasant natured and enjoys the company of children as much as he does his master and hunting cronies.

HAMILTONSTÖVARE
Hamilton Hound

PORTRAIT: This sleek tricolor foxhound boasts a rather long and elegant head, with ears that lie flatly and are not too pendant. He is robust and hardy. His possessions include: deep chest, well-tucked flanks, and high-toed feet. The coat is double, becoming thicker as the Norwegian winter approaches. His musculature and composition are clean in appearance. Height: 20–24 inches (51–61 cm). Weight: 50–60 pounds (22–27 kg).

DEVELOPMENT: In the late 19th century, A.P. Hamilton, in an attempt to achieve the superlative working hound, crossed three Germanic dogs of noteworthy ability with his English foxhounds. The Teutonic hounds included the Curlandish Hound, the Hölsteiner Hound, and the Heiderbracke. Hamilton Hounds are hunted singly and possess many universal hunting dog qualities, as they are able to trail, flush, and bay upon finding the wounded quarry. Today the breed is also popular in the show world.

RECOGNITION: FCI, KCGB

CHARACTER: His optimistic, happy-go-lucky personality is a pleasure to have in the home. Some owners confess that he can be high-strung and overly excitable. He needs a good deal of exercise and is quite an outdoorsman, but he also enjoys time spent indoors.

HANOVERIAN HOUND
Hannoverscher Schweisshund

PORTRAIT: Low on leg and somewhat heavy, the Hanoverian is essentially a medium-large sized dog that is thick in appearance. The head carries its large, stiff ears high. Height: 24–27 inches (51–61 cm). Weight: 84–99 pounds (38–45 kg). His chest is large and round, and his build is thicker than that of many of his hound brothers. Colors vary in shades of red, with streaks of black creating a brindling effect. Dogs occur with and without black masks.

DEVELOPMENT: Hanover, Upper Saxony, marks the locale of this German breed's origin. Lighter Celtic dogs were crossed with heavy tracking dogs to yield the Hanoverian Hound. Like its forebears, the breed was primarily pack hunted and began the chase before the smaller dogs were allowed in. Today these dogs are used mostly as tracking dogs, and they are praised for their unfaltering noses.

RECOGNITION: FCI

CHARACTER: Not recommended for non-hunters, the Hanoverian is a dedicated sportsman who requires an equally committed enthusiast. Like the Bloodhound, he is a complacent and placid hound, with long-lasting patience and an unmistakably noble air.

HARRIER

PORTRAIT: This well-balanced, well-built, medium-sized foxhound comes in a full range of hound colors, although tricolors are most common. The level back, deep chest, and marvelously proportioned head mounted on a neck of ample length give this hound a sturdy, competent appearance. His square stance is supported by his straight legs and round cat-like feet. Height: 19–22 inches (48–56 cm). Weight: 48–60 pounds (21–27 kg).

DEVELOPMENT: The original West County Harrier was begot by skillfully combining the Beagle with the St. Hubert Hound. In the early 20th century, however, there was one single pack of Harriers reportedly left in West County, England. In order to preserve the type, locals crossed in the Foxhound with the existing true specimens. This addition of Foxhound blood made this slower, medium-sized dog considerably faster. Hare is his natural quarry.

RECOGNITION: FCI, AKC, CKC, ANKC

CHARACTER: Although the Harrier's popularity has been hindered by its slightly larger relative the English Foxhound, the breed enjoys its moderate status. Despite their strong natural instincts, the Harriers make fine home companions (especially for country dwellers) and are recommended for non-hunters and sportsmen alike.

HYGENHUND

PORTRAIT: A solid, tight build complements this short-coupled hound. The muzzle is pointed, and the body is elongated. Height: 19–23 inches (48–59 cm). Weight 44–53 pounds (20–24 kg). The coat is straight and dense, without being excessively short. The Hygenhund commonly comes in yellow with white markings, although red/brown and other colors also occur. Well boned and deeply chested, he is a picture of strength and endurance.

DEVELOPMENT: Hygen, a Norwegian breeder, wanted a "dog to call his own," so he crossed the old Hölsteiner Hounds with a potpourri of Scandinavian hounds (and probably a Germanic cousin here and there) to attain what we today call the Hygenhund. Although Hygen obviously got his way, this hound is not exceedingly popular and basically looks like any other Scandinavian hound, differing subtly in size and color. Nothing, however, can take away from this hunter's instinctive abilities and expertise.

RECOGNITION: FCI

CHARACTER: A dog of severe endurance, the Hygenhund is a hunter par excellence, with enough strength and courage to hold his own every time he hunts singly or otherwise in his native Norway. A personable and merry soul, this dog makes a hunter's best friend.

ISTRIAN HOUND
Itrski Gonič

PORTRAIT: The Istrian Hound's two coat types are separated into two individual breeds, with no interbreeding allowed. The Smoothhaired (Kratkodlaki) and the Wirehaired (Resasti) are each recognized individually. The Smooth weighs in from 35–50 pounds (16–23 kg) and stands 18–21 inches (46–53 cm) high. The Wire can exceed those measurements by about 3 pounds and a couple of inches. White with orange/yellow markings on the ears aptly describes both coat colors. The main difference, of course, is in coat type: the Smooth coat is short and fine; the Wire coat is 2–3 inches (5–8 cm) in length and comes with a woolly undercoat. Both breeds are racy and cat footed.

DEVELOPMENT: Crosses of Phoenician sighthounds and European scenthounds produced these Istrian hunters. These are the oldest of the Yugoslavian scenthounds. They are prized for their bloodtrailing abilities and admired for their bravura basso on the trail.

RECOGNITION: FCI

CHARACTER: Like their voices, these dogs are low-keyed and well-rounded. They are peaceful and reticent in the home. Their handsome appearances have earned them fanciers in show circles; however, these dogs still function primarily as hunting mates.

JRQuinn

KERRY BEAGLE
Pocadan

PORTRAIT: A dapper and close-coated hound, the Kerry Beagle appears as an unexaggerated Bloodhound: smaller, less wrinkled skin, less keen nose. Black/tan is the most common color pattern, although other varieties are. known, including tricolor, mottled, and tan/white. Height: 22–26 inches (56–66 cm). Structurally, this hound is strong and firmly built.

DEVELOPMENT: As its appearance should hint, this dog most likely has Bloodhound blood in its veins. Cynologists believe that the Kerry, although used initially on stag, was one of the first dogs used exclusively to hunt hare. Though a common sight around Tipperary and Kerry in past centuries, the Kerry Beagle stepped into the 20th century with but a handful of packs. Some of these Irish hounds were brought with immigrants into the U.S. where they contributed to other hound strains. Drag trials in Ireland have spurred resurgence in this ancient breed.

RECOGNITION: NR

CHARACTER: These dogs are true sportsmen, enjoying physical activity for health and enjoyment. The Kerry is gentle and gentlemanly. To this day, Irish and Irish-Americans alike muster a sprig of Eire pride at the mere mention of the Kerry (even though most of them have never seen one).

LEOPARD CUR
Leopard Tree Dog

PORTRAIT: A sinewy, muscular body empowers this hound of strength and character. The merle color in this breed is considered "leopard-spotted"; other colors include black/tan, blue, brindle, and yellow. The coat is dense and smooth. Weight: 45–77 pounds (20–35 kg). The muzzle is elongated; the ears are moderately sized.

DEVELOPMENT: A tough dog capable of protecting early American settlers from Indian attacks and helping to provide them with food explains the rise of the cur in America. North Carolina was the Leopard Cur's Mecca. European dogs (British and French primarily) probably contributed to the development of these dogs—few owners really know and most can not be bothered with extemporaneous speculation. That the dog works, and works well, is paramount.

RECOGNITION: NR

CHARACTER: A keen desire to please his master drives the Leopard Cur to perform amazing tasks. Perhaps not the best family dog, the Leopard Cur tends to be one-man oriented. His courageous and alert disposition, however, qualifies him as an indispensable watchdog.

LEVESQUE

PORTRAIT: A strictly tricolor scenthound of good size, the Levesque is a slender but muscular dog. Expression-wise, it is intelligent and lively. Height: 26–28 inches (66–71 cm). Weight: 55–66 pounds (25–30 kg). The coat is typically hound—short and smooth. The head is long and rather large, the ears are big and houndy, lying close to the head. The overall impression is imposing and memorable.

DEVELOPMENT: Melding three breeds, Rogatien Levesque brought forth this hound in 1873, attaching his name to the creation. Levesque's three-dog formula included the Bleu de Gascogne, the Grand Gascon-Sain-tongeois, and the English Foxhound. Swift and well-built, the Levesque was intended to work in packs on a variety of game. Today the Levesque is very rare, and few true specimens can be found even in France.

RECOGNITION: FCI

CHARACTER: The Levesque is sedulous and business-like on the field yet loving and never distanced in the home. He is uncanny in his reliability and devotion to his master. Exercise and outdoor living are key to the breed's continued good health.

LITHUANIAN HOUND

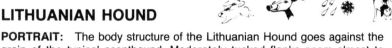

PORTRAIT: The body structure of the Lithuanian Hound goes against the grain of the typical scenthound. Moderately tucked flanks seem almost to contradict the sturdy, heavily boned body of this hound. He is an impressive sight: muscular, sleek and determined. Height: 21–24 inches (53–61 cm). Color is always black with limited tan markings. The dog possesses less heavy bone than many a hound his size. The Lithuanian's tail is rather long and held low.

DEVELOPMENT: In attempting to recreate the original-type Curlandish Hound, industrious Russian breeders crossed Bloodhounds, Beagles, Polish Hounds and a potpourri of native hounds to conjure the Lithuanian Hound. He is effective on boar, hare and fox. Joining the ranks of his hound *brats*, this Soviet worker is surely a fine addition.

RECOGNITION: NR

CHARACTER: This is a personable and exuberant hound who seems to have captured much of the verve and appearance of his long-lost prototype. In the hunt, he has unpassable speed and irreversible persistence. As a companion, he is agreeable and genial. No specimens are known outside of the Lithuanian Republic.

LUZERNER LAUFHUND
Lucernese Hound

PORTRAIT: The Luzerner Laufhund and his smaller cousin the Luzerner Neiderlaufhund (Small Lucernese Hound) possess tricolor, heavily ticked wire coats. The main difference between them is size: the Laufhund stands 18–23 inches (46–59 cm) tall and weighs 34–44 pounds (15½–20 kg); the Neiderlaufhund may stand from 13–16 inches (33–41 cm), but it can weigh up to 40 pounds (18½ kg). This latter dog is a shorter legged, sturdy-to-the-ground hound, while the former is taller and appears slighter in build.

DEVELOPMENT: These Swiss hounds were likely bred from the Petit Bleu de Gascogne of France, as they share many similar features. One inherited trait is the fine sense of smell. These dogs can be used on a wide variety of game, including roe deer and boar.

RECOGNITION: FCI

CHARACTER: Although merry and good-humored, the laufhunds of Switzerland are not named for their temperaments: *laufhund* loosely translates to walking dog. Committed and energized hunters, the Lucernese Hounds are even tempered and predictable. As pets, they are friendly and loyal.

MAJESTIC TREE HOUND

PORTRAIT: Massive and mountain-like, the Majestic Tree Hound epitomizes the large working dog. There is nothing cosmetic about this dog, and yet he maintains the dignity and nobility of any well-bred show champion. One hundred pounds (45 kg) of muscle, the Majestic can be 31 inches (79 cm) tall. His coat can be any combination of colors, usually arranged on a white sky; the coat is short, thick and dense.

DEVELOPMENT: Bred by American hunters to handle horse-killing big cats in the South, the Majestic had to be large and formidable. In creating this hound, hunters also subscribed to the old-type cold-nosed methodical worker. Although the Majestic couldn't be aptly described as a fast worker, he is unerroneously paced; and far be it from the well-witted fancier to suggest that he wastes time. The working Bloodhound is his closest pinpointable forebear.

RECOGNITION: NR

CHARACTER: Unlike the ferocious cats this dog trees, he is quite a kitten. His size is inarguably metaphorical of his heart: affectionate and demonstrative, he makes a beloved companion animal. Owners should be forewarned that this dog needs sufficient room for exercise and looks forward to mealtime with uncurbable verve.

MOUNTAIN CUR

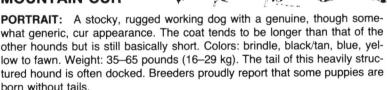

PORTRAIT: A stocky, rugged working dog with a genuine, though somewhat generic, cur appearance. The coat tends to be longer than that of the other hounds but is still basically short. Colors: brindle, black/tan, blue, yellow to fawn. Weight: 35–65 pounds (16–29 kg). The tail of this heavily structured hound is often docked. Breeders proudly report that some puppies are born without tails.

DEVELOPMENT: The European gene pool splashes soakingly on the American curs. Many hounds brought over with immigrants to America trysted with native curs. This unsurly, rather sordid combination of canine produces an off-beat hound able to adjust the exact rhythms of the polka to the untappable beats of the Indian war dance. This historic Ohio River Valley prowler is believed to possess a whiff of the Indian Cur's genetic smoke, in addition to the influence of other hounds and herders. He is used mainly as a treeing hound, but many are superb trailers as well.

RECOGNITION: NR

CHARACTER: This is not a submissive, easygoing hound. With the toughness to confront a very angry, very large cat, these curs have learned to be decisive and dauntless. Silent on the trail, they make consistent guard dogs but certainly are not ideal for suburbia, where there is no call to work.

OTTER HOUND

PORTRAIT: A fascinating and unearthly hound, the Otter Hound, with its webbed feet, extremely rough, thick double coat, and boisterous, meddlesome expression, is a monster among hounds. Height: 22–27 inches (56–69 cm). Weight: 65–115 pounds (29–52 kg). The body is well muscled and lean; the skin is thick; the coat is naturally stripped, and the undercoat is oily and waterproof. The Otter Hound comes in a wide variety of colors: generally grizzle, blue/white, wheaten, black/tan, liver/tan, tricolor, lemon/white, and reddish fawn.

DEVELOPMENT: The breed's ancestors, despite conjecture and obscurity, probably trace back to the Southern Hound and the Bloodhound, later crossed to the Water Spaniel to create what is effectively a carbon copy of the old Vendee Hound. The domed-shaped skull validates the Bloodhound's contribution, while the breed's swimming ability accredits the Water Spaniel's blood. Its original task of hunting otters no longer occupies the breed. It has adapted reasonably to trailing game. Otterhounds are, however, less inclined to riot after the game as would a Foxhound.

RECOGNITION: FCI, AKC, KCGB, CKC

CHARACTER: The patience and perseverance key to the Otter Hound's original occupation transfer well to current-day home life. He is a fun-loving, unpredictable companion who is unfailing in his devotion to his owner.

PETIT BASSET GRIFFON VENDEEN
Small Vendeen Basset

PORTRAIT: An irresistible, roughly coated little dwarf that is short-legged and efficiently constructed. The coat must be hard and rough to the touch; it reaches up to 2½ inches (6 cm) in length. A pure white background provides the woolly canvas for a palate of colors: orange, gray, tawny, and black/tan. Weight: 25–35 pounds (11–16 kg). Height: 13–15 inches (33–38 cm). The ears are graciously feathered and the merry tail is a sure barometer of his charm and appeal.

DEVELOPMENT: The smallest variety of the French Griffons of the Vendee area, the Petit was bred down from his larger *freres*. His terrifically tough coat and closeness to the ground make him ideal for hunting in rugged terrain. Hunting is instinctive, as it is with his Griffon relations. Although no newcomer to France, the Petit Basset is creating quite a stir in the U.S. and Great Britain, where active fanciers are promoting him. American television actress Mary Tyler Moore is one proud owner.

RECOGNITION: FCI, AKC, KCGB, CKC, ANKC

CHARACTER: The animated, sprightly personality of the PeeBee-GeeVees has earned them countless new fanciers. Their confident and gay carriage complete the perfect picture of this jaunty companion.

SCENTHOUNDS

PLOTT HOUND

PORTRAIT: A medium-sized, soundly put-together hound that is usually brindle. The coat, which is short, thick, and dense, may also make incidence in slate blue and buckskin; many with black saddles. Height: 20–24 inches (51–61 cm). Weight: 45–55 pounds (20–25 kg). A long, high-held tail and long ears characterize the breed. The conformation of the Plott Hound is lean muscled, rather thin boned and lithe. The tail is long and carried erect when alert. The ears are pendant and on the large side.

DEVELOPMENT: The breed's designated name honors its American founders and progenitors. Seven generations of Jonathan Plott's family, beginning in the 1750s, bred their dogs exclusively within the family. A mix of bloodhounds and curs reportedly comprised the original stock. The dogs' working claim to fame is coldtrailing bear. The Plott Hound is American through and through.

RECOGNITION: UKC

CHARACTER: The breed's "all-in-the-family" background makes it a fine companion. Southern owners report that they are quick to learn, quick to trail, and quick to love. Their personable natures are surely not evident on the trail. The courage and tenacity to play chicken with a 500-pound papa bear or a ticked-off boar are enviable.

POITEVIN
Haut-Poitou

PORTRAIT: In color the Poitevin, a Frenchman, is reminiscent of many English pack hounds. The breed is usually hound-marked, that is tricolored with a saddle, or orange and white. This is a racy fairly big hound with less earage than many a French packman. The Poitevin is greatly distinguished for his fine symmetry, appearing more perfectly balanced than most scenthounds. Height: 24–28 inches (61–71 cm). Weight: 66 pounds (30 kg). The body is tautly muscled and the skin is considerably tight for a hound. The head is handsomely sculpted, narrow with a well-pronounced occiput.

DEVELOPMENT: One of the longest established varieties of the French scenthounds, the Poitevin dates back to the early 1700s—probably further. The Marquis Francois de Larrye is revered as Pére Poitevin, the father of the breed. The Haut-Poitou region was well populated by working packs of these handsome hounds. In order to re-instate the breed after a devastating rabies epidemic in 1842, English Foxhounds were bred with the few remaining specimens. The post-epidemic Poitevin naturally resembles the Engllsh breed more so than did its predecessors. The breed was originally employed as an all-day pursuer of wolf.

RECOGNITION: FCI

CHARACTER: The Poitevin is by no means numbersome or cumbersome: this elegant dog is fancied by a small group of houndmen in France. He is genuinely friendly and attentive. His lively and intelligent nature endears him to those that work him.

POLISH HOUND
Ogar Polski

PORTRAIT: Massive and ponderous, the Polish Hound is efficiently built, though lighter than the flewy, large-headed St. Hubert. The general appearance of this hound is imposing. Height: 22–26 inches (56–66 cm). Weight: 55–71 pounds (25–32 kg). This hound's coat is usually black/tan or black and tan saddled. The breed carries its marvelously proportioned head with grace and pride.

DEVELOPMENT: Cynologists would agree that pinpointing the specific origins of ancient indigenous hounds is usually pointless. Thus, the Polish Hound, native to Poland, may or may not be related to tracking dogs of neighboring Germany and Austria. His movement at work is slow and consonant; he is a persistent and enduring tracker of various game over the most treacherous terrain. His inborn ability to locate game and his sense of direction are remarkable.

RECOGNITION: FCI

CHARACTER: A meek and mighty soul, the Polish Hound is a lovely family pet. Despite his enthusiasm on the field, it is advisable to provide him with substantial exercise to avoid obesity and irreversible slothfulness. No specimens are known outside of Poland, and at home, since the unkindliness of WWII and thereafter, he has become scarce. Some reveal that the dogs aren't particularly quick, but most owners don't seem to mind.

PORCELAINE

PORTRAIT: Evoking the refinement and elegance of fine porcelain, the Porcelaine's appearance is a pleasing sight to behold. The solid white coat is composed of very fine hairs of miraculously short length. The color can be interrupted by orange spots on the body but especially on its notably sizable ears. Weight: 55–62 pounds. (25–28 kg). Height: 22–23 inches (56–59 cm). The finely sculpted head and moderate but delicate build reinforce the appropriateness of his name.

DEVELOPMENT: Believed to be the oldest of the French scenthounds, the Porcelaine has roots in the now-extinct Montaimboeuf as well as some smaller laufhunds of Switzerland. The breed was necessarily reconstructed after the French Revolution but now stands on solid ground. Roe deer and hare are its specialties in the hunt.

RECOGNITION: FCI

CHARACTER: The Porcelaine is merciless and fierce in executing its hunting tasks. At home, however, this glistening white gladiator transforms into a serene and accommodating Snow White. Given the proper activities and exercise, this is an ideal fellow for the home.

POSAVAC HOUND
Posavaski Gonič

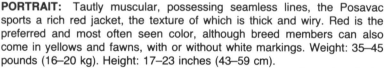

PORTRAIT: Tautly muscular, possessing seamless lines, the Posavac sports a rich red jacket, the texture of which is thick and wiry. Red is the preferred and most often seen color, although breed members can also come in yellows and fawns, with or without white markings. Weight: 35–45 pounds (16–20 kg). Height: 17–23 inches (43–59 cm).

DEVELOPMENT: Slavic hunters have appreciated and employed the alacrity and ability of the Posavac for many years. One legend says: in answer to a poor woman's plea to the Virgin, seven members of the breed miraculously came to her peasant family living near the shores of the Adriatic. These seven specimens looked significantly different from other Yugoslavian hounds and very much like today's breed. The family used them on hare and deer. Allegedly, these dogs saved this devout family from decimating poverty, sowing the seeds for today's breed and successfully escaping the pen of Mr. Ripley.

RECOGNITION: FCI

CHARACTER: As a hunter, the Posavac is accurate and no-nonsense. Obligatory and reliable as a family pet, the breed is a delight to all who own it. Exercise is an absolute must with these very active hounds. Although hunting instincts are strong, many are kept as companion/watchdogs and coexist positively contentedly.

RASTREADOR BRASILEIRO
Brazilian Tracker

PORTRAIT: The essential features of this feisty Brazilian include a flat head, which rounds with little apparent stop; metallic yellow eyes; a powerful deep chest; and a saber-like tail. This is a dog whose firm conformation is fashioned for endurance and power. The coat is short and rough to the touch. The ears are long and pendulous. Height: 25–27 inches (63–69 cm). Weight: 50–60 pounds (22–27 kg). In color the Rastreador is basically white (and sometimes brown) with blue, chestnut or black markings.

DEVELOPMENT: The breed was created by Brazilian hunter Oswalde Aranha Filho as a tracker of the South American jaguar. To pursue this mighty feline, a dog must be sufficiently powerful, absolutely fearless and endowed with the stamina to track for an average of six to seven hours over practically unsurmountable terrain—without losing a scent. Various varieties of American Foxhounds served as key ingredients; touches of American coonhounds were then added (Treeing Walker and Bluetick Coons are usually cited). Another source reports that German Shepherds were included. Regardless of the exactitude of the components, the breed is a formidable all-weather canine of superior abilities.

RECOGNITION: NR

CHARACTER: The Tracker doesn't trail any of his aggressive tendencies into the home—like the learned businessman, he leaves his problems at the office, so to speak. The Rastreador is ardent and industrious as a watchdog and companion.

REDBONE COONHOUND

PORTRAIT: A handsome, strong and robust coonhound, the Redbone stands 26 inches (66 cm) high. Weight can range from 50–70 pounds (22–31½ kg). This is a perfectly proportioned hound with an impeccable sniffer and sonorous voice. The coat is dense and short, rather hard to the touch. As the name may suggest, the Redbone is invariably solid red (with white marks not to be fussed over).

DEVELOPMENT: Breeders in the American South, Tennessee and Georgia to be precise, desired a hound with more speed and a hotter sniffer than many of the existing coonhounds. In formulating the Redbone, these breeders blended foxhounds and added a dash of "cur power." The results make the concoction seem trustworthy, as the breed's moderate size, foxhoundish appearance and fortitude comprise it to its marrow. He is used principally for treeing coon but can be adapted to other game, including big cat.

RECOGNITION: UKC

CHARACTER: The strong desire to fulfill his master's wishes and his even stronger ability to do so have made the Redbone an extensively used hunter. With the thrusting grit of a terrier and the pumping stamina of a husky, the Redbone is every hunter's hot-trailed dream come true. In the home, he is affectionate and kind.

RUSSIAN HARLEQUIN HOUND
Russian Piebald Hound, Gontchaja Russkaja Pegaja

PORTRAIT: This squarely built tricolor hound is sturdy and competent. The well-defined stop and noticeable flews distinguish him from other Soviet hounds, as does his piebald color. In height the Harlequin stands from 22–26 inches (56–66 cm). A strong head and well-developed teeth give this hound repute and respect.

DEVELOPMENT: The importation of English Foxhounds into Russia began some 250 years ago and is key in understanding the derivation of the Russian Harlequin Hound. Russian hunters bred their newly acquired Foxhounds with the Russian Hound to procure the Harlequin, which is smaller than the latter and heavier than the former. These creations were originally called Anglo-Russian Hounds. In 1951, the present name was adopted. The multi-colored coat distinguishes the dog from its quarry to eschew mishaps.

RECOGNITION: NR

CHARACTER: The Harlequin Hounds get on well with man—working, playing, and sharing the home. They are obedient and keen on pleasing their masters. These are handsome and obedient companions that are securing new fanciers daily.

RUSSIAN HOUND
Kostrome Hound, Gontchaja Russkaja

PORTRAIT: Appearing slightly longer than tall, the Russian Hound is a weighty-looking dog with a solid torso and back. Height: 22–27 inches (56–68½ cm). The coat is moderately short and unusually dense, possessing a thick undercoat. Usually drab yellow in color, the Russian Hound can vary from yellows into reds and possess a black saddle and small markings in white. The breed is even referred to sometimes as the Russian Drab Yellow Hound, but most do not favor this rather "colorless" translation. The dogs' wide-ranging voices are distinctive and expressive.

DEVELOPMENT: It is likely that Russian laikas crossed with indigenous scenthounds to create today's Russian Hound; the breed's undercoat and wedge-shaped head are thereby explained. Hare is this Russian's usual game, but an occasional fox or two may make his master's bag too.

RECOGNITION: NR

CHARACTER: Devoted to the hunt and his master, the Russian Hound has countless fans in the Soviet Union. Sportsmen favor him for his endurance and keen nose. Owners caution tyros to let pups bark at their leisure in order to develop their hunting voices. One hushing, rueful owner relays that her hound was destined to be a lyric tenor but now can only grovel in the basso range.

SABUESO ESPAÑOL DE MONTE
Large Spanish Hound

PORTRAIT: The Sabueso Español de Monte sports a white coat patched with red, which is hard and short. The breed weighs approximately 55 pounds (25 kg) and stands as high as 22 inches (56 cm). The skin, covered by glossy fine hair, is flexible and loose. The oversized ears hang freely and jocularly, and the flews and dewlap are in no scarcity. The patches on the coat vary in color (red or black), number and proximity.

DEVELOPMENT: The Sabueso's similarity to the St. Hubert Hound and his classic mastiff appearance can assure us that this is an ancient breed, if nothing else. It is believed quite assuredly that the breed is of Celtic origin and has existed on the Iberian peninsula for many years, where it has remained pure. Two varieties are still known. The smaller (Sabueso Español Lebrero) tends to be more uniformly colored and stands less than 20 inches (51 cm) high.

RECOGNITION: FCI

CHARACTER: The versatility of this Spanish dog makes him suitable for numerous functions: tracking, police work, line work. Although once hunted in packs, these hounds are used singly due to their temperamental and willful dispositions. They do not make good pets but are energetic and devoted to their huntmaster.

SCHILLERSTÖVARE
Schiller Hound

PORTRAIT: This short-bodied, long-legged hound appears more like a running sighthound than a full-bodied scenthound. The coat, which is self-colored in black and tan (with a saddle), is short, dense and smooth. The undercoat is thick. Height: 19–24 inches (48–61 cm). Weight: 40–54 pounds (18–25 kg). The body is square and gives this robust-looking hound a noble and compelling appearance.

DEVELOPMENT: This ancient hound was allegedly perfected by Per Schiller, the father of the breed. The desire of this Swedish breeder was a hound of lighter type, able to cover more ground with greater speed. The gene pool likely contains the German, Austrian and early Swiss hounds. This is a hunter and tracker of especial use on snow hare and fox. The Schiller Hound, however, has been employed effectively on quite a variety of land game.

RECOGNITION: FCI

CHARACTER: Despite the short coat, this is a particularly hardy dog, able to withstand the cold and prolonged journeys in the snow. He has gained quite a handsome following in the show ring, and his steady, obedient, and feline-like cleanliness prove him an ideal home companion. Minimal grooming and a lot of exercise are recommended to keep this hound in his best condition.

SCHWEIZER LAUFHUND
Swiss Hound

PORTRAIT: This is a rather lightweight dog that stands on rather lengthy, well-boned legs. The coat can come in either of two types: (1) a tight-fitting, dense, and short smooth variety; and (2) a stand-offish outer, soft inner, double coated roughhaired variety. Color for both varieties is white with either yellow, red or orange markings. Although red is reportedly less common, dogs with deep red markings have been found. Height is 18–24 inches (46–61 cm). Weight: 34–44 pounds (15½–20 kg). This is an attractive dog for one who prefers a more stream-lined, endurance-built hound. The smaller version, the Schweizer Neiderlaufhund is the spitting image of his brother but stands 13–16 inches (33–41 cm) high and weighs 30–40 pounds (13½–18 kg).

DEVELOPMENT: The Schweizer Laufhund represents one of the three basic Swiss hound types. He is, as are his close relatives of Switzerland, descended from the old French hounds—although some sources cite the Swiss hounds to be descendants of the ancient dogs that evolved into the French hounds, without the Swiss hounds coming from or through the French—and developed into a leaner, lighter, and generally smaller dog who is better able to work the Swiss terrain.

RECOGNITION: FCI

CHARACTER: The Schweizer is a dog with strong drive. His inner motive force is strong and needs a continuous outlet. He is a hunter and, to be contented, should be used in the hunt.

SEGUGIO ITALIANO
Italian Hound

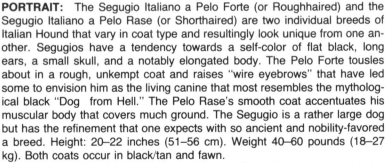

PORTRAIT: The Segugio Italiano a Pelo Forte (or Roughhaired) and the Segugio Italiano a Pelo Rase (or Shorthaired) are two individual breeds of Italian Hound that vary in coat type and resultingly look unique from one another. Segugios have a tendency towards a self-color of flat black, long ears, a small skull, and a notably elongated body. The Pelo Forte tousles about in a rough, unkempt coat and raises "wire eyebrows" that have led some to envision him as the living canine that most resembles the mythological black "Dog from Hell." The Pelo Rase's smooth coat accentuates his muscular body that covers much ground. The Segugio is a rather large dog but has the refinement that one expects with so ancient and nobility-favored a breed. Height: 20–22 inches (51–56 cm). Weight 40–60 pounds (18–27 kg). Both coats occur in black/tan and fawn.

DEVELOPMENT: Of very ancient origin, the Segugios are believed to be descended from crosses of the ancient Celtic and Phoenician dogs. Many believe the present type a fair representation of the early ancestors. The Italian Renaissance, with its revitalization of ancient beauty and value, brought the Italian Hounds to enviable popularity. They are still used on a variety of game over a great variety of terrain.

RECOGNITION: FCI

CHARACTER: The Segugio's having spent so many years with man has contributed to its warm and gentle way. Although still effective as a hunter, the Segugio is recommended as a pet to those looking for a docile dog with a touch of Italy and a spark of the ancient.

JRQuinn

SMALANDSSTÖVARE
Smalands Hound

PORTRAIT: This is the shortest yet stockiest of the Swedish hounds. His distinctively stövare body type is built upon well-boned, well-muscled legs. Besides his height, about 17 inches (43 cm), and visible thickness for a stövare—he weighs 33–40 pounds (15–18 kg), he is distinguishable from his Swedish cousins by his reliable color and black with tan markings on muzzle, possibly eyebrows and lower legs. Although his coat is thick, it is also smooth and requires little in the way of grooming.

DEVELOPMENT: As is true with many other canines, the Smalandsstövare gets his name from the area in which he originated, Smalands. The Smalands variety of the stövare type has probably been around since the early Middle Ages. Used with great success hunting in the forests of Sweden, the breed was taken seriously, and breeders worked hard to preserve and improve the dogs. They are still employed today as hunters of fox, hare, and other forest game in central Sweden.

RECOGNITION: FCI

CHARACTER: Although his relative smallness in size to other hounds may lead one to keeping him as a house or apartment dog, owners must remember that he requires much exercise and adequate outlet for his instincts.

STANDARD DACHSHUND
Normalgrossehteckel

PORTRAIT: A lengthy, low-to-the-ground hound with a deep chest and a compact muscular body. Six variations on this wondrous theme exist: two sizes and three coats. The Standard Dachshund weighs in from 15–25 pounds (6½–11½ kg); the Miniature Dachshund at less than 9 pounds (4 kg). The Smooth coat is short, thick and shiny. The Wire coat is uniformly tight, rough and coarse, complete with a beard and fine undercoat. The Long coat is soft, sleek and glistening. The breed's color possibilities can be one-colored (reds and yellows), two-colored (black, chocolate, gray with tan; white with yellow), or dappled (merle, harlequin and brindle).

DEVELOPMENT: The descendant of a race of long-backed, short-legged dogs that existed in Egypt at a very early date, this clumsy, egregiously eared 30-pound (14 kg) dog with the elegance of a pregnant otter, we learn, with certain embarrassment, to be the forebears of the multi-talented, well-versed Dachshund of today. In type, this is a true hound although many of his functions defy mere hound abilities: in addition to tracking and scenting, Miniature Dachsies can go to ground like the most tenacious of terriers, and Longhaired Dachsies have been known to retrieve in water, giving many a setter a swim for the mallard. The Dachshund's quarry obviously extends past the badger, its German breeder's original intention, to include rabbits, fox, deer, ferret and stoat.

RECOGNITION: FCI, AKC, UKC, KCGB, CKC, ANKC

CHARACTER: The Dachshund is as intelligent and clever as he is clean and industrious. One of the most hardy of dogs, the breed ideally is energetic and active. Owners are encouraged to be disciplinarian and discretionary. The long back opens up physical problems, thus dogs should not be allowed to jump off furniture. The breed's greedy and manipulative nature, if uncurbed, will transform a perky, active pup into a one-year-old, spoiled, fat homebody.

Standard Dachshund, Longhaired.

Miniature Dachshund, Wirehaired.

Standard Dachshund, Smooth.

Miniature Dachshund, Longhaired.

STEPHENS STOCK
Stephens Cur

PORTRAIT: A small, compact hound-like mountain cur that standardly comes in black (with white markings permissible); colors other than black disqualify. Height: 16–23 inches (40–59 cm). Weight: 35–55 pounds (16–25 kg). He is lean and short coated. A small head and a narrow muzzle complement his sleek look. The breed has a distinctive rat tail. The body shows every indication of developed musculature—it is sinewy and taut, with no sign of excess.

DEVELOPMENT: Hugh Stephens's "little blacks," after one hundred years of breeding pure, were deemed a single breed in 1970. These dogs are among the five "recognized" strains of mountain curs in the American South. Their vocal versatility and love of the hunt make the Stephens strain preferred by many hunters. Although too small to work alone on mountain lion or bear, these are mighty and courageous hunters.

RECOGNITION: NR

CHARACTER: Sensible and trainable, the Stephens Stock hounds are responsive to proper and sensitive treatment and do more than well as home companions. These dogs possess a strong desire to work and therefore are not recommended to non-hunters who might otherwise be attracted to their small size and easycare attributes.

STRELLUFSTÖVER
Danish Dachsbracke

PORTRAIT: A close-coated, close-to-the-ground hound who occurs in any color, the Strellufstöver stands 12–15 inches (30–38 cm) tall; despite the diminutive size, this is a powerful and muscular dog. The chest is deep, and the head is cleanly sculpted. Tail is long; the coat is efficient and all-purpose.

DEVELOPMENT: Frands Christian Frandsen of Denmark selectively crossed three hounds to acquire the desired features. The three contributors include the Westphalian Dachsbracke, the Smalandsstövaren, and the Berner Laufhund. By the 1920s, the breed caused quite a ruckus in Denmark, with hunters quickly acclaiming the breed an instant expert on fox, hare and deer. Later the breed contributed to the make-up of the Drever, who ironically has become more popular.

RECOGNITION: FCI

CHARACTER: The steady, docile temperament of the Strellufstöver, combined with its consistency and pluck, makes the breed popular with hunters and companion-seekers alike. Owners report that these dogs are never tenacious or bad-tempered.

STYRIAN ROUGHHAIRED MOUNTAIN HOUND
Steirischer Rauhhaarige Hochgebirgsbracke, Peintinger Bracke

PORTRAIT: Quite a wee little tot for such a long name, this breed is also relatively long in the body. As his name purports to convey, it is a rough-coated hound—the coat is hard and coarse but not shaggy. The wire coat is inclined towards feathering. Alternatively, the breed can have a short straight jacket that is without shine. Height: 17–21 inches (43–53 cm). Weight: 33–38 pounds (15–17½ kg). The breed's coloration varies from red to wheaten; a white spot on the chest is permissible.

DEVELOPMENT: A fairly modern hound from the Austrian province of Styria, the Styrian Hound was developed from Germanic hounds to withstand the extreme climatic conditions under which he would have to work. Good voice and untiring stamina were required of this little hound that was to be used extensively on the hunt. He is also able to silent trail.

RECOGNITION: FCI

CHARACTER: The Styrian Hound is hardy and good-natured. In addition to maintaining a serious and tranquil existence, he is continually obsessed with the hunt. Not snappy or belligerent, this dog makes a consistent and reliable companion.

TRANSYLVANIAN HOUND
Erdelyi Kopo, Hungarian Hound

PORTRAIT: This sleek, short-coated hound comes in two size varieties: the Tall variety stands 22–26 inches (56–66 cm) and weighs up to 77 pounds (35 kg); the Short variety stands 18–22 inches (46–56 cm). The variation continues in color as well: the Tall is black and tan with a white chest; the Short is red and tan. The Tall is longer than he is tall and appears lean and elegant. Both sizes possess sleek appearances and stunning good looks. The tricolor pattern is particularly brilliant and the head masterfully crafted.

DEVELOPMENT: The very ancient Hungarian Foxhound was developed for hunting in the game-filled woods of the Transylvanian region. The larger variety, which is the less-endangered today, was used on bigger game, while the smaller hunted mainly hare and fox. The Tall was successfully trained as a retriever. The Short today is probably extinct since no known specimens exist.

RECOGNITION: FCI

CHARACTER: A one-man dog who is easily trained, the Transylvanian Hound is loyal and quiet. Placing few demands on his owner, this dog is an easykeeper and enjoys time spent with his owner, although many tend to be extremely independent.

TREEING TENNESSEE BRINDLE

PORTRAIT: The pithy, solid body of the Treeing Tennessee is muscular and square. The coat, which may vary in shades of brindle, is short and dense and smooth to the touch. Height: 16–24 inches (40–61 cm). Weight: 40–50 pounds (18–22½ kg). The legs are powerful and well developed, giving the dog speed and coordination.

DEVELOPMENT: Like most hunters, particularly in the American South, the Brindle enthusiasts were not overly concerned with naming or labelling the hounds that worked for them. Hunters employed these small brindle dogs for generations, never giving them a second thought. This is not to suggest that owners were not keenly aware of the dogs' exceptional open-trailing and locating ability. Coon, squirrel and opossum comprise the breed's list of quarry. Hunters cannot ask for more enduring and dedicated workers than these Treeing hounds.

RECOGNITION: NR

CHARACTER: Demonstrative and placid, the Brindles delight owners with their boldness and outward displays of affection. Puppies should demonstrate these qualities at an early age. The breed is rugged and easy to keep. Its intelligence eases its training but heightens its sensitivity to scolding or neglect.

TREEING WALKER COONHOUND

PORTRAIT: The Treeing Walker is a medium-sized, capably put together hound with an elastic and durable frame. The coat, like that of many other coonhounds, is tight, smooth and glossy. The tricolor pattern is preferred, although bicolor dogs are also acceptable. Height: 20–27 inches (51–69 cm). Weight: 50–75 pounds (22½–34 kg).

DEVELOPMENT: The English Foxhound begot the Walker Foxhound; the Walker Foxhound begot the Treeing Walker. This direct lineage brings us this efficient hunter. He still possesses a strong resemblance to the English Foxhound. An undying sense of game coupled with untiring speed and manly drive makes this coonhound unstoppable. The coonhound lineage doesn't really stop at the Walker: American hunters also employ other varieties as well. One such coonhound is known as the Running Walker (no kidding!).

RECOGNITION: UKC

CHARACTER: These dogs are intelligent and proficient. Training is accomplished with little trouble, as these dogs are able to learn from example. They are primarily workers/hunters that are a bit too anxious to lie idly around a suburban home or condo. Working, to the Treeing, is not work but sport and diversion. Hunters find that these dogs demand very little in the way of care or grooming. They do, however, thrive on consistent and ample attention.

TYROLER BRACKE
Tyrolean Hound

PORTRAIT: Standing no greater than 19 inches (48 cm) high, usually 18 inches (46 cm) or smaller, and being black and tan (sometimes red) with white markings infrequently vacationing on the chest, the Tyroler both resembles and differs from the various other European scenthounds. This dog comes in three coat types (rough, hard, and smooth), and each are sometimes registered as individual breeds. Regardless of texture, the coat of the Tyroler is thick and resistant to extremes in temperature. The rough variety may show slight fringing, otherwise the dog will have a moderately tight appearance. Weight: 33–48 pounds (15–21½ kg).

DEVELOPMENT: Originating in the western area of Austria, it is very likely that these dogs are the product of line and crossbreeding with various German, Austrian, French, Swedish, and possibly Swiss hounds. Although type probably was secured many years ago, the breed still shares a look common to many of the well-established hounds of the contributing countries.

RECOGNITION: FCI

CHARACTER: He is a good-natured hound to be trusted at all times when he is properly cared for—that is, when allowed the necessary exercise and excitement, preferably through activation of his hunting instincts.

WESTPHALIAN DACHSBRACKE
Westfälische Dachsbracke, Sauerlander Dachsbracke

PORTRAIT: This short, broad-chested hunter is set square on four stocky legs. He has good tuck-up, a thick neck, and a chiseled head; these features convey the image of thrusting power set with a low center of gravity. His height is between 12–14 inches (30–36 cm); he typically weighs between 35–40 pounds (16–18 kg). The coat has a clean, hard, and smooth appearance.

DEVELOPMENT: Through knowledgeable breeding of the Dachshund to various hounds, German breeders combined the best of two different hunter types: the strength and proven ground ability of the Dachshund and the speed and quickness of the more leggy dachsbrackes. Though opinion differs on the origin of the breed, evidence suggests that the breed has existed for centuries. The Dachsbracke was used on hare, fox, wild boar and rabbit in his native Germany.

RECOGNITION: FCI

CHARACTER: Known for his ability to persevere and proceed, this Dachsbracke is highly regarded by ardent German hunters. Although rare to nonexistent outside his native Germany, the Westphalian is recommended as a companion to those who can guarantee moderate exercise and stimulus to this personable dog.

JR Quinn

YUGOSLAVIAN TRICOLOR HOUND
Jugoslavenski Tribarvni Gonič

PORTRAIT: A brawny body carried on long straight legs, the Tricolor is a picture of sleek, running elegance. His coat, mostly tan with black areas and white on the front, distinguishes him from the similar Yugoslavian Mountain Hound, who is black/tan. This is essentially a medium-sized dog with a broad head and a rectangular-shaped body. Weight: 44–55 pounds (20–25 kg). Height: 18–22 inches (46–56 cm). The coat is flat, dense and brilliant.

DEVELOPMENT: The influence of the Phoenician sighthounds is evident in the conformation of this swift-moving hound, whose long legs and excellent vision enhance his hunting abilities. He is believed to share similar origins to the other hounds of his area and, like his fellow Slavs, hunts fox, hare and other small game. Today both the Tricolor and the Mountain Hound are very rare and not frequently seen, even in Yugoslavia.

RECOGNITION: FCI

CHARACTER: Although becoming quite rare in his native land, the Tricolor is an adaptable dog that enjoys human companionship. He is affectionate and gentle. A devoted hunter that loves the chase, he prides himself on pleasing his master. He is obedient and attentive.

Maltese.

TOYS

AFFENPINSCHER

PORTRAIT: This definitely terrier-type toy, with plush eyebrows that shadow his black-bordered eyelids and large penetrating eyes, is called monkeyish in expression by those who love him most. His head is round, achieved in part by the well-domed forehead. The large round eyes are black and brilliant. The ears are small and set high. The muzzle is short and tipped with a black nose. Though the upper jaw is a "pinsch" shorter than the lower jaw, the teeth should never show. Height should never exceed 10¼ inches (26–27 cm). Weight: 7–8 pounds (3–4 kg). The entire coat is harsh, wiry and medium long. The preferred color is black, but black and tan, red, and dark gray Affens are also seen.

DEVELOPMENT: It is arguably true that the Affenpinscher contributed to its own "demise" in posing as a key ingredient for the creation of the more popular Brussels Griffon, who with all its charms cannot rival the Affenpinscher in genuine loveliness. Doubtless the Affen is an old breed, with records dating back to the 17th century. Through the centuries the Affenpinscher has retained his true "terrierism," though his muzzle has shortened. Years ago, the Affenpinscher and the (smooth) Miniature Pinscher were considered two varieties of the same breed, differing only in coat type.

RECOGNITION: FCI, AKC, KCGB, CKC, ANKC

CHARACTER: This is not a dog that you can step on, though the unwary or unenamored may make the foolish attempt. He is sturdy and fearless, energetic and proud. The Affen makes a fine companion, contributing always to the playful days and serious times of life.

AMERICAN HAIRLESS TERRIER

PORTRAIT: In build, the American Hairless Terrier is identical to the medium sized Rat Terriers, from whom he is directly descended. The American Hairless is a well-muscled dog with a deep chest, strong shoulders, solid neck, and powerful legs. The ears are carried erect when the dog is alert; the tail is customarily docked. Height: 9–14 inches (23–36 cm). Weight: 7–14 pounds (3–6½ kg). The one thing missing is the coat, for he is hairless. The skin color can be pink with gray, black, golden, or red spots.

DEVELOPMENT: In 1972, a remarkable thing happened: in a litter of mid-sized Rat Terriers, a completely hairless female was born. It became the prized pet of Willie and Edwin Scott of Louisiana, U.S.A., who bred it and produced another pair, male and female, that was used to stabilize the new breed. The Scotts, working under the guidance of their geneticists and veterinarians, have spent years striving to produce the breed they've aptly named the American Hairless Terrier. These are not just freak dogs. They differ substantially from the hairless types of Asia and Africa in that no powderpuff variety is needed to obtain hairless pups, as the hairlessness gene is not semi-lethal dominant but autosomal recessive. Furthermore, these dogs do not have absent premolars or any of the breeding complications associated with the hairless breeds. For these traits, the Scotts' nude puppy and its progeny are truly remarkable and unique in the canine world!

RECOGNITION: NR

CHARACTER: The temperament of these dogs is pure terrier, although they are not really terrier-terriers. The lively, feisty, fearless nature found in the best of terriers is sure to mellow as ratting cannot be recommended, due to the increased vulnerability brought on by the lack of a protective coat; however, the breed still enjoys challenging games and outdoor romps.

BELGIAN GRIFFON
Griffon Belge

PORTRAIT: Despite the characteristically disheveled look, this square little dog is well balanced and well sprung under his long hard coat. Height: 7–8 inches (18–20 cm). In size the Belgian Griffon comes in two varieties: one weighing up to 6½ pounds (3 kg), and the other up to 11 pounds (5 kg). Color for either variety can be black, black/tan, or red/black grizzle. Griffons customarily receive a tail docking and an ear cropping, both to a short length.

DEVELOPMENT: The original Griffon resembled a small terrier, half-Barbet and half-Griffon (Affenpinscher). There was a silky tuft on the head, and the muzzle was long and tapered. In the 1800s, the English Toy Spaniel was used to decrease the size and shorten the snout; it also eliminated much of his working ability. As the breed gained in popularity, Barbets, Smoushonds, Yorkshire Terriers, and Pekingese were likely used to perfect the desired type. The Pug is known to have been introduced into the bloodlines, and this infusion brought about the short coat and, hence, the Petit Brabancon, a close relative.

RECOGNITION: FCI

CHARACTER: An ideal mate, the Belgian Griffon was bred for companionship. Once an avid worker, exchanging a day's ratting for a day's meal, the Griffon retains his energy and ability in the form of extroversion and obedience. His wire coat, though long, requires a minimum of grooming; his disposition is hardy, and his feeding requisites are small.

BICHON FRISE
Bichon Tenerife, Tenerife Dog, Bichon a Poil Frise

PORTRAIT: He is quite the dog-about-town in his naturally white loosely curling coat, with his tail carried like a plume over his rounded hind quarters. Besides the long soft and curly outer coat, the Bichon is protected by an undercoat, making this 9–12 inch (23–31 cm) dog resistant to the inclemency of the rain. Some kennel clubs allow cream or apricot markings on the white coat for dogs younger than 19 months. While the AKC frowns upon silky Bichons, this coat is caressed by the KCGB.

DEVELOPMENT: Centuries ago, the Bichon was popular in Spain—how it got there no one is certain. It was likely introduced to the Canary Island of Tenerife by Spanish sailors. An alternative position maintains that Phoenician sailors first brought the Bichon to Tenerife, and from this island the breed made its way to the Continent. In either event, the Bichon waned slightly for some time until it was "rediscovered" by sailors in the 1300s. By the 1500s, these dogs were enjoying royal patronage. By the late 1800s, the Bichon was no more than a common street dog. Post-WWI brought a revival that reinstated the breed to its former noble status. The show ring now flaunts countless well-bred Bichons.

RECOGNITION: FCI, AKC, KCGB, CKC, ANKC

CHARACTER: The Bichon is forever the happy little dog, with a lively, carefree approach to life. His bouncy stride and pleasant voice contribute to his irresistible appearance.

BOLOGNESE
Bichon Bolognese

PORTRAIT: Easy to care for and easy to carry, the Bolognese, at a weight of between only 5½–9 pounds (3½–4 kg), fits comfortably into any home (or pocket). The coat is long and soft to the touch. The hair is tufty, with no undercoat. Almost all Bolognese are white, though an occasional specimen with blonde markings is seen; the blonde markings, while not encouraged by the FCI, are considered acceptable. He is of square build and is solid for his size of only 10–12 inches (25–31 cm).

DEVELOPMENT: Another of the bichon types, the Bolognese is believed to have descended from the bichons of southern Italy and Malta. He takes his name from the city of Bologna in northern Italy, where he originated. Like the Bichon Tenerife, the Bolognese enjoyed popularity with the nobility from the 1500s. He was graced by the company of such greats as La Pompadour and Catherine of Russia. Through the years, the Bolognese has always been bred for companionship; it is without a doubt one of the closest bonding of dog breeds.

RECOGNITION: FCI, KCGB

CHARACTER: This is quite the typical Bichon dog, with a jaunty air, happy gait, and a friendly wag of the tail. His coat requires a daily brushing, with monthly grooming sessions recommended. The Bolognese will likely take well to these procedures, as he revels in the added attention.

BOSTON TERRIER

PORTRAIT: With typical Bostonian elegance and tea-party couth, the docile yet determined Boston Terrier is, surprisingly, bred down from various one-time fighting dogs. The large, round, dark eyes retain a scant glimmer of his ancestors' scrappy ways and combine it with a quaintness that is indelibly New England. The breed comes in three weight classes: lightweight, under 15 pounds (6½ kg), middleweight, 15–20 pounds (6½–9 kg), and heavyweight, 20–25 pounds (9–11½ kg). The coat is short and smooth, usually colored in brindle with white markings. Black with white markings is also seen. The skull is square, and the cheeks are flat. The muzzle is short, square, wide, and deep; it must be in proportion to skull.

DEVELOPMENT: The "original" Boston Terrier was a cross between the English Bulldog and the English White Terrier. American breeders (yes, in Boston) began this cross sometime in the 1800s. Considerable crossbreedings were soon conducted, and by 1893 emerged a dog bred down from the English Bull Terrier, the Boxer, the Pit Bull Terrier, and other pithy terriers. These early Bostons were once shown in the category of "Round-headed Bull and Terriers, any Color." They have both mellowed and acquired a more worthy nomenclature since then.

RECOGNITION: FCI, AKC, UKC, KCGB, CKC, ANKC

CHARACTER: Though you couldn't call him either pugnacious or aggressive, the Boston Terrier is a dog able enough to defend himself should the need arise. A Cambridgian charmer, the Boston is a well-bred, highly intelligent dog with no small amount of inbred self-importance.

BRUSSELS GRIFFON
Griffon Bruxellois

PORTRAIT: This red-coated griffon of Belgium, like his fellow griff, the Griffon Belge, has a long wiry coat of harsh rough hairs. His color is called "clear red." Brussels Griffons are squarely and solidly built dogs that weigh between 6–12 pounds (2½–5½ kg) and stand 7–8 inches (18–20 cm) high. They move with a free gait and push off with a good drive. The body is short backed, with well-sprung ribs, and a strong loin. The Griffon Belge (Belgian Griffon) is often shown as a variety of the Brussels Griffon.

DEVELOPMENT: The original Griffons looked more terrier than they presently do. This is not surprising, considering that various terriers were used in their creation. All three griffons of Belgium, including the smooth-coated Petit Brabancon, were at one time considered only variations on a theme, undulating size and color motifs. The Affenpinscher was likely the instrumental stock to the early griffon's composition. In the 1800s, the English Toy Spaniel was used to diminish the size and shorten the snout. As the breed gained in popularity, Barbets, Smoushonds, Yorkshire Terriers, and Pekingese were likely used to fine tune desired type.

RECOGNITION: FCI, AKC, KCGB, CKC, UKC, ANKC

CHARACTER: These are lively little dogs, shedding content moments of intense affection and respect upon their human companions. These are independent and highly discriminating dogs who are quite obedient, if properly trained; they should never be spoiled.

CAVALIER KING CHARLES SPANIEL

PORTRAIT: New and improved, the Cavalier is a revised and miniaturized edition of the classic larger headed spaniels. This British tot is active, graceful, and genuinely grand, and his expression is always gentle and giving. The highly important head is almost flat between the ears; the stop is shallow; the muzzle is well tapered. The eyes are noticeably large, dark, and round, but should never be too prominent. Height: 12–13 inches (30–33 cm). Weight: 10–18 pounds (4½–8½ kg). The coat is long, silky and free from curl. He should be free of trimming and have plenteous feathering. Colors: black/tan, ruby (solid red), Blenheim (red/white), and Prince Charles (tricolor).

DEVELOPMENT: It was in the 1920s that an inquisitive American, named Roswell Eldridge, queried into the existence of the "Blenheim Spaniels of the Old Type." So acute was his curiosity and so earnest his desire to "preserve" the type that he offered £25 for spaniels representing the "Old Type" at Crufts, England's most prestigious dog show. The breed gained Kennel Club status in 1944, and from that point it becomes a Cinderella story. The 1960s saw the breed in the arms of British royalty; the 70s, on the top 20 chart of British breeds; and the 80s, despite the Monroe Doctrine, settling in the White House snoozing with President Reagan.

RECOGNITION: FCI, AKC, UKC, KCGB, CKC, ANKC

CHARACTER: The Cavalier is a soothing dog; he is non-aggressive and never nervous. His congeniality and hardy constitution make him the ideal pet for those who enjoy the company of guests.

CHIHUAHUA

PORTRAIT: The Chihuahua is an unmistakable dog, with his apple-domed skull blending into his lean cheeks and jaws. The head is topped with large ears that are held erect when alert, but have their   position for repose (a 45°-angle flare at the sides). The body is level on the back and slightly longer than high. There are two coat types: Smooth, a close glossy coat of a soft texture; and Long, a flat or slightly curly, soft-textured coat with an undercoat preferred. Either coat type can be any color—solid, marked, or splashed. Weight: 1–6 pounds (½–3 kg). Height varies accordingly.

DEVELOPMENT: The Chihuahua, named after the state in Mexico, is the smallest canine in recorded history. Some sources trace the breed to South America; it is believed variously that the dog, or dogs similar to it in size and type, was revered by the Aztecs as a sacred dog, fostered by the 9th-century Toltecs when it was called Techichi, or developed and kept by the Incas. The origins of any canine on the South American continent invite problems to which countless natural historians have addressed themselves. If dogs indeed existed in the Americas, particularly in Incan civilization, they were saved by the Spaniards that arrived there. Other reports, however, indicate that the conquistadores only found tree-climbing, mute, mutant rodents in South America and surely these are not the forefathers of our beloved Chihuahua. The Chinese, some believe, had their hands in the breed as well, with their incessant fetish for bantamization. The Chinese contribution to the breed more likely occurred in a latter-day cross to the Chinese Crested. The breed as we know it today descends from selectively bred American stock.

RECOGNITION: FCI, AKC, UKC, KCGB, CKC, ANKC

CHARACTER: A swift little dog with a quick response, the Chihuahua can run circles around dogs twice his size. He has a lot of heart and a lot of energy contained in one handy-sized canine companion.

Left: *Chihuahua, Long coated.* Above right: *Chihuahua, Smooth coated.* Below: *Chihuahua, Long coated.*

CHINESE CRESTED
Chinese Crested Dog

PORTRAIT: Sure to be an eyestopper, this dog has no hair—or at least very little of it. There are no large patches of hair anywhere on the body. The skin thus becomes an important feature; it is fine-grained and smooth. In the variety known as the powderpuff, the coat consists of an undercoat with a soft veil of long hair; a veil coat is another possible feature; however, the veil-coated dogs do not display hairlessness but do carry the gene. Height: 9–13 inches (23–33 cm). Weight: 5–10 pounds (2–5 kg). The tail, as with the crested head, is coated, creating a plume-like impression. In the powderpuff variety, any color is accepted. The skin is from pink to black, including mahogany, blue, lavender, and copper; it can be solid or spotted.

DEVELOPMENT: Hairless mutations certainly have occurred thoughout the history of the dog. Mostly these dogs were culled, either through an inability to adapt to their environment, the impossibility of finding a mate, or extermination by humans who saw them as freaks. In recent centuries, however, dog fanciers in Africa, China, Spain, and Mexico have been intrigued by the uniqueness of the hairless dogs. Although rare in its native country of China, the Chinese Crested is enjoying ever increasing popularity with the Western World.

RECOGNITION: FCI, AKC, KCGB, ANKC

CHARACTER: This breed places special demands on its keeper, for its hairlessness makes it especially susceptible to ultraviolet rays, cold and dampness, and other environmental conditions. The loving Chinese Crested certainly makes up for any special care required with his outward affection, kindness, and lively nature.

CONTINENTAL TOY SPANIEL, PHALENE
Épagneul Nain Continental Phalene

PORTRAIT: Drop ears and less popularity are all that separate the Phalene (or moth) from the Papillon (or butterfly). For a small dog—he stands only 8–11 inches (20–28 cm) tall—the Phalene has a certain bigness about him. His long, usually profuse, coat, with the abundant flowing undercoat, gives grandiose emanation. Movement is light and free, suggestive of ethereal power and grace. The long tail is set high and well fringed. Color is primarily white, with patches of any color except liver; color should surround the eyes and cover the ears, leaving a white blaze on the foreface.

DEVELOPMENT: The Épagneul Nain of Belgium, a favorite of royalty, is the ancestor of both the Phalene and the Papillon. The Phalene has always been loved by a select few, but he never achieved prolonged popularity, as did the Papillon in France during the early 1700s. No sound evidence connects the Continental Toy Spaniels to the Chihuahua despite an obvious similarity to the long-coated variety of that breed. In France today, the Phalene is called le Chien Ecureuil, or Squirrel Dog, in honor of its tail, not its quarry. Incidentally, dogs of the breed have been effectively used as rabbiters and ratters.

RECOGNITION: FCI

CHARACTER: These are prime house and family dogs, genuinely hardy and alert. The Phalene is cat-like in his cleanliness and neat-footedness. He is surprisingly adaptable to a variety of climates but today is primarily an indoor dog.

COTON DE TULEAR

PORTRAIT: As the name suggests, the most conspicuous feature of this breed is the coat, which is cottony or fluffy rather than silky. The outer coat is long and white; no undercoat is present. Other than the preferred all-white dogs, specimens with champagne heads or body markings, as well as those with black and white, have helped to distinguish the breed from other members of the bichon family. Height: 10–12 inches (25–31 cm). Weight: 12–15 pounds (5½–7 kg). Under the fluffy coat, the Coton is a dog of balance and symmetry.

DEVELOPMENT: The Coton is a bichon type that developed in Madagascar and the surrounding areas. The original bichon type extends back possibly one thousand years or more. Bichon type was diversified as new areas were settled by the Europeans, and the breeding stock of the bichon in that area was necessarily limited. It is even possible in some cases that native dogs of other types were crossbred. The Coton has enjoyed considerable popularity with the Madagascar upperclass for some years. The breed gained FCI recognition in 1970 and looks forward to continued progress and popularity.

RECOGNITION: FCI

CHARACTER: The Coton is full of tricks and surprises to fulfill his master's every wish. Endearing dogs with cottony coats and teasing expressions, they will enhance any home willing to spend the few moments a day in the necessary play and grooming routines.

Toys

369

ENGLISH TOY SPANIEL
King Charles Spaniel

PORTRAIT: Bred to be small, these one-time gun spaniels now weigh 9–12 pounds (4–5½ kg) and stand 10–10½ inches (25–27 cm) tall. In appearance the King Charles is cobby, though his type is refined. The skull is rather large in comparison to body size, expressive of the old-type spaniels. The eyes are very large and set wide apart, and the ears are very long and set quite low. The preferred bite is slightly undershot, with never a protruding tongue. Coat: long, straight, and silky, with ample feathering on the ears, legs, and tail. Color: black/tan (King Charles); tricolor (Prince Charles); red and white (Blenheim); solid chestnut red (Ruby).

DEVELOPMENT: Prior to the 20th century, spaniels of various sizes and types occurred in the same litter; a single litter could theoretically contain a cocker, a springer, and a "toy." Breeds, as we conceive of them today, did not exist. These toys were not the toy spaniels we see today; they were merely small variations (runts) of the larger gundogs. Man, always in search of companionship, would occasionally keep one of these dwarfs. As the desire for small dogs increased, breeders realized the value of these one-time culls and began breeding smalls to smalls. Eventually type was fixed.

RECOGNITION: FCI, AKC, KCGB, CKC, ANKC

CHARACTER: This breed is known for its quiet contentedness. It is the ideal housedog, quickly learning the house rules and always enjoying a quiet afternoon curled in a favorite corner. The breed is also known for its kindness and affection—the King Charles Spaniel is always there with care.

FRENCH BULLDOG
Bouledogue Francais

PORTRAIT: The heavy bone, big ears, and well-muscled body all contribute to the exceeding handsomeness of the French Bulldog. The short smooth coat contributes greatly to the clean appearance and enhances the solid build. The Frenchie shows a certain relation to the old bulldogs of the 1800s, though he has less bulk, more bowed legs, and an exaggerated wrinkle to the head. His head is large and square. The muzzle is short and broad. He is born with a screw or straight tail. In weight, there are two varieties: under 22 pounds (10 kg) and 22–28 pounds (10–13 kg)—which is rather large for a toy. Colors include brindle, fawn (with or without white markings), piebald, and white.

DEVELOPMENT: Throughout the 1800s, the Bulldogs raged in the pits and in popularity around the world, including France. It was there, just across the Channel, that a new breed of Bulldog emerged, one to which the English fanciers took mixedly. Frenchies were first brought to England in 1893, but nothing was done to further support the breed. When the French Bulldog Club of England formed in 1902, there were very few dogs in England. Soon, however, the value of the Frenchie as a breed was realized and things took a turn for the better. The breed is widely recognized and fairly popular.

RECOGNITION: FCI, AKC, KCGB, CKC, ANKC

CHARACTER: The French Bulldog is known for his determination. Such driven energy and suave charm make this breed a bundle of irresistible rapture. He is obedient and loves to please. Sleek yet muscular, the Frenchie is both active and attractive.

HAVANESE
Bichon Havanais, Havana Silk Dog

PORTRAIT: Never primped, clipped or altered in any way, the Havanese gives a rugged impression in a diminutive dog. He stands 8–11 inches (20–28 cm) high and is nearly square in build. Weight: 7–12 pounds (3–5½ kg). The legs are strong and allow for free and easy movement. The profuse coat varies from wavy to curly. The Havanese comes in a wide range of possible colors, including cream, gold, silver, blue, black, and other colors. The breed is of solid physical type and sound constitution.

DEVELOPMENT: The Havanese is a member of the bichon family. His coat, construction, and jaunty manner all point to the little white dogs so popular with the Spanish centuries ago. These dogs probably found their way with the Spanish settlers of Cuba, where the breed attained a certain distinctiveness from the other bichons. The breed has been facing a crisis through the 1900s, but is presently on the rise in popularity, having some dedicated believers in the breed who are actively campaigning for its preservation in the U.S.A.

RECOGNITION: FCI

CHARACTER: Havanese are gentle, responsive dogs. Some dogs may exhibit some degree of shyness around strangers, but this is not characteristic of the breed. They bond closely with their human families and have a natural affinity for children.

ITALIAN GREYHOUND
Piccoli Levrieri Italiani

PORTRAIT: Lithe and light, the Italian Greyhound is elegant and graceful in a dainty sort of way. In overall impression, the Italian Greyhound resembles a miniaturization of the Greyhound proper. There are two varieties according to weight: 8 pounds (3½ kg) maximum, and over 8 pounds (3½ kg). Height: 13–15 inches (33–38 cm). The head is long, flat, and narrow. The ears are rose shaped, not pricked, soft and fine and placed well back on the head. The eyes, though rather large, are bright and attentive. Highly refined in appearance, the Italian Greyhound has an arched neck and a high-stepping gait, making it resemble quite resolutely the larger sighthounds.

DEVELOPMENT: Italian Greyhounds are likely the first dogs ever bred strictly for companionship. Their claim to the ancient is unquestionable; mummified dogs have been found in tombs of pharaohs, and they are depicted in ancient texts and paintings from centuries ago. Italian Greyhounds have marched with man through the past 30 or so centuries, often gracing the palaces of influential nobles and rulers. The breed enjoys a moderate popularity today, and many wonder why the breed has never regained the status it once enjoyed.

RECOGNITION: FCI, AKC, KCGB, CKC, ANKC, UKC

CHARACTER: The Italian Greyhound, though not shy, takes time to bond; he is a discerning dog, choosing his bed, his meals, and his friends with utmost care. He is both loving and lovable—the perfect companion for those looking for an intelligent, elegant dog with a definitive sense of history.

Toys

JAPANESE CHIN
Japanese Spaniel, Chin

PORTRAIT: The Chin comes in two classes according to weight: over 7 pounds (3 kg) and under 7 pounds (3 kg). In the latter case, the rule is: the smaller the better. The Chin has a large head and large, dark, prominent eyes set wide apart. The Chin is an ornate dog, with a profuse coat of long straight and silky hair. The thick feathering tends to the stand-offish, thus creating a visible mane; the feathering on the upper legs creates the effect of breeches. Color: black and white or red and white in a broken pattern.

DEVELOPMENT: In closely studying the notes of ancient Chinese temples and the ancient pottery and embroidery that still exist, it is nearly certain that the Japanese Chin traces back to the dogs similar to his type found in China centuries ago. How these dogs arrived in Japan remains speculative and a topic of debate among cynologists. Were they received by the Japanese emperor as gifts brought by a Korean emissary in 732 AD? Did they come with the Chinese monks and teachers who emigrated as early as 520 AD? Or is there another explanation? Perhaps. Whatever the story, the fact remains that Japanese breeders perfected the breed centuries ago and deserve the credit for its existence today.

RECOGNITION: FCI, AKC, KCGB, CKC, ANKC

CHARACTER: The Chin is stylishly serious, though loving in his own way. He is instinctively accurate in his interpretation of intentions, always knowing a friend and never trusting an enemy. He is a fine watchdog.

JAPANESE SPITZ

PORTRAIT: The Japanese Spitz has the classic northern appearance that appeals to so many canine fanciers. The plush white coat is long, thick and stand-offish, creating a warm impression, and the tail is carried curled over the back in nordic fashion. The coat is short on the bottom half of the legs, with breeches on the hind legs and feathering on the forelegs. The ears are carried prick; the muzzle tapers slightly; the eyes are dark, and the nose and lips are black, together contrasting with the pure white coat. Height: 15 inches (38 cm). Weight near 13 pounds (6 kg).

DEVELOPMENT: Not to be confused with the American Eskimo, the Japanese Spitz is an entirely different breed, originating in a different country and descending from different stock. Whereas the American Eskimo is the believed descendant of small German spitz types, the Japanese Spitz is believably descended from the native Siberian Samoyed. These Samoyeds were strictly bred for smallness, with the end result being the Japanese Spitz. Creation of the breed commenced in the late 1800s; the breed is of worldwide distribution today, but is still fighting to attain a sure-footed foothold.

RECOGNITION: FCI, KCGB

CHARACTER: This diminutive dog offers all the appeal of the toy dog in a distinctively northern package. The breed is lively and bold; no doubt, had you no object with which to gain perspective, you would swear this was a very big dog. The plush coat is moderately easy to care for, requiring little more than a daily brushing. The Japanese Spitz is a very tidy animal.

JAPANESE TERRIER
Nippon Terrier, Nihon Terrier

PORTRAIT: Presented is a smooth-haired, smooth-muzzled terrier that is predominantly white with sparsely distributed specks of black and tan. The refined, elegant type of this terrier evokes the affecting winds of the smaller sighthounds. A small docked tail and a proportionately small head placed on its well-muscled body give the breed a distinctive appearance. Height: 12–15 inches (30–38 cm). Weight: 10–13 pounds (4½–6 kg).

DEVELOPMENT: Early 18th-century Japan met a clan of prolific and complying Smooth Fox Terriers. Sowing the seeds of this Nipponese terrier, these Fox Terriers (which came from Holland) bred with indigenous dogs to create a new nippy terrier, a tad smaller than themselves. These little dogs, although small enough to warrant their being solely toy companions, can function effectively as gundogs as well as terriers. The Japanese Terrier is a respected retriever and a skilled water worker, able to retrieve a bagged duck or downed goose. Certain specimens were fostered exclusively as toys, to be carried about in pockets; these were often called Mikado or Oyuki (snowy) Terriers.

RECOGNITION: NR

CHARACTER: Light-hearted and spirited in the home, they make celebrated pets. Whimsical and affectionate, these jovial juveniles are Japan's jauntiest tea-time mascots.

KYI LEO

PORTRAIT: The Kyi Leo is a small but solid dog, having borrowed the best from each of his two component breeds. In height he stands 8–12 inches tall (20–31 cm), with 9–11 inches (23–28 cm) being preferred. He is well boned for his size with good muscle tone. He is light on his feet and quite agile. The coat is long and thick; it hangs straight or slightly wavy; there is a natural part that tends to form along the spine, contributing to the breed's neat and attractive look. Color is usually black and white particolor, but gold and white and self-colors are also seen; the color of some specimens may fade from black to slate.

DEVELOPMENT: The Kyi Leo is certainly one of the newcomers to the world of dogs. The "breed" was established in 1972, after an original cross with the Lhasa Apso and the Maltese and 20 years of linebreeding for the desired type. The Kyi Leo originated in California. This breed has entered the hearts of many fanciers and has an active group of supporters behind it. His small size and good disposition should take him far in a world of diminishing space and ascending condominiums.

RECOGNITION: NR

CHARACTER: Breeders focus on character and disposition. The Kyi Leo is gentle and bonds closely with his immediate family. He retains the Lhasa's wariness of strangers and thereby makes a good warning dog. He is not known to bark without reason nor to be shy of people. The coat will require brushing and a little trimming, but no clipping is involved.

LHASA APSO

PORTRAIT: Beyond the flowing veil lie dark brown eyes that, legend says, will reveal a different secret each time they look upon you—and thus are the mysteries of the mountains of Tibet revealed. The Lhasa is an exotically appealing dog, with his long dense coat of heavy hairs lying straight. Color can be golden, sandy or honey, preferably with black tips on the ears, tail, and beard; other colors include grizzle, slate, smoke, particolor, black, white, and brown. The well-feathered tail is carried over the back in a screw-like fashion. The head, well furnished with whiskers and beard, is narrow and moderately sized. Height is between 10–11 inches (25–28 cm).

DEVELOPMENT: Deep within the largest continent in the world, in the ancient land of Tibet, there existed brachycephalic dogs bred from the native terrier-type canines for the purpose of guarding the interiors of temples. These dogs became the foundation stock of the Lhasa Apso. It was not until the 7th century that these Lhasas were bred to emulate, at least in appearance, the revered lion. The Lhasa visually imitated the holy lion—the symbol of the Buddha's dominance of the animal kingdom. Tibetans were greatly respectful of these tiny dogs that they believed to be the reincarnation of their pious lamas (priests) that failed to attain Nirvana.

RECOGNITION: FCI, AKC, UKC, KCGB, CKC, ANKC

CHARACTER: The Lhasa remarkably retains some of his once-valued instincts for guarding the home and family; therefore, he tends to be wary around strangers. His lively though assertive nature is appreciated in the home as well as in the show.

LÖWCHEN
Little Lion Dog, Petit Chien Lion

PORTRAIT: This is the emblem of courage, the symbol of bravery; he, the Löwchen, ruler of the couch, conqueror of the pillow, stands 10–13 inches (25–33 cm) tall and weighs 8–18 pounds (3½–8½ kg). When clipped, the Löwchen can resemble the lion. His long silky coat is wavy but never curly. He can be any color or any combination of colors. The eyes are round, dark, large, and intelligent. The ears are long, pedantically pendant, and well fringed.

DEVELOPMENT: Such is the appeal of the Löwchen that several different countries claim him as their native. Whether his origin truly is in Russia, the Mediterranean area, or France is not certain, but it is known that the Lion Dog enjoyed popularity in Italy, Spain, France and Germany as early as the 1500s. This popularity continued through to the 1800s; Goya is but one of the great artists who chose to capture the Little Lion Dogs on canvas. With the coming of the 20th century and the two World Wars, the popularity of the Löwchen waned. By 1960, he was granted the title "rarest breed" by the *Guinness Book of World Records*. However, the pendulum soon swung again—the Löwchen is on the rise, enjoying his Kennel Club recognition.

RECOGNITION: FCI, KCGB, ANKC

CHARACTER: Fearless and gentle, the Löwchen is king of the small companions. The coat will require special care, whether or not it is kept in the lion cut. Lively and gay, the Löwchen loves romping around the yard and being with his family.

MALTESE
Bichon Maltiase

PORTRAIT: The pure white, profusely coated Maltese is essentially short and cobby. The body is well balanced, with good spring of rib. The coat is of good length but does not interfere with the dog's gait; the texture of the coat is silky and never woolly. The eyes are oval and lively, never bulging. The head is of medium length, in perfect proportion to the body. The tail wavers over the back: a longhaired plume carried gracefully. Height: not exceeding 10 inches (26 cm). Weight: 4–6 pounds (2–3 kg). A solid white color is preferred, although lemon on the ears is pardonable.

DEVELOPMENT: The ancient dog of Malta has long been a symbol of the opulence of the art-loving, highly bred island inhabitants. The beauty and petiteness of the friendly Maltese complemented the peaceful society in which it dwelled. In the time of Phidias, the Maltese was favored by the great ladies of the Roman Empire. The Maltese hasn't always been solely a show piece and home ornament: once called the Maltese Terrier, it was used on rats and had a particular distaste for felines. Were it not for the exuberant coat (prized today no doubt!), it would have done a number on badger as well.

RECOGNITION: FCI, AKC, UKC, KCGB, CKC, ANKC

CHARACTER: No frail or delicate dog, the Maltese is hardy and lively and able to withstand reasonable extremes in climes. He is described as sweet tempered, gentle mannered, sprightly in action, and vigorous. He is ideal for those looking for a little action in their pets.

MEXICAN HAIRLESS
Toy Xoloitzcuintli, Tepeizeuintli

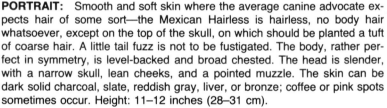

PORTRAIT: Smooth and soft skin where the average canine advocate expects hair of some sort—the Mexican Hairless is hairless, no body hair whatsoever, except on the top of the skull, on which should be planted a tuft of coarse hair. A little tail fuzz is not to be fustigated. The body, rather perfect in symmetry, is level-backed and broad chested. The head is slender, with a narrow skull, lean cheeks, and a pointed muzzle. The skin can be dark solid charcoal, slate, reddish gray, liver, or bronze; coffee or pink spots sometimes occur. Height: 11–12 inches (28–31 cm).

DEVELOPMENT: The hairless breeds developed most probably in Africa and, by one means or another, found their way to China and America. The Mexican Hairless was brought to Central America during the 17th century by traders. These dogs were once referred to as African dogs, and the irregular formation of their teeth and the absence of premolars on both jaws differentiate the Mexican Hairless from the least of his coatless brothers. The Aztec Indians favored these little hairless dogs and their larger brothers, the Xoloitzcuintlis, as night-time poncho warmers, general pets, and occasional sacrifices. As the breed developed in modern times, two types evolved. The more desired was the lighter, more active type as opposed to the cloddy untamed-appearing ones that invariably repulsed newcomers to the breed.

RECOGNITION: CKC

CHARACTER: The Mexican Hairless has perhaps raised more hair than any other dog (although never his own!). He is not a dog for everyone, requiring special attention to his skin, which is susceptible to the sun and to scrapes from objects around the house (including the cat). Otherwise he is a happy and alert canine, always willing to shed affection and not his coat upon his human family.

MINIATURE DACHSHUND
Zwergteckel

PORTRAIT: Long bodied, short legged, and low to the ground, the Miniature Dachshund is no squirt in boldness or confidence. The legs are crooked but do not give the dog a crippled, awkward, or cramped impression. The head tapers uniformly to the nose and is clean-cut. The ears fall hound-like (he is a hound) with animated carriage. Weight: 9–10 pounds (4–4½ kg). The coat can be long, wire, or smooth. The long is soft and straight, with abundant feathering. The wire, except for the head, is covered with short, straight harsh hair with no undercoat; the face is well but neatly furnished. The smooth is dense and short, with loose and supple skin. In color the Dachshund can be one-colored, two-colored or dappled.

DEVELOPMENT: The Miniature Dachshund was produced around 1900 by German hunters who desired a dog that could pursue and unburrow rabbits—not just any dog, but a Dachshund with his unparalleled German tenacity and inability to yield. Dwarf Pinschers and Black and Tan Terriers were first utilized, sacrificing some vim for the pint size. The result of the crosses was named the Rabbit Teckel for its doomed bunny quarry; it was also used on fox and an occasional badger.

RECOGNITION: FCI, AKC, UKC, KCGB, CKC

CHARACTER: The Miniature Dachshund has never lost his desire to go to ground—being so low to ground and all. He enjoys "regaling" his master by redesigning the tomato garden. He is a lot of energy in a little package. For the safety of his back, this energy should be curbed—jumping on the furniture cannot be tolerated.

TOYS 383

MINIATURE PINSCHER
Zwergpinscher, Reh Pinscher

PORTRAIT: The Reh Pinscher is so called because of his resemblance, structurally and animation-wise, to a very small species of deer. He is well balanced, short coupled, smooth coated and sensationally sleek. The head must be in correct proportion to the body, the ears set high and erect. He appears naturally well groomed and self possessed. Height: 10–12½ inches (25–32 cm). Weight: 8–10 pounds (3½–4½ kg). Colors available are black/-tan, chocolate/tan and stag red.

DEVELOPMENT: Not a dwarf of the Doberman Pinscher as some believe, the Miniature Pinscher is an ancient breed, and its resemblance to the Doberman is an *ex post facto* coincidence; namely, the doing of Herr Dobermann, who greatly admired the feisty MinPin in a big way. The MinPin was derived from large smooth-coated German Pinschers and was employed to keep down the rat population in the stables that it frequented. This ancient MinPin then looked very little like the refined tyke we hail today as the "King of the Toys."

RECOGNITION: FCI, AKC, UKC, KCGB, CKC, ANKC

CHARACTER: Modern society wouldn't dream of sending this noble miniature to ground, as he is a sublime house dog. He is a great alarm dog and amenable to discipline. The show ring is dominated by stag red dogs, but the inside scoop is that breeders can better sell the black/tan ones to pet owners and so use the red ones in the ring. Both colors make handsome and hardy companions.

MOSCOW LONGHAIRED TOY TERRIER
Moscovian Miniature Terrier

PORTRAIT: This diminutive newcomer to the world of dogs is a petite and elegant toy companion. His coat is long, with generous feathering on the ears and legs, a ruff to the neck, and tail that is docked. The tuck-up is substantial. The face tapers sharply and the ears are rather large. Height: 8–11 inches (20–28 cm). Weight: 4½–6½ pounds (2–3 kg). This Moscovian mite can be solid tan, black, brown, sable, fawn, all with tan points or in solid, and merle.

DEVELOPMENT: The most recent development in the Soviet dog world, the Moscow Longhaired Toy Terrier enters the scene as a hardy and minuscule house dog that doesn't need a lot of food to survive. The long-haired Chihuahua and some English toy terriers or Papillons are the likely candidates for the crossbreeds used to create the breed. The exact cross is, however, one of the better kept secrets of the U.S.S.R. The breeding efforts began in the late 1970s. So as far as dogs go, this is but an infant breed.

RECOGNITION: NR

CHARACTER: The latest craze in Russia, these Moscow Toys are the pick of senior citizens and urban dwellers. In a country where urban living quarters are rather cramped, a small dog with the Moscow stamp on it is sure to be the top toy in town for some time to come. He is easily trained and easy to care for.

PAPILLON
Épagneul Nain Continental Papillon, Continental Toy Spaniel Papillon

PORTRAIT. Finely boned and dainty, the Papillon flowers in elegance suitably French. Its distinguishing characteristic is its beautiful butterfly ears which stand straight up, like the widespread wings of a full-grown butterfly. It is not a cobby dog. The head is small and slightly rounded with a well-defined stop. The coat is abundant, silky and flowing—straight with a resilient quality. Breeches or culottes are noticeable. Height: 8–11 inches (20–28 cm). The Papillon is basically white, with patches of any color (except liver). Symmetrical facial markings are desired, including a white blaze down the face. Tail flows with plume.

DEVELOPMENT: The Épagneul Nain of Belgium, a favorite of royalty, is said to be the ancestor of the Papillon. The breed was popular in France during the early 1700s and has been brushed on canvas by many great artists. Famous owners include Marie Antoinette and Madame de Pompadour; ladies of exquisite taste and stature have always favored these charming French tarts. No sound evidence connects them to the Chihuahua, despite an obvious similarity to the long-coated variety of that breed. In France today, they are called le Chien Ecureuil, or Squirrel Dog, in honor of their tails, not their quarry. Incidentally, they have been effectively used as both rabbitters and ratters.

RECOGNITION: FCI, AKC, UKC, KCGB, CKC, ANKC

CHARACTER: These are prime house dogs and primarily indoor companions, genuinely hardy and alert. They are cat-like in their cleanliness and neat-footedness.

PEKINGESE
Peking Palasthund

PORTRAIT: Thick-set in appearance and dignity, the Pekingese preferably maintains a lion-like impression, as if walking out of a small cement temple statuette. He is ever alert and lively. The body is short with a broad chest. The head is wider than deep, and the skull is flat and deep between the ears. The profile is flat with the nose well set between the eyes. The coat is long and straight, with the profuse mane extending beyond the shoulders and forming a cape around the neck. The outer coat is coarse, the undercoat thick. Weight in three categories: under 6 pounds (2½ kg), 6–8 pounds (2½–3½ kg), 8–14 pounds (3½–6½ kg). Colors: red, fawn, black, black/tan, sable, brindle, white, and particolor. All dogs should be masked with spectacles around the eyes.

DEVELOPMENT: For thousands of years, the Pekingese has been associated with the Chinese devotion to Buddhism. The Budda lion became of great importance, worthy of great homage; and as such, the Pekingese enjoyed similar lauds. Bred by the chief eunuch, the tiny "Lion Dogs" were kept in the sacred temple. The Pekes preceded the emperor into the chamber of ceremonies and announced his arrival. Chinese vengeance is relentless, and punishment for theft or defamation of any of the emperor's dogs was slow death by torture (which no Peke was ever to witness).

RECOGNITION: FCI, AKC, UKC, KCGB, CKC, ANKC

CHARACTER: The Peke, despite his petiteness, is courageous and bold. His independence and confidence should imply combativeness rather than delicacy. The dog is accustomed to being unchallenged and foremost in his master's eyes. His coat requires extensive grooming.

PEQUEÑO PODENGO PORTUGUESO
Small Portuguese Hound, Portuguese Rabbit Dog

PORTRAIT: The Small Podengo Portugueso, actually a miniature sighthound type, appears like a very sturdy Chihuahua. It has a well-proportioned head, flat skull, pronounced stop, and straight muzzle. The eyes are small and oblique; they range in color from light honey to dark chestnut. The ears are pricked, triangular, and sizable. The back is level, the legs straight with cat feet. Height: 8–12 inches (20–31 cm). Weight: 10–12½ pounds (4½–6 kg). The breed occurs in two coat types: short coat, which is hard and longer than most sighthounds; and wire coat, which is medium long, shaggy and coarse. Yellow, fawn, and black with white markings are the color options.

DEVELOPMENT: Although hailed as the smallest hunting dog and bred for rabbit hunting, the Pequeño is an ideally sized companion dog. The Portuguese Podengos come in three size varieties. The Grande is the largest and therefore is able to cover the most ground. The Medio is probably the fastest of the three *hermanos* and has exquisite maneuverability on rough ground. The Pequeño, for all its petiteness, is still an eager hunter and even an able ratter.

RECOGNITION: FCI

CHARACTER: This Podenguito makes an excellent working dog and pleasant companion dog that is lively and even tempered. A potential owner with a love to hunt and a small abode can expect joy unparalleled—and a full bag of game—with the Pequeño at his side.

PETIT BRABANCON
Piccolo Brabantino

PORTRAIT: A smooth-coated griffon is an oxymoron in its very conception. *Griffon* of course translates to wirehair. Yet the American Kennel Club allows this paradox to persist in accepting Brussels Griffon in a smooth coat. The Petit Brabancon is that dog without the whiskers and wire jacket. The coat, which is short and dense, can be red, red/black, red/black grizzle, black or black/tan. These are squarely and solidly built dogs who weigh between 6–12 pounds (2½–5½ kg) and stand 7–8 inches (18–20 cm) high. The body is composed of a short back, well-sprung ribs, and a strong loin.

DEVELOPMENT: The original Griffons looked more terrier than they presently look. This is not surprising, considering that various terriers were used in their creation. The various Belgian "griffons" were all considered a single breed. The Affenpinscher (*pinscher* translates to terrier) was likely the prime contributor of component stock to the early Griffons. In the 1800s, English Toy Spaniel was used to decrease the size and shorten the snout; it also eliminated much of these dogs' ability. As the breed gained in popularity, Barbets, Smoushond, Yorkshire Terriers, and Pekingese were likely used to perfect desired type. The breed has enjoyed a healthy fancy in Italy.

RECOGNITION: FCI

CHARACTER: Companionable and playful, the smooth-coated Brabancons are lively and energetic in the house. They thrive on attention, when they are in the mood for it. Perhaps shy upon first meeting, the Brabancon eventually shows his chipper self and is sheer deiight.

POMERANIAN

PORTRAIT: Compact and short coupled, the Pomeranian possesses a well-knit tiny frame. The head and nose are foxy in outline, the skull is slightly flat. The ears are small and not too widely apart. The body is short backed and well ribbed, with a fairly deep chest. The coat is very abundant: the outer coat is long and perfectly straight, harsh in texture; the undercoat is soft and fluffy. In color the Pom is any of 12 colors: black, brown, chocolate, beaver, red, orange, cream, orange sable, wolf sable, blue, white or particolor. Height: 11 inches (28 cm) maximum. Weight: 3–7 pounds (3½–6½ kg).

DEVELOPMENT: Similar dogs to the Pomeranian were used as sheepdogs throughout the world, not just in northern Germany. These ancestors were obviously a few degrees larger than today's much-loved Lilliputian, being closer to the Keeshond in size. When the Pom first arrived in Britain, it was not well received, perceived as a "foreigner" with an unattractive, unkempt coat. Early breeders worked hard to master the Pom's coat. The breed is a descendant of the German spitzen and is the smallest from this sled-pulling family. At one time, white was *the* color for Poms, but these dogs were often a tad larger, and the smaller orange and sables moved into vogue.

RECOGNITION: AKC, UKC, KCGB, CKC, ANKC

CHARACTER: The Pom is a wonderful companion dog and show ring contender. The breed's docile temper and affectionate nature endear it to many; its vivacity and spirit make it well liked by persons who don't usually care for toy dogs.

PUG
Carlin, Mops

PORTRAIT: In appearance the Pug is decidedly square and cobby, with a compact form, well-knit proportions and hard muscles. The head is large and round with no indentation. The nose is snubbed. The muzzle is short, blunt and square, not upfaced. Wrinkles are clearly defined on the face. The coat is fine, smooth and soft, neither short nor woolly. Colors include apricot, black and silver-fawn. Height: 10–11 inches (25–28 cm). Weight: 14–18 pounds (6–8½ kg). The ears can either be rose or button.

DEVELOPMENT: Seemingly oxymoronical, the Pug is a miniature mastiff that finds its roots in the Orient, although it also found great favor in Holland, where it was called the Dutch Pug. The Dutch East India Company is believed to be this brachycephalic dwarf's ticket into Holland. As with many of the small breeds, the Pug is believed to have been larger at one time, and this pugnacious mush-faced Pug pushed his way into a few other British breeds (such as the Bulldog and Affenpinscher). During the reign of William III, the Pug found his way to Britain and into the favor of this monarch.

RECOGNITION: FCI, AKC, UKC, KCGB, CKC, ANKC

CHARACTER: *Multum in parvo*, the Pug certainly is a lot in a little package! He is sounder and more solid than most of his fellow toys and makes a hardy companion dog. Rumors of yore complained that Pugs snored and were greedy, making rotund, resonant, runty pets. This most assuredly is not true, and very few Pugs snore in reality.

SHIH TZU
Chrysanthemum Dog

PORTRAIT: With head held high, the Shih Tzu gaits with carriage well befitting his noble ancestry. The coat is luxurious, long and dense, with good undercoat. The breed is known for its chrysanthemum-like face. The head is broad and round, wide between the eyes. The muzzle is square and short but not wrinkled. The Shih Tzu enjoys an abundance of colors, and its white blazed tail is particularly prized. Height: 8–11 inches (20–28 cm). Weight: 9–16 pounds (4–7½ kg). The tail is heavily plumed, curved over the back and carried gaily.

DEVELOPMENT: "Will the real Lion Dog please stand up!" The Shih Tzu, like the Pekingese, is originally oriented in the Orient. The Shih Tzu was perfected in China and is likely a dwarfed Tibetan Terrier, that is, exaggerated beyond the Lhasa. The short face was much admired in China, and the Shih Tzu was derived by crosses between these bantamized Tibetan breeds and native Chinese miniatures. In its native land of China, the Shih Tzu enjoyed the unyielding admiration and love of the nation's emperor.

RECOGNITION: FCI, AKC, UKC, KCGB, CKC, ANKC

CHARACTER: Described as nearly human in his response to affection, the Shih Tzu is forthcoming and generous. One very tough home companion that is prized for his tremendous resilience and carefree big-dog attitude is described by his owner as "scary."

SILKY TERRIER
Australian Silky Terrier, Sydney Silky, Silky Toy Terrier

PORTRAIT: A lightly built, compact dog set moderately low—medium length with refined structure. Parted straight silky hair conveys the desired well-groomed appearance. The head is strong and wedge shaped, the skull is flat and moderately broad between the ears. The neck fits into the sloping shoulders with expected grace. The tail is set high and carried erect or semi-erect. Height: 9 inches (23 cm). Weight: 8–10 pounds (3½–4½ kg). The Silky Terrier's color is blue/tan. Pronounced diminutiveness is not desired since the general appearance should suggest the required substance of a small functional terrier.

DEVELOPMENT: Like his brother the Australian Terrier, the Silky was developed in Australia with British terriers during the 1800s. The breed's coat is worthy of note, and the first recorded blue/tan broken-coated terriers in Australia date to a show in Victoria in 1872. At some point, specimens were transported to England and bred to Dandie Dinmont Terriers to produce the dog we recognize today as the Silky Terrier. Not developed for the purposes of ratting or any hand-blistering task, the Silky is meant to be a companion.

RECOGNITION: FCI, AKC, UKC, KCGB, CKC, ANKC

CHARACTER: The Silky fills the bill of companion dog to the "tea." His coat requires great dedication, but not as much as some of the other long-coated toys. Although not bred to be a terrier, he maintains an assertive spirited terrier-like character.

TIBETAN SPANIEL

PORTRAIT: A well-balanced overall impression is complemented by the breed's gay and assertive expression. The body is slightly longer from the point of the shoulder to the root of the tail than at the withers. The tail is set high and richly plumed in a gay curl. The neck is embellished by a mane or "shawl" of longer hair. The top coat is silky but lies rather flat. The undercoat is fine and dense. Height: 10 inches (25 cm). Weight: 9–15 pounds (4–7 kg). The standard states no color preference, and all colors and combinations occur and are acceptable.

DEVELOPMENT: As a member of Tibetan monasteries, the Tibetan Spaniel earned his keep as a "Prayer Dog," turning the prayer wheel for intercessing monks. Prayers were written on parchment and put into a revolving box. The little monastery dwellers were trained to turn the wheels and simultaneously further the invoker's supplication (and gain a few plenary indulgences themselves). The purebred Tibetan Spaniel could only be found inside of the monastery, since the Tibetan people didn't much care about the romantic endeavors of their star-crossed crossbreeding dogs.

RECOGNITION: FCI, AKC, KCGB, CKC

CHARACTER: Perhaps leading a rather sheltered existence in times past explains the Tibetan Spaniel's shyness with strangers, which is variously interpreted as aloof or removed. With his own, he is gay and assertive. His intelligence is prayerfully proverbial.

TOY AMERICAN ESKIMO

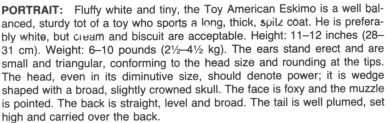

PORTRAIT: Fluffy white and tiny, the Toy American Eskimo is a well balanced, sturdy tot of a toy who sports a long, thick, spitz coat. He is preferably white, but cream and biscuit are acceptable. Height: 11–12 inches (28–31 cm). Weight: 6–10 pounds (2½–4½ kg). The ears stand erect and are small and triangular, conforming to the head size and rounding at the tips. The head, even in its diminutive size, should denote power; it is wedge shaped with a broad, slightly crowned skull. The face is foxy and the muzzle is pointed. The back is straight, level and broad. The tail is well plumed, set high and carried over the back.

DEVELOPMENT: This is the newest development in the American spitz types. The United Kennel Club is the lone registry for the two larger American Eskimos but has yet to recognize the toy variety. All varieties are measured against the same standard, except for size. The American Eskimos descended directly from the white German Spitz. United States breeders took a particular fancy to the white dogs and worked to develop only white spitzen. For many years, the breed was referred to in the U.S. simply as "Spitz," and many an AKC judge will use the term flippantly to refer to the American Eskimo, a breed with which they are scarcely acquainted.

RECOGNITION: NR

CHARACTER: The Toy American Eskimos promise everything their bigger brothers offer but in a smaller package. "Beauty without vanity" aptly describes the Eskies that have made flawless companions to Americans for generations.

TOY FOX TERRIER
American Toy Terrier, AmerToy

PORTRAIT: A well-put-together lively squirt, the Toy Fox Terrier is a handsomely balanced dog with a smooth easycare coat. The body is essentially square. The ears are pointed Vs and erect. The head is slightly dome shaped, never apple. The preferred coat is tricolor: white and black with tan trim. However, white/tan and white/black are acceptable as well. Height: 10 inches (25 cm). Weight: 3½–7 pounds (1½–3½ kg).

DEVELOPMENT: The Toy Fox Terrier is an American attempt to produce its own red, white and blue toy terrier. Despite having to settle somewhat for color, Americans happily have been more successful with the AmerToy than the British with the Toy Bulldog or Toy Bull Terrier, both of which were hindered by poor bone quality and weak conformation. The AmerToy, however, is bred down from the already small Smooth Fox Terrier, and therefore is quite free of these unfortunate complications. The originators of the Amer-Toy were Smooth owners who were fascinated by the "runts" in their litters, which consistently turned out to be scrappier than the other siblings. Crosses to the Chihuahua and the English Toy Terrier completed the mix that created the pint-sized AmerToy.

RECOGNITION: UKC

CHARACTER: A single armful, the Toy Fox Terrier is a comical and intelligent companion and surely the ideal toy dog for anyone desiring such a delightful mate. Puppyhood frivolity remains with him throughout his life; this, mixed with his scrappy nature, makes him a truly smile-evoking pet.

Toys

TOY GERMAN SPITZ
Zwergspitz

PORTRAIT: A minuscule cobby dog that is the perfect spitz in miniature. He is balanced and short coupled. His head is well proportioned to his body. The ears, mounted high on the head, are erect and triangular. The tail is typical of the spitz family, plumed and tossed over the back. The coat is double: the outer is long and coarse, with a glisten; the undercoat is dense and soft. Height: under 8½ inches (22 cm). Weight: under 7 pounds (3½ kg).

DEVELOPMENT: This is the smallest of the German Spitz family. The dog is easily mistaken for a Pomeranian, as is his next bigger brother, the Small German Spitz. In reality, these dogs (from Pomerania) acquired the name Pomeranian upon arrival into Great Britain. The Toy German Spitz, however, remains distinct, at least in name if not in lack of refinery to the biased eye, from the British toy. His ancestors are nordic dogs of Iceland and Lapland who have contributed to a number of modern day breeds, whose origins all sled side-by-side.

RECOGNITION: FCI

CHARACTER: Needless to say, the Toy German Spitz doesn't do much sledge pulling, although he does make the perfect fur mitt and always enjoys a pleasant sled ride with his master (having no qualms about being pulled around by his more appropriately sized brethren). He is indeed a wonderful home companion.

TOY MANCHESTER TERRIER
English Toy Terrier, Black and Tan Toy Terrier

PORTRAIT: Elegant and well-balanced, the compact Toy Manchester is a cleanly built and sleek toy with definite terrier attributes. The head is long and narrow with a flat, wedge-shaped skull. The ears are candle-flame shaped and carried erect. The coat is thick, and a considerable density of short hair is required. As its alternative name indicates, the Manchester is necessarily black and tan. The black is ebony, and the tan is a deep rich chestnut. Marks are clearly defined and brilliant. Height: 10–12 inches (25–31 cm). Weight: 6–8 pounds (2½–3½ kg). The ears are never cropped.

DEVELOPMENT: Enjoying the favor of Queen Victoria, the Toy Manchester Terrier fascinated the dog world by its minute size. Breeders got carried away for a while in their obsession with exaggerated smallness, and the breed suffered from breeding/physical problems. Exaggeration in the toy group is surely a vice of breeders since no working qualities need to be concerned with or preserved. General health, however, must always be paramount. The Manchester's ancestor, the long-extinct English Black and Tan, gives this particular toy quite a handsome lineage.

RECOGNITION: FCI, AKC, KCGB, CKC, ANKC

CHARACTER: Good looking and intelligent, the Toy Manchester is a favorite companion dog, although not overly popular in the United States. In England, the breed's fancy is more extensive. These are easycare, capital condo dogs with terrifically alert, self-assured personalities.

TOY POODLE
Caniche, Chien Canne

PORTRAIT: Elegant and proud, the Toy Poodle is well balanced and tiny. Every part of the dog must be in proportion to all other parts. The coat is profuse and clipped according to the traditional customs. All short hair is close, thick and curly. The Toy Poodle is a miniaturized replica of the Standard. Deep chest, long head, well sprung ribs, broad muscular loins and a customarily docked tail. Poodles can be in any solid color; particolor Poodles are not acceptable. Height: less than 10 or 11 inches (25–28 cm).

DEVELOPMENT: The Poodle was developed as an able-bodied water dog and hunter. The breed quickly became admired for its supercanine intelligence. Efforts in the past century to miniaturize the Miniature Poodle ofttimes resulted in a feeble-bodied smaller dog, which had a rather grotesque appearance and waned in comparison to their handsome forebears. 20th-century attempts were less scornfully accepted, and today's Toy Poodle is sturdily constructed. He was never intended for work and likewise lacks the necessary size to make him believable as a working dog. The clipping of his coat is purely traditional and doesn't feign to be more than ornamental.

RECOGNITION: FCI, AKC, UKC, KCGB, CKC, ANKC

CHARACTER: The Toy Poodle is quite gregarious and as such likes children and other little people quite a lot. He is really a delightful companion, if not spoiled. He tends to favor one family member, usually the lady of the house, and will defend her honor at all costs.

VOLPINO ITALIANO

PORTRAIT: A profusely coated, solid white spitz-type dog, the Volpino curls a sporty tail, with pointed erect ears and a foxy expression. It is a cobby, small dog with a short, small head. The skull is somewhat stretched from the ears and slightly rounded. The muzzle is short, straight and pointed. It is essential that the Volpino not resemble a toy spaniel. The eyes are large and rounded, dark in color; the ears are small and triangular. The coat is long and abundant on the entire body. Today the most common color is white, although times past enjoyed the Volpino in solid fawn, black and sable. Some sable dogs still exist. Height: 11 inches (28 cm). Weight: under 10 pounds (4½ kg).

DEVELOPMENT: Spitz dogs are certainly not exclusive to Germany. The dog-world inclination has been to tie every curly tailed, pointy eared, fox-headed dog to the German Spitz. Although the connection seems indicative, the moot issue is mottled with speculation. Early sources suggest that the Volpino is but an Italian Pomeranian, as white is certainly a color option in the German Spitz family. *Volpe* in Italian means fox, which is certainly descriptive of the breed. The Volpini have enjoyed popularity with Italian ladies for centuries and were decorated with ivory bracelets, symbols of their affection and affluence.

RECOGNITION: FCI

CHARACTER: For his small size, the Volpino makes an excellent watchdog. His bark is ten times his bite, and twenty times his size. He is an affectionate and good-natured dog who is amenable to fair discipline.

YORKSHIRE TERRIER

PORTRAIT: The Yorkie floats over the floor with a long coat of perfectly straight glossy hair hanging evenly down each side with a part extending from the nose to the end of the tail. The head is rather small and flat, not too prominent. The body is compact and well proportioned. The back is rather short with a level line. The tail is customarily docked to medium length and furnished with plentiful fur. Height: 9 inches (23 cm). Weight: 7 pounds (3½ kg) and less. The Yorkie color is blue/tan: the blue is steel, and the tan is darker at the roots; puppies are born black.

DEVELOPMENT: Produced by the working men of the West Riding region of Yorkshire, the Yorkie was created in the late 19th century as companion to the industrial classes (hence the *steel* blue coloration?). In order to produce a dog of this extreme petiteness, extraordinary and knowledgeable selective breeding was essential. Certain specimens (full-grown) weighed in at 2½ pounds (1 kg). As the breed was making its initial rounds, it was referred to as the Broken-haired Scotch Terrier, but this name was quickly replaced by the present one. Coincidentally, Yorkie pups look a great deal like Airedale pups—both breeds trace to the Airedale district.

RECOGNITION: FCI, AKC, UKC, KCGB, CKC, ANKC

CHARACTER: With a debonair and appealing demeanor, the breed is intelligent and vivacious with a goodly amount of terrier momentum. The Yorkshire requires regular grooming to keep his long coat looking its best. These are confident, outgoing companions that make fine alarm dogs.

Maremma Sheepdog.

FLOCK
GUARDIANS

AKBASH DOG

PORTRAIT: A solid white flock guard equipped with keen hearing and superior strength. The coat, which can be either smooth or long, is always double. Height: 28–34 inches (71–86 cm). Weight: 85–140 pounds (39–64 kg). Smooth-coated dogs, like long-coated, are sturdy protectors despite their misleadingly smaller appearance—they are actually the same size.

DEVELOPMENT: Accompanying wandering Eastern travelers to Turkey, the Akbash prototype was embraced by local shepherds and adapted to their specific needs. The alleged ancestors of the breed include various mastiffs and sighthounds; the contribution of the leggy, fleet hounds is apparent in the breed's ranginess and acute eyesight. The benefit of a flock guard's white coat is linked to the shepherd's ability to distinguish between dog and predator. The pure white Akbash has functioned in its native Turkey for thousands of years; he is used successfully in American flock-guarding programs and as a guard and utility dog around the world.

RECOGNITION: NR

CHARACTER: Bred to be a quick-thinking and independent protector, the Akbash often assumes an arguably prudent air, not to be mistaken for sluggishness or obtuseness. He is a handsome dog with a noble bearing—although more effective as a working dog than pet. He bonds more readily with animals than with humans and thinks twice upon receiving a command.

ANATOLIAN SHEPHERD DOG
Anatolian Karabash Dog

PORTRAIT: This well-built shepherd and guard possesses fine proportions and impressive musculature. The head should don a black mask, evident in its Turkish name (Karabash); other important features include a powerful jaw and moderate stop. Height: 27–31 inches (68½–79 cm). Weight: 85–150 pounds (39–68½ kg). The breed occurs in brindles, tricolors, and blacks; white dogs also occur, but color inheritance should be predictable.

DEVELOPMENT: Large working dogs have existed in Asia Minor for centuries. The Anatolian, bred from the most formidable guard dogs of the area, emerged as the dominant canine in Turkey. The size and accompanying strength reflect the breed's mastiff heritage. In its native Turkey, the breed is employed as a forefront defense line against the predators of its flocks. Once a hunter and gladiator, it combated big game—including lions.

RECOGNITION: KCGB

CHARACTER: A spiked collar worn by deserving dogs is the traditional indicator that an individual dog has tracked and downed a wolf. This ability suggests the breed's tremendously domineering and assertive temperament. The Anatolian is an individualist of undeniable intelligence and notable wariness. If acclimated to the family, the breed is suitable as a home companion, bonding closely to its immediate family and especially enjoying the company of children.

CÃO DE CASTRO LABOREIRO
Portuguese Cattle Dog

PORTRAIT: Centuries of hard work has made this cattle herder as hard as hooves. His steely muscles are densely ,packed, giving him well-built overall appearance. In length he is greater than in height. Despite his concentrated and slightly elongated appearance, he is exceedingly quick and mobile. Height: 21–25 inches (53–63½ cm). Weight: 50–75 pounds (23–34 kg). Coat: short, harsh, and waterproof. Color: various shades, most commonly gray to black-gray. The breed is built for endurance interspersed with bursts of high energy output. These dogs are rugged enough to be unaffected by the harshest terrain.

DEVELOPMENT: This very old breed is believed to have originated in Portugal, very likely near Castro Laboreiro, where it remains very popular. Selective breeding for a tough long-winded dog, fearless and feisty enough to combat wolves and other predators, yielded the Cão. He is highly regarded as a guardian of flocks and herds, and of late he has made an entrance into the show world—with a promising future, it may be added. His unique octave-climbing voice makes him a very effective watchdog as well.

RECOGNITION: FCI

CHARACTER: The breed is known for its unending dedication and love for work; dogs require vigorous daily exercise to remain contented. When well provided for, they are very loyal to the master and bond closely to the animals in their care; however, they remain wary of strangers and very aggressive towards potentially "predatory" animals.

CAUCASIAN OVTCHARKA
Caucasian Sheepdog, Kawkasky Owtscharka, Kaukasische Schaferhund

PORTRAIT: Although opinions vary about its ideal type, this very Russian canine is quite a large dog, usually standing between 25–28 inches (63½–71 cm) tall. Weight: 105–145 pounds (46–65½ kg). Contributing to its massive appearance is the profuse medium-long coat. There is heavy feathering and a bushy tail on these dogs as well. The weather resistant coat is especially effective at keeping out the cold. In its native country, the Ovtcharka's ears are cropped short, which gives the dog a soberingly wolf-like appearance. Never bred specifically for color, the breed varies in gray, fawn, tan, pied, brindle, and white. The FCI prohibits brown dogs.

DEVELOPMENT: The lack of organized kennel clubs and written standards partly explains why the Caucasian varies in type from country to country and even from locale to locale. Ovtcharkas are found primarily as working dogs throughout the Soviet Union, Turkey, and Iran. The most uniform specimens exist in the Georgian Republic of the U.S.S.R. Although exportation of the Soviet-bred dogs is prohibited, quality specimens have crossed the closed curtain into the aisles of both East and West Germany.

RECOGNITION: FCI

CHARACTER: The typical Ovtcharka is assertive, strong-willed, and intrepid. Unless properly socialized and trained, the Ovtcharka may exhibit ferocious and unmanageable tendencies. Some German fanciers employ the dogs as foremost guardians and deterrents.

CHIEN DE L'ATLAS
Aidi, Atlas Sheepdog, Kabyle Dog

PORTRAIT: The Aidi is smaller in size and less dominating in nature than most other flock guards. His height at the shoulder is between 21–25 inches (53–63½ cm). His lean yet thickly muscled body is protected by a coarse weather-resistant coat. The protection of the coat and the power of the muscles combined can rout the rowdiest wild combatant of Morocco. The preferred color is white; however, black, black and white, tawny, and a dilute red may also appear. The typical Atlas Sheepdog weighs about 55 pounds (25 kg).

DEVELOPMENT: The Aidi was originally bred to protect and guard the nomads of North Africa and their belongings; it was later that his use as a guard began with the flocks of sheep and goats in Morocco. The breed boasts versatile dogs that excel in their working ability. Having a good nose, the Aidi also finds employment as a hunter: an Aidi is usually paired with one of the sleek coursing hounds known as the Sloughi; the Aidi scents and finds while the Sloughi runs down and catches.

RECOGNITION: FCI

CHARACTER: In years past, the Aidi was almost exclusively a working dog, whether he was guarding flocks or peoples or hunting game. In recent years, however, he has found his way into more and more homes—mostly in the country. The Aidi can be acclimated to urban life if he is provided with challenging tasks and other diversions to keep his high-voltage disposition from over-charging.

ESTRELA MOUNTAIN DOG
Cão da Serra da Estrela, Portuguese Sheepdog

PORTRAIT: At an average height of 27 inches (68½ cm), with some specimens standing as tall as 29 or 30 inches (74 or 76 cm), the Estrela is an impressive dog. For his height, his weight is moderate, usually between 66 and 110 pounds (30–50 kg). The recognized colors by the KCGB are fawn, brindle, and wolf gray; although other colors may occur, they are deemed unacceptable. The skull is large and noticeably rounded. The overall appearance of the dog is that of mountain-moving power. The coat can be either of a long-type or a short-type; both are thick and medium-harsh.

DEVELOPMENT: The origin is uncertain, as is the component stock that went into the breed. Judging from its mastiffy appearance, one could argue that Spanish Mastin blood is traceable in its history. What is certain is that the Estrela was once used with great success as a guard for Portuguese flocks—there was no animal more fearless or determined. He was soon employed as an estate guard, and today he enjoys popularity as a guard, a companion, and a show dog.

RECOGNITION: FCI, KCGB

CHARACTER: This is an extremely strong dog who can be hard to handle if not properly socialized. Good owners, however, report no difficulty in directing the dog's instincts into acceptable behavior. Although not known to lavish affection, the Estrela is an obliging dog when treated with respect.

GREAT PYRENEES
Pyrenean Mountain Dog

PORTRAIT: Like the mountains whose name he bears, this dog is enormous and tremendously powerful. The snow white coat that this sinewy giant sports can also be patched with badger, gray, or tan, as is rather common in France and England. He is the largest of the flock guardians, standing as high as 32 inches (81 cm) and weighing from 90–130 pounds (41–59 kg). The medium-long, slightly coarse and undulating coat is equipped with a pure white undercoat, enabling this mountainous guard to withstand the most severe climatic conditions.

DEVELOPMENT: Only speculation exists upon the precise origin of the breed. Whether an offspring of the Anatolian, Kuvasz, or Maremma, this dog has undoubtedly worked flocks upon the French mountains for thousands of years. Early in the 20th century, the breed was scarce, and the efforts of Bernard Senac-Langrange and M. Dretzen are cited as bringing the torch of salvation to the nearly extinguished breed. Considered the strongest of the flock guards, this gentle giant is a flawless protector capable of slaying a threatening wolf. Today he is employed by farmers and ranchers on a variety of livestock. His bravery and strength have led to his conscription into war, just as his beauty and capacity have lured him into the show ring.

RECOGNITION: FCI, AKC, UKC, KCGB, CKC, ANKC

CHARACTER: Though deterring as a guard, he is docile and easygoing as a pet and especially patient with children. Compared to the Pyrs originally employed as guardians, today's dog has been domestically sweetened. He is, however, equally as noble, courageous, beautiful as his forebears.

FLOCK GUARDIANS   413

GREEK SHEEPDOG

PORTRAIT: A good-sized guardian of shepherd and sheep, the Greek Sheepdog fills its solid white coat with a sound and muscular body. Weight: 75–100 pounds (34–45 kg). Height: 25–28 inches (63½–71 cm). Distinguishing this white flock guard from both the Maremma and the Kuvasz (and any other big white sheepdog), the Greek Sheepdog traditionally has one ear cropped—a practice stemming from the Greek shepherds' forefathers' belief that doing so would improve the dog's already keen hearing. The uncropped ear sets dropped, creating an unbalanced appearance to the head, which admittedly suggests the discordant personality of the breed.

DEVELOPMENT: The area known as the Balkan foothills, located in Greece, is heavily populated with sheep. Centuries ago, migrators from Turkey likely brought their sheepdogs with them as they traversed the land, and similarities between the Greek Sheepdog and the Turkish Akbash Dog lead one to believe that such a derivation is probable. Years of breeding with local and semi-local stock produced the breed. This is a no-nonsense shepherd! Greek natives and the shepherds themselves describe the dog as fierce. This unrelenting ferocity calls for shepherds to attach logs to the dogs' collars to curtail their fanatical fervor.

RECOGNITION: NR

CHARACTER: The breed's fierceness doesn't detract whatsoever from its ability to protect the flock; on the contrary, its effectiveness in this field encourages its usage today. The modern Greek Sheepdog can be found guarding its flock and chasing unfamiliar passers-by or an occasional unsuspecting shepherd. This *is* not a pet but strictly a working dog.

KANGAL DOG
Karabash

PORTRAIT: Unlike the majority of breeds classified as flock guardians, the Kangal Dog is never white. Its black-masked head leads off a typical graying dun or chamois body. His limbs and body are expertly welded, yielding a sturdy balanced construction. His shoulders and thighs are especially muscled. The thick straight forelegs and powerful neck considerably contribute to this overall impression. Height: 28–35 inches (71–89 cm). Weight: 75–150 pounds (34–69 kg). The coat is dense while remaining essentially short and smooth.

DEVELOPMENT: The breeding of fine animals is of paramount importance to the region of eastern Turkey known as Kangal. The district's livestock is irreplaceable, as is this sturdy livestock guard. The component stock which shepherds utilized to create the breed has been effectively concealed; but the short coat and curled tail suggest more than a hint of the Nordic breeds. As a working dog, the Kangal is the epitome of performance. To observe a Kangal at work is to be amazed by an animal as exquisitely bred as an Arabian horse. In his work, he is truculent and intense.

RECOGNITION: NR

CHARACTER: Always at the side of the shepherd and surprisingly obedient, the Kangal is recognized by Turkish natives but never kept as a pet. Not as fierce as some flock guards, he is wary but willing to cavort with the shepherd's children. In this economically volatile era, the Karabash's untiring ability to perform at high intensity levels makes him better than the best blue-chip stock any shepherd could own.

KARST SHEEPDOG
Krasky Ovcar, Istrian Sheepdog

PORTRAIT: This iron-gray shepherd weighs in from 58–88 pounds (26–40 kg) and stands from 20–24 inches (51–61 cm) high. Hardy and muscular, the Karst Sheepdog can flourish in a rugged mountain climate. The breed has a relatively long water-resistant outer coat and an insulative undercoat. Like the Keeshond, the Krasky possesses "spectacles," lighter rings of coat around the eyes. The ears are high set and rather small. There is noticeable feathering on the angulated hind legs, the moderately tucked belly, the deep chest, and thick tail. The coat ideally has dark shadings throughout; the black mask is essential.

DEVELOPMENT: Like its surrounding European neighbors, Yugoslavia needs protection for its livestock and flocks. The Karst Sheepdog has filled the bill for centuries. He bears obvious similarities to the shepherds of Greece and Rumania but, being the oldest indigenous Yugoslavian breed particular to a given area, may actually antecede those guards. The Karst is rarely seen outside of his native Yugoslavian Alps, although he will make an occasional visit to a European all-breed show.

RECOGNITION: FCI

CHARACTER: Full of vim and energy, the breed is a pleasant—even delightful—companion dog. The typical Karst is smaller in size and less dominating and aggressive in character than most other flock guards. He has a distinctively serious air but can be delightfully playful. His loyalty must be earned as he is necessarily wary of new acquaintances.

KOMONDOR
Hungarian Sheepdog

PORTRAIT: The impeccable, impervious, imprescriptible Kom is a large, muscular dog that hints of strong limbs and back. A master of subtlety, the Kom is shrouded in a corded coat that covers his brawn and blends his presence into his flock. His secret is revealed to the unsuspecting predator only too late, for it is not many who escape the dedicated grasp of a protective Kom. His back is straight and strong; his chest deep; his hind legs well angulated; and his overall structure thick boned. Weight: 80–150 pounds (36½–69 kg). Standards specify height at 25½ inches (64½ cm) for dogs, although larger working specimens are common. The coat is invariably white; whether groomed or not, the coat should be corded.

DEVELOPMENT: Nomadic Magyars brought these dogs of Oriental origin with them to Hungary over one thousand years ago. Whether these nomads developed the breed or crossed their dogs with wolf cubs (as one colorful legend describes) must be left to conjecture. Nonetheless, the Komondor has guarded flocks in Hungary for countless years. The Komondor executes its work routine with grueling accuracy. Its lumpish, impenetrable jacket provides it with protection against predators' attacks and harsh weather. In the U.S., it has been effectively employed as a police dog and guard.

RECOGNITION: FCI, AKC, UKC, KCGB, CKC

CHARACTER: Dominating and assertive, the Komondor is innately protective and obedient. Although the exact origin of its name is not certain, in translation it may reveal much of the breed's character—somber, surly or angry. As a home companion, it is amenable. The show dog's coat requires many hours of preparation for the ring.

KUVASZ

PORTRAIT: A medium to large-sized, beautifully proportioned dog whose flowing medium-length coat glistens in white or ivory. Height: 22–26 inches (56–66 cm). Weight: 80–120 pounds (37–55 kg). The coat of the Kuvasz is plush and profuse. In addition to the dog's symmetrical carriage, the highlight of the dog's appearance is the head, with its handsomely majestic expression especially denoted in the dark glistening eyes. The broad skull begins after a mild stop. The powerful jaws are concealed behind an exquisite muzzle.

DEVELOPMENT: The history of the breed is traced back to Hungary, where Tibetan, Turkish, Hungarian, and possibly other dogs were crossbred to produce a definitive flock guard. The Kuvasz is excellent as a guard dog in almost any field, whether it be home, flock, estate, or lot; this dog tends to be touched deeply by its master and bonds closely to its immediate human family.

RECOGNITION: FCI, AKC, UKC, CKC

CHARACTER: Neither the ingrained independence necessary for a true flock guard nor the necessary ferocity and toughness have abandoned the companion/show Kuvasz of today. While the breed has mellowed considerably, it remains trustworthy and loyal. Owners must direct the inherent instincts of this natural guardian toward acceptable behavior. The Kuvasz is suitable as a companion, worker, or guard dog—so long as the instincts are properly directed, he is an unbeatable canine.

418   FLOCK GUARDIANS

MAREMMA SHEEPDOG
Pastore Abruzzese, Cane da Pastore Maremmano-Abruzzese

PORTRAIT: This profusely coated sheepdog is thickly boned and solidly muscled enough to deter the desperate burglar and slay the hungry wolf. Keeping with his flock guarding heritage, his coat must always be white; any yellow or orange coloration is tolerated on ears only. Very impressive are the large shoulders and thick legs. Height: 25–29 inches (63½–74 cm). Weight: 70–100 pounds (32–45 kg).

DEVELOPMENT: The longer bodied mountain dweller, the Abruzzese, and the shorter coated sheepdog, the Maremmano, combined to form to-day's Maremma. A direct descendant of early Asian guards, these two breeds, each from slightly different geographic regions, culminate in the Maremma.

RECOGNITION: FCI, KCGB

CHARACTER: Although not as large as many of its fellow flock guards, the Maremma possesses comparable endurance and strength, as well as the ability to feign the extra 50 pounds it lacks. Its alert and independent disposition presuppose an uninhibited majestic air. A flock guard of imposing dominance and lifelong dedication, the breed takes control over its flock and human family. As a pet, he is not doting or overly demonstrative, but his loyalty is surely undying. The Maremma is tame with man; breeders have adapted this rugged wolf-slayer into a marvelous companion, without losing its extraordinary working abilities.

MIDDLE ASIAN OVTCHARKA
Mid-Asian Shepherd

PORTRAIT: He is a dog without superfluous detail. His coat is short and dense, and his thick skin forms folds and wrinkles about the neck and head. His limbs denote strength but are not excessively muscled. Height: 23–28 inches (58½–71 cm). Weight: 80–110 pounds (37–50 kg). The coat is short and thick. Color may vary, but black, white, gray, and brindle are most common; color markings are also common.

DEVELOPMENT: The breed originated and is still primarily found in mid-Asia, more specifically, the mid-U.S.S.R., in the area between the Ukraine and Siberia. Some reports suggest that the dog may be found as far east as Mongolia and as far west as Germany. The breed is one of four from the Ovtcharka family; although they all are largely similar, they do possess differences in appearance and temperament. The Middle Asian is the medium-sized member of the group.

RECOGNITION: NR

CHARACTER: He is a bold and determined dog, fearless of almost every living thing. He is naturally quick to react and will adapt his behavior to fit the given situation. Used almost exclusively as a herder, and rarely seen playing the pet role, the Middle Asian does not yet have the "inborn" inclination to perform the role of premiere family companion and pet. He is, however, one of the outstanding herders of central Asia and, if given the chance, could surely perform in other locations as well.

OWCZAREK PODHALANSKI
Tatra Mountain Sheepdog, Owczarek Tatrazanski, Polish Mountain Dog

PORTRAIT: This magnificent Polish breed is solid white and massive. Its coat is long and dense—both straight and wavy varieties occur, as does either pure or creamy coloration. Height: 24–34 inches (61–86½ cm). Weight: 100–150 pounds (45–69 kg). Tatras are thick boned throughout their bodies and gifted with bounteous muscle mass. The dogs' obvious brawn, however, should not presuppose either slowness or lethargy. They are ever alert and quick to spring into action.

DEVELOPMENT: This skilled mountain worker is indigenous to Poland, sharing roots with east European flock guards of similar type. The credibility of past speculation connecting the Tatra directly to the Bergamasco falters as one recognizes the breed's many similarities with the flock guards of Hungary and Czechoslovakia, its more likely relatives. In Poland, he is used as a flock guard par excellence, holding his own against the most formidable foes, and as a cart puller. In the U.S. and Canada, he has been selected for military and police work.

RECOGNITION: FCI

CHARACTER: The Tatra is easygoing and cheerful but forever maintains that steady workaholic attitude for which he is so respected. His disposition is consistently independent; some specimens possess the typical aloofness that their intended work requires. As a home companion, he is an easycare dog who is rarely hard-up for affection.

PERRO DE PASTOR MALLORQUIN
Ca de Bestiar

PORTRAIT: The head, especially on the shorthaired variety, is sharply defined; the muzzle tapers slightly, contributing to the chiseled impression, and ends in a dark, solid-colored nose. Height: 19–22 inches (48–56 cm). Weight: 45–60 pounds (20½–27 kg). The ears should be left natural and the tail undocked. The legs should be of good length, insuring a steady, enduring stride.

DEVELOPMENT: A native of the Balearic Islands, just off ʹ the coast of Spain, this *perro* developed, through either selective breeding or genetic mutation (maybe both), the ability to work in extreme conditions of heat. He has been successful in various sorts of farm duty for many years on the islands and coastal areas of the Mediterranean. Owners primarily focus on utility and are less concerned with breed purity; therefore, it is difficult to be sure that one has a purebred Perro de Pastor Mallorquin.

RECOGNITION: FCI

CHARACTER: Somewhat pugnacious, the Pastor is readily willing to defend his home (of which he makes careful parameters in his mind). He is a brave dog and quite tolerant of pain—many a skirmish has ended in more than simple cuts and bruises. Overall, the dog is suited to rural life in temperate climates, where he can be kept outdoors and given plenty of plot to call his own.

PYRENEAN MASTIFF
Perro Mastín del Pireneo, Mastín d'Aragon

PORTRAIT: As revealed in his name, he is a sturdily built, powerful dog. Gray, brindle, black, or orange markings occurring on a white background describe his color. The coat is moderately long, longer on tail, neck and chest, and contributes to the massive appearance of this powerhouse. Height: 28–32 inches (71–79½ cm). Weight: 120–155 (55–70 kg). The head is very deep and excessive dewlap is not uncommon. The broad skull and prevalent flew are suggestive of the Saint Bernard. The thick powerful legs are no less than impressive.

DEVELOPMENT: The breed's history runs parallel to both the Great Pyrenees and the Spanish Mastiff, and the development of the breed, especially in the early years, specifically overlaps that history. It is quite probable that shepherds throughout France, Spain, and various adjacent regions traded and re-traded various of their flock guards. Finally, however, in the mid-19th century, motion was taken to delineate the Pyrenean Mastiff as a distinct breed. Today the dogs are gaining popularity, especially in Spain, both as good guards and as amiable companions.

RECOGNITION: FCI

CHARACTER: His rejuvenated popularity is not without reason, as the Pyrenean Mastiff has a fine-combed character of gentle affection and fearless loyalty. Never will he "love you and leave you"—this dog will prove a worthy companion and protector for life.

RAFEIRO DO ALENTEJO
Portuguese Watchdog

PORTRAIT: The Rafeiro is a stocky dog, having a short neck, thick chest, well-developed limbs, and a very strong, solid back. Height: 30 inches (76 cm). Weight: 95–110 pounds (43–50 kg). These features are not to be taken without regard; as they suggest, this dog is more canine than most can handle. The coat is medium-short and spotted; it can be composed of gray, brindle, black, red, or yellow in varying amounts. Besides its build, other notable features include heavily boned forepaws, oval feet, and a conspicuous dewlap.

DEVELOPMENT: Originating in the south of Portugal, the breed is probably a cross of various Spanish mastins (as is seen in its size) as well as established flock guards. This combustible combination produced a truly effective guardian with a natural affinity for flocks and herds. Although not a very common sight in the home, the Rafeiro do Alentejo is admired in the grazelands and on the farms of Portugal. In the U.S.A., he is currently used in flock-guarding programs.

RECOGNITION: FCI

CHARACTER: Although he may still be a man's best friend, this dog will choose to hold closely to its early canine heritage. He is hard to break to the *sapiens'* indoor ways and seems much more contented guarding a large estate or a dependent flock. He is a quick, determined dog who relies heavily on instinct.

RUMANIAN SHEEPDOG
Carpathian Sheepdog

PORTRAIT: A heavily boned, thickly muscled dog with a short stout neck, topped by a head composed of a large skull, deep-set eyes, strong jaw, and thick muzzle. Height: 23–26 inches (58½–66 cm). Weight: 70–98 pounds (32–45 kg). The dense coat is medium long in length. Color is usually white with a pied brown, sometimes all white; reports also suggest the occurence of brown dogs. A definitely brawny dog, he at once impresses fanciers with his quick reflexes and enduring stamina.

DEVELOPMENT: The roots of the breed are traced back to the eastern mountainous region of Rumania, where it is believed that various Slavic and possibly Turkish dogs were bred to produce a guard easily distinguishable from the common predator, the wolf. The result was a white, often pied, dog that was propagated as a useful guardian in the rough terrain. The Rumanian Sheepdog is quite rare today, however, and no dogs are known to exist outside their native land.

RECOGNITION: NR

CHARACTER: A bellicose dog with an imposing bark (and a bite to back it up), the Rumanian Sheepdog is a rough contender with whom most of us would not want to come into conflict. His territorial instincts make crossing his border a venturesome task. Although outstanding as a guard, he is not the kind of dog you'd like to bring home to mom.

SARPLANINAC
Sar Planina, Illyrian Sheepdog

PORTRAIT: The body is medium in size and bone; the feathering on the underbelly and legs and the bushy scimitar tail, however, give the appearance of a much stouter dog. Height: 22–24 inches (56–31½ cm). Weight: 55–80 pounds (25–37 kg). Coat: medium in length, quite dense, either rough or smooth. Color: tan, gray, white, or black; can be pure or blend. A keen, discriminating expression is characteristic.

DEVELOPMENT: The Sarplaninac has the honor of being one of only two dogs to be recognized by the Yugoslavian Kennel Club, the official club of his native land. Although not as old a breed as either the Greek Sheepdog or the Akbash Dog, its probable component stock, the Sarplaninac is one of the oldest breeds native to the area now part of Yugoslavia. Presently the Sarplaninac is gaining recognition as a hard-working, readily able flock guard in the U.S.A. and Canada.

RECOGNITION: FCI

CHARACTER: Not a brainless tailwagger, the Sarplaninac is a very discerning dog who chooses friends carefully and trusts no one completely. He is more obedient to his ingrained code of proper behavior than to command—except from his one master, to whom he is most loyal. His character demands a zesty, outdoor life.

SLOVAK CUVAC
Slovensky Tchouvatch, Liptok

PORTRAIT: The great white guard stereotype resulted in part from the Cuvac. He is truly an impressive dog. Height: up to 28 inches (71 cm). Weight: up to 105 pounds (48 kg). The plush coat is of medium length, with thick, wavy strands. Its color is ideally white. Although at first sight the Cuvac may be mistaken for the more common Kuvasz, the Cuvac is actually a noticeably leaner dog and his coat is less given to ivory coloration. While less stout, the Cuvac has power and speed that enable him to excel as a protector of flock and family.

DEVELOPMENT: A native to the mountainous regions of Czechoslovakia, the breed is the result of the great white guard prototype that made its way through Eastern Europe so many years ago. Whether intentional or not, the breed developed great speed. The combination of its unyielding courage and supreme dedication makes the Cuvac stand out as guard of great ability.

RECOGNITION: FCI

CHARACTER: One of the most industrious of the white shadows, the Cuvac is an incessantly alert dog who can perform well both day and night. He has proven his dual nature of dauntless ferocity and sweet affection time and again by warning of danger, deterring a bandit, and saving a life. His drives are strong, as he has been called both stubborn and independent. Others claim that he is ideally suited to family life, clinging closely to family members and keeping dedicated watch on a 24-hour basis.

SOUTH RUSSIAN OVTCHARKA
South Russian Sheepdog

PORTRAIT: An undeniably massive mammal, the South Russian Ovtcharka is one of the largest of the flock guards. Height: up to 35 inches (91 cm). Weight: 120–160 pounds (55–74 kg). The old adage, "The bigger they are, the harder they fall," does not apply to the Ovtcharka, for he never falls. The dog's rippling brawn, armor-like protective coat, and quick reflexes combine to create indomitability. Coat: long, dense, and double. The tail is long with a swirl tip; ears hang straight; bangs typically cover the eyes (unless trimmed).

DEVELOPMENT: This large, extremely strong, quick, and fearless dog is a result of the need to protect against the tremendously powerful wolves of the Ukraine. The long thick coat of the present-day Ovtcharka is suggestive of the corded and very heavy coat of its ancestors. The breed was meticulously bred for size, strength and courage, and remains today a very intimidating canine. Although no longer registered, this breed once enjoyed membership in the AKC Miscellaneous Class.

RECOGNITION: FCI

CHARACTER: The Ovtcharka extends himself to include his home, his family, and as much land as he can scentfully call his own. The possessive nature of this dog requires extensive property, a sizable family, and preferably other animals that he can protect. He has a dominating personality and can enforce his will upon other dogs with ease.

SPANISH MASTIFF

Mastin de Español, Mastin de Extremadura, Mastin de Leon, Mastin de La Mancha.

PORTRAIT: A large, rather lengthy dog with a massive chest and the power of a heavyweight contender. He has a large but shapely head, and a characteristic dewlap on the neck. These characteristics of the Mastin show clearly his mastiff type. Height: 26–29 inches (66–74 cm). Weight: 110–135 pounds (50–61 kg). Coat: short and dense. Color: fawn, brindle, black and white and red. The Mastin commonly sports a relaxed, carefree expression masking his ever watchful eyes.

DEVELOPMENT: The Mastin is a native of Spain. He was for some time populous in that country. He is a descendent of the ancient mastiff stock that made its ever-meandering way around the globe during the Roman, Phoenician, and other transworld traversings. The Mastin is a natural guard, and his inherent abilities led to many crossings with other breeds to perfect the lesser breed's type.

RECOGNITION: FCI

CHARACTER: He is a gentle dog around most non-canines—he is wary and often aggressive with other dogs. He is wonderful with people, and will bond inseparably with children if raised from a young age with them. Although appearing slightly slothful, he is quickly alerted and obedient.

Belgian Sheepdog, Tervuren.

HERDING DOGS

ARMANT
Ermenti, Egyptian Sheepdog, Chien de Berger Egyptian

PORTRAIT: The Armant is much canine compacted into a dog that stands 22 inches (56 cm) tall and weighs 50–60 pounds (22½–27½ kg). The sturdy, straight back and well-tucked belly give the body an accurate appearance of strength and virility. This dog is protected by a long woolly to shaggy rough coat, which adds to his ability and durability. Color is usually a shade of solid gray, although black, black with tan, and occasional white markings also may be seen. Other normally distinguishing features may vary, such as the ears, which are either prick or drop, and the tail, which is either long with a "shepherd's staff curl" or docked.

DEVELOPMENT: A native Egyptian, the Armant is named after his birthplace, a village in Upper Egypt. It was during Napoleon's invasion of Egypt that the breed began. The French army brought with it native dogs to guard supplies and livestock; some were left behind, some straggled, others were stolen. This resulted in these French dogs' breeding with the native local dogs of Upper Egypt and thus the Armant had its beginning. Its numbers today are uncertain.

RECOGNITION: NR

CHARACTER: The Armant is used today as a guard dog, shepherd dog, and occasionally as a sporting dog. Although no longer recognized by the FCI, these dogs can be found in their native Egypt. They are fine workers, but their tumultuous homeland has not been conducive to the continuation of the breed.

AUSTRALIAN CATTLE DOG
Australian Queensland Heeler, Blue Heeler

PORTRAIT: Symmetry, strength and substance prevail in this breed's appearance. The head is balanced with the body; the quarters are broad, blending and well developed. The chest is deep and muscular. The outer coat is medium short and medium textured; the undercoat is short and dense. The coat forms breeches behind the quarters and sufficient fur to make a "broom" of the tail.

Color should be blue or blue-mottled, with acceptable markings being black, blue or tan, preferably evenly distributed. Height: 17–20 inches (43–51 cm). Weight: 35–45 pounds (16–20½ kg).

DEVELOPMENT: Australian cattlemen needed a dog with very specific abilities to drive their livestock to market. Imported sheepdogs were not capable of the task, and the indigenous Dingo was too wild and incorrigible to employ. Six decades of crossing and crisscrossing various breeds yielded the Australian Cattle Dog of today. Infusing Bull Terrier, Dalmatian, and Kelpie with the Red Deer Dingo and the experimenter's blue-merle Collie created this silent, nipping but not distressing cattle herder. The Blue Heeler is so versatile that, in addition to cattle, he can work horses, goats, and even ducks, with skill and panache.

RECOGNITION: FCI, AKC, UKC, KCGB, CKC, ANKC

CHARACTER: Australian cattle farmers report, "The Australian Cattle Dog will eat anything that doesn't eat him first." The infusion of Dingo blood has slightly "undomesticated" the breed. He is 100% working dog, fearless and determined.

AUSTRALIAN KELPIE
Kelpie, Barb

PORTRAIT: A dog with little excess, the Kelpie's compacted body shows clearly his well-tempered, striated musculature upon strong well-developed limbs. He stands at a height of 17–20 inches (43–51 cm) and weighs 25–45 pounds (11½–20½ kg). Slightly longer than he is high, the Kelpie has a broad chest and firm hind quarters that contribute to his lithe, energized appearance. The double coat consists of a short and dense undercoat and a hard, straight and weather-repellent outer coat. Color possibilities include black and red, each with or without tan; and fawn, chocolate and blue.

DEVELOPMENT: Although many still believe that the Kelpie is a Dingo cross, more accurate documentation reveals the breed's development from English North Country Collies of the Rutherford strain. These hardy British working herders, like many sheepdogs, were imported to Australia during the latter half of the 19th century. Today nearly 100,000 Kelpies are employed on that continent. Despite their relatively small size, Kelpies are without limitations, capable of working cattle, goats, poultry and reindeer.

RECOGNITION: FCI, AKC, UKC, KCGB, ANKC

CHARACTER: These are devoted one-man dogs but far too work-oriented and energetic for a house or apartment existence. Their easy trainability and diligence on the job make them an indispensable component of the Australian work force.

AUSTRALIAN SHEPHERD

PORTRAIT: Sound and symmetrical in appearance, the Australian Shepherd has a somewhat long body and a moderately rough coat. The coloration varieties of this breed are brilliant—blue merle, red merle; black, liver, red, with or without tan markings—each pattern is unique and stunning. Height: 18–23 inches (46–58½ cm). Weight: 35–70 pounds (16–32 kg). The body is well balanced and well muscled. The combination of the whole is a sharp, beautifully put-together canine.

DEVELOPMENT: Not developed on the hills of Australia or New Zealand, this shepherd is an American creation. Imported Pyrenean Shepherds (Bergers des Pyrenees) crossed with various collie types generated the Aussie. The Border Collie, Collie, and Smithfield Collie are the most likely candidates. The Aussie has become requisite on countless American farms and ranches. He is able to steer the ovine multitudes and direct the trampling bovines, nipping at their heels while practically crawling on his belly.

RECOGNITION: UKC

CHARACTER: If the breed's "workaholism" ethic doesn't grab one's attention, its blue eyes and handsome looks most assuredly will. However, casual fanciers are religiously discouraged from taking on an Aussie. His strong herding instincts must be utilized or his true talents are wasted.

BEARDED COLLIE

PORTRAIT: A powerful dog of great activity and agility, the Bearded Collie should never appear heavy and lethargic or thin and weak. The body is of medium size, 40–60 pounds (18–27½ kg), and is covered with a medium long, harsh and dense, free flowing coat. Height: 20–22 inches (51–56 cm). Built for unending motion, the dog possesses a deep chest spaciously designed for cardio-vasculation, a level back, and very strong limbs. Acceptable colors are black, brown, fawn, and blue, with or without white markings. An alert, inquisitive countenance is characteristic of the breed.

DEVELOPMENT: The Bearded Collie, bearing enlightening similarities to the Old English Sheepdog and the Polish Lowland Sheepdog, may indeed be descended from like stock. These tousled gray dogs have been known in Scotland since the 16th century. Creative and romantic theories sail the Polish Nizinny (in baskets or from overturned vessels—?) to the shores of Scotland. Regardless, the Beardie is an adaptable, intelligent herder. His dense, harsh coat protects well against the elements.

RECOGNITION: FCI, AKC, UKC, KCGB, CKC, ANKC

CHARACTER: Possibly the up-and-coming sheepdog and straggly haired companion, the Beardie is blithesome and lighthearted and sometimes rambunctious. He is a joy in the home—affectionate and responsive.

BEAUCERON
Berger de Beauce, French Shorthaired Shepherd, Bas Rouge

PORTRAIT: Sturdy, powerful and large, the Beauceron is muscular but not clumsy—*au contraire*, this French sheep herder is limber and moves with grace. A robust dog: the neck is thick and muscular, the chest is deep, and the back is straight. The head is long and flat-topped or slightly rounded. Its coat must be short and close. On the head, the coat is smooth and flat-lying; the legs, tail, and flanks are slightly fringed. In color the exhibition-sanctioned Beauceron is necessarily black/tan, black, or harlequin. Previously the breed could occur in tawny, gray, or gray/black—although no less attractive animals, these colors have been banned from the show ring. Height: 25–28 inches (63½–71 cm). Weight: 66–85 pounds (30–38½ kg).

DEVELOPMENT: Contrary to what his name implies, this shepherd is not from the region of Beauce; instead, he shares Brie with his cousin (the Briard) as his hometown. The name was chosen to differentiate the two breeds—they do, by the way, exist in Beauce. Although in appearance the two seem quite different—the Briard is longhaired—they derive from the same general stock. A mastiffy workman, the Beauceron has foregone his boar-hunting days for a veritable grab bag of roles: sheepdog, guard, guide dog, and military assistant.

RECOGNITION: FCI

CHARACTER: A docile and quick-thinking shepherd, the Beauceron makes a fine companion dog. He is becoming an increasingly popular sight in the European show ring and a number of these mighty but meek dogs are finding their way across the Atlantic.

BELGIAN SHEEPDOG, GROENENDAEL
Belgian Sheepdog, Chien de Berger Belge

PORTRAIT: The dog is at once perceived as being strong, square, balanced and defined. The overall impression is one of canine nobility. The head appears finely chiseled and balanced. The skull is of equal length to the muzzle. The head is set upon a strong, slightly elongated neck. The neck is joined to a powerful squarely built body. Height: 22–26 inches (56–66 cm). Weight: about 62 pounds (28 kg). The coat is long, straight and abundant, with a medium-harsh texture. The color is black or black with limited, specified white markings.

DEVELOPMENT: Belgium has been copiously occupied by a variety of sheepdogs since time immemorial. The Groenendael, the black sheep (dog) of the family, is known in the U.S. simply as the Belgian Sheepdog. Regarded as the foster father of the breed, Nicholas Rose lived in the village of Groenendael. His black longhaired Belgians were decidedly the only black types that bred true. The Groenendael continues to prove a worthy and dutiful herding dog.

RECOGNITION: FCI, AKC, UKC, KCGB, CKC, ANKC

CHARACTER: The breed's inherent protective qualities make it an ideal watchdog and family guardian. Not apprehensive with strangers, the Belgian Sheepdog never shows timidity or fear. With his family, he is zealous for their attention and very possessive.

BELGIAN SHEEPDOG, LAEKENOIS
Laekense, Laeken, Chien de Berger Belge

PORTRAIT: The Laekenois's wire coat gives this shepherd a most unique appearance. In size and body type, the breed resembles his Belgian country canines. Height: 22–26 inches (56–66 cm). Weight: 62 pounds (28 kg). Coloration ranges from fawn to mahogany, with black overlay. The rough coat can measure over two inches in length. The body is sturdy and well proportioned. The ears appear small and are set high on the head. The muzzle and head are fringed, giving him a shaggy, woolly look.

DEVELOPMENT: This Belgian variety of sheepdog was developed as a watchman to guard the fields in Antwerp, where fine linens were bleached in the sun and rain. During the reign of Queen Marie Henriette, the breed was the favored sheep tender and "the dog to have." Today, however, it is the least plenteous of the four Belgian shepherds.

RECOGNITION: FCI, KCGB

CHARACTER: The Laeken is an adaptable companion dog with a very strong will. Owners are advised to initiate discipline and training at an early age. The breed's dominant personality and inborn guarding instincts combine to make a competent but wary canine.

BELGIAN SHEEPDOG, MALINOIS
Belgian Malinois, Chien de Berger Belge

PORTRAIT: Square and elegant in body, the Malinois is muscular and limber. This dog carries its neck and head with both pride and nobility. The head is clean cut, strong and in perfect proportion to the body. Rich fawn to mahogany is the standard color description. A black mask adorns the head and ears. Height: 24–26 inches (61–66 cm). Weight: 62 pounds (28 kg). He should not appear leggy or cumbersome. Gait is free and effortless. The triangular ears stand stiff and erect.

DEVELOPMENT: The first of the Belgian Sheepdogs to establish type, the Malinois became the gauge of his nearly indiscernible brothers, who were labeled *Berger Belge á poil court autre que Malinois* (that is, Belgian short-coated Sheepdog other than Malinois). Presently, the Malinois is hardly the single oracle of that country's herder. All the Belgian Sheepdogs developed from hardy working dogs, which ensures that the modern breeds are compatibly gifted on the field.

RECOGNITION: FCI, AKC, UKC, KCGB, CKC

CHARACTER: The Malinois is forever watchful but never shying. In temperament, he should demonstrate a steady, proud evenness. Nervousness and pugnacity are to be discouraged. The breed makes an easycare, delightful companion and family dog.

BELGIAN SHEEPDOG, TERVUREN
Belgian Tervuren, Chien de Berge Belge

PORTRAIT: The incarnation of grace and absolute symmetry, the Tervuren is a finely proportioned, dignified dog, never given to androgyny. This is a square and deep dog that should never appear bulky or cumbersome. Height: 22–26 inches (56–66 cm). Weight: 62 pounds (28 kg). The coat, which ranges from red to fawn to gray, with the characteristic black overlay, is moderately long. The neck is adorned by a ruff, and the legs are fringed. The male is longer coated than the female.

DEVELOPMENT: Brewer M. Corbeel is noted as the founder of the Tervuren variety, whose fawn dog was bred to a black longhaired dog, owned by M. Donhieux. The result of this cross became the prototype for the Tervuren standard. Even though his popularity is steadily increasing, his physical bearing is so similar to the German Shepherd Dog that he may never be a top-ranking canine. The Tervuren is agile and multi-talented and is used as a police, military and guide dog worker.

RECOGNITION: FCI, AKC, UKC, KCGB, CKC, ANKC

CHARACTER: The Tervuren is among the most delightful of the shepherding breeds. He is a jack of all trades: a joy to train and an able protector. He should be led with a strong hand—owners find him affectionate and responsible once trained.

BERGAMASCO
Bergamaschi, Bergamese Shepherd,
Cane da Pastore Bergamasco

PORTRAIT: A heavily muscled body under a heavily corded coat, the Bergamasco is able and agile, despite his somewhat impeded appearance. The coat, his most pronounced distinction, is bountiful, lengthy and corded. Height: 22–24 inches (56–61 cm). Weight: 57–84 pounds (26–38 kg). Color can be all shades of gray, including salt and pepper (flecked with various colors).

DEVELOPMENT: This rustic mass of matted cord and rug-like matter has resided on the mountains of northern Italy since ancient times. It is commonly believed that these dogs are related to Eastern sheepdogs and were transported by the peripatetic Phoenicians to the Bergamo area. Underneath his plaster-like coat is a dog who some believe resembles the Briard of France. To uncover the truth of this matter would require raking through hundreds of years of history and thousands of cords of coat. Few breeds of dog possess the heavy corded coat. On the Bergamasco, it provides him with warmth and insulation while creating an impenetrable buffer zone against attacking predators.

RECOGNITION: FCI

CHARACTER: Intelligence, loyalty, and proficiency at his task have scarcely saved this remarkable canine from extinction. Shepherds attest to the breed's uncanny nose, which can differentiate between lambs for the purposes of the master.

BERGER DES PYRENEES
Pyrenean Shepherd, Petit Berger

PORTRAIT: A handy-sized, fairly heavy-coated shepherd, whose muscular frame is considerable for his size and gyroscope-like in construction. Conducive to his given chore, a low center of gravity places this herder unteeteringly on his axis. Height: 15–22 inches (38–56 cm). Weight: 18–32 pounds (8–14½ kg). The Pyrenean Shepherd can be found in a number of varieties, each differing slightly in coat length and color. The three most commonly seen types include the longhaired, which is shaggy and will cord if not attended to; the goathaired, which is medium in length and considered the typical breed coat, equipped with cuffs and breeches; and the smooth-muzzled variety, which has a medium shaggy coat, with minimal hair on the face and front legs. Each variety can occur in fawn, brindle, gray, or blue, with white points; additionally, the smooth variety can be harlequin in color.

DEVELOPMENT: The Pyrenean Mountains have been graced by a fabulous team of canine shepherds since ancient times: the Berger des Pyrenees as the herder, and the Great Pyrenees (or Pyrenean Mountain Dog) as flock guard. This is an unstoppable duo capable of executing their flock tasks with enviable talent. The Petit Berger is bred for quickness and agility, as well as the ability to withstand the worst of weather conditions with infrequent fuelings. The varieties are the results of the relative isolation created by the terrain and the shepherding conditions in the Pyrenean Mountains.

RECOGNITION: FCI

CHARACTER: Perhaps charged with more than his share of machismo, as is a younger brother in the presence of the elder, the Berger is tough and assertive—with a little help from the Pyr. A worker at heart, in the presence of strangers the Petit Berger is shy and reserved.

Below left: *Berger des Pyrenees*, longhaired. Right: *Smooth-muzzled Berger des Pyrenees*. Below right: *Berger des Pyrenees*, goathaired.

BERGER DU LANGUEDOC
Farou, Cevennes Shepherd

PORTRAIT: The shepherding personnel of the Languedoc area in France are grouped under the name *Le Chien de Berger du Languedoc* and in reality consist of five types of Languedoc herders. These include the Camargue, the Larzac, the Grau, the Farou, and the Carrigues. In height these dogs range from 16–22 inches (40½–56 cm). For the sake of protection, these dogs are double coated. Their outer coat offers a varied fawn, often dark, spotted on the head and forehead; the undercoat usually includes white hairs.

DEVELOPMENT: The proficient Cevennes Shepherds are the bigger, stronger, more vigorous *chiens* of the French herding family. Principally employed in Lower Languedoc and Lower Provence, these dogs necessarily developed to be as hardy as any member of the herding group and as compatibly formidable as the strong mountain guards. These multi-functional canines worked alone with the shepherd and his allotted 450 sheep.

RECOGNITION: NR

CHARACTER: Hardly approachable and very independent, the Berger du Languedoc cannot be deemed a reasonable pet owner's prospect. Shepherds rarely complain about their helper's personalities, since they are deeply indebted to their services. Badly tempered and aggressive, these are not your typical lovable, domesticated pooches.

BERGER PICARD
Picardy Shepherd

PORTRAIT: This shaggy, surly shepherd conveys a natural, rustic appearance. One of the tallest of the herding group, he is in possession of good legs and a long back. Height: 21–26 inches (53–66 cm). Weight: 50–70 pounds (23–31 kg). His head is somewhat narrow and the ears, which are described as necessarily small, stand prick-like and are widely based. The rough, tousled coat is his distinctive characteristic. The coat is colored in various shades of fawn or gray. White is a discouraged coat color, but specimens have been known to occur.

DEVELOPMENT: Ninth-century France was graced by the entrance of the Berger Picard. These rather tall shepherds arrived with visiting Celts. The assertion that they are kinsmen of the Briard and Beauceron is dogmatic. Today he can be found working his flock in the Pas-de-Calais region in northern France. In his shepherd role, he is efficient and capable. He is not populous in France and very few specimens are to be found elsewhere in the world.

RECOGNITION: FCI

CHARACTER: Despite his somewhat pugnacious temperament, the Picardy Shepherd can be a fine home and family guardian. He is unfaltering in his assertiveness but is equally untiring in his affections.

BLUE LACY

PORTRAIT: This quintessential, all-accommodating, "blue collar" ranch hand is both lean and sturdy. The common cur appearance occurring typically in the herders of the American South well befits this rugged cowboy. Weight: 40–50 pounds (18–23 kg). The "blue" in the Lacy's name might be a mite deceptive: it occurs in tan, black/tan, yellow, cream, and the elemental gunmetal gray. Although the breed is known for its solid-colored coat, bicolors and tricolors occur; regardless, the coat is tight, sleek, and exceptionally clean in appearance.

DEVELOPMENT: Acquiring his name from his inherited blue-color gene, the Blue Lacy is likely a combination of feral pariah dogs that frequently inhabited the southeastern U.S. The Blue Lacy is used for both herding and droving tasks. Their gentle sureness ensures them the requisite versatility to handle the surliest of hogs and the most jittery of hens.

RECOGNITION: NR

CHARACTER: Easy to train and easy to handle, Lacys are spectacular workmen and pets. These are energetic and dedicated dogs capable of outworking the most indefatigable clan of ranchers.

BORDER COLLIE

PORTRAIT: Of typical Collie type, the Border Collie shows sufficient grace in proportion and substance to convince any onlooker that here is an active working dog of great ability and versatility. The skull is moderately broad with the muzzle tapering to the nose. Each are approximately equal in length, giving added distinction to his overall bearing. Height: ideally 21 inches (53 cm), with bitches slightly less. Neither heavy nor thin, the Border Collie weighs in at 30–45 pounds (14–20 kg). The coat may be either of two varieties: medium long or smooth coated. Both must possess a weather-resistant double coat. Color varies considerably; white, however, should not predominate.

DEVELOPMENT: The fertile grazing border area between Scotland and England has been patrolled and managed by the "working collie" for hundreds of years. The term "collie" finds renewed and rightful meaning in the Border Collie. The original collie types of Scotland closely resembled today's Border. His herding method, entrancing like himself, is strong-eyed. A strong-eyed dog moves the flock as it wills by staring it into submission. To avoid the unfaltering (unblinking) glare of the herder, the paranoid flock moves along. Present-day breeders stress the working qualities essential for the dogs to function to their inborn capacities.

RECOGNITION: FCI, AKC, UKC, KCGB, CKC, ANKC

CHARACTER: The Border Collie is a rugged dog full of love, life, and independence. He would sacrifice all for his ability to work the ranging lands where flocks and herds roam. His instincts are razor sharp, and his intelligence is superb.

BOUVIER DE ARDENNES
Ardennes Cattle Dog

PORTRAIT: Occurring in a variety of colors and a wide divergence in size as well, the Bouvier de Ardennes represents a mid-sized Belgian herder, that in size is intermediary between the hard-coated Belgian shepherds and the larger, more rugged bouviers. The head is somewhat large but in proportion to its somewhat stocky body. It is lower on the leg than the "bodacious" bouviers of Flanders. The coat is of moderate length. The ears are sizable and are never cropped; they stand upright and fold ever so slightly forward. The tail is never docked. The front legs are straight and the rear are slightly angulated. Height: two varieties; up to 24 inches (61 cm), and over 24 inches (61 cm). Weight: 55 pounds (26 kg).

DEVELOPMENT: The Bouvier de Ardennes is one of the surviving bouviers of Belgium. It developed from the standard stock that produced the more popular Bouvier des Flandres as well as the now-extinct Bouvier de Rouler, Bouvier de Moerman and Bouvier de Paret. Once called *chiens de vacher* or cowherd's dogs, these dogs are closely related and may in fact be thematic variations on the most popular Belgian ox-droving melody of the day. The Ardennes Cattle Dog, which does not resemble its Flemish neighbor, now teeters on extinction and is very rare in its homeland.

RECOGNITION: FCI

CHARACTER: A bold and valiant soul arms this hard-working, effective canine. Smarter than your average cow herder, this Bouvier is a specialist of extraordinary natural talent. With strangers, he is vigilant and wary; with his own, he is warm and welcoming.

BOUVIER DES FLANDRES
Belgian Cattle Dog

PORTRAIT: Power emanates from the body of the Bouvier. He is of concentrated construction and rugged appearance. Of considerable importance is the tousled double coat. The outer hairs are rough and harsh, and the undercoat is soft and dense; together they form an all-weather protectress. Color is anywhere from fawn through black, including salt and pepper, gray, and brindle. At a height of between 24 and 27 inches (61–68½ cm) and a weight of around 88 pounds (40 kg), the Bouvier is equally impressive in his free and proud gait as he is in his solidly square stance.

DEVELOPMENT: *Bouviers*, or cow herders, are historically an important component of the livestock industry of Belgium. These cow dogs varied substantially in type and all were plenteous throughout the country. In 1910, self-beckoned fanciers "deigned" to notice the ancient herders of Flanders and answer a familiar-sounding echo by consenting to further interest in the bouviers. This bouvier survived thanks to these fanciers and today is still a workman-like performer. Many other Belgian bouviers have since faded from existence. Once the discrepancy of type was resolved, the Flandres dog was able to thrive again, as it did before the discrepancy was invented.

RECOGNITION: FCI, AKC, UKC, KCGB, CKC, ANKC

CHARACTER: The Bouvier of today enjoys an unprecedented devoted fancy that perceives him as a handsome canine. Ironically, Belgian farmers historically viewed the breed unappreciatively as a homely, dirty-bearded peon. As a family pet and protector he is reliable and affectionate, never taking his job lightly.

HERDING DOGS

BRIARD
Berger de Brie

PORTRAIT: Here is vigor and virility in a humbly handsome form. Without ever appearing coarse or overdone, the Briard combines strength of muscle and sturdiness of bone with free movement and agility. Intelligent in expression, the eyes are bright and wide open and must always appear dark. They are complemented well by the coarse, dry, and hard coat covering the deep-chested, muscular body. The Briard comes in black, various grays, and tawny, with deeper shades preferred and white seriously discouraged. In height he stands from 22–27 inches (56–68½ cm) at the withers. Ideal weight is 75 pounds (34 kg).

DEVELOPMENT: For as long as the shepherd has needed to control expansive herds and flocks, there have been rough-coated sheep herders. In days of yore, the Briard accompanied nomadic herdsmen, making its exact origin ridden with uncertainty (and basically impossible to trace). In body type the Briard is a goat-haired Beauceron; these two French shepherds were once considered two varieties of a single breed. The Berger de Brie is found in most French provinces, managing the unruly woolly masses. Likewise, it is a familiar sight in show rings and competitions in both Europe and America.

RECOGNITION: FCI, AKC, UKC, KCGB, CKC, ANKC

CHARACTER: Dutiful and intelligent—an adorable gentleman: he is likable in his quiet or boisterous moods; he is charming in his foppish and willy-nilly approach to his daily routine; he is buoyantly French in his discretion in matters of etiquette and taste.

CARDIGAN WELSH CORGI

PORTRAIT: The first thing one notices about this herder is his low-set frame that is long in proportion to his height. Do not pre-judge, however, for the Welsh Corgi is heavy boned and in good possession of muscle strength and mobility. He is an all-weather dog, thanks much to his dense double coat: harsh outer, soft and thick inner. The overall coat appearance is smooth. The legs must be short and slightly bowed for best utility in his herding field. Height: 10½–12½ inches (27–32 cm). Weight: 25–38 pounds (11½–17½ kg). In addition to possessing the fox-like tail which his cousin the Pembroke does not, the Cardigan is considerably heavier and longer. Lack of balance and oversize or undersize are severely discouraged.

DEVELOPMENT: Until the 1850s, the Corgi was the only dog of any kind to dwell among the peoples of certain areas of Wales. Few dog lovers (and fewer Welshmen) dispute the antiquity of the enchanted Corgi. The earliest known reference to these dwarf-like cow dogs, dated 920 AD, is found in a Welsh statute which referred to cattle dogs. The Corgi's natural task is the driving and penning of mountain ponies, which he accomplishes by barking at the pony's heels, ducking and jumping with tremendous dexterity out of the path of the inevitable, oncoming pony punt. His perfect size makes him untiring and enduring in his work.

RECOGNITION: FCI, AKC, UKC, KCGB, CKC, ANKC

CHARACTER: These are active and loving companions. Truly the big dog in the small package, the Cardi is inflated with the helium of unmitigated self-esteem. He is gentle and amicable with family and friends.

CÃO DA SERRA DE AIRES
Portuguese Sheepdog

PORTRAIT: A surly but efficiently built herder. For his moderate size, the dog appears rather high on the leg. His feet are particularly adaptable to rough terrain. His legs are strong; his chest deep. In color this dog comes in shades of fawn, gray, wolf, black, brown, or yellow. Particolor and white are frowned upon. The coat is long and given to waviness. The hair is longer on the head, giving the dog bangs and a banged-up tousled look. Height: 16–22 inches (40½–56 cm). Weight: 26–40 pounds (12–18 kg). Ears are sometimes cropped.

DEVELOPMENT: A herder indigenous to the southern plains of Portugal, this dog has reportedly worked with flocks for generations. Owners relay that these little "monkey dogs" have been a part of the farming operation and family life for as long as they can remember. Although he appears similar to the Berger des Pyrenees and the Catalan Sheepdog, no reliable evidence is forwarded to suggest a direct line of ancestry.

RECOGNITION: FCI

CHARACTER: One of the most devoted and clever of sheepdogs. He can be willful and has therefore always been a challenge for shepherds to train. Once trained, this dog is more reliable than any owner could possibly wish.

CATAHOULA LEOPARD DOG
Catahoula Hog Dog, Catahoula Cur

PORTRAIT: Defying the herder type, this stock dog is rather houndy in appearance, although not lacking any of the physical strength or agility vital to the proficient herding dog. The coat is short and dense and is colored in a merle or black/tan pattern. Height: 20–26 inches (51–66 cm). Weight: 40–50 pounds (18–23 kg). Color is an especially notable feature in this herder: eye color and coat color working in a very complementary and expressive way.

DEVELOPMENT: A varied ancestry befits this multi-faceted herding dog. He is the believed result of crosses between Spanish mastiff-type war dogs and the generic-type Indian curs that roamed the American South. The state of Louisiana is cited as the point of origin, particularly the area of Catahoula. The breed's appearance indicates a certain amount of hound blood infused to acquire the houndy drop ears and various but distinct points in the dog's conformation. This dog is used expressly on the difficult task of driving and rounding hogs and unruly cattle.

RECOGNITION: NR

CHARACTER: This dog, although affectionate with his master, is not recommended for the casual pet owner uninterested in allowing the dog to function in his intended capacity. For the right owner, this is a protective yet dominating canine.

CATALAN SHEEPDOG
Perro de Pastor Catalan, Gos d'Atura Catala

PORTRAIT: Distinguished by a large, square tail and memorable for his whimsical flowing beard and mustache, the Catalan Sheepdog is a bit smaller than an English Springer Spaniel. Height: 18–20 inches (46–51 cm). Weight: 40 pounds (18 kg). The ears are often cropped to stand erect. The coat is usually lengthy and wavy, although a seldom seen short-coat variety exists. In color the Catalan can be fawn with black tips, black, black/tan, grizzle or brindle.

DEVELOPMENT: Historically, the Gos d'Atura Catala is a versatile dog filling a cornucopia of tasks: a herder of sheep and cattle, a police dog, and a messenger dog in times of war. The breed is native to Spain but is utilized in an area settled by French, not Spanish. Their natural guardian instincts combined with their ability to herd make these dogs capable of handling a flock by themselves. When necessary, the 20 inch (51 cm) tall Gos can look twice his size in confronting a potential enemy.

RECOGNITION: FCI

CHARACTER: His disposition and handy size suit him ideally for a house dog and companion. He is fierce, unafraid and effective as a herder—owners are not recommended to pamper and spoil this dog, for his natural instincts must become part of his personality. As a working companion he is a more well-rounded and even-tempered pet.

COLLIE
Scotch Collie

PORTRAIT: Collies present a dignified impression marked by certitude, alertness, and intelligence. The lithe working body is marked by a clean, firm, sinewy neck that carries one of the most expressive heads in dogdom. Of special importance are: the eyes (obliquely set and almond shaped), the skull in proportion with the body, and the tipped ears in proportion with the skull. The coat may be either rough or smooth, with the former being long and dense and the latter being short, smooth, and double. Color can be sable and white, tricolor, blue merle, or white. Height is between 22 and 26 inches (56–66 cm), and weight varies between 50 and 75 pounds (23–34 kg), always with good proportion, never oversized or undersized.

DEVELOPMENT: The essentiality of pastoral pursuits for Scottish mountain dwellers deemed the breeding of fine working collies tantamount to survival. Originally primarily black in color, the "Colley" acquired its name from the Anglo-Saxon word *col*, meaning black. Queen Victoria's fancy ignited in 1860 brought this humble shepherd's dog to the public's eye. Even in the breed's 19th-century heyday, the classic "Lassie" coloration (sable/white) was scarce. The two coat types developed side by side, without the intervention of any other canine and likely as a natural variant. Although there is no questioning that the show Collie is a handsome, impressive animal, he would not compete with his working Collie cousins and would scarcely recognize their wool-laden charges. Nonetheless, the show ring somehow chooses to emphasize a select and ephemeral aesthetic detail (the all-important tipped ear) instead of the breed's original instincts and abilities.

RECOGNITION: FCI, AKC, UKC, KCGB, CKC, ANKC

CHARACTER: Never timid or sullen, the ideal Collie is blessed with an expression that is absolutely distinctive to his breed. The ineffable mysticism and perfection of this expression crystallize the essence of the Collie character.

HERDING DOGS

CROATIAN SHEEPDOG
Hrvaški Övcar

PORTRAIT: This breed is known for its mobility, and this trait is evidenced in the dog's construction. The chest is wide but not excessively deep to impede vertical movement. The hind legs are lean and muscled and have marked angulation, which allows for unilaterally free direction. The back is level; the body has a slight tuck-up. The dog is well muscled overall—never thin or rangy. This athletic body is somewhat veiled by the medium-long, dark-colored coat, which is given to feathering and density. Color is often black or black-gray, with white markings accepted on the legs, feet and chest. Height: 16–21 inches (40½–53 cm). Weight: 30–45 pounds (13½–20½ kg).

DEVELOPMENT: Probably related to the latter-day Hungarian Water Dog and the increasingly popular Puli, the Croatian Sheepdog has been a recognizable entity for about one thousand years. The Hrvaški Övcar is indigenous to the area of Croatia in Yugoslavia. He is smaller and more agile than his flock's sturdy guardian, the Karst Sheepdog. As a herder, he is a fast and active performer with strong instincts and reflexes. His stand-offish approach to the flock may be less conventional than some herders but surely no less effective.

RECOGNITION: FCI

CHARACTER: The Croatian is a virtually weatherproof canine with a comparably adaptable disposition. He is most trainable and rather on the wary side.

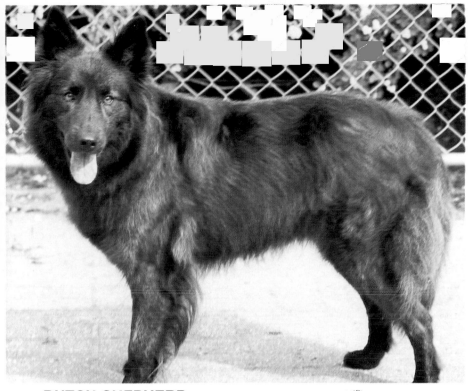

DUTCH SHEPHERD
Hollandse Herdershond

PORTRAIT: The Dutch Shepherd is a strong, enduring, and agile worker. His mass is well proportioned in relation to his bone structure. The combination of the strong, chiseled jaw; the solid carriage; the keen expression; and the round, tapered neck is elegant. Height: 23–25 inches (58½–63½ cm). Weight: 66 pounds (30 kg). The Dutch Shepherds come in three very different coat varieties, each of which is recognized by the FCI. The Longhaired's coat is long, straight, flat and harsh; the Roughhaired's jacket is medium long and wiry; the Shorthaired's hair is fine and dense. Although the coat types vary, the color possibilities remain the same for each: various shades of brindle, including gray, yellow, silver, red or gold brindle, and blue.

DEVELOPMENT: The Dutch Shepherds are remarkably similar to their Belgian cousins. In fact, the two breeds are judged by the same standard requirements, except for color. It is very probable that the Belgian and the Dutch Shepherds are descended from very close stock, with the Dutch Shepherds receiving a definite infusion of German Shepherd blood. Type for the Dutch Shepherd was fixed in the first half of the 18th century. They have remained true to type since that time, although their sharp decline in popularity during the late 19th to early 20th century resulted in slackened breeding practices and subsequent registrations.

RECOGNITION: FCI

CHARACTER: The Dutch Shepherds are among the most competent of all shepherd dogs at such tasks as guard work, herding, field trialing, and companionship. They are noble and very intelligent dogs.

EAST EUROPEAN SHEPHERD
Byelorussian Ovtcharka

PORTRAIT: Here is a solid working dog, set nearly square, with a strong back, deep chest, and substantial hips. The body is covered with a dense double coat capable of insulating the dog from the worst of Russian winters. The head is cleanly chiseled as it is on the German Shepherd Dog; however, the East European has a thicker skull and muzzle. Colors can be black and black/tan (with saddle); whites and brindle are allowed but rarely seen. Height: 24–29 inches (61–74 cm). Weight: 78–105 pounds (35–48 kg).

DEVELOPMENT: The East European Shepherd is a direct descendant of the German Shepherd Dog. The origin of the East Euro can be set near 1920, when the first German Shepherds to take root were introduced into the Soviet Union. The original center of distribution was Byelorussia, whence comes the alternative name. Today, however, these dogs are one of the most popular breeds in western U.S.S.R. It did not take long for the original stock to acquire traits that made it more suitable to the Russian habitat. The breed is now more square, slightly brawnier, and in possession of a denser coat.

RECOGNITION: NR

CHARACTER: A courageous companion and worker, the East Euro is pleasant, personable, intelligent and determined. No specimens exist outside the Soviet Union, so don't go to your local pet shop for this one.

ENGLISH SHEPHERD

PORTRAIT: English Shepherds have a slightly thick-set, very solid appearance. Their muzzle is medium short and tapered to the dark pigmented nose. The ears are rather high set and button. The eyes are clear and dark. The facial expression should be caring and attentive. The forelegs are straight, and the hind legs are slightly bent; they denote the power and quickness necessary for an effective herder. The coat is short on front of face and legs but medium long on body and tail; feathering is noticeable. The color possibilities include black and tan, tricolor, sable and white, and black and white. Height is medium, 18–23 inches (46–58½ cm), and weight is moderate, 40–60 pounds (18–27 kg).

DEVELOPMENT: Although the original breed may well trace its roots back to early Rome, the English Shepherd of today is a well-conceived conglomeration of the old-type collies, the Scotch Collie, the Border Collie, and other proven herder types. Although quite happy with the Shepherd of old, American farmers always strove to better their assets—the result of this striving was the agile, hardy, pliable worker, who herds loose-eyed with the degree of physical action adjusted accordingly to the individual stock members.

RECOGNITION: UKC

CHARACTER: Owing to his acute sensory perception, the English Shepherd is an alert, responsive dog. He is level-headed and never given to aggression or lethargy. He makes a good companion but must receive adequate exercise to maintain his appealing disposition and instinct.

HERDING DOGS

GERMAN SHEPHERD DOG
Deutsche Schaferhund, Alsatian

PORTRAIT: Active and enlivened, the German Shepherd Dog immediately impresses with strength, agility, and form in a medium-sized, deep bodied, smooth and substantial animal. The ideal dog denotes at once noble bearing and quality performance. The cleanly chiseled head carries moderately pointed well-proportioned ears, hold erect when alert. Weight. 75–95 pounds (34–43 kg). Height: 22–26 inches (56–66 cm). The dog has a medium-length double coat. Strong rich colors are in preference.

DEVELOPMENT: First exhibited in Great Britain as a German Sheep Dog, this familiar breed is of true German origin. During World War I, it was used by the French and called the French Police Dog. The British called the jaunty herder the Alsatian Wolfdog after the War. It would be inaccurate to limit the German Shepherd Dog's talents to the prairie, in attendance to a flock (a role it is still able to fulfill). The breed's finesse and sagacity at a myriad of tasks speak well of its unshakable popularity. A guard dog, guide dog, Red Cross worker, police assistant, military and messenger dog as well as flock herder paint a more complete portrait of the breed's abilities. The German Shepherd's overpopularity had taken a toll on its quality, affecting both temperament and physique. Fortunately, responsible breeders have worked toward replenishing the lost quality with substantial success.

RECOGNITION: FCI, AKC, UKC, KCGB, CKC, ANKC

CHARACTER: The breed's litany of virtues can degenerate into vice if this dog's energy and talents are not properly channeled. Its quick-thinking mind and agile body need a master cognizant of potential and dedicated to the attainment of that potential. Overall, these dogs are all one can possibly desire in a canine companion.

GIANT SCHNAUZER
Riesenschnauzer

PORTRAIT: In muscular composition and robustness, the Giant Schnauzer cuts a daring and dauntless figure of canine power. The body flourishes in agility and might. Its concentrated, short-coupled, and powerful frame accommodates an effortlessly free and driving gait. Height: 23½–27½ inches (59–70 cm). Weight: 70–77 pounds (32–35 kg). The coat is of medium length with a harsh texture and a stand-offish lay. The undercoat is woolly. In color the Giant can be solid black or pepper and salt. The ears are V-shaped and set high. In the United States, they are customarily cropped; in England, they are not. Uncropped ears are becoming more common in the States as well.

DEVELOPMENT: Developed for utilization as a cattle and drover dog, the Müncher Dog, as he was once called, is the largest of the Schnauzers and also the most powerful. His extraordinary size gives his terrier capabilities an impressive though perverse air—crunching monster rats without batting an eye. As a drover, the Giant Schnauzer was favored and widely used until the Industrial Revolution locomoted into Munich. Cattle droving dogs became virtually obsolete, so these acromegalic terriers sought work as guards—butchers and brewers, their newfound employers, replaced the farmers as breeders and owners.

RECOGNITION: FCI, AKC, UKC, KCGB, CKC, ANKC

CHARACTER: This is one of the hardiest of working dogs known to man. He is vigorous in body and mind and adaptable to all kinds of weather and living conditions. Despite his grand size, he needs relatively less exercise and obedience training than do many of the other large breeds.

HOVAWART

PORTRAIT: The fairly large Hovawart is a powerful herder. The average weight of this working dog is between 65–90 pounds (30–40½ kg). The body is well balanced, equipped with a strong topline, deep brisket and moderately deep loins. The head is broad and free from wrinkles. The eyes are usually dark and oval in shape. The coat can be black/gold, black or blonde, and the standard is quite explicit in its detail of the breed's color pattern. The coat is long in appearance but short on face and forelegs. Height: 24–28 inches (61–71 cm).

DEVELOPMENT: Two opposing theories exist regarding the Hovawart's origin in its present state. One theory contends that the breed is simply the re-discovered direct descendent of the Hovawart of the 1800s; a dedicated group of fanciers entered the potentially Hovawart-warted Black Forest and the Harz region in the early 20th century in search of the said canine; they exited both successfully and excitedly with both arms success-filled. A second theory states that breeds such as the German Shepherd, Newfoundland, Kuvasz, and possibly others were crossbred to produce the believed accurate type, based on artwork dating as far back as the 15th century. It is known with certainty that the Hovawart was an esteemed guard of the German aristocracy up until the 1800s. Today he is safely established with the dog fancy of Germany and England.

RECOGNITION: FCI, KCGB

CHARACTER: Loyal and protective, watchful and willing, the Hovawart is a fine watch and guard dog. Gentle, patient, and tolerant, he is also an excellent companion.

LANCASHIRE HEELER
Ormskirk Terrier, Ormskirk Heeler

PORTRAIT: This is a diminutive, low-set working dog of superior strength and broad instinctive abilities. The body possesses well-sprung ribs, and the topline is firm and level. The head is always in proportion to the body; the skull is flat and wide between the erect ears. Drop ears are undesirable. The tail is set on high and left natural. The coat is seasonally long or short—wintertime reveals a plush coat with a visible mane; the summer, a sleek shiny coat. Height: 10–12 inches (25½–30½ cm). Weight 6–12 pounds (2½–5½ kg).

DEVELOPMENT: The modern-day Lancashire is a "new" breed of dog. It has been bred to exhibit outstanding herder characteristics. It is somewhat surprising that a new working breed should emerge at a time when herding and other such canine employment is dwindling in demand. Largely a cross-breed of Welsh Corgis and Manchester Terriers, the Lancashire Heeler emerged in its present state in the 1960–70s. He is a herder of outstanding ability and great promise. He herds cattle, goats, horses, etc., and is also a fantastic rabbit hunter, ratter, and watchdog.

RECOGNITION: FCI, KCGB

CHARACTER: Besides their proven strength and nimbleness and their ability to work in inclement weather, these dogs possess the quick-witted, friendly personality that makes them enjoyable companions.

LAPINPOROKOIRA
Lapland Reindeer Dog, Lapponian Herder, Lapponian Vallhund

PORTRAIT: A spitzy looking herder, the Lapponian is a dog of moderate leg and overall medium size. The head is somewhat pointed and the ears stand wide and erect. Rather long in the back and double coated, the Lapinporokoira varies in color from white with dark shadings to black and black/- tan, the latter combinations being more popular. The outer coat is glossy, long and hard; the undercoat is soft and woolly. Height: 19–22 inches (48– 56 cm). Weight: 66 pounds (30 kg) maximum.

DEVELOPMENT: This Finnish breed was developed by crossing the local Lapphund with good-sized shepherds, such as the German Shepherd and Collie. This cross was activated to accommodate herdsmen who needed a worker to round up domesticated reindeer. The perfect crystallization of the assets of the Nordic breeds and the herders, the Lapinporokoira is an efficient and enthusiastic worker, able to withstand the most dastardly of weather conditions.

RECOGNITION: FCI

CHARACTER: A true herder today, the breed has lost most of its ancestor's hunting instincts. This "loss" is to the sheer gain of his herding capabilities. His attention and concentration on his work are unshakable. The Lapinporokoira is an easycare, well-mannered pet.

MUDI

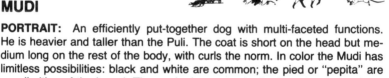

PORTRAIT: An efficiently put-together dog with multi-faceted functions. He is heavier and taller than the Puli. The coat is short on the head but medium long on the rest of the body, with curls the norm. In color the Mudi has limitless possibilities: black and white are common; the pied or "pepita" are peculiarities of the breed. The pepita is an evenly distributed collage of colors. Height: 14–20 inches (35½–51 cm). Weight: 18–29 pounds (39½–13½ kg).

DEVELOPMENT: Despite this breed's wide assortment of abilities, it has never been excessively popular, even in its homeland of Hungary. Much of the reason for this can be attributed to the ever-present Puli and Komondor, older and more popular Hungarian working breeds. The Mudi's versatility is astounding: both herder and guard, he is capable of handling his own flock without the assistance of a third paw; a terrier and hunter of passion—roles he fills for the sheer fun of working; a farm hand and family companion.

RECOGNITION: FCI

CHARACTER: The few owners who do employ and favor the Mudi find him incomparable. His seemingly unending list of talents combined with his pleasant disposition make him a top dog among canines. He is truly a rare dog; his proud owners reveal that as rare as he is, a moody Mudi is even more scarce!

470   HERDING DOGS

OLD ENGLISH SHEEPDOG
Bobtail

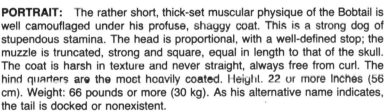

PORTRAIT: The rather short, thick-set muscular physique of the Bobtail is well camouflaged under his profuse, shaggy coat. This is a strong dog of stupendous stamina. The head is proportional, with a well-defined stop; the muzzle is truncated, strong and square, equal in length to that of the skull. The coat is harsh in texture and never straight, always free from curl. The hind quarters are the most heavily coated. Height. 22 or more Inches (56 cm). Weight: 66 pounds or more (30 kg). As his alternative name indicates, the tail is docked or nonexistent.

DEVELOPMENT: Probably a descendant of the large Russian sheepdogs or the Bearded Collie, the Old English Sheepdog can be reliably traced to the mid-1700s. The popular belief that these dogs descended from the rather hound-like Himalayan sheepdogs is probably faulty in light of the conformation and ever-consistent type associated with the OES. The origination of the breed's "Bobtail" designation can be traced to the dog's work as a drover dog; he was among the canines exempt from taxation and the docked tail was the indicator of this privilege. As a drover, he is active and compellingly accurate.

RECOGNITION: FCI, AKC, UKC, KCGB, CKC, ANKC

CHARACTER: Faithful and protective, the Old English Sheepdog is intelligent and trainable. His rather disdainful expression is well hidden under shaggy bangs, giving him a light-hearted yet watchful air. He is a capital companion and guardian dog.

PEMBROKE WELSH CORGI

PORTRAIT: Set low, strong, and solidly built, the Pembroke evokes the impression of substance and stamina, efficiently packed into a small space. The head must be particularly fox-like in shape and appearance but never sly in expression. The face is nicely chiseled, giving a somewhat tapered muzzle. The ears are erect and firm, coming to a slightly rounded point. The coat is medium in length, short, and thick; it is double—the outer is longer and coarser. On the body the length varies. Height: 10–12 inches (25½–30½ cm). Weight: 30 pounds (13½ kg) or less. Oversize and undersize are severely penalized. The tail is docked as short as possible—this trait in addition to the foxy expression distinguishes him from the Cardigan.

DEVELOPMENT: The Pembroke is a very old breed, with written references to this cattle drover cited as far back as 920–1107 AD. The most commonly spun yarn about the Pembie's first coming to Britain refers to Flemish weavers. These weavers were brought to the British Isles by Henry I of England and established themselves in Wales. They were dutifully attached to their colorful Corgis and brought them along. Breeders in the 19th century routinely crossed the Pembroke Corgi with the Cardigan—this explains readily why the breeds appear so similar today. Such crosses diminished the differences that may have once been noteworthy. Today, breeders are determined to keep the two highly enchanting, low-set herders distinct. Pembies are often born tailless, Cardigans never.

RECOGNITION: FCI, AKC, UKC, KCGB, CKC, ANKC

CHARACTER: A bold and kindly expression well befits this home-loving and energetic little dog. Despite his wee size, this Welshman is a vigilant and responsible watchdog. He is affectionate with his own and greatly admired for his superior intelligence.

POLISH LOWLAND SHEEPDOG
Polski Owczarek Nizinny, Valee Sheepdog, Berge Polonais de Vallée

PORTRAIT: A strong, cobby, muscular dog with a fairly shaggy thick coat. The head is medium in size and in proportion to the body. The profuse hair on the forehead, cheeks and chin makes the head appear larger than it really is. The coat can occur in any color, including piebald. The body is rectangular rather than square from the side—it is neither flat nor barrel shaped. Height: 16–20 (40–52 cm). Weight: 30–35 pounds (13½–16 kg).

DEVELOPMENT: The necessity of producing a working dog functional on the Polish landscape and unaffected by the harsh climate spurred the probable crossing of the Puli with other mountain herders to produce a smaller dog that retained the weather-resistant coat. This crossing surely occurred centuries ago (likely during the 16th). The Nizinny has been used as component stock for other breeds, i.e., the Bearded Collie. Although nearly sinking into extinction during the Second World War, the breed now enjoys well-deserved recognition.

RECOGNITION: FCI, KCGB

CHARACTER: This breed's inherent herding instincts have been well adapted to homelife—the dog is affectionate, possessive, a good guard and a trainable companion.

PULI
Hungarian Puli

PORTRAIT: The woolly, seemingly shapeless cords that fringe the tightly knit body of the Puli have become this handy herder's trademark. He is a compact, squarely built dog with a well-balanced frame. The head is slightly domed and medium broad. The muzzle is only a third of the head length, ending in a nose of good size. The dog is medium sized, with a moderately broad chest. The coat is dense and profuse on all parts of the body. Wavy or curly, the outer coat is never silky; the undercoat is soft. The coat clumps naturally and forms cords on the adult dog. Height: 14–19 inches (35½–48 cm). Weight: 20–40 pounds (9–18 kg). In color the Puli is usually dark—black, rusty black, and gray—but can be apricot or white as well.

DEVELOPMENT: That the Puli is a smaller version of the ancient Tibetan Dog is an assertion that stands up most to conjecture. Resembling the Tibetan Terrier in color and conformation, the Puli may indeed be a less sizable Komondor. As the Chinese blurt frothily, Tibetans have produced both "the most beautiful women and the worst-tempered dogs." The Puli that migrated with the Magyars to Hungary retained much of this Tibetan choler. His fervor and assertiveness transferred well to his flock detail. His size and energy made him an eager herder, and his innate belligerence (since mellowed) deemed him a fearless and confident guard. The Puli's dark and incessantly matted coat affords protection from both weather and attackers.

RECOGNITION: FCI, AKC, UKC, KCGB, CKC, ANKC

CHARACTER: Today's Puli is acrobatically lighthearted and decidedly sound. His coat can require a dedicated comber to keep it uncorded. More commonly, he is kept unkempt—of course, keeping him unkempt keeps his keeper busy cleaning his long cords.

PUMI

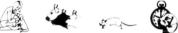

PORTRAIT: The gremlin-like and totally adorable Pumi is a small terrier-type dog with semi-erect ears and a curl-covered medium-small sized body. The coat is moderately long; the curls never cord. Any solid color except white is acceptable: shades of silver, dove gray and slate are most common. Height: 13–19 inches (33–48 cm). Weight: 18–29 pounds (8–13 kg). The tail is a fair indicator of the breed's temperament, always merry and carried high.

DEVELOPMENT: A spin-off of the Puli, the Pumi was produced by crossing his Hungarian cousin with French and German drover's dogs, likely of Pomeranian or Hutespitz roots. After three centuries of perfecting the type, the Pumi today is gaining in fans and employers. The long coat (without the cords) is inherited from the Puli; the ear carriage and volatile temperament are derived from his drover-type relations. Like the Mudi, the Pumi is a multi-functional dog. He is primarily a cow herder but can also double as an exterminator and triple as a watchdog.

RECOGNITION: FCI

CHARACTER: While the Puli is busy maneuvering the flocks of the high plains, the Pumi is duly occupied as a town dog. His personality lends itself to being near the family and master. He is obedient and watchful and takes reprimand with grace.

SAARLOOSWOLFHOND

PORTRAIT: This breed clearly resembles the wolf, from which it is descended. Many features, and especially the temperament, however, are tempered by its German Shepherd Dog lineage. It is a medium-large dog with a solid carriage, showing excellent strength and mobility. The skull is moderately broad, sloping from ears to eyes. The muzzle has a definite taper to the solid dark nose. The ears are large (like the German Shepherd Dog's) and carried erect. Height: 27½–29½ inches (70–75 cm). Weight: 79–90 pounds (36–41 kg). The coat is medium short and very dense; the neck is covered with a ruff. Color should indicate the wolf ancestry, being either agouti, wolf gray, or wolf brown, with limited white markings possible.

DEVELOPMENT: Although the idea may be quite old, its successful execution is definitely a 20th-century reality. During the 1930s and through to his death in 1969, Leendert Saarloos crossed stock obtained from crossing the domesticated German Shepherd Dog with a zoo-kept wolf. The first dog-to-wolf crossing was unsuccessful. Through continued attempts and sedulous selection, near success was achieved—the breed was not recognized by the Dutch Kennel Club until 1975, six years after Leendert Saarloos's death.

RECOGNITION: FCI

CHARACTER: This dog is only for the lover of the canine ways of old, as it retains in a modified state some of the wolf-like and/or ancient canine ways—including an intense pack instinct, a tendency towards shyness, and a need to roam (or at least to have adequate space).

SCHAPENDOES
Dutch Sheepdog

PORTRAIT: This is a dog whose body is longer than it is high. The back is long and straight and exceptionally strong; the chest is deep and the undercarriage perceivably tucked-up. Angulation is an important feature in the hind legs. The thick tail is long for the dog's height and covered with long hair. Height: 17–20 inches (43–51 cm). Weight: 33 pounds (15 kg). The head is also covered with long hair; the ears lie flat and are set well back. The skull is broad, as is the bearded muzzle. The coat is long, dense, and harsh to the touch. Many specimens have a wave to their coat. Coat colors are ideally between blue-gray and black; all colors, however, are acceptable.

DEVELOPMENT: The Dutch Sheepdog is undoubtedly a very old breed of similar descent to that of the Briard, the Bergamasco, and even the Bearded Collie. He was never known to be popular with the aristocracy, and there is now no record of his early history. With less and less employment for herders, this once exceptionally hardy, vigorous, and dedicated worker is becoming pure pet.

RECOGNITION: FCI

CHARACTER: Still retaining some of its herding characteristics, this breed requires considerable exercise and a family of which to feel a part.

HERDING DOGS

SHETLAND SHEEPDOG

PORTRAIT: A miniature Collie look-alike, the Sheltie is a small, rough-coated dog that is sound and sturdy. He is wholly symmetrical, with no part out of proportion to his tight frame. The coat, double and harsh, is abundant, complete with mane and frill. The shapely head and sweet expression combine to present the ideal. The head is refined and the ears are lipped. Height: 13–16 inches (33–40½ cm). The Sheltie can be black, blue merle or sable, marked with varying amounts of white (in Irish pattern) or tan. Smooth-coated specimens are most undesirable.

DEVELOPMENT: The fertile Shetland islands blessed by miniature four-legged dwellers—ponies and sheep—also yielded this tot-like working collie. The Sheltie should not be written off as a smaller version of the British (Scotch) Collie; it is a separate, though diminutive, entity. Many years ago, it is likely that Collies were brought to the island, and crosses or bantamization shed the Sheltie. A move some decades ago by British breeders wreaked potential havoc on this ancient herder. A miniature Collie was developed (many of which resembled an inflated Papillon more than a Sheltie) and was shown with the Shelties. These contrived miniatures created a second type and much dissension. A third Collie type was dwarfed—a toy—to add further to the sod-ridden matter. Neither of these had the working abilities of the Shetland. Today's Sheltie may have a bit more of these mini-Collies in him than did his ancestors, but his herding abilities are still intact.

RECOGNITION: FCI, AKC, UKC, KCGB, CKC, ANKC

CHARACTER: The Sheltie expression, sweet and unaffected, reveals this breed's gentle and unceasingly loyal personality. These are merry, well-mannered, and plain bloody adorable companions, fully deserving of their increasing popularity.

STANDARD SCHNAUZER
Schnauzer

PORTRAIT: Hardy and heavy set, the Standard Schnauzer is sturdily constructed and square in build. A harsh coat, sinewy composition, and rugged build add to his workman-like appearance. The arched eyebrows over his willful eyes and the bristly mustache and luxuriant whiskers on his broad "snauz" give him that distinctive Schnauzer air. The head is broad between the ears and narrows towards the eyes; it is rectangular and elongated. The forehead is flat and without wrinkles. The coat is wiry and weatherproof and as thick as possible. Color: pepper and salt, solid black. Height: 18–20 inches (46–51 cm). Weight: 33 pounds (15 kg).

DEVELOPMENT: References in art and literature verify that the Schnauzer has been an active native of Germany since the 15th century. Likely, these dogs are as ancient as any modern breed, barring a sighthound or two. The probable cross to achieve the Schnauzer involves the black German Poodle, the Gray Wolfspitz and roughhaired pinscher types. At home, Schnauzers are used as cattle drovers and watchdogs. Not to be overlooked, they are also energetic ratters. Breeders encourage these inborn qualities, adding to the breed's versatility.

RECOGNITION: FCI, AKC, UKC, KCGB, CKC, ANKC

CHARACTER: This is an alert and reliable canine, ideally sized and tempered. He is a popular and handy house dog that doesn't require a lot of exercise. A likeable, never pugnacious personality is nearly indiscernible through his intense beetling brow.

SWEDISH VALLHUND
Vasgotaspets, Swedish Cattledog

PORTRAIT: The dwarf-like Vallhund is sturdily built and powerful, with a fine efficiency of energy and drive. The pointed, prick ears sit on a rather long and clean-cut head, rather blunt and wedge-like. A fox-like expression is paramount. A well-defined mask is highly desirable, with lighter hair around the eyes, on muzzle, and under the throat. The coat is medium in length and harsh in texture. The top coat is close and tight. Height: 13–16 inches (33–40½ cm). Weight: 20–32 pounds (9–14½ kg). In color the Vasgotaspets can be steel gray, grayish brown, grayish yellow, reddish yellow, or reddish brown. A fractional amount of white markings are tolerated.

DEVELOPMENT: Sport-loving cynologists have jousted for years over the origin of the Vasgotaspets. This little Vallhund, closely resembling the Pembroke Corgi in conformation, may have been transported by Vikings to Britain or spurned from imported Pembies brought to Sweden. Although to Western eyes the Swedish Vallhund is less eye-catching than the Pembie, as its color is drabber and lacks the Corgi zing, he is no less a utility dog. The *Vallhund* , translating as forest dog, is a canine of many talents: a cattle drover, watchdog, ratter and versatile farmhand. He is a more and more common sight at European exhibitions.

RECOGNITION: KCGB

CHARACTER: A responsive and even-tempered companion, the Vallhund is intelligent and affectionate. He loves attention and can be gaily garish and show-offish. Owners are never disappointed in his multi-faceted ability or his spontaneous sense of fun.

TIBETAN TERRIER
Dhokhi Apso

PORTRAIT: Compact and powerful, the body is sturdy, medium sized and generally square in outline. The coat is double: the top coat is profuse and fine, not silky nor woolly; the undercoat is fine and woolly. The skull is neither broad nor coarse, neither domed nor absolutely flat between the ears. The head is furnished with long hair that drapes generously over the eyes. The lower jaw is bearded. The ears are pendant and V-shaped, not too close to the head—always well feathered. The forelegs are straight; the hocks well let down. The ribs are well up; the loins slightly arched. Height: 14–16 inches (35½–40½ cm). Weight: 18–30 pounds (8–12 kg).

DEVELOPMENT: Raised as mascots or talismans, the Tibetan Terrier is one of the two small native breeds of Tibet. The Lost Valley, a virtually inaccessible area, employed these monastery-raised tykes as St. Christopher medals (of sorts), given to adventuresome travelers as good luck charms (pets). The breed's alleged ancestors include the North Kunlun Mountain Dog and the poodle-like Inner Mongolian Dog. Many dogs herded sheep in the Tibetan hill country, with the massive Tibetan Mastiff on guard duty. The smaller specimens, too petite for the rugged task of herding, were given to Tibetan lamas to raise. Some Tibetan Terriers were and still are employed as watchdogs or lost article retrievers ("when any possession falls over the khud and lands in a place inaccessible to man or dog"). To the AKC, the Tibetan Terrier is a fairly recent addition, entering the Stud Book in 1973. All colors occur and are accepted by all registries. The Tibetan people did not discourage the multitude of color possibilities but rather concentrated on the physical soundness of the dogs.

RECOGNITION: FCI, AKC, KCGB, CKC, ANKC

CHARACTER: Equally prized in Tibet as herders and companions, these tiny shag-covered dogs are insightful and industrious. Although they are not terriers, they can be fearless and assertive. Their long coats require some attention—incidentally, a Tibetan summer finds these dogs clipped (like the sheep they herd) and their hair mixed with yak's hair to be woven into fine, impervious cloth.

Jack Russell Terriers.

TERRIERS

AIREDALE TERRIER

PORTRAIT: Largest terrier of the Western World, the Airedale is a well-muscled, fairly cobby dog with a durable wire coat. Riding this tan hard coat is a classic saddle, which is characteristic of the Airedale breed and the only acceptable color pattern. Height: 22–24 inches (56–61 cm). Weight: 44 pounds (20 kg). Side-saddling the long, rather narrow head are smallish, folding V-shaped ears. The slackless body is supported by column-like, straight fore legs, complemented by well-bent hind legs, giving the dog free, propulsive movement.

DEVELOPMENT: In the mid-19th century, otter-hunting sportsmen conceived of crossing various working strains of ratting terrier (all larger than today's Fox Terriers) with the Otter Hound to obtain a dog of substantial weight and substance to tackle larger foes, and then provide security for their homes. Later, the introduction of Irish Terrier (and possibly Welsh Terrier) blood led towards the setting of size and type. The Airedale's versatility is enviable: as a terrier, he can "kill rats as fast as you can wink" and give hell to badgers, rabbits, etc.; as a gundog, he is superb in setting, retrieving and flushing; as a water dog, his swimming ability is olympic; as a warrior, he is unstoppable.

RECOGNITION: FCI, AKC, UKC, KCGB, CKC, ANKC

CHARACTER: By reason of his intelligence and his natural instincts, he is the easiest of all terriers to train. Unobtrusive, patient and perfectly mannered, he is a gentleman in the home.

AUSTRIAN SHORTHAIRED PINSCHER
Österreichischer Kurzhaariger Pinscher

PORTRAIT: Relative to his medium-short body, this terrier's broad head and wide ears contribute to the general deception that he is much bigger than he is. Standing at most 20 inches (51 cm) and usually smaller, the Austrian Shorthaired Pinscher possesses a wide, developed chest, inducing the dog's width to apparently exceed its height. The breed can be red, black, brown, fawn, brindle or black/tan, with limited white markings common. The tail is docked or left to curl over the back.

DEVELOPMENT: Without acquiring a following outside of its native Austria, this working terrier has been known at home for many years. The breed is probably similarly rooted with the German Pinscher, if one hypothesizes principally on type and geographic similarity. This breed is becoming increasingly scarce, despite the efforts of a few enthusiasts.

RECOGNITION: FCI

CHARACTER: A tad high strung, this terrier is most content in the country where he can put his instinctive abilities to work. His big bark does not make him ideal for urban life. Fearless and attentive, this dog makes a terrific watchdog.

AUSTRALIAN TERRIER

PORTRAIT: A feisty, low-set, unfalteringly sturdy dog, long in proportion to his height, rugged and hard bitten in appearance. He is essentially a working dog, as his features denote. The head is long; the skull flat and of moderate width. The muzzle is strong and powerful. The soft silky topknot protects the eyes when working or when going to ground. The body is of solid construction; the ribs are well sprung; the chest is moderately deep and wide. Height: 10 inches (25½ cm). Weight: 12–14 pounds (5½–6½ kg). Coat: harsh, straight, and dense. Color: blue/tan or clear sandy.

DEVELOPMENT: A combustible blend of the best terriers that northern England and Scotland had on tap. British settlers of Australia quickly recognized the need for a dog hardy enough to brace the demanding climate, combat the problemsome varmints, and keep watch over the homestead in its new and different home. Selective breeding was soon initiated, and the environment lent a hand in weeding out the weak. Type was show-bench ready by 1872, though British acceptance of the breed did not come until 1936. The Aussie was slow to leave his native land, possibly because his rowdy energy so well suited him to the virgin terrain, or simply that the settlers were tight-fisted in giving up their pie.

RECOGNITION: FCI, AKC, UKC, KCGB, CKC, ANKC

CHARACTER: The Aussie remains a lot of bang in a little fur. His instincts are strong; he's a fine ratter, a dutiful watchdog, and a tireless farm hand. His antics and obedience make him a fine companion as well.

BEDLINGTON TERRIER

PORTRAIT: This obviously ovine presence, despite his chiefly sheeply appearance, is unadulterated canine. A light-made lathy dog, not weedy or shelly, he is strong, hard and muscular—conformation is of utmost importance. Fairly long in the body with natural arched loin and a long rat tail. The natural coat is a blend of hard and soft hair with a tendency to curl (often appearing as wool). Height: 15–17 inches (38–43 cm). Weight: 17–23 pounds (7½–10½ kg). Coat color possibilities include blue, liver, sandy, or each with tan.

DEVELOPMENT: The most common contention is that the Whippet was crossed with the Dandie Dinmont and Otter Hound to produce this distinctive terrier. Known as the Rothbury Terrier until 1820, the Bedlington was once a very hardy game dog used by gypsies in northern England as poachers and pit fighters. The dogs, fancied by many walks of life, including miners and pitmen, hunted rats, otters, and badgers alike. The fast-paced industrialization that swept Europe forced this overly snarly contender to mellow and concede to the more fanciful fancier's type.

RECOGNITION: FCI, AKC, UKC, KCGB, CKC

CHARACTER: Possibly too sheepishly clown-like for the real terrier man, the show Bedlington falls prey to foppish fashion, costuming all too well what is left of his game terrier heart. Although hunting abilities have faded, many working Bedlingtons still faithfully comply to their age-old task of ratting. As a pet, the breed is affectionate and personable and may indeed be for "ewe."

BLACK RUSSIAN TERRIER
Chornyi, Terrier Noir Russe

PORTRAIT: A dramatically strong and robust conformation is boasted by the Black Russian Terrier. The body is square and powerful. The coat is coarse and thick and measures as long as four inches (10 cm). As the name indicates the most common color, the breed also occurs in salt and pepper. Height 25–28 inches (63½–71 cm). The head, facial furnishings and flop V-shaped ears conjure images of the Giant Schnauzer all too vivid to overlook. Structurally, he is heavier boned and thicker overall.

DEVELOPMENT: In an effort to create a mighty monster-like terrier to call their own, Soviet breeders crossed three Western breeds of whom they thought highly. These purebreds included the Giant Schnauzer (popularly called the Russian Bear Schnauzer in the U.S.S.R.), the Rottweiler and the Airedale Terrier. Used primarily as guards and protectors in Russia, the breed is hardy and aggressive. Its thick coat provides ample protection from the severe Soviet winter.

RECOGNITION: NR

CHARACTER: This Soviet creation is not bound to show up on any Westerner's doorstep in the near future. Owners therefore need not contemplate how he would get along with their three Toy Poodles. He is reported, by the way, to be potentially quite ferocious but this terrorizing terrier can make quite an unsurpassable watchdog. Considering the disposition of his forebears, he should be a reasonably sound and personable dog.

BORDER TERRIER

PORTRAIT: Efficiently put-together, the Border Terrier is medium boned but strong and active. The jacket, ranging from red to wheaten, is slightly broken, tightly fitting and excessively wiry. This is a working dog and the conformation is utterly dependent on its functional abilities. No aesthetics should interfere and, despite its otter-looking head, it is by no means an unsightly little dog. Weight: 11½–15½ pounds (5–7 kg). Height: 11 inches (28 cm).

DEVELOPMENT: The first written record of the breed dates back to 1880—an article describing the terriers of Northumberland and Westmorland. Its original purpose was the work of digging out foxes from the rocky rugged country. He has worn a number of caps for the various localities in which he dwelled: the Reedwater Terrier and the Coquetdale Terrier. Sufficiently legged to keep pace with the horses on the hunt yet squat and plucky enough to go to ground, the Border is truly an ideal worker.

RECOGNITION: FCI, AKC, KCGB, CKC, ANKC

CHARACTER: Gameness is this terrier's game. He is agile and alert, steadfast and hard. In the home, he is amiable and affectionate. This dog's instincts are strong and cannot be ignored. Owners are encouraged to provide him with plenty of exercise time.

CAIRN TERRIER

PORTRAIT: Tousled, tiny and tousy, the Cairn Terrier possesses a fox-like facial expression and a rough double coat. Its undocked tail and pointed ears are carried erect. Height: 9–12 inches (23–30½ cm); Weight: 13–16 pounds (6–7½ kg). The muzzle is short and the head is proportioned to body. This is a compact and natural-appearing workman.

DEVELOPMENT: Said to resemble most expressly the original Highland Terrier, today's Cairn Terrier is the general stock from which the Westie, Skye and Scottie arose. The Highland Terrier lived to decimate vermin: badgers, otters, foxes, setting the example for all his descendants. The road to the present breed name was rocky but "Cairn" was chosen for the little terrier's ability to retrieve intruders from the small openings in stone grave markers (the cairns).

RECOGNITION: FCI, AKC, UKC, KCGB, CKC, ANKC

CHARACTER: Happy to be alive, independent and smart, the Cairn continues to delight owners and adapts well to apartment living. Although a terrier at heart, the breed thrives in a suburban environment. Owners are warned to keep an eye on him since he has a natural proclivity towards excavating and redesigning flower beds. Owners in Kansas attest to the dog's uncanny ability to find its way to (there's no place like) home.

CZESKY TERRIER
Bohemian Terrier

PORTRAIT: A terrier of both gameness and grace, the Czesky vests in a fine, silky coat that comes in blue-gray or light coffee. He has drop ears and well-furnished eyebrows and beard, a long head with a moderately full muzzle. Robust and hardy, the Czesky weighs in at 20 pounds (9 kg), the average being closer to 16 pounds (7½ kg). Height: 10–14 inches (25½–35½ cm).

DEVELOPMENT: Convinced that the German Hunt Terrier could not fulfill their needs, Czechoslovakian sportsmen sought a terrier to go to ground and yet be strong enough to undo either fox or badger. Crosses between the Scottish Terrier and Sealyham Terrier, orchestrated by geneticist Frantisek Horak, generated the Czesky Terrier. Horak was pleased with the dog's working attributes and attractive looks. Some of the breed's unique traits may point to a dose of Dandie Dinmont as well.

RECOGNITION: FCI

CHARACTER: A breed of character and good nature, the Czesky is a sensational home companion. His obedience combined with his good looks have made him the choice of many new fanciers. The breed is becoming more popular in the States as Americans begin to cash in on this Czech's distinctive looks and terrier abilities.

DANDIE DINMONT TERRIER

PORTRAIT: Longer than he is tall, the Dandie Dinmont ambles on short, crooked legs, cocks a round head, topped by a soft, buffy hairpiece, and shakes a wiry tail. The body is long, flexible, and well built. Height: 8–11 inches (20–28 cm). Weight: 18–24 pounds (8–11 kg). The coat is crisp and is comprised of both hard and soft hairs. Penciled or piley, the coat is pepper (bluish black to silvery gray) or mustard (reddish brown to pale fawn).

DEVELOPMENT: Existing for many years before receiving its name, this terrier was dandily knighted "Dinmont" by Sir Walter Scott. Scott's *Guy Mannering*, published in 1814, provided that name. These dogs are off-springs of the rough-coated Border area terriers, created through crosses between the Dachshund and Otter Hound. What the relationship is between the Dandie and the Bedlington has been so intricately weaved into obscurity that no real conclusions can be drawn—so we won't pretend. Badger and otter are the breed's designated foes.

RECOGNITION: FCI, AKC, UKC, KCGB, CKC, ANKC

CHARACTER: Bolting after badgers requires a bolder terrier than the serene Dandie of today. The breed makes a fine companion—it is intelligent and industrious. It should be added that it is also strong willed, obdurate, and not keen on obedience. Show dogs tend to be better behaved but readily broadcast condescending waves to their fellow former rat-chompers.

DUTCH SMOUSHOND
Hollandse Smoushond

PORTRAIT: The straw-colored Dutchman known as the Smoushond is a diminutive stable dog with a coarse wire coat. This jacket of medium length must come in yellow, preferably dark straw, and is complete with facial accoutrements—the beard, mustache and eyebrows giving the dog a carefree, untidy appearance. Height: 14–17 inches (35½–43 cm). Weight: 20–22 pounds (9–10 kg). The body is well balanced and close to the ground.

DEVELOPMENT: When German dog fanciers pooh-poohed the yellow-colored German Coarsehaired Pointers being whelped, a Dutch entrepreneur called Abraas transported specimens to Amsterdam, Holland. The little yellow tykes soon became favored as a vogue companion dog. World War II was not kind to the breed so post-War efforts were made to restore its former status. The breed is not known outside of the Netherlands, and Dutch breeders express little interest in promoting him abroad.

RECOGNITION: FCI

CHARACTER: An easycare and compliant household dog, the Smoushond is genial and winsome as a companion. The Smoushond tends to be quiet with those he doesn't know, but is lovingly boisterous with his own.

GERMAN HUNTING TERRIER
Deutscher Jagdterrier

PORTRAIT: A mighty lot of might in a mighty little tot. The Jagdterrier is small and game, standing no taller than 16 inches (40½ cm). Bigger than a number of terriers though, this dog is well muscled and vigorous. This breed can come in one of two coats: the shorter is smooth and coarse; the rough is very wiry and broken. In color, it can be black/tan, red, or chocolate/tan. Clearly visible cheeks and a sturdy muzzle give its angulated head a determined look. Its ears are V-shaped and sit much like a Fox Terrier's. Weight: 20–22 pounds (9–10 kg).

DEVELOPMENT: Another case of European sportsmen, this time Bavarian, being ill-satisfied with their terrier stock and setting out to create a hunter of their own. The Hunting Terrier was created through crossing Welsh Terrier and the old-fashioned Broken-Coated Terrier, a black and tan British dog. Its progeny was crossed with both varieties of Fox Terriers: this latter cross explains the breed's two coat types. The result is a tremendously plucky terrier capable of working most game, with a wondrous nose. He can also double as a land or water retriever, should the need surface.

RECOGNITION: FCI

CHARACTER: The pet world has made little ground in softening this tough tyke—he remains solely a working dog, one of the few terriers that can clasp and tackle that claim to fame. Thus, he is not recommended for owners who desire only a companion. For the terrier man, however, this is a one-man devoted worker and an outstanding watchdog.

GLEN OF IMAAL TERRIER

PORTRAIT: The wee Imaal Terrier is a dog of distinctive bearing and appearance. Its dwarf-like size deceives its abilities—the long body insures the image of great substance. Height: 14 inches (35½ cm). Weight: 35 pounds (16 kg). A soft undercoat underlies a rough-textured, medium-length coat which is tidied to project a clean outline. The Imaal can be wheaten, blue, or brindle in all shades.

DEVELOPMENT: Unlike many other terriers, the Imaal is compact enough to go to ground after badger or fox and game enough to fight its chosen vermin to the death. Inhabitants of eastern Eire, especially in the Glen area of County Wicklow, have always known of the presence and ability of the Imaal Terrier but, outside the tavern, have never been able to explain his actual beginnings. Good sources, however, reveal that at one time the dogs were used in fighting matches and that specimens could weigh up to 50 pounds (22½ kg).

RECOGNITION: FCI, KCGB

CHARACTER: This is a hardy, adaptable terrier. The harsh, raw Glen area required a dog of substance and vigor and today's Imaal still maintains these traits. Moderate size and good health make him an ideal home or apartment dog.

HARLEQUIN PINSCHER
Harlekinpinscher

PORTRAIT: Well muscled and dry, the Harlequin's body is square without a cobby appearance detracting from its elegant lines. A sufficiently deep chest and a slightly tucked belly give the dog a brawny but sleek appearance. Height: 12–14 inches (30½–35½ cm). Weight 22–26 pounds (10–11½ kg). Its short smooth coat is spotted gray, or black, or dark on a white or clear ground, with or without tan markings. Like most other pinschers, the ears are cropped to a point and the high-set tail is docked.

DEVELOPMENT: This smaller spin-off of the Standard Pinscher, swirled with a touch of small Pyrenean Shepherds for the unique coloration, was selectively bred and promoted as a "new" German breed, categorized as a "dog for pleasure." Breeders were apparently not interested in the dog's working abilities and beauty contests of sorts were held to boast this harlequin knockout.

RECOGNITION: FCI

CHARACTER: The Harlequin Pinscher makes a beguiling and agreeable companion, who thrives on indoor living. Despite his dormant terrier instincts, the breed is active and awake in many other ways. The roguish and attentive look that characterizes the variety so well explains his desirability as a companion; today, however, he has become dangerously scarce.

IRISH TERRIER
Irish Red Terrier

PORTRAIT: Harmonious and symmetrical, the Irish Terrier conveys its greatly animated character. Its moderately long body is slackless and strong and should not appear cloddy. The head is also long, in proportion to the body. Drop V-shaped ears are characteristic of the breed, as is a well-trimmed beard, neither profuse nor absent. Height: 18 inches (45 cm). Weight: 25–27 pounds (11½–12½ kg). The coat is dense and wiry in texture, of rich quality with a broken appearance. The dog should be whole-colored in shades of red through wheaten.

DEVELOPMENT: Promoted by the Irish as the oldest breed of dog known to man, the first actual record of the Irish Terrier brings us to 1872 when Mickey Dooley's "Daisy" and "Fly" were entered in a pedigree-only dog show in Dublin, boasting the most unequivocal, proven history of any other living canine. Dooley and the leprechaun that handled his terriers (whom only he saw) caused much of a ruckus: the only consistency at his particularly strange medley of exhibits lied in that all the dogs were born in Ireland. So much for history, the breed is a rambunctious ratter and can be used as a hunter and retriever.

RECOGNITION: FCI, AKC, UKC, KCGB, CKC, ANKC

CHARACTER: Versatile and spirited, the Irish Terrier is stout-hearted and unrelenting in pluck and assertion. He is eager and able as a guard, hunter and companion.

JACK RUSSELL TERRIER

PORTRAIT: An elegant and sprightly little terrier that is well balanced and superlatively structured. Three coat types—broken, rough and smooth–all come predominantly white with tricolor, brown, or black markings. Two sizes—9–12 inches (23–30½ cm); 12–15 inches (30½–38 cm). Weight: 12–18 pounds (5½–8½ kg). The chest is not so broad to interfere with the dog's entering a fox hole. The body is longer than it is tall. The tail is docked, leaving approximately four inches (10 cm) on the adult specimen. The ears are dropped Vs. The muzzle is long and rather pointed.

DEVELOPMENT: Not the first clergyman to be obsessed with the canine sports, the Reverend Jack Russell desired the ideal terrier, one of compatible size to its quarry, the fox, but not so petite that it would fall behind the running hounds and need to be carried. A shorter legged, smaller terrier seemed elemental for the Reverend's needs. The result of Russell's unknown crosses was the Jack Russell Terrier. The exact ingredients to yield this plucky ratter and hunter are unknown but most sources point to the Bull Terrier and the Pocket Beagle's being added to other terriers. The present type is much thinner and more refined than the older type. The older type JRs are stocky and stubbly, very much like a disproportioned Bull Terrier.

RECOGNITION: NR

CHARACTER: These are affectionate and personable people dogs that require a lot of exercise. They are popular farm dogs but reportedly have a more limited life span than many terriers.

KERRY BLUE TERRIER
Irish Blue Terrier

PORTRAIT: Originally a bluish unbarbered bloke, today's upstandingwell-knit Kerry is still strong and well balanced. The Kerry's most distinctive feature is surely its square head, the show-groomed muzzle giving the dog a peculiarly uncanine appearance. The Kerry's coat is characterized by its dense, silky growth, soft and plentiful, and unusual eye-catching color. The breed's sturdy construction provides it with freedom of movement. Height: 17½–20 inches (44½–51 cm). Weight: 33–40 pounds (15–18 kg).

DEVELOPMENT: The Kerry mountains of Ireland have long been the home of this terrier. Natives of the region have been aware of the hardy, handy-sized terriers of superior sporting abilities for generations. The dog has always been an integral part of southern Irish country life, guarding homes, children and livestock and extirpating rats from land and water. The Kerry has a strong show following and fortunately purebred fanciers haven't exorcised the breed's natural instincts or abilities for the sake of gross exaggeration or inane fashion.

RECOGNITION: FCI, AKC, UKC, KCGB, CKC, ANKC

CHARACTER: Spunky, good-humored and typically terrier in temperament, the Kerry is a well rounded, much loved international purebred. He is no pushover and has not been entirely softened by pet life. A game worker and competent watchdog, he is the well-considered choice of many dog lovers.

KROMFOHRLÄNDER

PORTRAIT: A robust and well-proportioned dog whose coat type may vary from rough and wiry to medium-long and straight. In color the breed is mostly white with varying shades of tan marking on its head and saddle. The ears are pointed and fold over the top of the skull. The muzzle is not too pointed, with powerful jaws. Height: 15–17 inches (38–43 cm). Weight: 26 pounds (11½ kg).

DEVELOPMENT: The Kromfohrländer was created by Frau Ilse Schleifenbaum rather unintentionally. This Westphalian townswoman crossed what now seems to be a Griffon Fauve de Bretagne with a tousy, fawn-colored dog given to her by passing American soldiers in 1945. She so delighted in her first litter from the cross that she worked to perpetuate the type. Within ten years, the breed was established and recognized. It is a sound and useful sportsman.

RECOGNITION: FCI

CHARACTER: More of a companion dog than a bolting terrier, the Kromf is handy as a watchdog and pet. Of course, Frau Schleifenbaum wasn't interested in a terrier for terrier's sake and nurtured one of Germany's newest and most delightful companion dogs.

LAKELAND TERRIER

PORTRAIT: Soundly put-together and square in build, this workman is compact and well balanced. The head is also square: the length of the muzzle equaling that of the skull. The outer layer of its two-ply coat is hard, wiry and water-proofed. The undercoat is soft. Color: blue and tan, black and tan, red, wheaten, red grizzle, liver, blue or black. The tan on a Lakeland is light wheaten to straw. Height: 13–15 inches (33–38 cm). Weight: 17 pounds (8 kg).

DEVELOPMENT: For an untraceable length of time, the Lakeland Terrier has avenged and exterminated the destructive foxes from the English Lake District. These terriers are out to kill and are relied upon by farmers to rid their grounds of lamb- and poultry-killing scoundrels. In order to evict the quarry, the Lakelands were worked in packs in conjunction with hounds. They are not diggers but more untiring patrols, with the ability and license to kill.

RECOGNITION: FCI, AKC, KCGB, CKC, ANKC

CHARACTER: These are courageous workmen and yet affectionate dogs to have in the home. They are extremely devoted to their work, often coming to their masters bedraggled and toilworn—they are equally faithful to their owners. Regular grooming is recommended.

MANCHESTER TERRIER
Black and Tan Terrier

PORTRAIT: The breed's alternative name aptly describes the requisite coloration of this sleek, finely built terrier: jet black with rich mahogany tan markings, which do not blend into each other but abruptly form clear well-defined lines. Height: 15–16 inches (38–40½ cm). Weight is divided into two categories: 12–16 pounds (5½–7½ kg); 16–22 pounds (7½–10 kg). In the United States, the ears are often cropped to stand to an erect point; in Great Britain, the ears are left natural, hanging close to the head. The coat is short, firm, and glossy.

DEVELOPMENT: This individualistic terrier was favored by the British working classes in the heyday of the ratting sport. The Manchester was prized for its uncanny ability to sort through miles of rat carnage in a few mere seconds. This ability, perceived by our 20th-century sensibilities as inexcusably nauseating, was both entertaining and exciting to the Brits who fondly looked on. Ironically, it was the outlawing of *ear cropping* that takes responsibility for the breed's fall of popularity in England.

RECOGNITION: FCI, AKC, KCGB, CKC, ANKC

CHARACTER: Once referred to as the "Gentleman's Terrier," the Manchester is described as ardent, lively, and good-natured. His agreeable disposition, convenient size and minimal grooming needs make him an ideal companion.

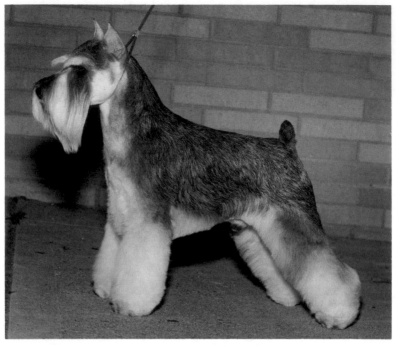

MINIATURE SCHNAUZER
Zwergschnauzer

PORTRAIT: This nearly square dog is sturdy and strong—conformation in a Miniature Schnauzer is considered more important than sheer appearance. A moderately broad chest, a strong straight back, well-muscled thighs, and a head of good length comprise the dog's structure. Colors include salt-/pepper, black and silver, and solid black. The coat is harsh and rough; fairly thick furnishings conspicuously adorn the head and legs. Height: 12–14 inches (30½–35½ cm). Weight: 13–15 pounds (6–7 kg). Ears may be cropped in America but are not tampered with in England. Tails are customarily docked.

DEVELOPMENT: This is not merely a diminutive Standard Schnauzer. Whether the Miniature Schnauzer was derived directly from the Standard or possibly from selectively crossing Miniature Pinschers and Affenpinschers, it is now a distinctive breed with a conformation and character all its own. The Miniature is the smallest of the three German Schnauzer breeds and the only one that is expressly a ratter. Its abilities in this arena were highly respected.

RECOGNITION: FCI, AKC, UKC, KCGB, CKC, ANKC

CHARACTER: This is surely the most elegant of the terriers and the well-kept home Miniature surely doesn't readily fit our concept of "terrier." The breed's instincts are dormant—whatever its forebears, the Mini today is seldom used as an unearthing earth dog. He is, however, one of the world's most popular companion dogs—stylish and friendly. He should never be overly aggressive or timid.

NORFOLK TERRIER

PORTRAIT: A stocky, short-legged, drop-eared dog, compact and keen. The coat should be harsh and flat lying; it is longer and rougher on the neck. The body is short-backed, level and of good substance. The Norfolk colors include various shades of red, wheaten, black and tan and grizzle. White marks are not desirable. Height: 10 inches (25½ cm). Weight: 11–12 pounds (5–5½ kg).

DEVELOPMENT: An enterprising sportsman, known as "Doggy" Lawrence, began selling little "Red Terriers" to Cambridge undergrads in the 1870s. These dogs, considered the forebears of the Norfolk/Norwich breeds, were nothing more than small Irish terriers. After the decimation of World War I, Frank Jones attempted to revitalize the hard-hit stock. He crossed Staffs and Bedlingtons with other small red Irish terriers to regenerate the lost Norfolk dwarf. For a while these were called Jones Terrier. At other times, the breed has been known as Cantab Terriers and Trumpington Terriers, and, of course, was one and the same with the Norwich until the 1979 split. The Norwich has prick ears, among other dissensions.

RECOGNITION: FCI, AKC, UKC, KCGB, CKC, ANKC

CHARACTER: Considered a "demon" for his size, the Norfolk is a feisty, active tyke, with a hardy, unquarrelsome disposition. He is recommended as a house or apartment companion. He does indeed need exercise and his coat should be plucked in order to keep him looking his best.

NORWICH TERRIER

PORTRAIT: A squat, keen dog of awesome power for his little size. Height: 10 inches (25½ cm). Weight: 11–12 pounds (5–5½ kg). Its prick ears are perfectly erect when aroused. The mouth is tight-lipped with scissor-biting teeth. The Norwich's gait should be true, low, and driving. The Norwich colors include various shades of red, wheaten, black and tan and grizzle. Extensive white marks are unpardonable.

DEVELOPMENT: The Cantab Terrier, the favored mascot of 19th-century Cambridge students, was a prick-eared little red terrier, one in the same with today's Norwich. The Norwich at one time (pre-1979) could either have drop or prick ears but today must have prick ears—the drop eared dogs are called Norfolk. Since this split, other conformation differences have arose—but frankly these can only be discerned by a trained, self-colored expert. Dog show people who become obsessed with the need to exaggerate a particular feature are adamant that these two breeds look decidedly different. The undecided, average viewer will probably notice nothing aside from the difference in ear carriage.

RECOGNITION: FCI, AKC, UKC, KCGB, CKC, ANKC

CHARACTER: Not just a pluck plucked show dog, the Norwich is still a working dog of considerable acclaim. Regardless of the politics involved with the Norfolk and Norwich clansmen, the Norwich, like its floppy eared brother, makes a delightful companion, capable of pleasing the least of canine fans.

PATTERDALE TERRIER
Black Fell Terrier

PORTRAIT: Cheeky and thicker than most any terrier, this well-built tiny stock dog stands only 12 inches (30½ cm) high and weigh s 12–13 pounds (5½–6 kg). Its small size can be used as a reverse scale to measure its gameness and tenacity. The coat is weather resistant and is short and coarse. Color: Black, red, chocolate, black/tan.

DEVELOPMENT: A product of the Yorkshire and Lake District of Britain, the Patterdale is a robust, sturdy working stock dog. The name Patterdale was chosen after a village in Cumbria, where the dogs are common. Breeders are solely interested in working abilities. Even today types vary somewhat. One breeder jests that show conformation (adhering to the subtle and undulating nuances of aesthetic pleasure) is so immaterial that, were it the case, a dog could work better with two heads, we would select immediately for that trait.

RECOGNITION: NR

CHARACTER: Although the Patterdale's diminutive size could qualify him as a toy dog, his abilities and gameness deem him solid terrier, his sheer stoutness and virility demand his inclusion in the mastiff group. This is not a dog for the non-terrier enthusiast or the faint-hearted. Exercise and a hardy stock of prey is the recommended way to satiate his hunting cravings.

PINSCHER
German Pinscher, Standard Pinscher

PORTRAIT: A smooth-coated, middle-sized dog with well-cut eyes of good size and high-set cropped ears. The most common color is shiny black with clear tan markings. Other colors include red, dark brown with yellow, fawn, red fawn, but not biscuit fawn. Higher on the leg than most terriers, the Standard Pinscher stands 16–19 inches (40½–48 cm) and weighs 25–35 pounds (11½–16 kg). Although well balanced with elegant lines, the breed is not as sleek and taut as the Doberman. The dog's back is straight and the tail is customarily docked.

DEVELOPMENT: Considered a German native, the Standard Pinscher, if not created in Germany, may indeed be a latter-day representation of the old Black and Tan Terrier which might have undergone "alterations" in Germany. The Doberman Pinscher and the Miniature Pinscher are said spin-offs and have both achieved strong followings outside the Motherland, unlike the Pinscher. The breed is too large to go to ground but makes a great farm hand and guard.

RECOGNITION: FCI, KCGB

CHARACTER: The Kennel Club of Britain, which includes the breed in the Working Group not the Terrier Group, describes the Pinscher as self-possessed and high spirited. He is playful and loyal and makes a well-behaved and delightful housemate.

RAT TERRIER
Feist

PORTRAIT: These smooth-coated "Feisty" terriers come in three different sizes: the Standard is 14–23 inches (35½–58½ cm) in height and 12–35 pounds (5½–16 kg) in weight; the Midsized is 8–14 inches (20–35½ cm) and 6–8 pounds (3–3½ kg); and the Toy is 8 inches (20 cm) and 4–6 pounds (2–3 kg). In color the Rat Terriers are tri-spotted, red/white, solid red, black/tan, blue/white, and red brindle. Their bodies are compact but meaty; the heads are tiny and the muzzles pointed.

DEVELOPMENT: Named by the perceptive Teddy Roosevelt, the Rat Terriers were developed in Great Britain originally from Smooth Fox Terriers and Manchester Terriers in 1820. These dogs were astounding in their ratting abilities and they soon climbed to the top of the rat-tailed carnage as the princes of the rat pits. One Rat Terrier is reported to have killed over 2,500 rats in the span of seven hours. The Rat Terrier is a most industrious farm hand, able to rid an infested barn of vermin lickety-split.

RECOGNITION: NR

CHARACTER: The Rat Terrier is a hardy and resourceful dog. The Standards are used for hunting expeditions as well as terrier work. The smallest variety was derived from the Smooth Fox and Chihuahua and make delightful, robust pets, capable of spending a good amount of time outdoors, with proper protection.

SCOTTISH TERRIER
Aberdeen Terrier

PORTRAIT: Possessing the strength and solidity of a big dog in the compass of a small one, the Scottish Terrier is well muscled and sturdy. The Scottie's head is long but not exaggerated in relation to the body, which is also elongated. The face wears a keen, lively expression. Although black may seem the most popular color, Scotties can be steel, iron gray, brindled or grizzled, sandy or wheaten. White is usually tolerated on the chest only. Height: 10–11 inches (25½–28 cm). Weight 19–23 pounds (8½–10½ kg). The outer coat, close lying and harshly wired; the undercoat, soft and short.

DEVELOPMENT: There were many Scottish terriers—that is, terriers in Scotland. The breed we know today as the Scottish Terrier came into being thanks to Captain Gordon Murray and S.E. Shirley who worked towards setting the type. Culling "mongrels with hair ten and a half inches long" from the show rings, Murray described the "Scottish Terrier" type in 1879, eliminating the "half-breed curs and their half-wit owners" from exhibition circles. Establishing type has certainly stabilized the Scottish Terrier's soundness and gratefully has never detracted from his natural gameness.

RECOGNITION: FCI, AKC, UKC, KCGB, CKC, ANKC

CHARACTER: Vigorous and hardy, the Scottie is no toy dog—he is able to withstand extremes in climatic variation, adaptable to both city and country living. Owners are encouraged to be firm with the Scottie; subduing his pest-control instincts may take a little doing. However, do not be too hard on your Scottie if he drags a mauled rat carcass home and expects a cookie!!

SEALYHAM TERRIER

PORTRAIT: Superbly balanced and elongated, the Sealyham Terrier boasts a unique appearance in the dog world. Its head is long and broad without coarseness. The breed's coloration is paramount to the Sealyham look—tan or badger patches marking the pure white head and ears (without exaggeration). Otherwise, the body is solid white. Height: 10–11 inches (25½–28 cm). Weight: 22–25 pounds (10–10½ kg). The outer coat is hard and wiry; the undercoat is weather-proof.

DEVELOPMENT: Seeking the perfect terrier companion for his pack of Otterhounds, the eccentric and aged Capt. J.O. Tucker Edwardes fashioned today's Sealyham Terrier. Edwardes's ideal terrier had to be light boned to keep up with the hounds, agile to maneuver over the rocky precipitous terrain, and utterly small enough to uncover and undo the otters hiding between the rocks. The breed type was set around 1848.

RECOGNITION: FCI, AKC, KCGB, CKC, ANKC

CHARACTER: Strong-willed and assertive, the Sealyham needs a firm hand to guide his way. Although the Sealyham feels he is quite capable of handling his day's household tasks, like a child, parental guidance is suggested. He retains much of his ancestor's gameness, but certainly makes an incomparable companion and show dog.

SKYE TERRIER

PORTRAIT: Profusely but elegantly coated, the Skye Terrier is the picture of dignity and fashion. Underneath his long, flowing outer coat and soft undercoat is a sturdy-boned, hard-muscled terrier. The breed's coat, however, is his claim to fame: the moderate-sized head is draped with long hard hair, veiling the eyes and forehead and edging the self-revealing prick ears. Height: 10 inches (25½ cm). Weight: 25 pounds (11½ kg).

DEVELOPMENT: Deriving its name from the "Misty Isle," the Skye Terrier has been recognized for over 400 years. Probably not confined to the Skye Islands these terriers enjoyed the favor of the aristocracy and didn't associate with the commonfolk and their common dogs. Today's Skye looks much different than its progenitors: 19th-century Skyes had less-feathered drop ears, smaller heads and weighed as little as 14 pounds (6½ kg). At work, he is resilient and ruthless in his expelling of squirmy undesirables.

RECOGNITION: FCI, AKC, KCGB, CKC, ANKC

CHARACTER: Exhibiting stamina and fearlessness, the Skye is the original one-man dog; to his one man, he offers undying devotion. He is merry and hearty with familiars but is stand-offish with strangers. He is an abundantly pleasing household chum.

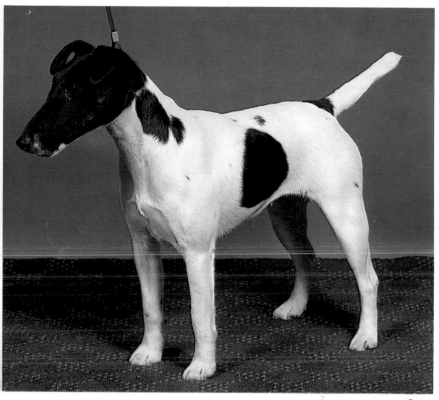

SMOOTH FOX TERRIER

PORTRAIT: The gentleman of the terrier world, the Smooth Fox Terrier is a well-made sportsman and hunter. The importance of good bone cannot be understated. The legs cannot be too long nor too short in order for the Fox Terrier to project the proper appearance. The avoidance of cloddiness and coarseness is sovereign. He must be short backed with a moderately narrow skull. The foreface is chiseled somewhat, the jaws are punishing. Height: 15½ inches (39 cm). Weight: 16–18 pounds (7½–8½ kg). The all-important coat is smooth—hard and flat and abundant.

DEVELOPMENT: Smooth-coated terriers were always an indispensable accoutrement of the fox hunt, as were untiring pack hounds. The Smooth Fox Terrier answers this call to work with a surly vengeance. A cornered rat, in its last snarling attempt to escape, will wrap itself around the terrier's head to inflict a potentially mortal, invariably ugly wound. In response to the rat's kamikaze effort, the Smooth Fox becomes even more vicious. The dogs are also lethal against badger and, of course, fox!

RECOGNITION: FCI, AKC, UKC, KCGB, CKC, ANKC

CHARACTER: Energetic and "on tip toe of expectation," the breed is an eager-to-please hunter and companion. His general gay and light-hearted disposition, in addition to his over-and-above-the-call-of-duty work ethic, make him the choice of numerous canine advocates.

SOFT COATED WHEATEN TERRIER

PORTRAIT: A true oddity to the terrier family, the Soft Coated Wheaten Terrier flaunts an expansive, soft, flowing, silky coat, gently waving a field of gentle wheaten. The coat is profuse, never harsh, with a generous amount of loose curls. The body, rectangular in appearance, is compact and relatively short coupled. The head, with its bales of warm wheaten, is also rectangular in appearance, with no indication of coarseness. Height: 18–19½ inches (46–49½ cm). Weight: 32–45 pounds (14½–20 kg). A light clear wheaten is most desirable.

DEVELOPMENT: One of three large terriers indigenous to Ireland, this terrier has a long, although unrecorded, history boisterously boasted by its Irish owners. Many a tavern mug has been lifted to the Spanish Armada which allegedly sunk off the coast of Ireland and from which those celestial blue dogs swam ashore to progenerate the Wheaten. It is an all-purpose dog: cattle drover, guardian of home and stables, and exterminator.

RECOGNITION: FCI, AKC, UKC, KCGB, CKC

CHARACTER: Although overall happy and peace-admiring, he can be assertive and straight forward. As a home companion, he is choice: affectionate and devoted. Also great with children and very athletic.

WELSH TERRIER

PORTRAIT: This is a medium-sized terrier with a square body appearance. Its coat is wire-textured and colored black and tan. He is long-legged for a terrier, his topline is level, and he possesses excellent substance. Height: 14–15½ inches (35½–39 cm). Weight: 20 pounds (9 kg). The jacket is double coated, close fitting, with furnishings on muzzle, legs and quarters. The ears, like the Airedale and Fox Terriers among others, are V-shaped and drop.

DEVELOPMENT: Although the Welsh Terrier looks a great deal like the ancient Old English Terrier (or Broken-Coated Terrier), there is no reason to doubt that the breed is purely indigenous to the principality of Wales and is not an offspring of that long-gone English breed. Lengthy Welsh pedigrees and reasonably credible accounts verify this assertion. Its original name, the Carnarvonshire Welsh Terrier, indicated the breed's founding principality. For well over two and a half centuries, the breed was used for the pack hunting of otters and badger.

RECOGNITION: FCI, AKC, UKC, KCGB, CKC, ANKC

CHARACTER: Not shy or timid, the Welshie is of a gay, volatile nature. He is game and fearless, but never vicious or overly pugnacious. He tends to be curious and energetic and loves the company of children. Suitable as a companion and workman.

WEST HIGHLAND WHITE TERRIER

PORTRAIT: A foxy-faced head and a compact body, the West Highland White Terrier is pure white. The coat, the breed's hallmark, is rarely seen to perfection: a double coat, properly blending the two-inch outer coat of straight hard hair with the plenteous, soft undercoat. Silkiness and curliness are insufferable. A flattish side appearance is supported by a level back and deep, well-arched ribs. The desired appearance possesses both a high-esteemed and "varminty" quality, unknown in any other terrier.

DEVELOPMENT: The prejudice of Cairn Terrier hunters against white puppies paves the way for the Westie. The Malcolms of Poltalloch began collecting and breeding these white outcastes. These once-called Poltalloch Terriers ("white Cairns") were then crossed with Sealyhams in order to generate a longer bodied, white terrier. This cross was ill-conceived, as the longer body was not suitable for game terrier work. Selective breeding helped to restore the breed which today looks more like a Cairn in body type than the Sealyham.

RECOGNITION: FCI, AKC, UKC, KCGB, CKC, ANKC

CHARACTER: Self-reliant and adaptable to a variety of lifestyles, this energetic and pleasing terrier makes an all-around companion dog. Pugnacity and timidity are discouraged. The show Westie requires a considerable deal of grooming. To keep the pet Westie looking his best, regular grooming is advised. In America, the Westie is popular on both coasts.

WIRE FOX TERRIER

PORTRAIT: The keystone to a terrier's anatomy is indisputably the overall balance and proportion of the dog. The Wire Fox Terrier is the epitome of the desired anatomical terrier type. Its balanced conformation and straight-legged movement give it propulsive power, the quintessence of terrier gait. The proper coat appears broken and feels "crinkly"; the hairs have the tendency to twist and are wiry, "like coconut matting." Height: 15½ inches (39 cm). Weight: 16–18 pounds (7½–8 kg). The dog is predominantly white; liver, brindle, red, or slaty blue is objectionable.

DEVELOPMENT: Far be it from cynologists today to pretend to pinpoint the origins of a dog as ancient and unblemished as the Fox Terrier. Accounts of similar type dogs date back to 55 B.C. Britain, likely the old black and tan wirehaired terriers that were used to create today's Wire Fox. The Wire Fox's attainment of perfection is not hyperbolic—this breed has gone more times Best in Show at Westminster and Crufts than any other dog.

RECOGNITION: FCI, AKC, UKC, KCGB, CKC, ANKC

CHARACTER: The Wire Fox is decidedly not for uncouth owners. He is a dog of majesty and unstinted character. His abilities on the field, comparable to his show wins, are undeniable and astounding. This dog demands an owner who is dedicated to his way of thinking—he enjoys his world and loves the human who decides to make him his own.

Dingo.

PARIAHS

BASENJI
Congo Dog

PORTRAIT: Creasing in alertness, the Basenji is a finely built, light dog with gazelle-like grace. The ears are pointed, erect and slightly hooded, sitting well forward on the top of the head. Facial wrinkles, fine and profuse, appear on the forehead when the ears are pricked. The body is balanced with a short, level back. The tail is set high, curls tightly over the spine and lies close to the thigh in a single or double curl. The coat is sleek and close; the skin pliant. Height: 16–17 inches (40½–43 cm). Weight: 21–24 pounds (9½–11 kg). Accepted colors include red, black/tan and black, all with white markings. In their native Zaire, however, Basenjis occur in merles and brindles as well.

DEVELOPMENT: Assertions that the Basenji derives from the spitz family can be amply substantiated if one considers the breed's general physical similarities (the curled tail and prick ears). Yet many believe that it is more likely that the Basenji developed from central African pariah types into a highly efficient hunting dog, a function that comes quite naturally to him. The Basenji was designated variously by Western explorers in the late 1800s as "Congo Terriers," "African Bush Dogs," and "Lagos Bush Dogs." These explorers commented on the dogs' inability to bark. Basenjis emit soft and low growl-like noises, peculiar to this breed alone, although some other African natives make similar sounds. In the Congo, Basenjis could be found with bells on, hunting in packs and steering game into nets. It is believed that some were used as vermin exterminators, hence the "Congo Terrier" appellation.

RECOGNITION: FCI, AKC, UKC, KCGB, CKC, ANKC

CHARACTER: As a home companion choice, the Basenji is a sublime candidate. His short coat requires little to no grooming; additionally he is cat-like in his daily primping. These are stylish and intelligent pets with panache and good looks. Basenjis tend to scrap with other dogs but are entirely affectionate with their human charges.

BEDOUIN SHEPHERD DOG
Ishtarenhund

PORTRAIT: A rugged, stalwart canine with a solid frame and unyielding durability, the Bedouin Shepherd Dog is a medium-sized pariah-type dog. The coat is equally durable and stands up well to the desert sun and sand storms. The skull is broad; the muzzle tapers; the ears, set high, drop to shield the blowing sand. The chest is deep and moderately broad, with a noticeable tuck to the underbelly. Hind legs are sufficiently angulated. In color the Bedouin dog can be any of a variety of solids or merles. Height: 20–24 inches (51–61 cm). Weight: 40–55 pounds (18–25 kg).

DEVELOPMENT: The desert dwellers of the vast Sahara desert and the Arabian peninsula are known as Bedouins. These nomads roam with their camels, asses, and herds of goats and sheep in search of water and pasture. Although of lesser importance to the shepherds than their camels, the Bedouin Shepherd Dogs are a noteworthy component to the survival of these peripatetic peoples that must move across unirrigated land with their irritated, discontented flocks. These dogs, semi-domesticated from wandering pariahs, must survive on the shepherd's meager diets of millet, mutton, and dates, supplemented by an occasional locust or lizard.

RECOGNITION: NR

CHARACTER: These shepherd dogs are somewhat neglected by their keepers, who rarely attend to their coats which often mat and remain unkempt. The dogs are accepted more as a necessity than embraced as a companion. These dogs, due to their long history of undomestication, do not bond to their flocks as would a European flock herder. Their instincts toward the flock are essentially territorial and protective in nature.

CANAAN DOG
Kelef K'naani, Israel Canaan Dog

PORTRAIT: A medium-sized, notably delicate dog, well proportioned and of a general spitz type. The head is blunt and wedged, the skull slightly rounded. The body is strong with a straight topline and is tautly muscled throughout. The coat is medium short, harsh and straight; the tail is bushy and curled over the back. Colors include sandy to red brown, white and black. Dark and white masks are acceptable. Gray and black/tan are frowned upon. Height: 19–24 inches (48–61). Weight: 35–55 pounds (16–25 kg). A sharp, fast trot is characteristic of the breed.

DEVELOPMENT: Legend has it that a Canaan Dog was tied to the dais of Queen Jezebel by a golden chain. The Canaan Dog is the national dog of Israel and has been known in the Middle East for centuries. He is a pariah in origin, although many communities of non-wild (semi-domesticated) Canaans have existed in the Negev Desert and have been employed by the Bedouins and other nomadic tribes as herders and sentry dogs. The Basenji is surely one of the Canaan's relatives. Dr. Rudolphina Menzel of Israel is chiefly responsible for the salvation and stabilization of the breed.

RECOGNITION: FCI, AKC, CKC

CHARACTER: A non-aggressive but resourceful watchdog, the Canaan is a protective and companionable dog that is quickly gaining ground in the United States. He is a hardy canine but is mostly an indoor dog.

PARIAHS 527

CAROLINA DOG

PORTRAIT: A lightly constructed pariah-type dog with pointed ears, thick neck, wedge-shaped muzzle and smallish head, compared to its somewhat stout, well-muscled body. The chest is well developed and the coat, short and dense, is yellowish gold. Height: 22 inches (56 cm). Weight: 30–40 pounds (13½–18 kg).

DEVELOPMENT: The Carolina Dog comes out of the American Deep South and is of an ancient pariah type. A number of such pariah types exists in the United States. Many of these dogs were favored by Indians and used for various tasks, herding for one. The Kentucky Shell Heap Dog and the Basketmaker Dog are examples of ancient pariahs on the North American continent. Down South, the Carolina Dog is affectionately named "Old Yaller," be it for his coat color, quality of his howl, or just a passing literary allusion.

RECOGNITION: NR

CHARACTER: With proper socialization, the Carolina Dogs are proven to be amenable companion dogs. They are easily trained and enjoy hunting small game, a task they do with grace and quickness. Wild specimens are still known, so this is not a completely domesticated canine. Many dogs are known to be extremely shy around people and resent a lot of handling.

DINGO
Australian Native Dog, Warrigal

PORTRAIT: Although the Dingo looks like your everyday domesticated pooch, the Dingo actually is a wild dog. The Dingo's head is characterized by rather small rounded ears, carried erect. The tail is well furred, appearing bushy. The coat's length, density, and texture vary according to climate. In color the Dingo is commonly tawny; however, they can be any color from white through black, including an occasional brindle; albinos are also reported. Height: 19–23 inches (48–58½ cm). Weight: 50–70 pounds (23–32 kg), although dogs up to 120 pounds (55 kg) are documented.

DEVELOPMENT: A feral animal brought to Australia by primitive man in a semi-domesticated state, the Dingo reached Australia during the late Pleistocene period. With the Europeans' introduction of domestic sheep and rabbits, the Dingo population flourished. Because of the Dingo's preying on man's livestock, the relationship between the two has been untidy and quarrelsome. Man's interference in Australia's perfectly balanced ecology has been essentially blamed on the Dingo.

RECOGNITION: NR

CHARACTER: The Dingo communicates by a distinctive yelp or howl. Families of Dingos can be heard vocalizing together before a hunt. The Dingo may hunt alone or in family units, but rarely in packs. Dingos shy from man and have reverted to the wild. Good pets they're not.

HAWAIIAN POI DOG
Ilio, Poi Dog

PORTRAIT: Pudgy and numb, the Poi Dog of Hawaii is the original "couch pineapple." This is a dog of no nobility who feigns no grace. Clumsy but playful, this short-coated pariah is no taller than four stacked coconuts and comes in a variety of colors. Weight: over—*Slightly more precooked.* The body is low and barrel-shaped, piled on shortened legs. The head became large and flat due to the lack of chewing.

DEVELOPMENT: Pardoning the authors' light-hearted portrait, the Hawaiian Poi Dog is one of the most fascinating canines anyone will encounter in the world of cynology. The dog has become extinct but at one time was an important part of the Polynesian people's lifestyle. The females in the tribe took care of the dogs and even nursed Poi puppies, believing that this would increase their protective instincts. They were obviously prized as companions, especially for children. The twist comes out of the Polynesian's custom of feeding the dogs only poi (a granular paste based on the taro root) to fatten them for the purpose of consumption. It was not uncommon for a child to dine over the dog he slept with the previous night. The dogs became obese and slothful (not undesirable traits in a dog to the islanders) and often hobbled about with the hogs.

RECOGNITION: NR

CHARACTER: Aside from being friendly, the Hawaiian Poi Dogs essentially lack any of the positive qualities that one normally associates with a canine pet. This is not to say that the Poi Dogs were low-quality pets for the Polynesians who kept them. The dogs, however, couldn't be aptly described as dedicated or sprightly companions, since their soft-skulled mentalities could only facilitate tumbling with the children who delighted in tossing island fruits at the dogs, whose papaya-covered muzzles weren't quick enough to open and catch the ricocheting globes.

INCA HAIRLESS DOG
Peruvian Hairless Dog

PORTRAIT: The Inca Hairless Dog comes in three size variations: the small, 9–18 pounds (4–8 kg); the medium, 18–26 pounds (8–12 kg); and the large, 26–55 pounds (12–25 kg). Height varies accordingly. The skin is scaly and soft to the touch. In color the skin should be dark. Coated dogs can vary in color, with lighter colors and fawns often occurring. On the top of the Hairless Dog's head is a fuzzy tuft of hair. Smaller tufts occur on the edge of the ears, feet and tail.

DEVELOPMENT: Hairless dogs, possibly occurring sometime during the pariah's alleged evolution to sighthound, have been deemed "freaks of nature" by many persons (many of whom are also dog lovers). The hairless "breeds" survive through selective breeding with the ever-important coated variety within each breed. In order to cut the effect of the lethal homozygous gene, the coated dogs are essential to the propagation of the breed. Hairless dogs as such have existed in Peru for centuries. The dogs were highly prized companions of the Incan civilization.

RECOGNITION: FCI

CHARACTER: Like all other hairless breeds, the Inca Hairless Dog needs daily care for his skin, since it is very vulnerable to the sun's rays and to nicks and cuts. For the dog lover that is allergic to pet hair, a hairless dog may be the perfect option.

Above right: *Inca Hairless Dog.* Below right: *Inca Hairless Dog, coated.*

NEW GUINEA SINGING DOG

PORTRAIT: This medium-sized pariah is a hardy and well-balanced dog with erect ears and an average to long coat. In color he is red or shades of red, with or without symmetrical white markings. Height: 14–15 inches (35½–38 cm). Weight: 20 pounds (9 kg). The head is fairly broad and the body duly muscular. The medium-length tail is well plumed.

DEVELOPMENT: This dingo-type dog took residence on the island of New Guinea. The climate of the island varies greatly and this pariah who roams there is a versatile and adaptable one. It dwells with natives in the lowlands as well as in the mountains. The breed acquired its name from its howl, which is an undulating and modulating series of tones that blends into a swelling portamento. The musical quality of the sound is unlike that of any other dog—even the most beautifully voiced of the scenthounds. The breed is quite rare in New Guinea today but can be seen in a number of zoos around the world.

RECOGNITION: NR

CHARACTER: Essentially a wild dog, the New Guinea Singing Dog is presently tame enough to tolerate the handling of humans. He will not, however, put up with this on too regular a basis. Opera singers have expressed a particular interest in this vocally dexterous canine, but his character is even more aloof than those of the divas whose attention he attracts.

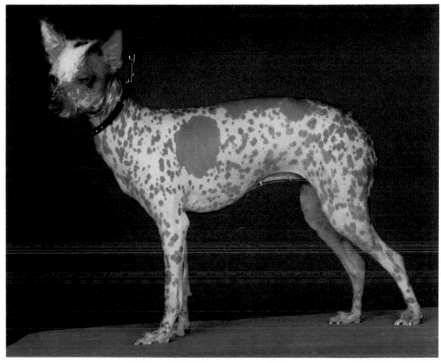

PERUVIAN INCA ORCHID
Perro Flora, Moonflower Dog

PORTRAIT: Perhaps not the most handsome of canines, the Peruvian Inca Orchid is a thin and lightly boned dog that resembles a tiny short-legged baby deer (without hair, of course). Height: 20½–25 inches (50–65 cm). Weight: 26–50 pounds (12–23 kg). The skin is heavily mottled in any color, in combination with a pink background, or it can be solid colored. The skin is soft and pliable. The eyes tend to squint in the daylight due to over-sensitivity. As with most other hairless breeds, a coated variety exists and is full-coated in any color.

DEVELOPMENT: This vestless Peruvian dog was discovered by Spanish explorers visiting Peru. These Moonflowers were nighttime dogs that didn't like the light of the day nor the rays of the sun. Their original Incan owners practiced selective breeding and only produced light-colored dogs. This breed has tooth and skin problems and the coated variety is essential to keeping these disorders to a minimum. This is not peculiar to the Peruvian Inca Orchid breed but is true for most other hairless dogs created with the dominant, semi-lethal gene for hairlessness. Today the breed is growing in the Americas with some dogs participating in coursing.

RECOGNITION: FCI, UKC

CHARACTER: For the right owner, the Peruvian Inca Orchid is an exotic treat. He will require special care to maintain his very sensitive skin and is often very bouncy in the evening, after the sun goes down. As a companion, he is quick-witted and calm.

TELOMIAN

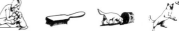

PORTRAIT: An efficiently sized pariah-type dog with a sleek and amiable appearance. The Telomian has a medium-sized head topped by slightly rounded ears, always erect. Height: 15–19 inches (38–48 cm). Weight: 18–28 pounds (8–13 kg). The coat is short and smooth and can occur in any shade of sable with white. Speckling may occur in the white areas. The Telomian's face is wrinkled similarly to the Basenji, with whom it shares many physical likenesses and ancestors.

DEVELOPMENT: Perhaps the missing link between the Basenji and the Dingo, the Telomian is an ancient breed of dog that originated in Malaysia, and there was fostered by the aborigines. The aborigines and the Telomian shared many aspects of everyday life. In order to sleep with his master, the Telomian had to climb a ladder each night to the aborigine's stilt-standing hut. His diet, the same as his master's, consisted mostly of tapioca, fish and fruit. The Telomian's great intelligence and lack of fear made him an ample protector (from snakes and other slimy, injurious types) and an avid catcher of fish. Dogs today grow to be a tad larger than the Telomians of yesterday, due to their more substantial diets.

RECOGNITION: NR

CHARACTER: The breed is extremely sociable with humans if acclimated to people at an early age. These are clever and uncannily smart dogs that are a constant source of diversion and delight for their masters. One American owner tells of his Telomian's super affinity for Jello® chocolate pudding.

TAHLTAN BEAR DOG
Chien d'ours de Tahltan

PORTRAIT: The Tahltan Bear Dog resembles a cross between a fox and a terrier, with a distinctive, and comical shaving-brush tail standing at attention and glassy electric eyes dancing wildly in their sockets. The coat is short and dense. The color is black/white or blue-gray/white. Height: 12–16 inches (30½–40½ cm). Weight: 15 pounds (6½–7 kg). The tail, the Tahltan's flag of uniqueness, is long, thick, carried erect, and finishes with rather an explosive-cigar effect. The dogs usually had solid-black heads with irregular black-and-white patches over their bodies.

DEVELOPMENT: The Tahltan's small size is no indication of its hunting abilities or fearlessness. The Tahltan Indians that bred him were very protective of their dogs and passed the breeding stock down from generation to generation. The Indians used the dogs to hunt black bears and grizzlies, as well as lynx. The Tahltan's hunting style was to distract the victim by circling it and pelting it with its staccato yelps. The Indians felt it necessary to engage in preparatory hunting rites to rouse the Tahltans for the kill. This ritual involved stabbing the dogs in the hind quarters with a wolf's fibula bone and then canvas-sacking the dogs until bear tracks were sighted. The "missing" Mrs. Harriet A. Morgan was the last breeder of Tahltans in Canada before she picked up herself, sacked her Tahltans, and moved to California in 1951. No one knows what became of Mrs. Morgan and her odd kennel of Indian dogs. No new dogs have been registered since that time.

RECOGNITION: CKC

CHARACTER: The Tahltan Dogs were extremely hardy and adaptable. Their attributes as pets were suitable for their original keepers, but even if they did exist today, they would make dubious companions and be bored with no grizzlies to girdle or grope and no masochistic rituals in which to partake.

XOLOITZCUINTLI
Standard Mexican Hairless Dog

PORTRAIT: The foremost characteristic is the total or nearly total absence of hair. Its calm, graceful way has a harmonious effect. The body is rather long in comparison with the height. The head is somewhat broad and strong; the stop is not very pronounced; the nose is blunt. Both the Xolo and Toy Xolo (Mexican Hairless) are devoid of premolars. The ears are large and expressive—long and thinly textured. The neck is carried high, flexible with the grace of an antelope. The skin is smooth and soft. Uniform dark colors are preferred—charcoal, slate, dark reddish gray, liver or bronze. Pink and coffee stains occur (areas that lack pigmentation). Height: 13–22½ inches (33–57 cm).

DEVELOPMENT: As far back as the 17th century, the ancestors of the present-day Xoloitzcuintli and the Chihuahua were transported to South America by traders from China. The Aztec Indians, who may have acquired the dogs from South America, called the hairless dogs "Biche," which meant naked. These dogs fulfilled rather peculiar tasks for the Indians and were used as bed warmers, communion to the gods, and general delicacy. These pets were also revered for their palliative powers, capable of curing rheumatism and other physical unpleasantries. The general body type of this hairless dog suggests relation to the pariah group.

RECOGNITION: FCI

CHARACTER: It takes a special owner to love a Xolo. Adults are often quiet and tranquil, howling and growling only under provocation. The character is in no way sad or cowardly. The skin requires daily attention to keep it soft and healthy.

Above right: *Xoloitzcuintli.*
Below right: *Xoloitzcuintli, coated.*

PARIAHS

Contributors and Owners

The authors and staff of T.F.H. Publications wish to acknowledge all persons who have contributed to the completion of this volume. The following list represents a compilation of the owners of the dogs portrayed in this book. To these rightly proud dog people, we wish to extend our thanks and congratulations. These owners continue to cooperate with our photographers and correspondents, and for their never-ending support, we are grateful. In addition to Isabelle Francais, the principal photographer for this *Mini-Atlas*, John Ashbey, Sandra E. Brisbin, Lois Constantine, William Gilbert, Earl Graham, Ernest Hart, Mueller Studios, Patulio Studios, Vladimir Pcholkin, Robert Pearcy, Fritz Prenzel, Joe Rinehart, Vincent Serbin, Arthur Sorkin, and Ken Walters have each made contributions of their work. The following doggie amalgamation lists owners by breed; T.F.H. extends its sincerest apologies to any owners who have been accidentally excluded or incorrectly identified. Many thanks to all!

Perfectly synchronizing the appeal and exquisiteness of the Poodle breed are Dancer Poodles, owned by Joy Grouf of East Northport, New York.

This growing Cocker of the English breed (right) belongs to Corky Meck of Lancaster, Pennsylvania, patiently sitting as Ms. Francais focuses. This distinctive Chinese Crested Powderpuff (below) graces the home of Arlene Butterklee of Ronkonkoma, New York.

Extending unreserved French affection for mistress Jo Ann Duarte are her two beau bouledogue beaux; Ms. Duarte, of Bayshore, New York, heads a family of champion French Bulldogs as well as Bullmastiffs. Three Fingertail Shar-Pei pups (left) belonging to Jo Ann Webster of Raritan, New Jersey.

This bouncy Nizinny (above right) lives with acting-shepherdess Anna Helfrich in Saxonburg, Pennsylvania. The Polish Lowland Sheepdog continually levitates in numbers and appeal. These two eye-catching Chow Chows (below right) share their home in Oceanside, New York, with owners Robert and Mindy Costanza.

Dorothy and George O'Neil of Rhode Island join the ranks of our proud owners with "Leslie," a six-year-old Field Spaniel of astonishing beauty.

Affenpinscher, Josephine M. Harkin ◆ Afghan Hound, Joann Bottega ◆ Afghan Hound, Mrs. C. Derraugh ◆ Airedale Terrier, Sandra Hamer ◆ Akbash Dog, Dee Gannon ◆ Akita, Gayle Pierce ◆ Alapaha Blue Blood Bulldog, Lana Lou Buck ◆ Alaskan Malamute, Bonnie Sue O'Neill ◆ Alaskan Malamute, Dee Schindler ◆ Alaskan Malamute, Joyce Pessel-Yaskoski ◆ Alpine Dachsbracke, Ingeborg Klose ◆ American Blue Gascon Hound, Herrick Mountain Kennels ◆ American Bulldog, Steve Leclerc ◆ American Cocker Spaniel, Geraldine Drayer ◆ American Eskimo, Faye and Myrl Stone ◆ American Eskimo, Miniature, Elizabeth and Joseph Daoust ◆ American Eskimo, Monica Sellers ◆ American Foxhound, Mrs. Ashlyn Cannon ◆ American Hairless Terrier, Willie Scott ◆ American Pit Bull Terrier, Charles M. Kopenhafer ◆ American Pit Bull Terrier, Peggy Allen ◆ American Staffordshire Terrier, Nelison Kennel ◆ American Staffordshire Terrier, Sigrid Reisiger ◆ Anatolian Shepherd Dog, Mr. Emanuel ◆ Anglo-Francais de Petite Venerie, Michel Thiery ◆ Appenzeller, Nysen Wilcy ◆ Ariégeois, Frans Reyns ◆ Australian Cattle Dog, Kathleen M. Spivey ◆ Australian Kelpie, Outi Liukkonen ◆ Australian Shepherd, Joe Hartnagle ◆ Australian Shepherd, Patricia M. Poroz ◆ Australian Terrier, Esther C. Krom ◆ Austrian Brandlbracke, Dr. Paul Richter ◆ Austrian Shorthaired Pinscher, Andreas Steghofer ◆ Azawakh, Ingrid Klgeldinger ◆ Barbet, Yves Masse ◆ Basenji, White Kennels ◆ Basset Artesien Normand, J. Eisenoble ◆ Basset Bleu de Gascogne, M. Vulvin ◆ Basset Fauve de Bretagne, Louis Le Helloco ◆ Basset Hound, Kitty Sue Kaffke ◆ Basset Hound, Martine Ouimet ◆ Bavarian Mountain Hound, W. Stadler ◆ Beagle, Mrs. Catherine Sutton ◆ Beagle, Sarah Russo ◆ Beagle Harrier, Aimé Defois ◆ Bearded Collie, Barbara Wilk ◆ Bearded Collie, Sheila Green ◆ Bearded Collie, Thomas M. Davies ◆ Beauceron, Manuel Olciva ◆ Bedlington Terrier, Nancy Rappaport ◆ Belgian Griffon, M. Guimard ◆ Belgian Griffon, Petit Brabancon, Milor ◆ Belgian Sheepdog Laekenois, D.V. Boel ◆ Belgian Sheepdog Malinois, Danny Van Huffel ◆ Belgian Sheepdog Tervuren, Albert C. Galera Ibañez ◆ Bergamasco, C.M. Beenen ◆ Berger des Pyrenees, Jacques Bezançon ◆ Berger des Pyrenees, Paul Redam ◆ Berger des Pyrenees, Smooth-muzzled, Ilse Tschopp ◆ Berger Picard, Bruno Henaff ◆ Berner Laufhund, Ozdikmen Faruk ◆ Berner Neiderlaufhund, Aügli Werner ◆ Bernese Mountain Dog, Dennis and Lillian Ostermiller ◆ Bernese Mountain Dog, Judith Parr ◆ Bichon Frise, Florence Erwin ◆ Billy, M. Machenaud ◆ Black and Tan Coonhound, Christopher Mars ◆ Black Forest Hound, Vogel ◆ Black Mouth Cur, Howard Carnathan ◆ Black Russian Terrier, Kirsti Pitkänen ◆ Bleu de Gascogne, Basset, M. Backa-Greeven ◆ Bloodhound, Donna Emery ◆ Blue Lacy, Paul and Pam Wilkes ◆ Bluetick Coonhound, Martin Fortin ◆ Bolognese, Deleu Vansteenkiste ◆ Border Collie, Ken Sigel ◆ Border Terrier, Wayne and Joyce Kirn ◆ Border Terrier, Joanne and Craig Francisco ◆ Boston Terrier, Lt. Col. Jim Cronen ◆ Boxer, Felice Burton and Suzy Chait ◆ Boxer, Richard Tomita ◆ Boykin Spaniel, Boykin Spaniel Society, photo ◆ Bracco Italiano, Mergio Vittorio ◆ Braque d'Auvergne, M. Campagne ◆ Braque du Bourbonnais, Jacques Dremaux ◆ Briard, Robert Bloom ◆ Brittany, Alida Edwards ◆ Brussels Griffon, M. Guimard ◆ Bulldog, Deville and Baron ◆ Bulldog, Roberta Arnold ◆ Bullmastiff, Emgallant Elitz ◆ Bullmastiff, M. Bahlman ◆ Bull Terrier, Irene and Tom Lecki ◆ Cairn Terrier, Karen Zarobinsky ◆ Canaan Dog, Hinda B. Bergman and Tabatha Chafkin ◆ Canary Dog, Carl Semencic, photo ◆ Cão da Serra de Aires, Joao Bessa ◆ Cão da Serra de Aires, W. Marleen van Wolferen ◆ Cão de Castro Laboreiro, Francisco Parrinha ◆ Cardigan Welsh Corgi, Eugenia B. Bishop ◆ Carolina Dog, Dr. I. Lehr Brisbin, Jr., photo ◆ Catahoula Leopard Dog, M. Morgan ◆ Catalan Sheepdog, Pepa Reichs Matelouge ◆ Caucasian Ovtcharka, Fritz Rasch-Gründing ◆ Cavalier King Charles Spaniel, Carousel Kennels ◆ Cavalier King Charles Spaniel, Shelia Millward ◆ Chesapeake Bay Retriever, Marie Whitney Bonadies ◆ Chien d'Artois, Josette Gilat ◆ Chien Francais Tricolore, Hubert Bigot ◆ Chihuahua, Smoothhair, Patricia Lambert ◆ Chihuahua, Longhair, Eric and Annette Mellinger ◆ Chihuahua, Longhair, Mary M. Silkworth ◆ Chihuahua, Smoothcoat, Betty Hayden ◆ Chinese Crested, Arlene Butterklee ◆ Chinese Crested, Dottie Thompson ◆ Chinook, Mr. and Mrs. Neil K. Wollpert ◆ Chow Chow, Cindy Attinello ◆ Chow Chow, Mary Ellen Kandybowicz ◆ Chow Chow, Pam Burnside ◆ Clumber Spaniel, Charlotte Stanton ◆ Clumber Spaniel, Eunice Bailey ◆ Clumber Spaniel, George and Dorothy O'Neill ◆ Collie, Rough, Mr. G. Catalano ◆ Collie, Smooth, Smith ◆ Continental Toy Spaniel, Phalene, M. Studer ◆ Czesky Terrier, Carousel Kennels ◆ Dachshund, Longhair, Leah Farr-Williams ◆ Dalmatian, Eric and Ardith Dahlstrom ◆ Dalmatian, Charlotte Katz ◆ Dalmatian, Michael Manning ◆ Dandie Dinmont Terrier, Joan Thomas ◆ Danish Broholmer, M. Weiss ◆ Deutsche Bracke, Deutscher Bracken Klub, photo ◆ Deutsche Wachtelhund, Theodor Mangold ◆ Dingo, Native Dog Training Society of New South Wales, photo ◆ Doberman Pinscher, Carol A. Kepler ◆ Doberman Pinscher, Kristin Marie King ◆ Doberman Pinscher, Cec Ringstrom ◆ Doberman Pinscher, Mrs. B. Rowland ◆ Doberman Pinscher, William Mackay ◆ Dogo Argentino, Gabriel Moyette ◆ Dogue de Bordeaux, Peter Curely ◆ Dogue de Bordeaux, Robin Marcelle ◆ Drever, Leino Eino ◆ Dunker, Norske Harehundklubbers, photo ◆ Dutch Smoushond, H.R.C. Schay ◆ East Siberian Laika, Barbara Erhard ◆ English Cocker Spaniel, Nancy McFadden ◆ English Coonhound, United Kennel Club, photo ◆ English Foxhound, Suzy Reingold and Richard Reynolds ◆ English Setter, Shawnine Hogan ◆ English Shepherd, Diana L. Karr ◆ English Springer Spaniel, Franz Wagner ◆ English Springer Spaniel, Joan Howe ◆ English Toy Spaniel, Karen Abbott Henderson ◆ Entelbucher, E.P. Kerkhof ◆ Entlebucher, Lindinger Hans ◆ Épagneul Bleu de Picardie, Jean Moron ◆ Épagneul Picard, Jean Moron ◆ Épagneul Pont-Audemer, Mme. Leseigneur ◆ Eskimo Dog, Mike Cooper ◆ Estrela Mountain Dog, Francisco Parrinha ◆ Finnish Hound,

Reino Sartila ♦ Finnish Lapphund, Spitz Club of Finland, photo ♦ Finnish Spitz, Judith L. Dolan ♦ French Bulldog, C. and G. Secher ♦ French Bulldog, Beth and Mark Carr ♦ Galgo Espagñol, Juan A. C. Albaronte ♦ German Hunting Terrier, Michael Lucero ♦ German Longhaired Pointer, Remko and Elmer Yntema ♦ German Shepherd Dog, Karen Squire ♦ German Shepherd Dog, Louise Morneau ♦ German Shepherd Dog, Raymond Filiatrault ♦ German Spitz, Fritz Gerber ♦ German Spitz, Mrs. J. Gunnell ♦ German Spitz, Miss Russell Smith ♦ German Wirehaired Pointer, Drahthaar, Albert Louis ♦ German Wirehaired Pointer, Judith E. Ford ♦ German Wirehaired Pointer, Patricia Laurans ♦ German Wirehaired Pointer, Robert A. Koppel ♦ Giant German Spitz, Gerber Fritz ♦ Giant Schnauzer, Ben Bleckley ♦ Giant Schnauzer, Caro Thurdsen ♦ Glen of Imaal Terrier, Jean Clarke ♦ Golden Retriever, Joan Young ♦ Golden Retriever, Stuart Schwartz ♦ Gordon Setter, Virginia Radonis ♦ Grand Anglo-Francais, Marchis Pudognon ♦ Grand Basset Vendeen, J. Huisman ♦ Grand Bleu de Gascogne, F.W.A. Vael ♦ Grand Gascon-Saintongois, Equipage de Bramofam, photo ♦ Grande Podengo Portugueso, S. Contera ♦ Great Dane, Lisa Saks ♦ Greater Swiss Mountain Dog, Helmut Jöhle ♦ Great Pyrenees, C. Fargas ♦ Great Pyrenees, Gregory Siner ♦ Great Pyrenees, Rhonda Dalton ♦ Great Pyrenees, Laurie Scarpa ♦ Greenland Dog, Annelise J. Stampe ♦ Greenland Dog, Krogfeh ♦ Greyhound, Patti Clark and June Matarazzo ♦ Griffon Nivernais, Daniel Duede ♦ Hamiltonstövare, Ann Bevan ♦ Hanovarian Hound, Dr. Kahl ♦ Havanese, A. Haarlem ♦ Hertha Pointer, Jyette Weiss ♦ Hovawart, A. Sinnema ♦ Hovawart, Silvia Moser ♦ Hygenhund, Norsk Kennel Klub, photo ♦ Ibizan Hound, Judith E. Ford ♦ Ibizan Hound, Wirehair, Alfonso Tout Condra ♦ Iceland Dog, Frances Federighi ♦ Inca Hairless Dog, Latulippe ♦ Irish Red and White Setter, M.M. Knox ♦ Irish Terrier, Rod Umlas ♦ Irish Water Spaniel, Gregory Siner ♦ Irish Wolfhound, Marilyn C. Munroe ♦ Istrian Hound, Smoothhaired, Benŏić Zarko ♦ Italian Greyhound, Kerri Baronowski ♦ Jack Russell Terrier, Dr. John Lowery ♦ Jack Russell Terrier, Jack and Terri Batzer ♦ Jack Russell Terrier, Kenneth Williams ♦ Jack Russell Terrier, Sean and Elizabeth McCarthy ♦ Jämthund, Bertil Barhammar ♦ Japanese Chin, Mark J. Berkel ♦ Japanese Spitz, Jeanette Paton ♦ Jura Laufhund, Bruno, Daniel Gaston ♦ Kangal Dog, Nelson Kennel ♦ Karelian Bear Dog, Kim Dokter ♦ Keeshond, Tom and Ellen Crewe ♦ Kerry Blue Terrier, Ruth Gettings ♦ Kooikerhondje, A.J. Roossien ♦ Kromfohrländer, Wirehaired, M. Blankenagel ♦ Kuvasz, Nancy L. Eisenberg ♦ Kyi-Leo, Margaret E. Keim ♦ Labrador Retriever, Fran Opperisano, Joan Huebel, and Janet Farmilette ♦ Labrador Retriever, John and Sheri Buhagiar, Jr. ♦ Labrador Retriever, Stephen Wojculewski ♦ Lakeland Terrier, Cees Van Benthem ♦ Lancashire Heeler, Mary Genovese ♦ Lapinporokoira, Spitz Club of Finland, photo ♦ Large Münsterländer, Mrs. Dorothy Hunter ♦ Leonberger, C. Delhorne ♦ Leopard Cur, J. Richard McDuffie ♦ Lhasa Apso, Helen Hailes ♦ Lhasa Apso, Rachel Slater ♦

Luzerner Laufhund, Heiderer Fritz ♦ Magyar Agăr, C. Werk ♦ Majestic Tree Hound, Lee Newhart, Jr. ♦ Maltese, Ann Glenn ♦ Maltese, Mrs. A. Dallison ♦ Manchester Terrier, Janet A. Caporale ♦ Maremma Sheepdog, Edward Pugielle ♦ Maremma Sheepdog, R. Coppinger, Hampshire College, photo ♦ Mastiff, Winterwood Kennels ♦ Mastiff, Charles B. Boyer ♦ Mastiff, John and Donna Bahalman ♦ Mexican Hairless, Mary Fernandez ♦ Miniature Bull Terrier, Donly Chorn ♦ Miniature Dachshund, Longhair, Edith M. Nelson ♦ Miniature Dachshund, Wirehair, Mr. and Mrs. Groves ♦ Miniature Pinscher, M. D'Errico ♦ Miniature Pinscher, Rose J. Radel ♦ Miniature Poodle, Marion and Mary Ellen' Fishler ♦ Mountain Cur, Kenneth Jones ♦ Neapolitan Mastiff, Sherilyn Allen, D.V.M. ♦ Norbottenspets, Norbottenspets Club of Sweden, photo ♦ Norfolk Terrier, Gregory Siner ♦ Norfolk Terrier, M.S. Baird ♦ Norwegian Buhund, Lynne Robson ♦ Norwegian Elkhound, Bobbie Chatlos, Beverly Labraire, and Anthony Attalla ♦ Norwegian Elkhound, Margaret Mott, Sara and Lillian Kletter ♦ Norwich Terrier, Ellen Shannon ♦ Nova Scotia Duck Tolling Retriever, Nete Wunsch ♦ Nova Scotia Duck Tolling Retriever, Rochelle Yuspa ♦ Old Danish Bird Dog, V.G. Kristensen ♦ Olde English Bulldogge, Karen and Dominic Campetti ♦ Old English Sheepdog, Margaret J. Trenholm ♦ Old English Sheepdog, Marilyn Mayfield ♦ Otter Hound, Robin Anderson ♦ Owczarek Podhalanski, E.M. Helm ♦ Pekingese, Jeannine Joyal ♦ Pembroke Welsh Corgi, JoAnn Schmidt ♦ Pequēno Podengo Portugueso, J. Beso ♦ Perdiguero de Burgos, José Drago Ryeza ♦ Perdiguero Navarro, Faus Ferreira Ramalho ♦ Perdiguero Navarro, M. Contera ♦ Perro de Pastor Mallorquin, Juan Antonio Cabezas ♦ Peruvian Inca Orchid, Page Mitchell ♦ Petit Anglo-Francais, Jean Yves Postollec ♦ Petit Basset Griffon Vendeen, Thelma Vlas-Zandstra ♦ Petit Basset Griffon Vendeen, Valerie Link ♦ Petit Brabancon, Pontois Yves ♦ Pharaoh Hound, Sue M. Sefscik ♦ Pharaoh Hound, Wirehair, Alfonso Tout Cendra ♦ Pinscher, Gloria Cutmbert ♦ Plott Hound, United Kennel Club, photo ♦ Poitevin, M. de la Rochefoucauld ♦ Polish Lowland Sheepdog, Anna M. Helfrich ♦ Pomeranian, Joy Brewster ♦ Porcelaine, Maurice Guyonard ♦ Portuguese Water Dog, Deborah Gressle and Jennifer Male ♦ Pudelpointer, Pohn Hermann ♦ Pug, Lorraine Getter ♦ Puli, Patricia B. Giancaterino ♦ Pumi, Arthur Sorkin, photo ♦ Pyrenean Mastiff, Rafael Accrudo ♦ Rafeiro do Alentejo, Josi da Costa Botto ♦ Redbone Coonhound, United Kennel Club, photo ♦ Rhodesian Ridgeback, Dudley Hackney ♦ Rottweiler, Ann Wasserman ♦ Rottweiler, Donna E. Saul ♦ Saarlooswolfhond, E. Pielanen-Degenhardt ♦ Sabueso Espagnōl de Monte, Ruisanchez Oqueranza ♦ Saint Bernard, Anita Poisson ♦ Saint Bernard, Smooth, Wayne Ferguson ♦ Saint Bernard, Woodraska Kennel ♦ Samoyed, Dianne Sorrentino ♦ Samoyed, Novon Glosky ♦ Sarplaninac, Claude Milliand ♦ Schapendoes, Mayts Geloler ♦ Schipperke, Diane E. Solarski ♦ Schweizer Laufhund, Peter van Liempt ♦ Scottish Deerhound, Shawnine Hogan ♦ Scottish Terrier, Joan Toomey and Dorothy

Greenhouse ◆ Sealyham Terrier, France Bergeron ◆ Segugio Italiano, Guerrini Nadir ◆ Shar-Pei, Margaret Kastner ◆ Shar-Pei, Pat Leone ◆ Shetland Sheepdog, Margaret and Walt Huening ◆ Shiba Inu, Richard Tomita ◆ Shih Tzu, Louis and Wanda Gec ◆ Shih Tzu, Kathy Kwait ◆ Siberian Husky, Bunadunna ◆ Siberian Husky, Margaret Cook ◆ Siberian Husky, Nancy Wolfe ◆ Siberian Husky, Sylvia Roselli ◆ Silky Terrier, Angelica C. Mazzarella and Lisa Saks ◆ Slovak Cuvac, Paul and Pam Wilkes ◆ Small Münsterländer, D. Scheer ◆ Smooth Fox Terrier, Cherie DiLorenzo ◆ Soft Coated Wheaten Terrierm Lise Lockquell ◆ Spanish Mastiff, Teresa Casas ◆ Spinone Italiano, Dr. Storace ◆ Spinone Italiano, Guerrini Nadir ◆ Stabyhoun, D.C. Bakelaar ◆ Staffordshire Bull Terrier, Joe LeBlanc ◆ Standard Dachshund, J. Vink ◆ Standard Dachshund, Longhair, Mrs. Dorothy Poole ◆ Standard Dachshund, Smoothhair, N.J. and G.D. Cowie ◆ Standard Dachshund, Wirehair, Pat Leone ◆ Standard Poodle, Dr. and Mrs. Samuel Peacock ◆ Standard Poodle, Ivy and Ken Soutter ◆ Standard Poodle, Joy Grouf ◆ Standard Poodle, V. Jean Craft and Margaret M. Klotz ◆ Standard Schnauzer, Hanaraan Kennel ◆ Standard Schnauzer, Karen Ann Fine ◆ Standard Schnauzer, Margaret Platt ◆ Stephens Stock, Hugh Stephens ◆ Strellufstöver, Dansk Stöverklub, photo ◆ Styrian Roughhaired Mountain Hound, Ernst Stachel ◆ Sussex Spaniel, Walter Stewart ◆ Swedish Vallhund, Ernie and Nicky Gascoigne ◆ Telomian, Jody R. Nathan ◆ Tibetan Mastiff, Donald and Louise Skilton ◆ Tibetan Spaniel, Carousel Kennels ◆ Tibetan Terrier, Eileen J. King ◆ Toy American Eskimo, Carolyn Jester ◆ Toy Fox Terrier, Orpha Sauceda ◆ Toy German Spitz, Fritz Gerber ◆ Toy Manchester Terrier, Helene Reich ◆ Transylvanian Hound, Tall, Jawsky Jirsf ◆ Treeing Tennessee Brindle, Glascow Kennels ◆ Tyrolean Smoothhaired Hound, Viktor Wöhry ◆ Vizsla, P. Boelte ◆ Volpino Italiano, S. Giuntini ◆ Weimaraner, Parke Kennel ◆ Welsh Springer Spaniel, Karen Ertyl and Pat McCoy ◆ Welsh Terrier, M. Lussin ◆ Welsh Terrier, Nancy Kozma ◆ West Highland White Terrier, Barbara Stiles ◆ West Highland White Terrier, Joseph P. Engers ◆ Westphalian Dachsbracke, Evelyn Schweiz ◆ West Siberian Laika, Dr. Arabadjian Kevork ◆ Wetterhoun, Saskia Mulder ◆ Xoloitzcuintli, Angela Wills ◆ Xoloitzcuintli, coated, S. Mitchell ◆ Yorkshire Terrier, Patricia Scagliotti and Sandy Mandarino

Index

Page numbers in bold indicate major breed articles or group chapter openings.

English Toy Spaniel, 358, 362, **370**, 391
English Toy Terrier, 398, 400
English Water Spaniel, 216
English White Terrier, 123, 361
Entelbucher, **130**
Entelbucher Sennenhund, 130
Entelbuch Mountain Dog, 130
Épagneul Bleu de Picardie, **225**
Épagneul Breton, 211
Épagneul Francais, 225, **226**
Épagneul Nain Continental
—Papillon, 387
—Phalene, 368
Épagneul Nain of Belguim, 368, 387
Épagneul Picard, 225, **227**
Épagneul Pont-Audemer, **228**
Erdelyi Kopo, 348
Ermenti, 432
Eskimo Dog, **163**
Esquimaux, 163
Essig, Herr Heinrich, 135
Estonian Hound, **304**
Estrela Mountain Dog, **411**
Eurasian, 164
Eurasier, **164**
Evolution of dog, 9
Exercise, 49, 61–62
—and the older dog, 75
—for flock guardians, 34
—for scenthounds, 30
—for sighthounds, 22
—water requirement and, 62
—when selecting a dog, 12
Exercise necessary, symbol, 78
Eyes, care of, 66
Farou, 446
Fats, 59
Fédération Cynologique International, 44
Feeding, 49, 59, 60

—mastiffs, 24
—puppy's requirements, 51
—variety and, 60
Females, when selecting a dog, 47
Feral dog, symbol, 79
Field Spaniel, **229**
Fila Brasileiro, 63, **131**
Filho, Oswalde Aranha, 333
Finlandskaja, 175
Finnish Cock-eared Hunting Dog, 166
Finnish Hound, **305**
Finnish Lapphund, **165**, 194
Finnish Spitz, 26, 74, **166**, 175
Finsk Spets, 166
Finsk Stövare, 305
Fitzinger, Dr., 171
Flat-Coated Retriever, **230**
Fleas, 58, 70
Flock Guardian, symbol, 78
Flock Guardians, 36, **405**
—group discussion, 34
Flusher, symbol, 79
Flushing, 28
Food
—canned, 59
—commercial, 59
—fresh, 59
Foxhounds, 31, 233, 235, 253, 285, 289, 315
Fox Terrier, 116, 486, 496
—smooth, **517**
—wire, **521**
Frandsen, Frands Christian, 346
French Bulldog, 13, **371**
French Hound, 298
French Mastiff, 129
French Pointer–Gascony type, 207, 207
French Pointer–Pyrenees type, 206

Recommended Reading

T.F.H. Publications, Inc., continues to provide the dog community with the best literature possible. The following books by respected authors in their field prove reliable, informative and entertaining.

The Atlas of Dog Breeds of the World By Bonnie Wilcox, DVM, & Chris Walkowicz (H-1091)
Traces the history and highlights the characteristics, appearance and function of every recognized dog breed in the world. 409 different breeds receive full-color treatment and individual study. Hundreds of breeds in addition to those recognized by the American Kennel Club and the Kennel Club of Great Britain are included—the dogs of the world complete! The ultimate reference work, comprehensive coverage, intelligent and delightful discussions. The perfect gift book. *Hard cover, 9" × 12", 912 pages, 1,106 color photos. ISBN 0-86622-930-2*

Dog Training By Lew Burke (H-962)
The elements of dog training are easy to grasp and apply. The author uses the psychological makeup of dogs to his advantage by making them want to be what they should be—substituting the family for the pack. *Hard cover, 5½" × 8", 255 pages, 64 black and white photos, 23 color photos. ISBN 0-87666-656-X*

The Complete Dog Buyer's Guide By Dr. William Bruette & Kerry V. Donnelly (H-989)
Plots the advances in veterinary care and genetics of the last fifty years by incorporating descriptions of the breeds as they are today. Many of the photos illustrate Best In Show winners and top and historical dogs. Individual complete sections on breeding, selection, caring, etc. *Hard cover, 5½" × 8", 608 pages. Illustrated. ISBN 0-86622-026-7*

Dog Owner's Encyclopedia of Veterinary Medicine By `Allan H. Hart, B.V.Sc. (H-934)
Written by a vet who feels that most dog owners should recognize the symptoms and understand the cures of most diseases of dogs so they can properly communicate with their veterinarian. This book is a necessity for every dog owner, especially those who have more than one dog. *Hard cover, 5½" × 8", 186 pages, 86 black and white photos. ISBN 0-87666-287-4*

Dog Breeding for Professionals By Dr. Herbert Richards (H-969)
For dog owners who need and actively seek good advice about how to go about breeding their dogs whether for profit or purely because of their attachment to animals. *Please note* that the breeding photography is sexually explicit and some readers may find it offensive. *Hard cover, 5½" × 8", 224 pages, 105 black and white photos, 62 color photos. ISBN 0-87666-659-4*

Dogs and the Law By Anmarie Barrie, Esq. (DS-130)
A practical and reliable survey of laws pertaining to our dogs. Advice concerning liability, licenses, impoundment, vehicles, insurance, wills, vaccinations and many other useful and often entertaining topics. Full color cartoon illustrations add a delightful twist. *Hard cover, 6" × 9", 160 pages, over 55 color illustrations, appendices, charts. ISBN 0-86622-088-7*

Pit Bull Terriers and Other Man-Stopping Guard Dogs by Dr. Carl Semencic
Dog man Carl Semencic is lucid and penetrating in his survey of today's most effective man-stoppers. For potential dog owners desiring the most reliable and powerful of the world's canines, this book is invaluable. Complete coverage of over 20 of the best possible protection breeds, focusing on each breed's abilities, characteristics and shortcomings. Pit Bull Terriers, Rottweilers, Doberman Pinschers, German Shepherds, French Mastiffs, Fila Brasileiros and many others included.
Full color photography throughout.

The following books published by T.F.H. focus on specific breeds on which readers may desire more detailed discussions. All books are illustrated generously with color photography and are insightfully definitive texts on the breeds they present.

The Basset Hound/Marcia Foy/PS-815/ISBN 0-86622-044-5

The Beagle/Marcia Foy and Anna Katherine Nicholas/PS-811
ISBN 0-86622-042-9

The Boxer/Anna Katherine Nicholas/PS-813/ISBN 0-86622-028-3

The Book of the Bulldog/Joan McDonald Brearley/H-1071/ISBN 0-86622-027-5

The Chihuahua/Anna Katherine Nicholas/PS-827/ISBN 0-86622-977-9

The World of the Chow Chow/Dr. Samuel Draper and Joan McDonald Brearley

The Book of the Cocker Spaniel/Joan McDonald Brearley/H-1034
ISBN 0-87666-737-X

The Collie/Anna Katherine Nicholas/PS-825/ISBN 0-86622-723-7

The Dachshund/Anna Katherine Nicholas and Marcia Foy/PS-822
ISBN 0-86622-158-1

The World of Doberman Pinschers/Anna Katherine Nicholas/H-1082
ISBN 0-86622-123-9

The Fox Terrier/Anna Katherine Nicholas and Marcia Foy/PS-858
ISBN 0-86622-931-0

The German Shepherd Dog/Ernest H. Hart/PS-810/ISBN 0-86622-031-3

The German Pointer(Shorthaired and Wirehaired)/Anna Katherine Nicholas
PS-816/ISBN 0-86622-150-6

The Golden Retriever/Jeffrey Pepper/PS-786/ISBN 0-87666-668-3

The Great Dane/Anna Katherine Nicholas/PS-826/ISBN 0-86622-122-0

The Labrador Retriever/Dorothy Howe and Anna Katherine Nicholas
PS-805/ISBN 0-87666-487-7

The Lhasa Apso/Anna Katherine Nicholas/PS-854/ISBN 0-86622-932-9

The Maltese/Anna Katherine Nicholas/PS-803/ISBN 0-87666-569-5

The Book of the Miniature Schnauzer/Anna Katherine Nicholas/H-1080
ISBN 0-86622-151-4

The Pekingese/Anna Katherine Nicholas/PS-857/ISBN 0-86622-929-9

The Poodle/Anna Katherine Nicholas/PS-814/ISBN 0-86622-033-X

The World of Rottweilers/Anna Katherine Nicholas/H-1083/ISBN 0-86622-124-7

The Rottweiler/Richard F. Stratton/PS-820/ISBN 0-86622-732-6

Rottweilers/Anna Katherine Nicholas

The Samoyed/Anna Katherine Nicholas/PS-855/ISBN 086622-820-9

The Shar-Pei/Ellen Weathers Debo/PS-818/ISBN 0-86622-803-9

The Book of the Shar-Pei/Joan McDonald Brearley

The Book of the Shetland Sheepdog/Anna Katherine Nicholas/H-1064
ISBN 0-86622-036-4

The Book of the Shih Tzu/Joan McDonald Brearley and Rev. D. Allan Easton
H-996/ISBN 0-87666-664-0

The Book of the Siberian Husky/Joan McDonald Brearley

The Book of the Yorkshire Terrier/Joan McDonald Brearly/H-1066
ISBN 0-87666-940-2